Advanced WordPerfect®

Series 5 Edition

Advanced WordPerfect®

Series 5 Edition

Eric Alderman

and

Lawrence J. Magid

Osborne **McGraw-Hill**
Berkeley, California

Osborne **McGraw-Hill**
2600 Tenth Street
Berkeley, California 94710
U.S.A.

For information on translations and book distributors outside of the U.S.A., please write to Osborne **McGraw-Hill** at the above address.

A complete list of trademarks appears on page 453.

Advanced WordPerfect®, Series 5 Edition

1234567890 DODO 898

ISBN 0-07-881289-5

To Rachelle and Sophia, for their love and inspiration
—E.A.

To Patti, Katie, and William, for their love and patience
—L.M.

CONTENTS

PREFACE

Much has changed in the two years since we wrote *Advanced WordPerfect: Features and Techniques*. WordPerfect has changed, WordPerfect Corporation has changed, the industry as a whole has changed, and not least of all, we have changed. Luckily, everything has changed for the better.

WordPerfect itself has grown dramatically since version 4.1, the subject of our first edition. Version 4.2 added many new features, but it is 5.0 that has really enhanced WordPerfect. Some truly impressive features have been added in this release, including outstanding laser printer support, styles, the ability to edit in reveal codes, letters for menu choices, a general revamping of the program's various menus and screens, and a powerful macro command language.

Version 5.0 is a very major revision. Unlike those of its predecessors, its changes encompass almost all of the program's features. In addition, the program's macros, which are a primary topic of this book, have changed drastically. As a result, this edition took about as long to write as the first edition. It was a big job, but we think that the information we were able to compile, especially about the macro language, will be very helpful for those intending to exploit WordPerfect's advanced features.

WordPerfect Corporation has grown with phenomenal speed into one of the industry's leading software suppliers. When the first edition of our book hit the market, there were about 250,000 registered WordPerfect users. Today, this enlightened group numbers well over 1.1 million. Back then, it was still possible to get a quizzical look when you asked someone in the industry about WordPerfect. Not much chance of that happening these days.

Not only is WordPerfect the uncontested leader in word processing software, it has at times during the last few years unseated the formidable Lotus 1-2-3 as the best-selling business program of any kind. In addition, the company has expanded its line to include versions of WordPerfect for the Apple Macintosh, Apple IIGS, Atari ST, Amiga, and VAX computers. The company's goal was to have a version of the program running on every significant hardware platform on the market, and so far they have achieved this goal.

The industry has seen many changes as well. The past couple of years have brought about a growing acceptance of graphic displays and laser printers, creating a demand for software that cares about form as well as content. Fueling that demand has been the development of a whole new type of computer application. Desktop publishing has sparked people's imaginations, empowering PC users to perform tasks that were once the province of trained graphics professionals.

Although WordPerfect 5.0 is not a full-fledged page composition program, it incorporates some of the features most sought after for desktop publishing. These include the ability to place a graphics image on a page and have text wrap around it automatically, a graphics page preview that shows varying fonts, font sizes, and graphics, and impressive laser printer support.

Finally, the past two years have seen some changes in our lives. Eric has become a WordPerfect Certified Instructor, and has written several other word processing books. In addition, he's currently a partner in LAW Services, a firm providing WordPerfect consultation, training, and customization for law offices in the San Francisco Bay area. Larry, meanwhile, has become Senior

Editor for "The Computer Show," a nationally syndicated television program which features topics of interest to all computer users. Both of us continue to write articles and columns for various newspapers and computer magazines.

As it happened, this edition was written at a time when Larry was deeply involved in several other projects. As a result, Eric is primarily responsible for the new material on version 5.0, and for the reorganization of the book.

Eric Alderman and
Lawrence J. Magid

ACKNOWLEDGMENTS

Although she was not involved in this edition of the book, we are still grateful to Gail Todd, the technical editor, for the first edition. Her contribution to this book's contents, even in its currently revamped form, is still plainly felt.

Her counterpart for this edition, Kevin Shafer, has also been a great asset. His perseverance through late nights of tediously checking and rechecking menu choices and long macro listings helped make the book as accurate as possible.

Nancy Carlston and Lindy Clinton contributed greatly to this book's rapid progress. Without them, we probably would've only written two chapters by this time.

In addition to thanking those who helped the book as a whole, we each would like to express our gratitude:

To Arthur Naiman, for continuing to be an invaluable, accessible veteran.

To Steve Michel and Dale Coleman, for advice and encouragement throughout.

To my wife Rachelle DeStephens, who provided (and continues to provide) stability, comfort, and undying encouragement. Her example of strength, perseverance, and chutzpah have helped me reach for opportunities that may otherwise have passed me by.

And, to my chunky six-month old daughter Sophia Marie, who taught me that WordPerfect is nice but is no comparison to the ultimate new release.

Eric Alderman
Oakland, California

To Burt Alperson, who, despite his undying loyalty to Microsoft Word, helped me through some of the more interesting challenges that found their way into macros and techniques in the book.

To my wife, Patti, and my children, Katie and William, for their patience, understanding, and companionship.

And finally, to the late Andrew Fluegelman (1943-1985), my friend and collaborator, who helped teach me the meaning of excellence.

Lawrence J. Magid
San Francisco, California

INTRODUCTION

This book is primarily meant for the WordPerfect user who, after using the program's basic functions for some period of time, has decided to explore some of its more advanced ones. While the book's main emphasis is on WordPerfect's macro programming language, as well as on its merge facility, the book discusses each of the program's "high-powered" functions.

After you have properly installed WordPerfect for your system (as described in the WordPerfect manual), you should consider running the TUTOR program provided with WordPerfect. This book is intended for those who have used WordPerfect for some period of time, or who are already somewhat computer literate. The tutorial, on the other hand, is especially helpful for those new to computers in general.

Another source of information is available with WordPerfect's Help key (F3), which leads you to the program's Help screens. If you need more help with a particular subject, refer to the appropriate section in Chapter 1, "Basics Refresher." While this chapter does not cover all of WordPerfect's basic functions, it does give a detailed description of the most important ones. It also provides some general rules and guidelines that every WordPerfect user should follow.

At the end of the book is a chapter entitled "Macro Library." This chapter contains over 20 complete, documented macros in such areas as document translation and office automation. One of the most important things it will teach you is how a complete macro application is constructed—for example, how you can use the macro commands to build menus and prompts.

Before using the applications found in "Macro Library," you should understand the general process of naming, defining, invoking, and editing a macro. If you need help, refer to Chapter 2, "Macros." The advanced concepts described there are put into practice in the "Macro Library."

WordPerfect is a unique product in that it has attracted both beginners and advanced users. While not overwhelming for the first-time user, it has provided an ever-increasing number of professional features. These features remain in the background until needed—this book will help you lure them into the open.

NOTATION CONVENTIONS

The following conventions are used throughout this book:

	Example
User input is shown in **boldface**	Type **letter**
WordPerfect keys (which are identified on the keyboard template) are enclosed in <angle brackets>	Press the <Bold> key
WordPerfect keys are followed by the keys you actually press the first time they are mentioned in a section	Press the <Center> key (SHIFT+F6)
Standard PC keys are shown in SMALL UPPERCASE LETTERS	TAB
Keys that are struck together (you hold down the first, then press the second) are separated by a plus sign	CTRL+ENTER

	Example
Keys that are pressed in succession are separated by a comma	HOME,HOME, UP ARROW
Menu selections are indicated by their *numbers*, followed by the actual text of the menu choices.	Type **6** for "Line Spacing"
Menu *letters* are not used in this book. (We had to pick one, and numbers is it.)	

The SHIFT key is indicated by SHIFT, and the ALT key by ALT. The CONTROL key, however, is indicated by CTRL.

WORDPERFECT RELEASES

WordPerfect Corporation frequently releases updates to WordPerfect, usually once every few months. These updates fix minor problems with previous releases, and add support for new printers. Each update is identified by the date it was released. To determine the release date of your copy of WordPerfect, start the program, and then press the <Help> key (F3). In the upper-right corner of the screen will be the release date.

This book is as accurate as possible through the 05/05/88 release of version 5.0.

ORDERING A DISK

To receive a disk containing all of the macro routines found in Chapter 13, "Macro Library," among others, as well as several merge examples and other useful WordPerfect tidbits, send a check for $19.95 (plus 7% sales tax for California residents) to:

Alderman/Magid
48 Shattuck Square, Suite 13
Berkeley, CA 94704-1140

You can also use the order form following this Introduction.

Disk Order Form

You can order a disk that contains all of the macros, procedures, and BASIC programs found in this book. The disk contains:

1. **All macros listed in Chapter 13, "Macro Library"**
   Each of these macros can be used immediately as-is, or customized using WordPerfect's macro editor. The macros are fully commented, so you can easily modify their steps.

2. **Additional Macros**
   In addition to the macros described above, several other macros will be included on the disk. For example, an RTF macro, which translates a WordPerfect document into Microsoft Rich-Text-Format for transfer to Microsoft Word on the PC or Macintosh. Also, a more advanced Paragraph Document Assembly routine than is shown in Chapter 13 is included. Several advanced macro editing tools in the form of Shell 2.0 macros are included, such as a one to facilitate printing the steps of a WordPerfect macro, and another to transfer the steps of one macro into another.

3. **Primary Merge document examples**
   Some Merge document examples for labels and reports.

4. **The Line Feed Strip program**
   The Line Feed Strip BASIC program (in both source .BAS and compiled .EXE formats) listed in Chapter 12.

To order the disk, complete this form, and send it with a check for $19.95 to:	***WordPerfect 5.0 Disk Order Form***
Alderman/Magid **48 Shattuck Square, Suite 13** **Berkeley, CA 94704-1140**	Name: _____ Street: _____ City: _____ State: _____ Zip: _____
CA residents add 7% ($1.40) sales tax.	

1

BASICS
REFRESHER

This book is a guide to WordPerfect's advanced features, most notably to macros and merging. However, Chapter 1 will serve as a refresher for those familiar with the product as well as an accelerated tutorial for experienced computer users who are new to WordPerfect.

This chapter is not meant to be used as an introductory tutorial on WordPerfect. If you are new to computers, work through the TUTOR program included with the program. This self-paced tutorial takes a basic, step-by-step approach to learning Word-Perfect.

Throughout the remaining chapters of this book, we will assume that you have mastered the basic editing skills discussed in this chapter. If you are currently a WordPerfect user, reading this chapter may help you to understand some aspects and basic concepts of the program that you have overlooked.

THE EVOLUTION

In the beginning there was the cursor. Soon there were columns and rows, letters and symbols. Then menus and prompts appeared, followed closely by hidden codes and keyboard templates. In the end, there were macros and merge, columns and math, indexes and tables of contents, styles and master documents.

As the program has evolved, many of its features have been improved with added functions and increased speed. There have also been a dramatic number of features added to the program since its birth. Its most basic editing concepts, however, have remained the same—a tribute to their popularity.

THE CONCEPTS

The key to fully mastering WordPerfect lies neither in memorizing the location of the function keys nor in trying to learn what they all do. Rather, mastery requires an understanding of the three basic concepts that underlie the program's operation. If you learn WordPerfect with these concepts in mind, you will ultimately have both an appreciation of the program's power and the ability to use this power efficiently.

The "Clean Screen" Concept

As a modern writer, you recognize the benefits of using a word processing program. You are prepared to dive headlong into the world of *block moves* and *line formats*. You accept that you will be spending some time operating the word processing program instead of actually writing.

But when the time comes to put thought to screen, what do you want to be looking at? Do you want a cluttered screen with a program menu at the top? Do you want control characters and other unintelligible squiggles intermixed with your text? Do you want two-letter codes indicating an indented paragraph or a change in line spacing? Or would you rather see *your writing*—underlines where you have underlined, emphasis where you have emphasized, and indents where you have chosen to indent?

WordPerfect provides a "Clean Screen": only the text you enter is displayed, with a single line of document information at the bottom. Some formatting commands, such as boldfacing and margin changes, are immediately reflected on the screen. Others, such as page formatting and printer controls, are inserted with a *hidden code* that you can't see unless you need to.

The result is a pleasant environment for writing, one that shows only what you want to see: your words.

The "Unnamed Document" Concept

When you start WordPerfect you are presented with a blank editing screen. From this screen you enter new text or retrieve any document and then save the document with any name. This flexibility has a number of advantages.

To Save or Not to Save

There will be times when you want to create a document that will never be saved. For example, if you are writing a quick personal letter or memo, you may want to print the document without saving it to disk. With WordPerfect, you can print a document without saving it first. After it has been printed, you can just clear the screen and you'll be ready for the next document.

Another advantage of WordPerfect is that you don't need to determine a document's name until after it has been created (or at least started). This is often useful, because when you begin writing a document, you don't always know what its file name should be.

A Document by Any Other Name

In WordPerfect, you can save a document with any name, at any time. This means that you are never "locked in" to any one file name, as you are with many other programs. You might want to exploit this capability by maintaining standard documents or formats. For example, you could retrieve a document as a standard form, fill it in appropriately, and then save it under a different name. Or you might be modifying a document when you realize that you want to keep the original version intact. You can save the revised version under a different file name. In many word processing programs these tasks might require several steps.

Clearing and Retrieving

When you retrieve a document in WordPerfect, it appears on the screen at the current cursor position. If the screen is clear, this is of no consequence. If, however, you are already editing a document, the text of the retrieved file will be inserted in the text of the current file, at the current cursor position.

This can initially cause confusion, especially if you are used to programs that automatically clear the screen when a new file is loaded. With a little practice, however, you will learn to use this handy WordPerfect feature to combine documents easily. If you forget that documents are *combined* when the screen isn't cleared before retrieving a file, your documents will seem to increase mysteriously in size. Therefore, if you do not mean to combine two documents when you retrieve a new one, always remember to *clear the screen* first.

To clear the screen, press the <Exit> key (F7), type **N** for "No Save" or **Y** for "Yes Save" (whichever is appropriate), and then type **N** for "No Don't Exit WordPerfect."

The "Hidden Codes" Concept

When you use one of the WordPerfect function keys to modify your text in some way, or when you press either the TAB or the ENTER key, the program automatically inserts a *hidden code* in your text. To see these hidden codes, you press the <Reveal Codes> key (ALT+F3). The lower half of the screen is then altered to display your text intermixed with the various codes that were previously invisible.

If you are a first-time WordPerfect user, this can be a frightening experience, but don't let it scare you away. Once you understand what is going on, you will see why it is important to use the <Reveal Codes> key frequently.

For many of the formatting features, the code specifies a particular format that will remain in effect until another such code is entered. For instance, when you use the <Format> key (SHIFT+F8) to change your left and right margins to 1.25 inches on either side, the program inserts a code that looks like this:

`[L/R Mar:1.25",1.25"]`

Why don't you see that information on your screen? The reason is that it is a hidden code, so it is visible only when Reveal Codes is active. These margins will remain in effect until you make another margin change.

It's important to keep in mind that every time you make a format change, another hidden code is generated. If, for instance, you indecisively change the margins four times in a row before you start to type, four codes are generated in succession. The first three are superfluous, since only the last will actually affect any text. It is important to use Reveal Codes to delete unnecessary codes. A document with unnecessary codes is a messy document.

The Reveal Codes function is discussed in more detail later in this chapter.

THE CARDINAL RULES

There are three cardinal rules that you should always keep in mind using WordPerfect:

- *Always exit WordPerfect with the <Exit> key (F7) before turning off the computer or restarting it with the CTRL+ALT+DEL key sequence.* After exiting, you will usually see the WordPerfect Shell menu or the DOS prompt, which is usually A>, B>, or C>.

- *Always make sure the screen is clear before retrieving a new document.* To clear the screen press the <Exit> key, and then type **Y** to save the current document if you haven't yet done so or type **N** if you don't want to save it. Then answer **N** to the prompt "Exit WP (Y/N)?" and the screen will clear.

■ *If the printer doesn't print when you tell it to, don't tell it to print again.* There is most likely some problem that needs to be corrected. Refer to the section on "Managing the Print Queue" later in this chapter.

USING HELP

Software companies expend a lot of energy (and spend a lot of money) designing and building comprehensive on-line Help facilities for their programs. Manuals and books are good ways to learn about a product because they can go into depth about its various features, but they can never be as convenient as a good Help facility for jogging the memory. Many people, though, use a program's Help facility only occasionally or not at all. Instead they riffle through a book, trying to find the right chapter, or they just give up and call the local computer store.

WordPerfect's Help has been continually expanded and improved since the program's introduction. Although not what is classically considered "context-sensitive" (that is, the program knows what you are trying to do when you ask for help), it is nonetheless an excellent Help system. Anyone learning WordPerfect should use Help.

To use the Help system, press the <Help> key (F3) any time WordPerfect is displaying the normal Document Editing screen. If you are using a floppy-based computer system, you may have to insert the Learning Disk in one of the disk drives and then tell WordPerfect where to find the Help file by pressing the drive letter. When you press the <Help> key, you will see a message explaining how to use the Help function. Press ENTER or SPACE BAR to exit the Help function.

CURSOR CONTROL

WordPerfect has many commands that let you move the cursor around the screen and through your document. It can be overwhelming to look at a complete list of them. However, you should learn the most important ones as soon as possible, since they will probably be the most used of WordPerfect's functions. No matter which of the program's features you intend to use, you will *always* need to use the cursor positioning controls to move quickly through your text.

Rigidity or Freedom?

There are essentially two types of word processing programs: *rigid* and *free-form*. Rigid programs limit movement of the cursor to areas that already contain text. Free-form programs allow the cursor to be positioned anywhere on the screen.

WordPerfect is a rigid program. It will only let you move the cursor to a part of the screen containing text, spaces, tabs, or other text-positioning codes. As you move the cursor through your text as described in the following sections, you will see the cursor jump to the end of a short line, rather than move out into the "void."

If you are looking at a blank screen and you decide that you want a centered title in the middle of the screen, you must generate the correct codes to get there. You cannot simply move the cursor to where you want the title to appear and start typing. You have to press the ENTER key several times to move to the middle of the screen and then press the <Center> key to move to the center of the line.

Short Trips

The four arrow keys on the keyboard generally move the cursor one character or line in the direction shown by the arrow. If the cursor jumps to a different column position when you move it to a short or blank line, it will return to its original column position when you move onto a line that is long enough.

When used in combination with the CTRL key, the RIGHT ARROW and LEFT ARROW keys move the cursor by whole words instead of by individual characters. This is a useful way to move quickly through a line.

The gray − (minus) key on the far right side of the IBM keyboard is the <Screen Up> key, and the gray + (plus) key is the <Screen Down> key. These keys position the cursor at the top or bottom of the screen the first time they're pressed, and then they scroll the text in screenfuls (usually 24 lines at a time). This is the best way to scroll the document when you want to read the text on the screen.

The HOME key serves many purposes, but only in combination with other keys. By itself, it does nothing. Pressing the HOME key once puts WordPerfect into a "Short Cursor Trip" mode. The next key that you press determines where the cursor will go. After you press HOME,

- The LEFT ARROW key moves the cursor to the beginning of the line, or if you're using wide margins, to the left edge of the screen.

- The RIGHT ARROW key moves the cursor to the end of the line, or if you're using wide margins, to the right edge of the screen. (If you're using normal margins, pressing the END key performs the same function as pressing the HOME, RIGHT ARROW key sequence.)

- The UP ARROW and DOWN ARROW keys move the cursor to the top and bottom of the screen, respectively. (Pressing the <Screen Up> or <Screen Down> keys performs the same function as the HOME, UP ARROW or HOME, DOWN ARROW key sequence.)

Long Distance Trips

While the <Screen Up> and <Screen Down> keys move the cursor by *screenfuls*, the PGUP and PGDN keys move by *pagefuls*. PGDN moves the cursor to the top of the following page, and PGUP moves it to the top of the previous page. This is a good method of scrolling when you want to move in bigger jumps than a screenful at a time.

Pressing the HOME key twice puts WordPerfect into a "Long Distance Trip" mode. Pressing the UP ARROW key next moves the cursor to the top of the document (but after any hidden codes at the top); the DOWN ARROW key moves it to the bottom of the document. To move the cursor to the *absolute* top of the document, press HOME, HOME, HOME, and UP ARROW.

The CTRL+HOME key sequence performs the "Go to" command. As with the HOME key, the action this sequence initiates depends on the next key you press, as follows:

- To move to a particular page, press <Go to> (CTRL+HOME), type the page number, and press ENTER.

- To move the cursor to wherever it was before the last cursor movement command, press the <Go to>,<Go to> key sequence (CTRL+HOME,CTRL+HOME) or hold down CTRL and press HOME twice.

This sequence is convenient when you are moving or copying blocks of text. For example, let's say you are somewhere in the middle of a document and you want to copy a paragraph to page 23. After copying it, doing a <Go to> page 23, and retrieving the text, you can use the <Go to>,<Go to> sequence to return the cursor to its original position.

- To place the cursor at the start of your most recent block (even if the block is no longer highlighted), press the <Go to> key (CTRL+HOME) followed by the <Block> key (ALT+F4).

This sequence is useful if you want to perform more than one procedure on the same block of text. Since all of WordPerfect's block commands automatically turn Block mode off, the text will no longer be highlighted. To rehighlight a block after issuing a Block command, press <Block>, followed by the <Go to>, <Block> sequence.

TEXT EDITING

This section will discuss basic text editing techniques, including methods for deleting, copying, and moving text. It will also discuss the Undelete function.

Basic Text Editing

There is very little to learn about WordPerfect's basic editing procedures. When you see the program's "Clean Screen," you simply begin typing. The program will wrap your text at the default right margin. You end paragraphs by pressing the ENTER key. You can also generate blank lines with the ENTER key.

The key marked INS on the numeric keypad toggles WordPerfect between two modes, Typeover and Insert. In Typeover mode, letters typed on the keyboard replace letters at the cursor position. At the bottom-left of the screen will be this message:

Typeover

In Insert mode, no message is shown. Letters typed on the keyboard are inserted at the cursor position, and all characters to the right of the cursor are pushed to the right to make room.

When you reach the end of a page, WordPerfect inserts a Soft Page Break (displayed as a row of dashes across the screen). If you wish to start a new page before you have reached the bottom of the current one, press the Hard Page Break key (CTRL+ENTER). The Hard Page Break is displayed as a row of equal signs across the screen.

Marking a Block

Various sections in this book discuss the Block command, which designates a section of text for a particular purpose. WordPerfect can perform about 20 different functions on a block of text, including underlining, spell checking, and deleting. To see a complete list of these functions, press the <Help> key (F3) and then the <Block> key (ALT+F4).

To mark a section of text as a block, position the cursor on the first letter you wish to include in the block and press the <Block> key (ALT+F4). The message:

Block on

will begin flashing on the screen. Use any of WordPerfect's cursor positioning commands to move to the character *following* the last character you want included in the block. The blocked text will appear highlighted (shown in reverse video).

If you type any single character while defining a block, the cursor will move forward to the next occurrence of that character (within the next 2000 characters). By pressing the ENTER key or a period, you can easily define a paragraph or sentence as a block. You can use the Search function to extend the end of the block to the next occurrence of any code or text in the document.

You can also define a block by starting with the cursor positioned *after* the last character to be included in the block and moving it backward in the text *onto* the first character.

While the text you want is highlighted and the "Block on" message is flashing, you can perform any block action.

Deleting Text

There are several methods of deleting text in WordPerfect. The method you choose depends on how much text you want to delete. Some of the major deletion commands will ask for confirmation before actually performing the command. Even after you confirm the deletion of the text, however, you can still bring it back to life with the Undelete function discussed later in this chapter.

Deleting Small Amounts of Text

The following two keys are used to delete characters one at a time:

DEL (Delete)   This key is usually located at the bottom of the numeric keypad on the right side of the keyboard. It deletes a single character *at the cursor position* and moves the following text to the left to close up the space.

BACKSPACE   This key is usually above the ENTER key and is marked with a left arrow. It deletes a single character *to the left of the cursor position* and moves the following text to the left to fill in the missing space.

Deleting Larger Amounts of Text

There are four key sequences for deleting larger amounts of text:

<Delete Word> (CTRL+BACKSPACE)   This key sequence deletes the word at the current cursor location. You can place the cursor anywhere within, or on the space following, the word. After the word is deleted, the cursor is positioned at the first letter of the following word, making it convenient to delete several words *forward*, in succession.

<Delete Word Left> (HOME, BACKSPACE)   This key sequence deletes the word that *precedes* the word at the current cursor location. (If the cursor is positioned in the middle of a word when you first press the key sequence, WordPerfect will delete the letters in the word that precede the cursor.) You can use this key sequence to delete several words *backwards*, in succession.

<Delete EOL> (CTRL+END)   This key sequence deletes all text from the cursor position to the end of the current line. If the line ends with a Soft Return (a return automatically generated by WordPerfect when the cursor reaches the right margin), text from the following line is brought up to the cursor position. In this way, you can delete several lines of a paragraph in succession.

<Delete EOP> (CTRL+PGDN)   This key sequence deletes all of the text from the cursor position to the end of the current page. The command will ask for confirmation before deleting the text.

Deleting Sentences, Paragraphs, and Pages

You can have WordPerfect help you delete a single sentence, paragraph, or page by using the Move function. To do this, position the cursor anywhere within the sentence, paragraph, or page, and press the <Move> key (CTRL+F4). Type **1** to select a sentence, **2** for a paragraph, or **3** for a page. Then type **3** to delete the selected text.

Using the Block Function to Delete Text

You can also use the Block function to delete text. To do so, use the steps outlined in "Marking a Block" to define the block, and while the "Block on" message is flashing, press the DEL or BACKSPACE key. WordPerfect will ask for confirmation before deleting the text.

Moving and Copying Text

To move text from one place in WordPerfect to another, or to duplicate text, use the Move function. When you *move* or *copy* text, you can either proceed to *retrieve* the text in another location, or you can leave it in a buffer (a holding area) until you are ready to retrieve it somewhere else. The text can be retrieved anywhere in the current document, on a blank screen, or in another document that you retrieve from disk. There is only one buffer, so each time you execute a Move or Copy command, the previous buffer contents are automatically cleared. Both Move and Copy place text *into* the buffer—the only difference between them is that Move also deletes the text from its original position.

You can use the <Move> key with *block definition off* or with *block definition on*. The menu that appears at the bottom of the screen will differ, depending on which method you are using.

If you press the <Move> key but have not marked a block, you can only move or copy a single sentence, paragraph, or page. As long as the cursor is positioned anywhere inside any of these units, the Move command will automatically highlight the amount of text you choose to move. You can then choose whether to move or copy the text. (As discussed earlier, you can also choose to delete the selected text.) Next, you can select the position that you want the text to go to.

You can move any amount of text (not just one sentence, paragraph, or page) by defining a block before pressing the <Move> key. First, mark the block as specified in "Marking a Block." Then, while the "Block on" message is flashing, press the <Move> key. Type 1 for "Block," and a menu will appear at the bottom of the screen, allowing you to either move or copy the text. After you choose one, you can select the position that you want the text to go to.

After choosing to move or copy the text, you'll see the message "Move cursor; press Enter to retrieve." at the bottom of the screen. Move the cursor to where you want the text to be placed. You can clear the screen and load a new document before retrieving, or use the <Switch> key (SHIFT+F3) as described later in this chapter. When you have positioned the cursor where you want the text to appear, press ENTER. If you want to go on with your typing and retrieve the text whenever you're ready, press the <Cancel> key (F1) instead of ENTER. The buffer will retain the moved text until you either perform another Move command or exit WordPerfect.

When you are ready to retrieve the text, press the <Move> key, type 4 for "Retrieve" and 1 for "Block." (You can also press the <Retrieve> key (SHIFT+F10), and simply press ENTER when prompted for a file name.) The text will be placed at the cursor position.

Undeleting

WordPerfect has a unique, three-level Undelete function that lets you restore text deleted by mistake. Given all of the methods the program has for deleting text, it is inevitable that you will one day accidentally hit the wrong key sequence and delete some portion of text that you want to retain. At this point you will truly appreciate the Undelete feature. It allows you to edit documents quickly, because you don't need to worry about inadvertently deleting text.

No matter how much text you deleted, and no matter which method you used to delete it, you can retrieve it with Undelete.

WordPerfect will save up to three levels of deletion in separate buffers. The determining factor in what constitutes a deletion is *cursor movement*. If you deleted four words in a row, they would all be considered one deletion. If you were then to move your cursor to the beginning of a line and execute the <Delete EOL> (CTRL+END) key sequence, the entire deleted line would be considered the second deletion. If you moved your cursor again and deleted four characters you would have the third deletion. If you were to make yet another deletion, the first deletion would be "pushed off the stack" to make room for the newest selection of deleted text.

To activate Undelete, press the <Cancel> key (F1) when there is nothing to cancel—in other words, when there are no menus or prompts visible and there is no other function taking place. The first time the key is pressed, the most recent deletion is inserted and highlighted at the cursor position. A menu gives you the choice of either restoring the displayed text or viewing the previous deletion. You can cycle through all three deletions before deciding to undelete one. (The UP ARROW and DOWN ARROW keys can also be used to cycle through the deletions.)

Press **1**, "Restore," to restore the deleted text. You can cancel the Undelete function by pressing <Cancel> a second time.

You can also use the Undelete function as a sort of "quick and dirty" Move function. For example, you can easily delete three words, move the cursor to where you want the words to be pasted, and undelete them. This is frequently faster and more convenient than taking the time to mark a small amount of text as a block.

Text Embellishments

You can add emphasis to your text by adding underlining or bold-facing. There are two ways to do this, depending on whether you have already typed the text to be embellished.

If you have not yet typed the text, press the appropriate function key (F8 for underline or F6 for bold) once, type the text you want emphasized, and press the same key again to turn the emphasis off.

If the text already exists, mark it as a block using the block procedures discussed earlier and, while the "Block on" message is flashing, press the appropriate emphasis key.

You can embellish your text with a variety of other attributes, depending on the capabilities of your printer. For example, you can use the <Font> key (CTRL+F8) to change the size, font, and color of the text, or to cause the text to appear in italics, small capital letters, double underlined, and so on. These all work in the same way as the Bold and Underline commands. That is, you select the option once from the menu to turn on the attribute, type the text you wish to be affected, then select the option a second time to turn the attribute off.

Note that WordPerfect does not actually insert the Begin code for an attribute (such as underlining) the first time you select it, and then the End code when you select it a second time. Instead, the program inserts both the Begin *and* the End codes when you request the attribute the first time, and the cursor is left between the codes. As you type text, it pushes the End code along. When you select the attribute a second time, it simply moves the cursor *past* the End code, and thus out of the area where the attribute is in effect. (You could do the same thing manually by simply pressing RIGHT ARROW.)

You can also use the Normal command to turn off any number of attributes at one time, although it does not in fact insert a code of its own. Instead, it moves the End codes for all active attributes to just before the current cursor position, thereby turning them "off" at that point in the text.

To format text you've already typed, mark as a block the part you wish to affect, then press the <Font> key and select an option. The appropriate Begin and End codes will be placed around the marked text.

WORKING WITH REVEAL CODES

Working with the <Reveal Codes> key (ALT+F3) can sometimes be traumatic for first-time users of WordPerfect. Suddenly, the nice "Clean Screen" turns into a mess of seemingly unintelligible abbreviations. Yet the use of the Reveal Codes function is such an important part of working successfully with WordPerfect that you must clear this cloud of confusion.

When you press the <Reveal Codes> key, you see a split screen as in Figure 1-1. The top portion of the screen displays your text as usual, and the bottom portion displays your text with its codes revealed. There are now two cursors on the screen: the normal one in the top portion of the screen, and a "highlight" block cursor in the Reveal Codes screen.

–

Doc 1 Pg 1 Ln 1 Pos 10

Press Reveal Codes to restore screen

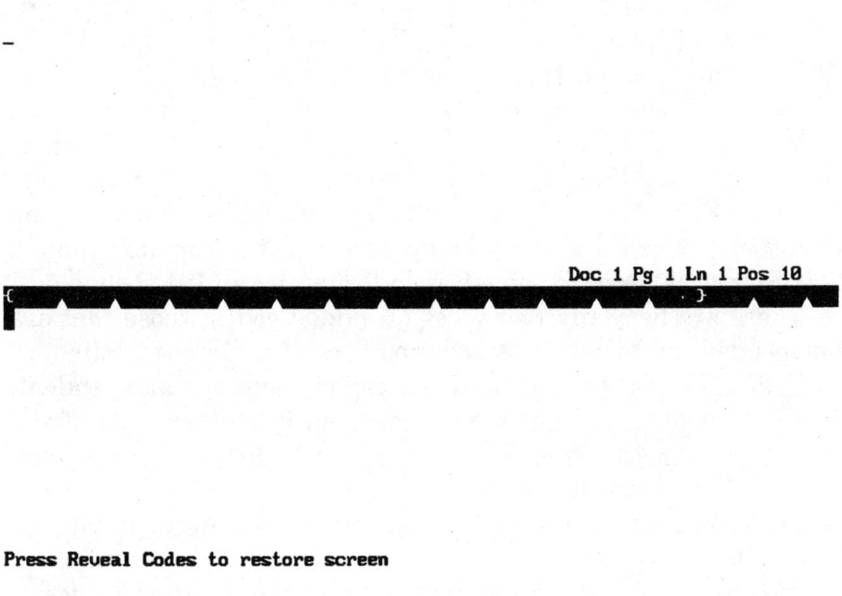

Figure 1-1.   The Reveal Codes screen

You can move the cursors using all of the normal cursor movement commands; both will move simultaneously.

You can easily see where you have made formatting changes in your text on the Reveal Codes screen. These changes are represented by bolded codes surrounded by square brackets. As you move the cursor onto a code, the block cursor will expand to cover the entire code. WordPerfect considers all the characters between each set of brackets to be a single code, although the code may be made up of many characters on the screen.

While the Reveal Codes screen is active, you can perform any commands that you normally would if it were inactive. As you make formatting changes to your text, you'll see the codes appear in the lower portion of the screen. To delete a code or character on which the block cursor is resting, press DEL. To delete the code or character that precedes the one on which the cursor is resting, press BACKSPACE. When you want to turn off the Reveal Codes display, press the <Reveal Codes> key a second time. The original screen display will be restored. (See Chapter 13, "Macro Library," for a trick that allows the Reveal Codes screen to be "temporary," as it is in older versions of WordPerfect.)

While Reveal Codes is active, you can see an [HRt] code wherever *you* pressed the ENTER key in your text. [HRt] is an abbreviation for Hard Return. When *WordPerfect* decides where a line should end (when it automatically wraps text to the next line), a Soft Return is inserted, which is indicated by an [SRt] code.

There are basically two types of hidden codes: those that are independent and those that are members of a Matched Pair.

Codes like margin, tab, and spacing changes are independent. They affect all text that follows them until another code of the same type is encountered. Figure 1-2 shows a Reveal Codes screen containing an independent code.

Codes for underlining and boldfacing are examples of Matched Pair codes. These typically use all uppercase letters to designate the beginning of the function and all lowercase letters to designate its end. For example, try pressing the <Underline> key, typing some text, and pressing the <Underline> key again. Be sure Reveal Codes is active (press <Reveal Codes> if necessary). At

This is a test

Doc 1 Pg 1 Ln 1 Pos 20

[L/R Mar:2",2"]This is a test

Press Reveal Codes to restore screen

Figure 1-2.   An independent hidden code

the point in your text where you first pressed the <Underline>
key, there appears an [UND]; and where you pressed it again,
there appears an [und]. Tab Align, Flush Right, Center, Bold, and
all other print attributes are examples of functions that generate
similar Matched Pair codes.

To remove format choices like these from the text, simply
remove either one of the matched pair; its match will be automatically deleted. Figure 1-3 shows a Reveal Codes screen containing
Matched Pair hidden codes.

With either type of hidden code, it is easy to leave behind a
trail of unneeded, potentially troublesome codes. You can see in
the following example how this would be a bit of a mess:

[UND][BOLD][und][bold][UND][BOLD]Hello[bold][und][HRt]

This is <u>underlined.</u> _

                                                         Doc 1 Pg 1 Ln 1 Pos 29

This is [UND]underlined[und].

Press Reveal Codes to restore screen

Figure 1-3.   Matching Pair hidden codes

In this case, the user was obviously confused and pressed the bold and underline keys too many times, generating a lot of unnecessary codes. These unnecessary codes should be deleted, even though the text may look fine. In fact, if the user had not used Reveal Codes, the codes might never have been discovered at all. Nevertheless, excess codes should always be found and deleted, since they make the Reveal Codes display much more confusing to understand, and they may cause problems when you print the document.

Here is another example of unwanted codes:

[L/R Mar:1",1"][L/R Mar:1.2",1"][L/R Mar:1.2",1.2"]Hello

The user in this case was simply indecisive and tried several different margin settings before finding a satisfactory one. Since the [L/R Mar:] code only affects text that follows it *until the next [L/R Mar:] code*, the first two settings do not affect any text at all and should be deleted.

The Search and Reverse Search functions are useful for locating hidden codes in the text while Reveal Codes is active. (The Search functions are described later in this chapter.) If you mark a block when Reveal Codes is active, you will see a [Block] code, which temporarily marks the beginning of a block.

LINE FORMATTING

Tabs, margins, and line spacing are essential elements of your document's format.

Tabs

When you first use WordPerfect, it uses a default tab setting with a tab stop every half inch. You can change the tab setting at any point in a document by using the Line Format menu. The [Tab Set:] code you generate affects all [Tab] codes that follow it—until the program encounters another [Tab Set:] code. By generating a new [Tab Set:] code before a section of the text that contains [Tab] codes, you can quickly adjust the position of the text.

To insert a new tab setting (define new tab stops), first position the cursor at the place in your document where you want the new tabs to take effect. Then, press the <Format> key (SHIFT+F8), type **1** for "Line," and **8** for "Tab Set." You will see the Tab Setting area at the bottom of the screen. This area is marked with measurements representing the distance from the left edge of the paper. (Although WordPerfect is initially set to use inches as units of measurement, you can easily switch to centimeters, points, and so on. See Appendix A, "Using Setup.") A row of periods represents the area of the document currently visible on the screen. As you move the cursor past the edges of the screen to the left and right, the setting area will scroll, allowing you to set tab stops for wider margins.

Tab Stop Alignment

There are four types of tab stops: left-aligned, centered, right-aligned, and decimal-aligned. These are represented in the Tab Setting area by the letters L, C, R, and D, respectively. Decimal-aligned tab stops actually align text to the current align character, which normally is a decimal point. (See the section "Align Tabs" for a description of decimal-aligned tab stops.)

Setting Tab Stops

Before setting tab stops, you may want to erase the existing default tab stops. To do so, see "Deleting Tab Stops" later in this chapter.

There are three ways to set tab stops: free-form, direct, and incremental.

To use the free-form method, move the cursor with the RIGHT ARROW and LEFT ARROW keys to the desired position for the tab stop, and type the appropriate letter (**L, R, D,** or **C** in either lowercase or uppercase).

To enter tab stops with the direct method, type any number (representing a measurement) and press ENTER. The cursor will move to the specified position and insert a left-aligned tab stop. (If you don't want a left-aligned tab stop, you can press the appropriate letter after pressing ENTER.) You can enter as many tab stops in succession as you like with this method.

Because the default measurement is in inches, you can type **2.5** and press ENTER, and WordPerfect will set a left-aligned tab stop 2.5 inches from the left edge of the paper. You can also specify measurements in hundredths of inches.

Finally, the incremental method allows you to specify a starting tab position and an incremental value. Simply enter the two values separated by a comma. For example, entering **2,1** would place left-aligned tab stops at one-inch intervals beginning at position 2. To set incremental tab stops of a type other than left-aligned, you need to manually insert a tab stop of the desired type at the starting point of the series, and then enter the two values.

Tab Stops with Dot Leaders

You can make any of the tab stops (except center tab stops) use a "dot leader" by positioning the cursor onto any L, R, or D tab stop, and typing a period (the letter will be highlighted). When a tab stop uses a dot leader, the space before each tabbed item is filled with periods, rather than being left blank.

Deleting Tab Stops

To delete a tab stop in the Tab Setting area, position the cursor on the tab stop you want to delete and press the DEL key. You can also delete many tab stops at once by using the <Delete EOL> command (CTRL+END). This command will delete all of the tab stops to the right of the cursor. (You may first want to position the cursor on the left edge of the Tab Setting area with HOME, HOME, and LEFT ARROW.) This is useful for clearing away all existing tabs.

Using Tabs

When you are through changing tab settings, press the <Exit> key (F7) to return to the Line Format menu, then press <Exit> again to return to the Document Editing screen. To move the cursor to a tab stop while you are typing your text, press the TAB key. This key is usually positioned above the CTRL key on the left side of the keyboard and marked with two opposing arrows.

The precise hidden codes that are placed in the document when you press the TAB key depend on the type of the next defined tab stop. If it is a left-aligned tab stop, a [Tab] code is inserted. For right-aligned or decimal-aligned tab stops, [Align] and [C/A/Flrt] Matched Pair codes are placed around the aligned text. (You can also decimal-align text by pressing the <Tab Align> key, as discussed in the next section.) For a centered tab stop, [Cntr] and [C/A/Flrt] Matched Pair codes are placed around the tabbed text.

To display a ruler at the bottom of the screen which displays your current tab settings, see the section titled "Windows" later in this chapter.

Align Tabs

Align tabs line up text at the occurrence of a particular character, rather than at the left edge, right edge, or center of the tabbed text. Align tabs are most frequently used to line up a column of numbers properly. However, Align tabs are flexible enough to be used for many different purposes.

You can use Align Tabs in two ways: you can either define a decimal-aligned tab stop using the steps outlined in the previous section, and then use the TAB key each time you want to use an Align Tab; or, you can use the <Tab Align> key (CTRL+F6) to use an Align Tab with any type of defined tab stop. The first method is better when you know you'll be entering a lot of data, as in a table. The second method is helpful when you only occasionally need to use an Align Tab, or if you don't want to change your tab settings.

Whichever method you use, the program will display

`Align Char = .`

Enter the text to be aligned. All the characters you type will move to the *left* of the tab stop until you type a decimal point. Then the characters you type will start appearing to the right of the tab stop. For example, if you enter **1,298.79**, the characters 1,298 would be moved to the left of the tab stop, the decimal point would be lined up right at the tab stop, and the characters 79 would appear after the tab stop. This allows a column of dollar amounts to be lined up correctly on the decimal point. If you want to end the Tab Align function before you have pressed the align character, press TAB, <Tab Align>, or ENTER.

You can change the Tab Align character from a period to any letter, number, or punctuation mark. To change the character, first position the cursor at the place in your document where you want the new align character to take effect. Then, press the <Format> key (SHIFT+F8), type **4** for "Other," and then **3**. Type the character you want to use for alignment. Next, type the character you want WordPerfect to use to separate thousands in numbers (usually a comma, but it can be a period). Press the <Exit> key (F7) to return to the Document Editing screen. From this point on in the document, the Tab Align function (and decimal-aligned tab stops) will respond to the specified character. This versatility allows the Tab Align function to be used for a variety of text applications as well as for lining up numbers.

For example, here's a table where the equal sign was used as the align character:

```
     belief = croyance
       boat = bateau
      bulky = volumineux
butterscotch = caramel au beurre
```

Another use for changing the align character would be to have the function use a comma for alignment because in many countries a comma is used as a decimal point.

Left and Right Margins

WordPerfect's left and right margins are set by specifying a distance from either side of the paper. Both are initially set one inch from the edge. This means that on a typical letter-size page you will have 6 1/2 inches of room for text across the page.

To change the margins, position the cursor at the left edge of the first line you want to affect. If you do not position it at the left edge, an [HRt] code (Hard Return) will automatically be inserted before the margin code. Press the <Format> key (SHIFT+F8), type **1** for "Line," and **7** for "Margins." The current margin settings are shown in the current measurement unit (initially inches). Type the measurement for the left margin and press

ENTER, then type the measurement for the right margin and press ENTER. Press the <Exit> key (F7) to return to the Document Editing screen. An [L/R Mar:] code is inserted in the document at the cursor position, and all text from that point on, until another [L/R Mar:] code is encountered, will be formatted with the margins you have specified.

If your margins are wider than the screen, your text will automatically scroll left and right as you type. You can manually scroll the text using the arrow key sequences discussed earlier in "Short Trips."

Spacing

WordPerfect has two commands that control the spacing between lines: Line Spacing and Line Height.

Line Spacing

WordPerfect initially produces single-spaced text unless you've modified the program's Initial Settings (see Appendix A, "Using Setup"). To change to another spacing, begin by positioning the cursor where you want to begin the change. Then, press the <Format> key (SHIFT+F8), type **1** for "Line," and **6** for "Line Spacing." The prompt shows the current spacing value. Type the number you want (for example, **2** for double spacing), and press ENTER. Press the <Exit> key to return to the Document Editing screen. A [Ln Spacing:] code is inserted in the text at the cursor position.

The screen displays, as closely as possible, the spacing as it will appear when your document is printed. For example, there is no way the screen can show half spacing—however, the Line Indicator at the bottom of the screen will keep track of half lines. The line spacing shown on the screen will be the next whole number after the value you enter. Specifying one-and-a-half line spacing (1.5), for example, would produce double spacing on the screen.

If you have a graphics display, the Print View command will show you line spacing exactly as it will appear when you print the document. See "Previewing a Document" later in this chapter.

Line Height (Leading)

Although line spacing is always entered in lines, the actual distance between lines—that is, from the bottom of one, to the bottom of the next—is based not only on the current line spacing, but also on the current line height (or leading). Normally, Line Height is set to Auto, which means it will be adjusted automatically for each line to allow for the largest character on the line. Each font size has an associated default value for its line height.

If you wish, however, you can specify a fixed Line Height of any measurement. In this case, spacing between the text will remain consistent, regardless of the size of the characters on each line. If you use text larger than the space specified between lines, it will print on top of the text above it.

To change the line height, press the <Format> key (SHIFT+F8), type **1** for "Line," and **4** for "Line Height." If you want automatic line height, type **1** for "Auto." To specify a fixed line height type **2** for "Fixed," then type a measurement, and press ENTER. Press <Exit> to return to the Document Editing screen.

Centering

As with text embellishments, centering may be specified either before or after you have typed the text to be centered.

To center a line before you type it, simply press the <Center> key (SHIFT+F6), type the line, and press ENTER. WordPerfect inserts matched pairs of [Cntr] and [C/A/Flrt] codes around the centered text. To center a line that has already been typed, position the cursor on the first character of the line and press <Center>. Then, when you move your cursor down, the line will reformat and be properly centered. You can also center many lines at once by marking them as a block and, while the "Block on" message is flashing, by pressing the <Center> key. The program will ask you to confirm the centering before it completes the command.

To center text over a column of text or numbers, use a center tab stop (see the earlier section "Tabs").

Indenting Paragraphs

You can use the Indent functions to effectively increase the left and right margins for just one paragraph at a time. The Left Indent function increases the left margin, and the Left/Right Indent function increases both margins evenly by bringing the text in on both sides. WordPerfect uses tab stops to determine how far to indent the paragraphs. Because tab stops are set at half-inch intervals by default, you usually indent a paragraph in increments of half an inch.

Many people think of an indented paragraph as one in which only the first line is indented. To create this type of paragraph, you should use the TAB key as described in the earlier section, "Tabs."

To indent the left margin of a paragraph, simply press the <Left Indent> key (F4) before typing the text of the paragraph, and the cursor will move to the first defined tab stop. You can press the <Left Indent> several times, until your cursor is positioned where you want the left margin of the paragraph to be. At first, it may seem that the Indent function performs the same function as pressing the TAB key. However, when you begin to type the paragraph, you will see that the second and subsequent lines wrap to the same location as the first line. The cursor returns to the left margin when you press ENTER.

To indent an existing paragraph, position the cursor on the first character in the paragraph, and press the <Left Indent> key. You may need to press the DOWN ARROW key to have the screen reflect the indentation.

You may wish to type a paragraph number, or some other text, before indenting the paragraph. Then, when you press the <Left Indent> key, the remainder of the paragraph is indented to the next tab stop. You can also press the TAB or <Left Indent> key before entering the paragraph number, useful for numbered sub-paragraphs.

The Left/Right Indent function works exactly the same as the Left Indent, except that the right margin is increased by the same amount as the left margin. Tab stops are only used to determine the increase for the left margin—the right margin simply mirrors the indentation on the left. Therefore, you control the position of both margins only by the location of the tab stop with which the left margin aligns.

For example, to enter a quotation that is evenly indented one inch on both sides—when your tab stops are set at half-inch intervals—simply press the <Left/Right Indent> key (SHIFT+F4) twice, type the paragraph, and press ENTER.

PAGE FORMATTING

WordPerfect's page formatting options allow you to control elements such as top and bottom margins, page numbering, and headers and footers.

You should begin by positioning the cursor at the very top of the first page on which you want to start the new format. If your cursor is anywhere on the desired page, you can do this quickly by pressing CTRL+HOME (the <Go to> key) followed by UP ARROW. If you are on the previous page, press PGDN. If you are on the following page, press PGUP. All of these commands position the cursor at the beginning of the page, before all text and codes. You can also position the cursor manually using Reveal Codes.

The editing screen will not reflect page formatting changes made in the text. For example, you will not see page numbering or footers on the screen. However, WordPerfect will automatically compensate for these elements when it calculates the amount of text to allow on a page. You can also use the Print View command to see the pages of the document exactly as they will appear, with all page numbering, headers, footers, and so on. (See "Previewing a Document" later in this chapter.)

Top and Bottom Margins

The top and bottom margins of the pages in a document are defined, respectively, as the distance between the top edge of the paper and the top of the first line of text on the page, and the distance between the bottom edge of the paper and the bottom of the last line on the page. Initially, both are set to one inch.

To change the top and bottom margins, begin by positioning the cursor at the top of the first page you wish to affect. Then, press the <Format> key (SHIFT+F8), type 2 for "Page," and then 5 for "Margins." The current top and bottom margin settings will be shown. Type a measurement for the top margin, press ENTER, then type a measurement for the bottom margin, and press ENTER. Measurements are normally entered in the default unit of measure, initially set to inches. However, you can use a different unit by following the number with an appropriate symbol, and WordPerfect will instantly convert it to the default unit. (See Appendix A, "Using Setup.")

Press the <Exit> key (F7) to return to the document editing screen. A [T/B Mar:] code will appear in the document at the cursor position. This code affects the top and bottom margins from this point to the end of the document, or until another [T/B Mar:] code is encountered.

Page Numbering

There are two methods for placing page numbers in your document. You can either choose a specific location for just the number using the Page Numbering command, or you can create a header or footer that contains the page number. Using a header or footer allows you the flexibility of including some text with the number, such as the word "Page" (as in "Page 3"), or two hyphens (-3-). (See the next section, "Headers and Footers.")

To specify just a page number, begin by positioning the cursor at the top of the first page on which you want the number to appear. Then, press the <Format> key (SHIFT+F8), type **2** for "Page," and then **7** for "Page Numbering." The Page Number Position screen will appear, as shown in Figure 1-4.

You can see that you have quite a few choices for the position of the page numbers. Type **1**, **2**, **3**, **5**, **6**, or **7** to place the page numbers in one of the four corners of every page, or at the top center or bottom center of every page. Type **4** or **8** to have the page numbers appear on alternating pages—typing **4** causes the numbers to appear in the upper-left for even pages, and upper-right for odd pages; typing **8** causes the numbers to appear in the lower-left for even pages, and lower-right for odd pages. To stop page numbering which you've set previously, type **9**.

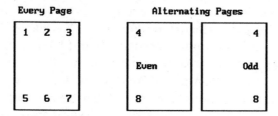

Figure 1-4.   Page Number Position screen

After you make a selection, you'll return to the Page Formatting screen. Your page numbering choice is shown next to option 7. Press <Exit> to return to the Document Editing screen. A [Pg Numbering:] code is inserted in the document at the cursor position.

You can choose to suppress the printing of a page number on any one page by using the Suppress function. (See "Suppressing a Page Format" later in this chapter.)

Headers and Footers

You can have WordPerfect automatically place some text at the top or bottom of every page in your document by using the Header or Footer command. You can also choose to have the text appear only on odd or only on even pages.

To begin creating a header or footer, position the cursor at the top of the first page on which you want the header or footer to appear. Press the <Format> key (SHIFT+F8), and type **2** for "Page," then **3** for "Headers" or **4** for "Footers." Next, type **1** for Header or Footer A, or **2** for Header or Footer B. You can have two headers or footers defined simultaneously (A and B) and then switch between them at will. You can also have the two headers or footers alternate on odd and even pages. You might, for example, want a chapter title and a flush-right page number on odd pages, and a flush-left page number and a book title on even pages. You can easily create this format by specifying that Footer A should appear only on odd pages, and Footer B on even pages.

Once you've selected which header or footer to work with, another menu appears at the bottom of the screen. To have the selected header or footer appear on every page, type **2** for "Every page." To have it appear on odd pages, type **3**. To have it appear on even pages, type **4**.

When you have specified an option, you'll see the Header/Footer Editing screen. Enter whatever text you want in the header or footer. (You can type several lines of text if you like.) For example, let's assume you selected Footer A on every page. To place a centered book title at the bottom of every page, you'd press the <Center> key, type the title, and press ENTER. To include the page number in the header or footer, simply press CTRL+N at the place where you want the number to appear. You'll see a $^\wedge$N appear on the screen. WordPerfect will replace this code with the appropriate number on each page. (You can also use CTRL+B for this purpose, in which case you'd see $^\wedge$B instead.)

When you've entered the desired text for the header or footer, press the <Exit> key (F7), and you'll be returned to the Page Format screen. Next to the "Header" and "Footer" options, you'll see abbreviations of the headers and footers currently defined, along with the placement you've selected for each one. For example, "HA" represents Header A, and "FB" represents Footer B.

Press <Exit> to return to the Document Editing screen. A [Header] or [Footer] code is inserted in the text at the cursor position. You can preview the appearance of the header or footer on the page by using the Print View command. (See "Previewing a Document" later in this chapter.)

WordPerfect automatically separates the text of a header from the first line of a document with one blank line. This assumes that you *do not* press ENTER at the end of the last line in the header. If you *do* press ENTER, you'll be adding an additional blank line of space below the header. Each time you press ENTER, you'll add another blank line. This also reduces the amount of text allowed on each page.

The text of a footer is also automatically separated from the text of the body of the document by one blank line. By pressing ENTER before the text in the footer, you can increase this space.

Suppressing a Page Format

You can have WordPerfect suppress a header, footer, or page number for any single page using the Suppress command. This is useful, for example, on the first page of a letter, book chapter, or legal pleading.

To suppress a page format, begin by positioning the cursor at the top of the relevant page. Then, press the <Format> key (SHIFT + F8), type **2** for "Page," and then **9** for "Suppress." The Suppress screen will appear. WordPerfect displays "Yes" or "No" for most of the options, to show which ones have already been suppressed for the current page. To change any of the options, type the appropriate number, then type **Y** or **N** to indicate whether you want that option suppressed.

When you've finished changing the suppression options, press the <Exit> key to return to the Page Format menu, then press the <Exit> key again to return to the Document Editing screen. A [Suppress:] code is placed in the document at the cursor position. This code must appear before any text on the page if it is to have effect. The specified headers, footers, and page numbering will not appear on the current page, but will resume on the next page.

Restarting Page Numbering

You can have WordPerfect restart page numbering with any number, on any page in the document. You can also choose whether to use Arabic or lowercase Roman numerals for the numbers. (For example, you may want the preface of a book to be numbered in Roman numerals, and have the body of the book start over in Arabic numerals.)

To restart page numbering, begin by positioning the cursor at the top of the first page you want to number. Then, press the <Format> key (SHIFT+F8), type **2** for "Page," then **6** for "New Page Number." The current page number is displayed at the prompt, using the current number style. Type the desired page number for the current page, using the style that you want for the printed numbers. For example, type **i** (a lowercase "I") to indicate that the current page should become Page 1, with page numbering in lowercase Roman numerals. Type **47** to have the current page become Page 47.

Press ENTER after you've typed the desired number. Press the
<Exit> key to return to the Document Editing screen. A [Pg
Num:] code is placed in the document at the cursor position.

You can also force the current page to be numbered with an
odd or even number. This is useful, for example, on the first page
of a new chapter in a book. Typically, you would want this page to
always be an odd page, appearing on the right-hand side of the
book. The Force Odd/Even Page command will skip a page
number if necessary to force a page to be numbered odd or even.

To force the numbering in this way, begin by positioning the
cursor at the top of the page you want to affect. Then, press the
<Format> key (SHIFT+F8), type **2** for "Page," then **2** for "Force
Odd/Even Page." Type **1** to make the current page an odd-
numbered page, or **2** to make it even-numbered. Press the
<Exit> key to return to the Document Editing screen. A
[Force:Odd] or [Force:Even] code is placed in the document at the
cursor position.

SEARCHING

WordPerfect has a Search function that looks through your text to
find any word, phrase, or series of letters and codes that you specify. You can have the program search from the cursor position
forward (toward the end of the document) or backward (toward
the beginning). It is very important to position your cursor appropriately before you issue the Search command.

Using Search

To start the search, press the <Search> key (F2), and enter the
search string (the text you wish to search for). If you have previously used Search since starting WordPerfect, the program will
suggest the previous search string. You can either type a new
search string, or you can edit the previous one. When you have

entered the desired search string, press <Search> again or ESC. The cursor will then be positioned *after* the next occurrence of the search string. To search for more occurrences of the same text, just press the <Search> key twice. To search backward, follow the same steps as above, using the <Search Left> key (SHIFT+F2) to start the process.

Replacing

Use the Replace function to search for one string of text and replace it with another. This function can be useful if you have consistently misspelled a name or incorrectly typed a phrase. The Replace function works in a similar fashion to the Search function; however, it only works in a forward direction.

To start the Replace procedure, press the <Replace> key (ALT+F2). The program asks whether you want it to stop at each occurrence of the search string and ask for confirmation. If you are sure you want to replace all occurrences, you don't need confirmation, so type **N**. If only some of the occurrences will need to be replaced, type **Y** for confirmation.

You will then be prompted for the search string, which you entered exactly as you would for the Search command. You can press any of the Search keys or ESC to end the search string. When you do, you will be prompted for a *replacement string*. Enter the text that will replace the search string and press any of the Search keys or ESC again.

If you don't enter anything for the replacement string, all occurrences of the search string will be replaced with nothing— that is, they will be deleted. The function can also be used to strip a document of certain codes, such as underlining and boldfacing.

To perform the Replace function on a specific amount of text rather than the entire document, simply use the Block function to mark the text before starting the Replace. Only the occurrences of the search string that are found within the blocked text are replaced with the replacement string.

Searching for Hidden Codes

You can search for codes as well as for text. If you mistakenly try to start a search by pressing the ENTER key, [HRt] appears in the search string. This happens because the [HRt] code is *searchable*— that is, you can use the Search function to find the code in the text. This can be useful if, for example, you want to find a phrase that appears on a line of its own (such as a title), you want to find all paragraphs that begin or end with a certain word, or you want to find a certain number of blank lines between paragraphs.

To insert other codes into the search string, you can usually press the key sequence that you would normally use to generate them in the text. However, sometimes the sequence of keystrokes needs to be slightly modified. For example, to search for the next occurrence of a margin change in your document, press the <Search> key (F2), then enter the [L/R Mar:] code into the search string by pressing the <Format> key (SHIFT+F8), and typing **1** for "Line," and **6** for "Margins." Most codes can be entered in this manner, although the menus that appear might look a little different than those that each key would normally produce.

Appearance options such as underline, bold, italics, and small caps all use matched pairs of hidden codes. To enter the code that turns the function on (for example, the [UND] or the [BOLD]) into the search string, press the appropriate function key or choose the option from the Appearance menu. To enter the code that turns the function off (for example, the [und] or the [bold]) into the search string, press the appropriate function key (or choose the option) once, press BACKSPACE, and then press the key or choose the option again.

Searching for Words

Sometimes a search can turn up unexpected results. For example, if you search for "man," the Search function will not only find all occurrences of the word *man* but also *woman, manager,* and

Comanche. One way to limit a search to entire words is to put a space before and/or after the word in the search string. However, this will not always work. For example, some occurrences of the word might start a new paragraph, in which case they will be preceded by an [HRt] instead of a space; they may end a sentence, which means they would be followed by any of a number of different punctuation marks; or, they may be enclosed in quotation marks.

Ultimately, there is no good way to limit a search to entire words, as opposed to parts of larger words, without compromising the reliability of the search. The best bet, then, is to put up with the inaccurate findings, so that you are sure of finding all of the occurrences.

This problem is especially troublesome with the Replace function. Let's say you want to replace all occurrences of *man* with *person*. If you performed a Replace operation without confirmation, you'd probably end up with words like *woperson* in place of *woman*. On the other hand, confirming each replacement might be very time consuming if you're working with a large document.

One solution would be to perform two Replace operations. The first, with no confirmation, would search for *man* with a space before and after it, and replace it with *person* with a space before and after it. This would replace the bulk of the legitimate occurrences of *man*. The second, with confirmation, would search for *man* by itself and replace it with *person* by itself. This would take care of any of the exceptions mentioned above (such as words in quotes, or those followed by punctuation).

Using Wildcards

Another feature of the Search and Replace functions is that the search string can include a *wildcard* character that will match any single character. To insert the wildcard character into the search string, press CTRL+V and then CTRL+X, and you will see ^X appear. The search string "ra^Xt," for example, will find raft, rant, and rapt.

Extended Search

Normally, the Search and Replace functions locate text and codes that appear only in text that is visible on the editing screen. The Extended Search (or Replace) extends the scope to include text in headers, footers, footnotes, endnotes, and graphic boxes.

To use the Extended Search, simply press the HOME key before pressing the <Search>, <Search Left>, or <Replace> keys. If an occurrence of the search string is found within a header, footer, footnote, or endnote, the Search will end (or the Replace will pause) within the appropriate screen.

FILE MANAGEMENT

File management consists of the process of saving and retrieving documents to and from disk, as well as deleting, renaming, and copying documents currently on disk. File management functions are simply housekeeping tasks that keep the files on your disks organized.

Saving and Retrieving Documents

All WordPerfect documents are given a file name when they are saved on disk. These file names can be any legal DOS file name; that is, they can consist of a name of from 1 to 8 characters, a period, and an extension of from 1 to 3 characters. The characters can be any letter or number, as well as any of these punctuation marks:

$ ( ) & ' − @ # { } % ~ ! — ^

You can use the extension to specify a type of document. For example, .LTR might specify a letter, while .AGT might specify an agreement. The <List Files> key, discussed later in this chapter, could then be used to search through all your files to find only your letters or agreements.

Saving

To save the current document on disk, press the <Save> key (F10), type a file name, and press ENTER. If you have previously saved the current document (thereby giving it a name) or you have retrieved the document from disk (instead of creating it from scratch), the Save command will first suggest the known name. If you want to save the document with this name, you can simply press ENTER. Otherwise, you can use the cursor control keys to edit the name, or just type a new name and press ENTER. If a file with the name you specify already exists on disk, the program will ask if you want to replace the file with the current document. Type **Y** to replace the file or type **N** to specify another name.

It is a good idea to save a current version of your document periodically while you work, not just when you are done. This is truly a quick and painless procedure and one every computer veteran does on a frequent basis. The hassle of pressing the <Save> key, ENTER (use the same name), and typing **Y** (to confirm the replacement) is trivial compared to the horror of losing a file because it wasn't saved to disk when the lights went out.

It's also a good idea to use WordPerfect's Timed Backup feature, described in Appendix A, "Using Setup."

Retrieving

You can retrieve a document into memory (onto the screen) at any time. If the screen is clear when you retrieve, you will see the new document. If the screen already contains a document, you will insert the contents of the retrieved document at the cursor position.

There are two ways to retrieve a document from disk: using the <Retrieve> key (SHIFT+F10) and using the <List Files> key (F5).

Using the <Retrieve> key can be quicker, but you must remember the entire file name. To retrieve a document this way, press the <Retrieve> key (SHIFT+F10), type the file name, and press ENTER.

The <List Files> key allows you to display a disk's directory and simply point to the file you want to retrieve (see the next section). *Don't forget that unless you want to combine documents, you should clear the screen before retrieving a new document.*

When you retrieve a document created with WordPerfect 4.2 or an earlier version (using either List Files or the Retrieve key), you'll see the message "Document conversion in progress" while it translates the document's format. If you try to retrieve a document that was created with a more recent version of WordPerfect than the one you're using, you'll see the message "Incompatible file format." If you didn't clear the screen before using the List Files function, you'll see the message "Retrieve into current document?" Type **Y** to combine the documents, or type **N** to cancel the command.

List Files

With the <List Files> key (F5) you can retrieve and print documents as well as perform DOS-like commands like renaming, deleting, and copying files. In addition, a Word Search function finds documents that contain specific text, or that were saved or created within a certain date range. A Look command lets you take a "quick look" at a document without actually retrieving it.

When you press the <List Files> key (F5), you will see a display like this at the bottom of the screen if you are using floppy-based computer system:

Dir B:\×.×   (Type = to change default Dir)

If you are using a hard disk, you will see a display similar to this:

Dir C:\WP\DATA\×.×   (Type = to change default Dir)

At this point WordPerfect is displaying the current *default directory* —that is, the disk or directory that files are retrieved from and stored to, unless you specify otherwise.

There are four actions you can choose from at this point:

- Press ENTER to work with the files on the default directory.

- Edit the directory name, or type a new drive or directory, and press ENTER to work temporarily with the files from that drive or directory.

- Press = (equal sign), and then edit the directory name, or type a new drive or directory, and press ENTER to *change* the default directory. WordPerfect will again display the directory prompt, so you can repeat any of these actions.

- Enter a *filename template*, which is usually a combination of valid DOS file name characters and the two DOS wildcard symbols, ? and *. This template allows you to specify a subset of your current disk or directory files that the List Files function will use. For example, to work with all of your letter files, you could enter *.**LTR** to specify all files with an .LTR extension, or you could enter **GR*.*** to specify all files beginning with GR. (Refer to your DOS manual for a complete description of the wildcard symbols.)

After selecting some combination of these four choices, you will see the List Files display. At the top is some useful information: the current date and time, the displayed disk or directory, the filename template you specified, the size of your current document, the amount of free space on your current disk, the amount of space used by the files shown, and finally, the total number of files shown. Below this information will appear a list of the files you've specified, in alphabetical order from left to right.

You will see a bar located on an entry labelled ". <CURRENT>" at the top of the column on the left. This bar indicates the file on which an action can currently be performed. If there are more files in the list than can be displayed on one screen, a small down arrow (▼) appears at the bottom of the center dividing line. After you begin scrolling down through a long list, you'll see an up arrow (▲) appear at the top of the dividing line, indicating that there are more files above the list currently shown.

You can use the arrow keys to move around the list, as well as <Screen Up>, <Screen Down>, and several other cursor positioning controls. To locate a file quickly, you can use Name Search. To do this, type **N** for "Name Search," or press the <Search> key (F2), then begin typing the file name. The bar will immediately move to the file that most closely matches the letters you type. Most of the time it will find the file you need after you type the first few letters. Press SPACE BAR or ENTER to exit Name Search.

Nine different actions are listed at the bottom of the screen (in addition to Name Search). Pressing a number from 1 to 9 causes the action to be performed, usually on the selected file. You can also perform an action on several files at a time either by marking them individually (positioning the cursor bar and pressing the * key) or by marking all files with the <Mark Text> key (ALT+F5). Once all files have been marked with the <Mark Text> key, you can unmark individual files by positioning the cursor bar and pressing the * key. Marked files can be deleted, copied, printed, and searched. To move the cursor bar to the next marked file, press TAB; to move to the previous marked file, press SHIFT+TAB.

Let's discuss the nine actions individually:

Retrieve   Retrieves the selected file in the same manner as the <Retrieve> key. Remember to clear the screen before retrieving a new document. If you don't, a message will ask whether you want to retrieve the document into the current document.

Delete   Deletes the file from disk. The program will ask for confirmation before completing the command.

Move/Rename   Prompts you for a new name for the selected file. The name cannot be the same as another file name on the disk or in the current directory. If you specify a new directory on the same disk, the file will be moved to that directory.

Print   Prints the selected file. This is one of the three methods of printing documents. Printing is discussed later in this chapter.

Text In   Retrieves the selected file as an ASCII file. This command is discussed in detail in Chapter 12, "Integration with Other Products."

Look   Lets you "look" at the selected file or directory. (You can also use the ENTER key to perform this action.) This is a quick way to check the contents of a file without actually retrieving it and disrupting your current editing workspace. It is also much faster than retrieving the file. Once you are looking at a file, you can use the UP ARROW and DOWN ARROW keys, the <Screen Up> and <Screen Down> keys, the PGUP and PGDN keys, or HOME, HOME, UP ARROW and HOME, HOME, DOWN ARROW to view the file. You can also use the <Search> key (F2) to locate text. When you are through looking, press the <Exit> key (F7) to return to the List Files screen.

If the bar is currently highlighting a directory name instead of a file name when you press ENTER or type **6**, you will first be prompted for a filename template, and then you will "look" at the directory. That is, you will see the contents of the directory in the List Files display, but the directory will not become your default directory.

Other Directory   Allows you to change the default directory and filename template while remaining on the List Files screen.

Copy   Copies the selected file to a specified disk or directory. You can also use Copy to make a duplicate of a file with a different name. This command performs the same action as the DOS COPY command.

Word Search   Presents a menu which allows you to search through all the files currently listed on the List Files display for a specific word or phrase and/or a date range. A complete discussion of how this function is used can be found in Appendix B, "Using Word Search."

Type **0**, or press the <Cancel> key (F1), the <Exit> key (F7), or SPACE BAR, to exit the List Files screen and return to your document.

WORKING WITH TWO
DOCUMENTS AT A TIME

There are times when you will want to work with two documents simultaneously. Perhaps you're creating a document and need information contained in another WordPerfect document. You may, for example, be writing a letter and need access to a previous letter you have written about the same subject. If you are writing a magazine article, you may want your outline or notes in one file and the article itself in another. Or you may be working on a document and need to write a quick memo or take notes on a phone conversation. WordPerfect makes it easy to edit two documents at once. You can even copy (or move) and retrieve information between two documents with this feature.

To switch from a document you are working on to a second document, press the <Switch> key (SHIFT+F3). The screen will be clear except for the document information in the lower-right corner. Instead of "Doc 1," it now says "Doc 2."

At this point you can begin typing a new document or retrieve an existing file. All WordPerfect commands function exactly as they do when you are working with only one file.

What happened to the first file you were working on? Don't worry. It is still there, even if you have not saved it to disk. If you press <Switch> again, you are returned to your first document, exactly where you left off. The <Switch> key acts as a toggle, taking you back and forth between the two documents.

You can work with each document independently, or you can transfer information back and forth between them using the Move command. Simply use the <Switch> key after copying or moving text, but before retrieving it.

Windows

With the Windows function, you can view both Document 1 and Document 2 on the screen at the same time. The separate sections of the screen that show the two documents are called *windows*.

To split the screen into two sections, press the <Screen> key (CTRL+F3) and type **1**, for "Window." You will be prompted for the "number of lines in this window." Type any number from 1 to 24 (WordPerfect allows for 24 lines of text on a full screen), and press ENTER.

Once you select the window size, you will notice a thick horizontal bar across the screen. This is called the *ruler*, and it shows you the current tab and margin settings according to your cursor position. The little triangles in the middle of the line show the positions of the tab stops. The left and right margin marks are normally displayed as left and right square brackets, but if a margin mark falls at the same place as a tab stop, it is displayed as a curly bracket.

If the tab stop triangles are pointing up, you are working in Document 1, the top window. If they are pointing down, you are working in Document 2, the bottom window. The <Switch> key (SHIFT+F3), as always, toggles you between Document 1 and Document 2.

The ruler and the two lines of document information for each window take up a total of three lines. Since there are 25 total lines on the screen, this leaves you with 22 lines of text to be shared by both windows. When you size one window, WordPerfect automatically sizes the other window to 22 lines minus the size of the first window. For instance, if you change one window to be 10 lines, the other window is automatically 12 lines. (Because of this, you can create two equal-sized windows by specifying that either window contain 11 lines.)

To change the size of either window, press the <Screen> key, type **1** for "Window," and enter the number of lines that you want the window to contain. Instead of entering the number directly, you can also use the UP ARROW and DOWN ARROW keys to position the separating ruler higher or lower on the screen. When you are satisfied with the number you've entered, or the position of the ruler on the screen, press ENTER.

You can eliminate windows altogether by sizing either window to 24 lines. When you do that, the other window (the one that you are not actively working in) disappears from view, but the document is still in the computer's memory. You can switch to that document at any time by pressing the <Switch> key.

To get the ruler on the screen without displaying a window, set the size of either window to 23 lines. The ruler will be displayed at the bottom of the screen. Use the <Switch> key to switch between the two documents.

Working with windows can require quite a few keystrokes, but you can automate the steps with macros (see Chapter 13, "Macro Library").

SAVING BLOCKS

You can save a portion of a file by marking it with the <Block> key. There are two ways to save the block: as a file by itself or added to the end of another file.

Saving a Block to a File

To save a block as a separate document, highlight the text with the Block command. While the message "Block on" is flashing, press the <Save> key (F10). WordPerfect will display the "Block name:" prompt. When you enter a file name, the block will be stored on disk as a separate file. Just as with the Save command, if a file with that name already exists, you will be prompted to confirm the file replacement. The block will remain in its original location in the document you are working on.

Appending a Block to Another File

WordPerfect's Block Append command lets you add a block of text to the end of another file. This can be useful, for example, for collecting bits and pieces of text into a sort of "scrapbook" file.

To perform the Block Append command, highlight the text with the Block command. While the "Block on" message is flashing, press the <Move> key (CTRL+F4), then type **1** for "Block," and **4** for "Append." Type the name of the file to which you wish to append the block, and press ENTER. If the file you name does not already exist on disk, WordPerfect creates a new one for you.

CONTROLLING PRINTERS

When you tell WordPerfect to print a document, it generates a *print job*. This print job is placed at the end of the *print queue*, which is simply a list of the documents waiting to be printed.

You manage the print queue from the Printer Control screen, which gives you a complete account of what is going on with your printer: Is it printing? What is it printing? How far along is it? The Printer Control screen provides the answers.

Printing

There are three ways to print a document. All have the same result: they generate a print job, which is added to the print queue.

Printing the Current Document

This method is the easiest because it does not require that the document be saved to disk or that a file name be entered. When you are through typing the text you want printed, press the <Print> key (SHIFT+F7) and type **1** for "Full Document" to print the entire document currently in memory, or type **2** to print just the page the cursor is on.

The other two methods of printing require that the document be stored on disk in the condition in which you want it printed. This means that if you are editing a document on screen and want to print it using one of these methods, you must first save the file on disk. *You must also have saved the document with the Fast Save option turned off.* (See Appendix A, "Using Setup.") You can be editing any document when either of these print commands is issued.

Printing with List Files

To print with List Files, first go to the List Files display by pressing the <List Files> key (F5) and pressing ENTER. Then position the bar on the file you want to print and type **4** for "Print," to generate a print job. You will be prompted for the page(s) to print.

You can either press ENTER to use the default (printing the entire document) or you can enter individual page numbers or ranges of pages (see the section "Specifying Page Ranges" in this chapter).

Printing a Document by Name

To print a document with this method, press the <Print> key (SHIFT+F7), and type **3** for "Document on Disk." Then enter the name of the file you wish to print. When you enter the file name, you will be prompted for the page(s) to print. You can either press ENTER to use the default of printing the entire document, or you can enter individual page numbers or ranges of pages.

Specifying Page Ranges

To print individual pages, enter each number separated by a comma. For example, you can type **2,9,15** and press ENTER to print pages 2, 9, and 15 of the specified document. To print a range of pages, enter two page numbers separated by a hyphen. For example, you can type **5-10** and press ENTER to print pages 5 through 10. If you omit the first number, printing will start at the beginning of the document. If you omit the second number, printing will continue to the last page of the document.

You can also combine individual page numbers with page ranges. For example, you can type **5,10-15,20** to print page 5, pages 10 through 15, and page 20.

If you have used the New Page Number command to start new sections within a document—for example, to restart numbering for chapters within a book or sections within a manual—you can refer to these sections when printing a range of pages. To do this, simply precede the number of the page within a section with the section number and a colon. For example, to print page 3 of the second section in a document, type **2:3** and press ENTER. To print pages 5 through 9 from the third section, type **3:5-9** and press ENTER.

Managing the Print Queue

Once you generate a print job, it is added to the end of the print queue. After it is printed, the document is removed from the queue. You can inspect and manage the print queue by pressing the <Print> key (SHIFT+F7) and typing **4**, for "Control Printer." At the top of the screen is a status display showing what is currently happening in the print queue. In the middle of the status display is a list of the three print jobs at the top of the queue, and at the bottom is a menu of commands for controlling the queue. To see a list of all print jobs in the queue, type **3** for "Display Jobs."

If you will normally print only one file at a time, the process of managing the print queue is incidental, unless you encounter problems during printing. However, you can still check the Control Printer screen for information on the status of a print job.

If you generate a print job and the printer doesn't start printing, *don't tell it to print again*. Something probably needs correcting before the print job can be restarted. If you generate too many print jobs, you can end up with quite a mess. Instead, check the Control Printer screen to see if you can determine what the problem is, so that you can fix it and restart the print job.

Here is an explanation of the menu choices on the Control Printer screen that affect printing:

1. **Cancel Job(s)**   This command cancels a specific print job by number. You can also cancel all the active print jobs either by typing * here and pressing ENTER or by exiting WordPerfect and responding **Y** to the prompt "Cancel all print jobs?"

2. **Rush Job**   This command prompts you for a job number, and then puts it at the top of the print queue.

3. **Display Jobs**   This command clears the screen and displays a list of all print jobs in the print queue.

4. **Go (start printer)**   If you need to stop printing (if the printer cover opens or you run out of ribbon, for example), use the Stop command that follows. The Go command will then start things rolling again, beginning with whatever page you specify. The Go command also starts printing for each page when you are operating in hand-fed mode. This process can be simplified by using a macro, as discussed in Chapter 13, "Macro Library."

5. **Stop**   This stops WordPerfect from trying to print. Because many printers have memory buffers that hold a page or more of text, printing may not stop immediately. It may be necessary to type 5 and then turn off the printer—or reset it, if possible—to actually stop printing immediately. Use Go to start printing again.

Print Options

There are several commands on the Print menu which allow you to set such options as adding a binding width, printing multiple copies of a document, or affecting the quality of the output. Changes to any one of them will remain in effect for all future print jobs until you reset them, or until you exit WordPerfect. No hidden codes are generated by the following commands.

S Select Printer   This allows you to select the active printer. You can also add printers to the available printer list with this command. See Chapter 11, "Using Printers," for a description of the printer selection process.

B Binding   The binding width is a page offset that moves even pages to the left and odd pages to the right. This allows documents to be bound in book format. Enter a measurement for the offset. You can use any measurement unit, but the value you enter will be converted into the default measurement unit (see Appendix A, "Using Setup").

N Number of Copies   Enter a number indicating how many copies of the document should be printed. Note that most laser printers will print each page in succession the specified number of times. Otherwise, WordPerfect prints the entire document once before printing the second copy, and so on.

G Graphics Quality   Choose "Do Not Print" from the menu if you want your printed document to contain only text. Otherwise, choose "Draft," "Medium," or "High" to select the quality of the output. These options are only relevant if your printer has such quality levels.

T Text Quality   Choose "Do Not Print" from the menu if you want your printed document to contain only graphics. Otherwise, choose "Draft," "Medium," or "High" to select the quality of the output. These options are only relevant if your printer has such quality levels. For example, most dot matrix printers have both a draft print and an NLQ (Near Letter Quality) print. Most laser printers, on the other hand, have only one quality of print for text, so on them this command would have no effect.

Previewing a Document

WordPerfect does not display on the editing screen such document elements and formatting features as headers, footers, footnotes, endnotes, page numbering, line numbering, and right justification. Instead, these are normally visible only when you print a document. However, the Print View function allows you to see these things on the screen, without the need to print.

If you have a graphics display, the Print View function will also show you all of the print attributes, such as italics, superscript, and so on, as well as font and size changes. In addition, you'll see all graphics placed as they will appear when printed.

To preview a document on the screen, press the <Print> key (SHIFT+F7), and type **6** for "View Document."

If you do not have a graphics display, you'll see the top of the page on which the cursor was resting when you issued the Print View command. If you do have a graphics display, you'll see a graphic representation of the full page, and a menu will appear at the bottom of the screen. In either case, you can use the cursor keys to move around the page and the document. The status indicators in the lower-right corner will let you know which document and page you're viewing.

With the graphics preview, some additional options are provided in the menu. Type **1** to see the page at 100% of its actual size. Type **2** to zoom in further to 200% of actual size. Or, type **3** to zoom back to full page size. While you're viewing the document at 100% or 200%, you can use the arrow keys to view different parts of the page. You can also elect to view facing pages simultaneously (for example, two facing pages in a book or brochure). To do this, type **4** for "Facing Pages."

When you have finished looking at the previewed text, press the <Exit> key (F7) to return to the Document Editing screen.

SPELL CHECKING

WordPerfect's built-in spell checker has a 125,000-word dictionary that allows you to check the spelling for an entire document, a page, a single word, or a marked block of text. Before initiating the spell-check procedure, floppy disk users may have to insert the Speller Disk in one of the disk drives.

Checking Text

To begin the spell-checking procedure for the entire document, press the <Spell> key (CTRL+F2) and type **3** for "Document." The cursor may be positioned anywhere when you issue this command. To check the current word or page, position the cursor accordingly, press <Spell>, and choose "Word" or "Page." To check a block of text, mark the text first with the <Block> key (ALT+F4) and then press <Spell>.

WordPerfect will begin to read through the selected text, checking each word against its own dictionary and your personal dictionary. If it finds a word that isn't in one of the dictionaries, it tells you that the word was "Not found" and presents you with a list of alternative spellings. You must first determine if the word is indeed misspelled or if it is a proper name or other correctly spelled word that is not in WordPerfect's dictionary. If the word is correct, press **2** to skip over that word or press **3** to add the word to your personal dictionary. Once a word is added to your personal dictionary, WordPerfect no longer considers it a misspelling.

You will be presented with a list of possible spellings. If you see the correct spelling, simply select the letter adjacent to the word; WordPerfect will make the correction for you and continue checking the document. (If the same misspelling is found again in the document, it will automatically be replaced with the correction you selected for the first occurrence.)

If you do not see the correct spelling in the list, you can select **4** for "Edit," and make the correction yourself. (You can also simply begin to move the cursor using one of the arrow keys, and you will enter Edit mode automatically.) In the Edit mode, you can move the cursor to the left and right and delete and insert characters. Press ENTER to return to the spell check.

If the spell checker highlights a word that contains numbers, you have the option of editing the word, skipping it, or ignoring words that contain numbers for the rest of the spell check.

WordPerfect also notifies you if it finds two identical words in succession, which is a common typing error. If it does, you will have the option of skipping the double words, deleting the second word, editing the text, or disabling double-word checking. You can also edit the text in the same manner as with a misspelling.

When the spell checker is finished it tells you the total number of words in the document. This feature is handy for writers whose documents must contain a specific number of words. Pressing any key returns you to the Spell menu. To generate a word count without checking the spelling of a document, choose "Count" from the Spell menu.

If you need additional help to correct misspellings, you can use WordPerfect's Look Up function. If the Spell function is displaying the message "Not found," you can choose "Look Up" from the menu.

Alternatively, you can press the <Spell> key (CTRL+F2) and choose "Look Up" from the menu. In either case, the program will prompt you for a "Word or Word Pattern:". If you enter a word, the phonetic search will begin. If you enter a word pattern, the program will perform the Look Up procedure. (See the following section.)

Using Look Up

Look Up allows you to search for the correct spelling of a word based on how it sounds. For example, if you don't know the correct spelling of "straight," you can press the <Spell> key, choose **5** for "Look Up," and enter **strate**. WordPerfect will present you with a list of words that are phonetically similar, including "straight." When WordPerfect is highlighting a misspelled word, choosing "Look Up" will start a search based on the word.

Look Up also allows you to type in part of a word so that WordPerfect can provide you with a list of correct words that contain those letters. You do this by using the question mark (?) and the asterisk (*) as wildcards. The question mark is used to represent any single character and the asterisk is used to represent any number of characters. (You can also use a hyphen to represent any number of characters.)

For example, say you don't know how to spell "necessary" but you know that it begins with "nec". Choose "Look Up" from the Spell menu and enter **nec***; you will see a list of about 80 words that begin with "nec". "Necessary," incidentally, is the seventh one on the list. During a spell check, you can simply type the letter adjacent to the word, and WordPerfect will automatically make the correction.

If you know the end of a word, you can precede that string with an *. For instance, if you don't know how to spell "alkaloid" you can enter ***oid** and get a rather long list of words ending in "oid".

You can even use this feature for letters that appear in the middle of a word. Specifying ***mand*** will find all words with "mand" in the middle, including "archimandrite." Entering **pres*ed** will present a list of all words that begin with "pres" and end with "ed".

You can limit the words that will be displayed even more by using the question mark. Entering **??ed** would produce a list of just the four-letter words that end in "ed". Entering **lik??** would produce a list of words that start with "lik" and that have no more than five letters.

PASSWORD PROTECTION

WordPerfect can help you keep your secrets. By using the program's File Encryption feature, you can "lock" your files so that no one can retrieve or print them without entering the correct password.

To lock a document with File Encryption, begin by having it displayed on the screen. Then, press the <Text InOut> key (CTRL+F5), type 2 for "Password," and then 1 for "Add/Change." The program then asks you to enter a password. Select any word or phrase of up to 75 characters (no text is displayed as you type), and press ENTER. You are then prompted to reenter the password. You need to type the password exactly as it was first entered and press ENTER. This is WordPerfect's way of verifying that you have entered the password correctly. You are returned to the Document Editing screen. From now on, whenever you save this document, it will be locked using the password you have provided.

You retrieve locked files as you do all WordPerfect files, except that WordPerfect will ask you to "Enter Password:". If you fail to enter the password correctly, the program will say "ERROR: File is locked," and you will be prevented from accessing the file. Without the password, you cannot use WordPerfect to edit or print the file, nor can you read it from within DOS. There is no known way to access a locked file without knowing the password. Therefore, if you are going to lock your files, make sure you remember your password. Even WordPerfect Corporation cannot help you access a locked file without it.

If you decide to remove the password protection from a document, begin with the document on the screen. Press the <Text In/Out> key, type 2 for "Password," and then 2 for "Remove." You are then returned to the Document Editing screen. Now save the document in its new, unlocked state. The next time you retrieve the document, you'll see that it no longer prompts you for a password.

When you password-protect a document, WordPerfect also automatically protects all of the temporary editing files and backup files used for that document. Therefore, the text you type in a locked document will never be recorded in a readable form on the disk, and so is quite secure.

2

MACROS

Imagine driving your car and seeing a sign that says: "Remove foot from the accelerator, depress brake pedal, look for oncoming traffic, wait for the traffic to clear, remove your foot from the brake, depress accelerator, proceed." Fortunately, you have been programmed to perform all those tasks when you see a sign that simply says "STOP."

A macro is like that Stop sign—simply a shortcut. It is either a typed word or a keystroke or two that can substitute for any longer sequence of keystrokes.

Built into WordPerfect is a macro facility that lets you store keystrokes—whether for commands or text—and play the keystrokes back at any time, for any number of times. You can think of a macro as a "typing robot": if you teach it to perform a task once, it will remember the steps and automatically repeat them for you. With WordPerfect's macro command language, you can even give the robot some brains.

When you create a macro to perform a task, all the keys you press are stored on disk in a file with the name of your choice. You can specify whether the macro will be started with a single keystroke or with a name. The keystroke method is faster, but the more descriptive name method helps you remember what the macro does.

You can use macros either to type commonly used phrases like long company names or to execute a sequence of formatting commands, such as margin and tab changes. You can also use macros to perform procedures that would be too tedious to perform by hand. For example, newspaper articles often need special typesetting codes inserted in the text before they are submitted. You could create a macro to go through each finished article and add all the appropriate codes.

Macros are one of WordPerfect's most powerful features. The more you learn about the program, the more you will discover uses for them. They can help with day-to-day tasks as well as with infrequently performed, complex procedures. Once you are familiar with the basics of macro naming, definition, and invocation, you will find macros an invaluable tool in the writing process.

MACRO NAMES

WordPerfect allows you to specify a name and a description for each macro, which is stored as a file on disk with a .WPM file extension. (You can also choose to attach a macro to any key on the keyboard. See "Keyboard Definition" later in this chapter.) You can execute a macro at any time, regardless of which document you are currently editing. This allows you to use the same macro with many different documents.

Macros are normally stored on (and retrieved from) the disk or directory that you've specified with the Setup function (see Appendix A, "Using Setup"). However, if you have not specified a disk or directory with this function, macros are stored on (and retrieved from) the *default* drive or directory. If you change the default disk or directory after creating a macro, WordPerfect will no longer be able to find it.

Another way to ensure that macros are always found is to store them on the *system* disk or directory (where the WordPerfect program files are stored). The macros will then be accessible no matter what your default directory. To do this, change the default directory to the system disk or directory before starting the macro definition.

On a floppy disk system, the system disk is usually the one that is kept in the A drive. You don't normally want to store files on the system disk, but macros are typically small enough not to cause a problem. On a hard disk, the program files are normally stored in a directory called C:\WP50 or C:\WORD.

On a hard disk system, then, there are essentially two different strategies for storing macros. If you want all of your macros to be stored in the same location, and to be always accessible no matter which disk or directory is the default, specify a special macro directory with the Setup function. (You can always override this by entering a specific pathname at the "Define Macro:" prompt.) If you want the flexibility to store macros in different directories (useful when you have different macros for specific applications), you would not specify a special macro directory.

There are two ways to name a macro: with the ALT key, or with a full name. You can also create a temporary macro with no name.

ALT Key Macros

Use the ALT key to n ame macros which you plan to invoke frequently, because ALT+*key* combinations require the fewest keystrokes. To use this method, hold down the ALT key and type any single letter while the program is displaying the "Define Macro:" prompt. (It is not necessary to then press ENTER.)

Even though you can include a description with each macro, it would be a good idea to keep a written record of the ALT key macros you've defined. Otherwise, you may be lost trying to remember the single letter you use for a forgotten macro.

You can specify up to 26 ALT key macro names for each hard disk directory or floppy disk—one for each letter of the alphabet. Use a letter that indicates the macro's purpose. A macro to control the printer, for example, might be named ALT+P while a macro to save a file might be named ALT+S.

ALT key macros are saved on the disk as ALT plus the single letter plus the .WPM extension. A macro named with the ALT key and P, then, would be stored as ALTP.WPM.

Remember, you can also attach any defined macro to any key on the keyboard (see "Keyboard Definition" later in this chapter). So, for example, you could use the F2 key, or a CTRL key combination, to begin a macro.

Full Name Macros

Use a full name for more complex macros that will not be invoked frequently. To name a macro in this way, type the name and press ENTER while the program is displaying the "Define Macro:" prompt.

The name can be one to eight characters long and can consist of any characters that are valid for DOS file names (letters, numbers, and some punctuation marks).

The disadvantage of using a full name is that it requires a minimum of four keystrokes, whereas the ALT key method takes only two. The advantage of this method is that you can pick a name that describes the macro's purpose. When you use a full name, the macro is saved on disk with the name you enter and the .WPM extension.

ENTER Macro

You will usually need to save your macros for future use, but you may occasionally want to create a macro for use during a single session only. To quickly create such a macro, simply press ENTER while the program is displaying the "Define Macro:" prompt. The ENTER macro is saved on disk with the name WP{WP}.WPM. However, WordPerfect does not ask for confirmation to replace this macro as it does for ALT+*key* and Full Name macros. If you decide that you want to retain the macro you have named with ENTER, you can use the List Files function to rename it.

See Table 2-1 for examples of macro naming methods.

Table 2-1.   Examples of Macro Names

You type		Result	Method
ALT+S	→	ALTS.WPM	ALT key method
find	→	FIND.WPM	Full Name method
ENTER	→	WP{WP}.WPM	ENTER Macro

DEFINING MACROS

To define a macro, first press the <Macro Def> key (CTRL+F10). You will see this prompt at the bottom of the screen:

Define Macro:

The program is asking you to provide a name for the macro. You can use any one of the three methods described earlier:

- *ALT key* To create a macro using the ALT key, hold down the ALT key and type any single letter. You do not need to press ENTER.
- *Full Name* To create a macro with a full name, type any name one to eight characters long and press ENTER.
- *ENTER Macro* To create the ENTER macro, press ENTER by itself.

If a macro named with the ALT key or the full name you specify already exists on the disk, you will be asked whether you want to replace the existing macro with the one you are about to define, or whether you want to edit the macro's steps (see "Editing Macros" later in this chapter). Be careful—it is easy to forget which function a macro performs: in choosing to replace the macro you might accidentally delete a lot of work with just one keystroke.

After you name the macro, WordPerfect will prompt you for a description (except with the ENTER macro). You can type up to 39 characters to describe the macro (using spaces and upper- and lowercase, if you wish). Then, press ENTER.

Once you've named the macro, this message will begin to flash at the bottom of the screen:

Macro Def

It will continue to flash for as long as you are defining your macro. (It may disappear if you enter one of WordPerfect's menus, but it will always reappear when you return to the document.) While the message is flashing, everything you type, including both text and WordPerfect commands, will be stored in the macro.

When you are through entering the keystrokes you want contained in the macro, press the <Macro Def> key again to stop the macro definition, and the macro will be stored on disk.

Clear the screen (by pressing the <Exit> key (F7) and typing **N** and **N**). Then try the following exercise using a full name to identify the macro:

1. Press the <Macro Def> key (CTRL+F10).

2. Type **respond** and press ENTER.

3. Type **Request for Response** and press ENTER. You will now see the flashing "Macro Def" on the screen.

4. Type **Please respond to our request**
   Include a space after the word "request."

5. Press the <Underline> key (F8).

6. Type **as soon as possible**

7. Press the <Underline> key again.

8. Type . (period) and press ENTER.

9. Press the <Macro Def> key again.
   The flashing "Macro Def" will disappear.

Your screen will look like Figure 2-1.

Here you have combined a frequently used phrase with the WordPerfect underlining function. When you pressed the <Macro Def> key the second time, the macro was saved on disk as RESPOND.WPM. You can use the <List Files> key (F5) to verify this if you are distrustful. (Remember that the macro will be stored in the special macro directory, if you have specified one with the Setup function.) In the next section, you will use the macro you just defined.

INVOKING MACROS

The procedure you use to invoke a macro (that is, to play back its keystrokes) varies, depending on the method you chose in naming it.

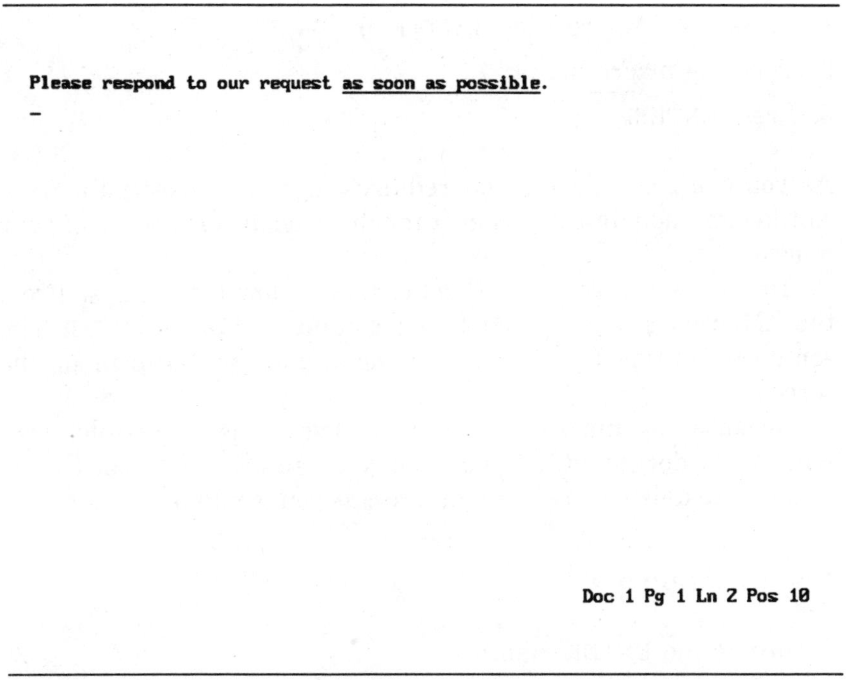

Please respond to our request <u>**as soon as possible**</u>.

Doc 1 Pg 1 Ln 2 Pos 10

Figure 2-1.   Creating a macro

ALT Key Macros

When you want to invoke a macro you've named with the ALT key, simply hold down the ALT key and type whatever letter you used to name the macro. All your keystrokes will be played back. As mentioned earlier, this is the quickest and easiest way to invoke a macro.

Full Name Macros

If you used a full name to name a macro, you can invoke it by following these three steps:

1. Press the <Macro> key (ALT+F10).

2. Type the macro name.

3. Press ENTER.

As you can see, this method requires more keystrokes than the ALT key method, but it makes it much easier to keep track of your macros.

To use the macro you defined earlier, follow these steps: Press the <Macro> key (ALT+F10), type **respond**, and press ENTER. The sentence you typed earlier, underline and all, will appear on the screen.

Because the macro is stored on disk, it is accessible from within any document. (If you wish, you can use the <List Files> function to delete or rename macros, as you would any other file.)

ENTER Macro

To invoke the ENTER macro,

1. Press the <Macro> key.

2. Press ENTER.

MACRO PRACTICE: UNDERLINE TO BOLD

Let's create a more complex macro. Suppose you have a document in which you've liberally used underlining to emphasize words and phrases, and you decide that you should have used boldface for emphasis instead. There is no built-in function in WordPerfect to perform this task. You cannot use the Replace function, because the codes you are replacing are Matched Pair codes—two codes would have to be replaced at once.

So what should you do? Spend hours going through your document to make the changes? You can use the Search function to locate each [UND] code, but you would still have to mark each boldface occurrence individually. Instead, you can use a macro to handle this situation.

The first step is to decide on the steps *you* would follow to perform the same procedure that the macro will perform. The best way, after moving the cursor to the top of the document, would be to

1. Use the Search function to find the [UND] code.

2. Turn Block on, and search for the [und] code.

3. Use the <Bold> key to boldface the word.

4. Press LEFT ARROW once to position before the [bold] code.

5. Press BACKSPACE once to delete the underline codes.

A macro will follow the same steps. It can also repeat the steps as you would until it can find no more occurrences of the given text. (This type of macro, called a looping macro, is discussed in the next section.) First, you will create a macro that boldfaces one occurrence at a time, using the steps just listed.

To start, let's enter some text to work with. (When typing the following text, be sure to underline the indicated words and phrases by pressing F8 once before typing the text, and again after typing the text.) Now clear the screen and type the following:

Inside the palazzo, the well-equipped royal guard anxiously watched the courtyard. A ring of horses slowly surrounded the palazzo. Beyond the duck pond, the palazzo gates were giving way to the thrusts of the angry mob. Soon, the palazzo would be overrun by screaming activists.

For the purposes of this exercise, imagine that this short paragraph is in fact a novel spanning over 350 pages in which you have used underlining a lot. Save the paragraph on disk with the name of your choice for later use in this chapter. Then position the cursor at the top of the document by pressing HOME, HOME, UP ARROW. Press the <Reveal Codes> key (ALT+F3), so that you'll be able to view the codes as you define the macro.

Now you need to decide on an appropriate name for the macro you're going to write. This is the type of macro which you may use in the future, but certainly not on a daily basis. So, let's give it the full name UND2BOLD.

Note: If you make a mistake while entering the steps of the macro, press the <Macro Def> key to stop the "Macro Def" message from flashing at the bottom of the screen. Then reposition your cursor at the top of the document and start again from step 1. You may also need to clear the screen and reload the paragraph from disk. When WordPerfect tells you the macro already exists, type **1** for "Replace."

1. Press the <Macro Def> key (CTRL+F10).
2. Type **UND2BOLD** and press ENTER.
3. Type **Underline to boldface conversion** and press ENTER.
    Now you will search for the [UND] code in your paragraph.
4. Press the <Search> key (F2).
5. Press the <Underline> key (F8) and press the <Search> key. The cursor will now be positioned at the beginning of the first occurrence of underlined text in the document (after the first [UND] code).
6. Press the <Block> key (ALT+F4).
    Flashing wildly at the bottom of the screen will be this message:

    Block on Macro Def

7. Press the <Search> key.
    We next need to search for the end of the underlined text.
8. Press the <Underline> key, press BACKSPACE, and press the <Underline> key again.
9. Press the <Search> key.
    The underlined text will now be highlighted.
10. Press the <Bold> key (F6).
    The text will now be boldface.

11. Press the LEFT ARROW key to position the cursor onto the [bold] code.

12. Press BACKSPACE to delete the [und] code (the matching [UND] code will be automatically deleted).

13. Press the <Macro Def> key to end the macro definition.

And that's it! While defining the macro, you boldfaced the first occurrence of underlined text in the document. Now let's use the macro to boldface the next one.

1. Press the <Macro> key (ALT+F10).

2. Type **UND2BOLD** and press ENTER.

If everything goes as planned, the next occurrence of underlined text will be boldfaced. Try the macro a few more times to boldface the remaining occurrences.

In the preceding example, you located the text, marked it as a block, boldfaced it, and removed the underlining codes. More precisely, you taught WordPerfect how to perform for you what would otherwise have been a laborious task. Are your fingers still tired from pressing the <Macro> key, though? In the next section, you will see how a macro can perform even more of the work.

LOOPING MACROS

You can instruct a macro to perform its task once and then repeat itself. The instruction that tells a macro to repeat itself is always the last instruction in the macro.

The Search function prevents a macro from falling into an *endless loop*. This undesirable situation occurs when the macro is performed over and over, endlessly. When a search included as a macro step is no longer able to find the specified text, the macro is terminated. Thus, whenever the purpose of a macro is to find some text repeated throughout a document and manipulate it in some way, this termination feature will allow the macro to execute until all occurrences have been processed and then stop searching for that text.

This rule does not apply to the Replace command, which can be used several times within a macro without causing it to terminate.

Note that an alternative to writing a looping macro is to use one of WordPerfect's commands in its macro command language. For example, you could use the Label and the Go commands to repeat only a segment of a macro, rather than the entire macro. In addition, you can use the On Not Found command to handle a Search failure. (See "Macro Commands" later in this chapter.)

Trying Out the Looping Macro

The looping macro repeats a procedure as many times as necessary to complete a given task. For example, in the Underline to Bold exercise, you need a way for the macro to boldface *each* occurrence of underlined text until the Search function cannot find another occurrence. This would allow you to start the macro and then sit back while it churns away.

Let's create a looping macro to do this job. First, clear the screen and retrieve the original document with the underlined text. (You saved it, didn't you? If not, retype the text.) Again, make sure that the Reveal Codes screen is displayed. Position the cursor at the top of the document and follow these steps to redefine the macro:

1. Press the <Macro Def> key.
2. Type **UND2BOLD** and press ENTER. Type **1** to replace the existing macro.
3. Type **Underline to boldface conversion** and press ENTER.
4. Press the <Search> key.
5. Press the <Underline> key, then the <Search> key.
6. Press the <Block> key.
7. Press the <Search> key.
8. Press the <Underline> key, press BACKSPACE, and press the <Underline> key again.
9. Press the <Search> key.

10. Press the <Bold> key (F6).

11. Press the LEFT ARROW key.

12. Press BACKSPACE.

13. Press the <Macro> key, type **UND2BOLD**, and press ENTER. This additional step causes the macro to loop.

14. Press the <Macro Def> key to end the macro definition.

Now let's try out the macro. Clear the screen and retrieve the original document again. You can turn off Reveal Codes if you wish. Then press the <Macro> key, type **UND2BOLD**, and press ENTER. All occurrences of underlined text will now be in bold. Let's see how it happened.

First, the macro searched for the [UND] code. It found the first occurrence, marked it as a block, and boldfaced the text. The underline codes were then deleted. Finally, the macro invoked a macro—itself—and the steps were repeated until no more occurrences of underlined text could be found. Then the macro gracefully came to a halt.

AVOIDING MACRO PITFALLS

Before you begin creating your own macros, you should learn how to avoid some common pitfalls.

Assumptions

A macro may *assume* certain conditions when it is invoked. These can include the position of the cursor, whether the printer is ready, and even whether there is a document on the screen.

It is important to consider the conditions under which a macro is created. Will it rely on these conditions to work properly when it is executed? For example, will the macro assume that the cursor is at the top of the document, or will it move the cursor to the top as its first step?

As you know, a looping macro will repeat itself over and over as it goes through your text. If you include a HOME, HOME, UP

ARROW sequence as the first step of such a macro, the cursor will move to the top of the document each time a loop executes. This will probably disable whichever function the macro is trying to perform. In this case, then, you must *not* include HOME, HOME, UP ARROW. Instead, you must make the *assumption* that the macro will be started with the cursor already at the top of the document.

(A better alternative would be to use the Go macro command to repeat only a part of a macro. You could thus include the HOME, HOME, UP ARROW sequence at the beginning of the macro. See "Macro Commands" later in this chapter.)

Cursor Navigation

When you use the cursor control keys during normal editing, you can see where the cursor goes at all times. For example, you can tell which characters are being included in a block definition by noting the on-screen highlighting. If something unexpected happens because of your document layout, you can easily correct the situation. However, a macro cannot make corrections for you during execution. You will have to write macros that move the cursor appropriately in all text situations.

For example, say you need to write a macro that searches for a particular phrase, marks it as a block, and then makes it bold. However, one word in the phrase is underlined in some of the occurrences. As you know from the discussion on Reveal Codes in Chapter 1, "Basics Refresher," the cursor moves past a hidden code (like the Underline Begin and Underline End codes) as it would a letter. When marking the phrase as a block, then, you would have to use an arrow key two more times for an occurrence including an underlined word than you would for one that did not. A more reliable way to mark the phrase as a block would be to use the <Word Left> key in your macro instead of the arrow keys, because the cursor would then jump by entire words, avoiding the problem of hidden codes in the text.

There are many other situations where it helps to use cursor positioning controls that do not depend on your own decision making. Whenever possible, then, use the END, HOME, <Word Left>, and <Word Right> keys in macros to "feel" your way around the text.

PAUSE FOR INPUT

You can insert a pause in a macro that allows it to stop temporarily; it will wait for you to enter information from the keyboard before continuing. You can therefore write a macro in a general format and customize it each time it is invoked. For example, you can create a macro that issues the keystrokes necessary to go to a menu and then pauses to let you make your choice from that menu.

You can pause the macro at any point—for example, when WordPerfect needs a response to a menu choice or prompt. When you execute the macro, it stops at the pause and waits for you to enter something and press ENTER before it continues.

To insert a pause for input into a macro, create the macro in the usual way until you get to the place where you want the macro to pause for user input. Then press the <Macro Commands> key (CTRL+PGUP) and type **1** for "Pause." WordPerfect will now wait for you to enter an *example* of the text that will be entered. This example will not be stored with the macro. It is necessary only if your macro needs *something* entered here to work properly during the macro definition. When you are through, press ENTER to end the pause. If you do not need or want to enter an example, simply press ENTER after choosing "Pause" from the menu. In any case, you can now define the rest of your macro.

For practice, let's create a macro to change the Initial Font for a document. (A discussion of this and other printing topics can be found in Chapter 11, "Using Printers.")

1. Press the <Macro Def> key (CTRL+F10).

2. Press ALT+F (hold down the ALT key and press **F**).

3. Type **Change Document Initial Font** and press ENTER.
   This will create a macro called ALTF.WPM. If you have previously defined a macro with this name, the program will ask for confirmation to overwrite it.

4. Press the <Format> key (SHIFT+F8).

5. Type **3** for "Document," and then **3** for "Initial Font."

6. Press the <Macro Commands> key (CTRL+PGUP).

7. Type **1** for "Pause."

8. Move the cursor bar onto a font name as an example.

9. Press ENTER to end the example input.

10. Type **1** for "Select" to select the font.
    If you are using a printer with scaleable fonts (such as a PostScript printer), you'll now see a prompt for the point size of the font. You may want to include a pause for input for this prompt. Alternatively, the macro might simply assume a standard size, such as 10 or 12 points.

11. Press the <Exit> key (F7) to return to the document.

12. Press the <Macro Def> key to end the macro definition.

To run the macro, press ALT+F, position the cursor bar onto a font name, and press ENTER. You can see how much easier this is than entering all of the steps manually each time.

MACRO VISIBILITY

You can make a macro either "visible"—that is, text, menus, and prompts will be shown on the screen while the macro is executing—or "invisible"—which means the screen will clear and "* Please Wait *" will appear at the bottom of the screen. Unless you specify otherwise, macros are normally invisible.

To change the visibility of a macro while you are defining it, press the <Macro Commands> key (CTRL+PGUP), and type **2** for "Display." Type **Y** to begin visibility from that point on in the macro, or type **N** to begin invisibility.

If you type **Y**, WordPerfect inserts a {DISPLAY ON} command in the macro. If you type **N**, WordPerfect inserts a {DISPLAY OFF} command in the macro. (See "Macro Commands" in a later section.) Whenever you begin defining a macro, a {DISPLAY OFF} is inserted for you automatically at the beginning of the macro.

EDITING MACROS

WordPerfect has a built-in macro editor, which allows you to create and edit the steps of a macro. To do this, you must have first defined the macro by giving it a name and saving it on disk. (Note that this is unlike the creation of a document, where you can begin with a blank screen.)

There are two primary reasons for using the macro editor. First, it allows you to modify any steps which you performed when you created the macro "on the fly," as described earlier in "Defining Macros." Second, you can add special macro commands with the editor, which you cannot insert during Macro Definition.

Creating a Macro

Even a macro containing many macro commands is sometimes easier to initially define "on the fly." This allows you to record the bulk of the macro's steps, then go back and add commands using the editor. However, you'll frequently want to create a macro entirely with the macro editor.

To do this, you should define an empty macro with the name you want. For example, if you want to create a macro called LETTER using the editor, begin by pressing the <Macro Def> key (CTRL+F10), then type **LETTER** and press ENTER. Next type a description and press ENTER. "Macro Def" will begin to flash on the screen. Press the <Macro Def> key again to turn off Macro Definition. Now you've created an empty macro that you can edit as described in the next section.

Editing a Macro

When you're ready to edit the steps of a macro, press the <Macro Def> key, type the name of the macro, and press ENTER (or press an ALT+*key* sequence). A menu indicating that the macro is already defined will appear. Type **2** for "Edit" to edit the macro, and the Macro Edit screen will appear, as shown in Figure 2-2.

You can then either change the description of the macro, or you can edit its steps. Type **1** for "Description" to edit the description. Enter or edit the text for the description, which can be up to 39 characters long, then press ENTER. Type **2** for "Action" to change the steps of the macro. The cursor moves into the Macro Editing window (see "Using the Macro Editor" in the next section).

When you've finished changing the steps of the macro, press the <Exit> key (F7), and the changes you've made to the macro will be saved. If you decide as you're editing the macro that you don't want to save the changes you've made, press the <Cancel> key (F1) instead. A prompt will appear asking you to confirm that you want to cancel the changes. Type **Y** to confirm the cancellation. In either case, you need to press the <Exit> key to return to the Document Editing screen.

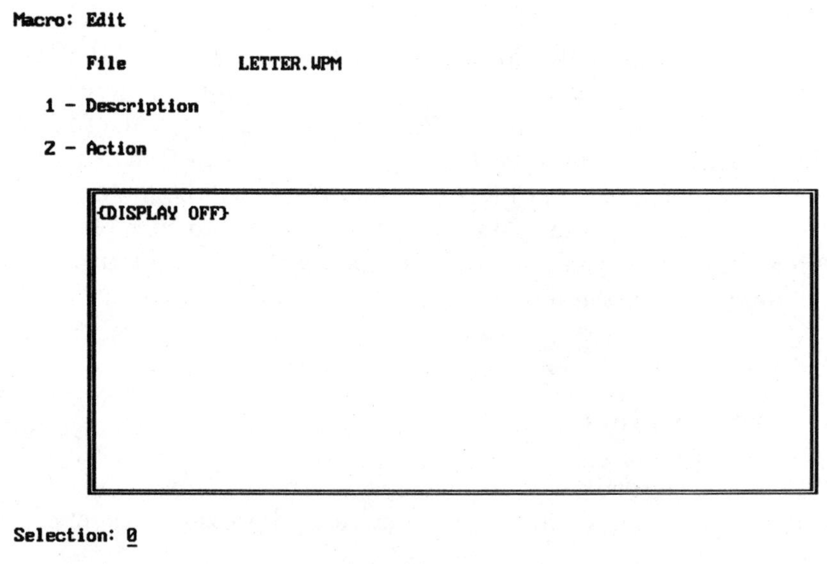

Macro: Edit

    File   LETTER.WPM

  1 - Description

  2 - Action

```
┌─────────────────────────────────────────────┐
│ {DISPLAY OFF}                                │
│                                              │
│                                              │
│                                              │
│                                              │
│                                              │
│                                              │
└─────────────────────────────────────────────┘
```

Selection: 0

Figure 2-2.   The Macro Edit screen

You cannot change the name of the macro from the Macro Edit screen. Instead, use the Rename command on the List Files screen. Remember to include the .WPM macro name extension.

Using the Macro Editor

Within the Macro Editing window, any WordPerfect keys you pressed when you created the macro appear in boldface between two curly brackets (for example, {**Reveal Codes**}). You may also notice that the steps of the macro have been wrapped to fit within the confines of the Macro Editing window. This continues to happen as you enter steps into the window, and will not affect the operation of the macro. Spaces on the Macro Edit screen appear as small, centered dots.

Cursor Control

Once the cursor has moved into the Macro Editing window, you can edit the steps of the macro using several editing keys. You can use the four arrow keys to move the cursor. You can also press CTRL+RIGHT ARROW to move right a word at a time, and CTRL+ LEFT ARROW to move left a word at a time through text in the macro (but not over a macro command). Press the <Screen Down> key, PGDN, or HOME, DOWN ARROW to move the cursor down one screen at a time. Press <Screen Up>, PGUP, or HOME, UP ARROW to move the cursor up one screen at a time. The HOME, LEFT ARROW and END key sequences work the same way as they do in a document, moving the cursor to the beginning and end of the line. Press HOME, HOME, UP ARROW to move the cursor to the beginning of the macro, and HOME, HOME, DOWN ARROW to move the cursor to the end.

You can delete individual steps of the macro with the DEL and BACKSPACE keys, and you can delete from the cursor position to the end of the current line by pressing CTRL+END.

Formatting the Macro

When you press ENTER while editing a macro, it does not cause the ENTER key to become a part of the macro (that is, no [HRt] code is inserted). You can therefore use the ENTER key to break lines to make the macro more readable. Pressing the TAB key allows you to indent sections of the macro, which also improves its readability. You have a four-space tab grid in the editing window to lay out the macro steps. To insert an actual ENTER or TAB in a macro, you need to include the {Enter} or {Tab} keyname as described in the following section.

You can also describe sections of the macro by including comments (see "Macro Programming Aids" in the "Macro Commands" section).

Inserting Key Names

To insert most of WordPerfect's key names into the macro, simply press the appropriate key. If the key has a purpose within the macro editor (such as the arrow keys or the TAB or ENTER key), you can insert its key name into a macro by first pressing CTRL+V, and then pressing the desired key. For example, to insert the {Enter} key name, press CTRL+V, ENTER. Use this method while editing when you need to insert just one or two key names.

You can also switch into a Macro Commands mode, where all keys insert their corresponding key names. To do this, press the <Macro Def> key (CTRL+F10). You'll see the message "Press Macro Define to enable editing." All keys now insert their key names, including the <Exit> and <Cancel> keys, and the cursor keys. Use this mode when you have a lot of macro steps to enter at one time. To resume normal editing, press the <Macro Def> key a second time.

Inserting Commands

To insert one of WordPerfect's macro commands (see "Macro Commands"), begin by positioning the cursor where you want the command to be placed. Then press the <Macro Commands> key (CTRL+PGUP), and a Command window will appear in the upper-right corner of the screen, as shown in Figure 2-3. Move the cursor bar onto the macro command you want to use. To do this, you can use the arrow keys, or the PGUP and PGDN keys. In addition, a Name Search function is active in the window, so you can simply begin typing the name of the command you want to insert.

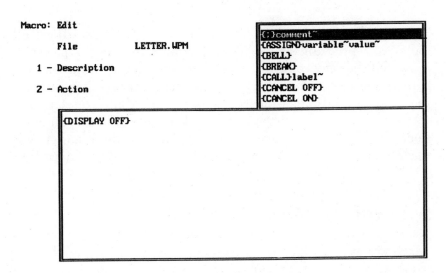

Figure 2-3.   The Macro Commands window

When you've positioned the cursor bar onto the desired command, press ENTER to insert it into the macro. If you decide not to insert a command, you can cancel the action by pressing the <Cancel> key (F1) or even the ESC key. Note that many macro commands require you to type a trailing tilde character (~).

Copying Macro Steps

While there are no provisions for copying steps between two macros with WordPerfect's built-in editor, there is one method you can use to insert all of the steps of one macro into another. To do this, you first need to attach the steps from the macro you want to copy to a key on the keyboard. (See "Keyboard Definition" later in this chapter.)

Once a key has the steps of a macro attached to it, you can use this key to insert those steps into any other macros. Simply press CTRL+V, and then press the key you've assigned. The steps will be inserted into the current macro at the cursor position.

Editing Macro with M-Edit

The WordPerfect Library (sold separately from WordPerfect) includes a program called M-Edit, which provides a powerful macro editing environment. M-Edit offers many editing features not available with WordPerfect's internal macro editor, such as the ability to edit two macros at once, the ability to copy and retrieve sections of a macro, and an Undelete function. In addition, WordPerfect's internal editor is not able to create or edit macros larger than 5K, whereas M-Edit has no such limitation.

VARIABLES

WordPerfect has ten *variables*—containers which can hold a value of some text or a number. These are named {VAR 0} through {VAR 9}. While variables are not used exclusively with macros, that is where they are most useful.

Once you put a value into a variable, you can use the variable name anywhere you would normally enter that value. For example, you can use the Text command (see "Macro Commands") to ask for the user's name. The entry could then be assigned to Variable 1. Then {VAR 1} could, for example, be inserted into the document, used for a Search, or entered as part of a file name.

Variables can contain text and a few of WordPerfect's codes. The [Tab], [→Indent], [HRt], [HPg], and [-] are all allowed in a variable. An [SRt] code will be translated into a space. An [SPg] code will be translated into either an [HRt] or a space, whichever is appropriate. All other codes are stripped out when you assign a value to a variable.

Setting Variable Contents

You can set the contents of a variable either in normal WordPerfect operation, or from within a macro.

Under Normal Operation

You can assign a value to a variable either by marking text within the document, or by entering the value at a prompt.

If you want to use text from within the document for the value of the variable, begin by marking the text as a block. Then press the <Macro Commands> key (CTRL+PGUP), and the prompt "Variable:" will appear at the bottom of the screen. Type a number from 0 to 9 to indicate which variable to use.

To enter a value for the variable at the bottom of the screen, begin by pressing the <Macro Commands> key. (You can be anywhere in WordPerfect when you do this, even at a menu or prompt.) At the "Variable:" prompt, type a number from 0 to 9 to indicate the variable to use. At the "Value:" prompt, which appears next, type the desired value for the variable. This can be up to 120 characters long. Press ENTER when you've finished.

After you've assigned a value to a variable, you can insert its contents at any point by pressing the ALT key in combination with the appropriate number. The value of the variable will be entered as if you had typed it.

Within a Macro

During Macro Definition, you can assign a value to a variable as you would under normal operation. The only difference is that when you press the <Macro Commands> key, you'll see a menu. Type **3** for "Assign," and continue as in normal operation.

Within the Macro Editing window, you can insert the Char, Look, Text, and Assign macro commands that assign values to variables. The Char and Look commands are used to accept from the user a single character, which is placed in a variable. The Text command is used to prompt the user for a word or phrase, which is also placed in a variable. The Assign command is used to have the macro simply set a variable to a particular value, or to the result of a math formula. (See "Macro Commands.")

You can also enter into a macro steps for assigning a block of text to a variable. That is, include the steps to mark the block, then include the {Macro Commands} key name, type **3** for

"Assign," and then type a single digit to represent the variable to use. A macro will then be able to make a decision based on text within the document.

Inserting Variable Contents

To insert the contents of a variable, simply press the ALT key in conjunction with a number from 0 to 9, using the keys along the top row of the keyboard. For example, to insert the contents of Variable 1, press ALT+1.

To insert this step into a macro, you insert a variable's *key name*. To do this in the Macro Editing window, first press CTRL+V. Then press the ALT key along with a number from 0 to 9, as described above. The variable's keyname notation is inserted at the cursor position. The key name for Variable 1, for example, is {VAR 1}.

When WordPerfect encounters the keyname notation during execution of a macro, it "expands" the notation to the current value of the variable. It then continues with the macro as if the actual value had existed there already. So when you enter the keyname notation into a macro, think about it as if it were a value that the variable will contain (for example, a name or number).

Using Variables in Macro Commands

Variables can also be used in several macro commands. For example, you can test the condition of a variable with the If or Case commands, and then perform different actions depending on the result. You might use the Char command to produce a menu at the bottom of the screen, and assign the entered character to a variable. You could then use the Case command to branch to different parts of the macro depending on the character typed.

Observe that the notation used to represent a variable is different with the various macro commands. For places where a variable name is expected (Assign, Char, If Exists, Look, and

Text), you simply type the numeric digit from 0 to 9 which represents the variable. The If, Case, and Case Call commands, however, normally expect constant text or numeric values. To use a variable in one of these, you need to include the keyname notation for the variable (as described above). If the value you're comparing is text, you also need to enclose the key name within quotes. Thus, an If statement to compare the contents of Variable 1 with the text "OK" would read

{IF}"{VAR 1}"="OK"~

See the next section, "Macro Commands," for a description of each of the macro commands.

MACRO COMMANDS

WordPerfect has a powerful and extensive macro programming language that can take your macros far beyond the simple repetition of keystrokes. In this section, each macro command's format and use is documented. In addition, examples are provided for each of the macro commands. You can find complete macro applications that use these commands in Chapter 13, "Macro Library."

WordPerfect's macro commands can be loosely classified into the following categories:

- User interaction
- Branching
- Conditional testing
- Exception handlers
- Macro file flow control
- Environment control
- Macro programming aids
- Timing

User Interaction

The commands described in this section perform functions that allow macros to interact with the user.

Char

The Char command displays a message at the bottom of the screen, and then waits for the user to press a single key. That key is then assigned to a specified variable. This command is especially useful for producing yes/no prompts, "Press any key to continue" prompts, and WordPerfect-like menus at the bottom of the screen. The format of the Char command is

{CHAR}*variable~message~*

where *variable* is a single digit from 0 to 9, and *message* is a message to be displayed on the screen. See the section "Message Strings" for more information on the potential contents of the message.

Any key which is pressed when the Char command is waiting for input is assigned to the specified variable. This includes not only letter and number keys, but any function or cursor keys as well. An exception is the <Cancel> key, which normally cancels the macro. To avoid this, you can include the Cancel Off command before the Char command. This enables "{Cancel}" to be returned when the <Cancel> key is pressed.

The following command will produce a horizontal menu at the bottom of the screen, and place the key pressed by the user into Variable 1:

{CHAR}1~1·Load·document;·2·Set·codes;·3·Begin:·~

To make this a working menu, you would need to add a command which specifies the program's response to the user entry. You might, for example, want this command to repeat the Char command (to redisplay the menu) if an invalid key is pressed. The

Case command works very well in this situation, because it enables the macro to check the user's entry against a list of potentially equivalent values (see "Case" later in this section). Here's an example of a fully implemented menu:

```
{LABEL}menu~
{CHAR}1~1·Load·document;·2·Set·codes;·3·Begin:·~

{CASE}"{VAR 1}"~                    \
    "1"~load~
    "2"~codes~
    "3"~begin~
    "{Cancel}"~end~
    "{Exit}"~end~
    "{Enter}"~end~~
{GO}menu~
```

(Note that the Case command branches to sections of the macro that are not shown in this example.) Here's an instance of a multi-line menu created with the Char command:

```
{CHAR}1~{Enter}{Enter}
What·should·we·do·next:{Enter}
{Enter}
1)·Load·document{Enter}
2)·Set·codes{Enter}
3)·Begin{Enter}
{Enter}
Enter·your·choice:·~
```

As this menu appears from the bottom of the screen, you'll see the text of the document scroll up. It's a good idea to include a {DISPLAY OFF} command before the Char command. Otherwise, the screen will continue to display lines from the menu after the menu has done its work. You can include a {DISPLAY ON} immediately after the Char command, if you wish.

There may be times when you want the macro to stop and wait for a single keystroke, but not to display a message. Although you can omit the message from the Char command, the cursor will still be positioned at the first character at the bottom line of the screen. The bottom line will be cleared (that is, any menu or prompt that previously was displayed on the bottom line will not appear while the Char command is awaiting input). If you would like the cursor to remain in the text and the last line to remain intact while the macro waits for a keystroke, try using the Look command within a loop (see the next section, "Look").

Look

The Look command works much the same way as the Char command, although it does not display a message. The main difference is that instead of waiting for the user to press a key, the Look command looks to see if a key that has not yet been processed has been pressed. That is, it checks to see whether the user typed a key while the macro was performing another action. If it finds a keystroke, it is placed in the variable. Then, whether the Look command found a keystroke or not, the macro continues with the next step. The format of the Look command is

{LOOK}*variable*~

where *variable* is a single digit from 0 to 9, indicating the variable to use. The variable is set to an empty value if no keystroke is detected. The If Exists command can subsequently be used to determine whether a keystroke was found. (See the section, "If Exists," later in this chapter.)

Like the Char command, the Look command provides a useful way to wait for a single keystroke. By placing the Look command within a loop that constantly checks for a change in the value of the variable, you can perform the same function as the Char command. The reason you would create such a loop, rather than use the Char command, is that the cursor can remain where it normally is—in the document or a menu, for example—and the bottom line of the screen would remain intact. If you don't need a prompt at the bottom of the screen (for instance, for a menu), the Look command within a loop is a cleaner way to wait for a single keystroke than the Char command.

For example, here's a routine which emulates the Char command to wait for a single keystroke:

```
{LABEL}start~
{LOOK}1~
{IF EXISTS}1~
{ELSE}
    {GO}start~
{END IF}
```

In this macro, the If Exists command is used to determine if Variable 1 has a value. If it does, no command is executed, and the macro ends. If it doesn't, then the Go command returns to the beginning to check for a key. You may want to save a macro which contains this type of routine, call it something like ONEKEY, and then use the Nest command to perform the process from within other macros (see "Nest" in a later section). The calling macro would then check the contents of Variable 1 after the Nest command.

Here's a macro which positions the cursor to the "Display Document Comments?" prompt within the Setup function, and then waits for either a "Y" or "N" response:

```
{Setup}33

{LABEL}start~
{LOOK}1~

{IF EXISTS}1~
{ELSE}
    {GO}start~
{END IF}

{CASE}"{VAR 1}"~
    "y"~yes~
    "n"~no~~
{GO}start~

{LABEL}yes~
Y{Exit}
{QUIT}

{LABEL}no~
N{Exit}
{QUIT}
```

Text

The Text command displays a message at the bottom of the screen, then waits for the user to respond by typing some text and pressing ENTER. The text is then assigned to a specified variable. The format of the command is

{TEXT}*variable~message~*

where *variable* is a single digit from 0 to 9, and *message* is a message to be displayed on the screen. (See the section "Message Strings" later in this chapter for more information on the possible contents of the message.)

You can use the Text command to request such items as names and file names. In addition, you can use the Text command to produce menus. While the Char command is better for producing menus that have single character responses, the Text command is useful for menus which require an entry of more than one character, ending with ENTER.

Let's say you want to customize a series of steps for a specific attorney in a law office. You might have a macro which creates a legal pleading or some other document with the attorney's name on it. Perhaps each attorney in the office uses a different format for documents, and therefore the document should be created with a specific style sheet. By using the Text command to prompt for the attorney's initials near the beginning of the macro, you'd be able to customize the remainder of the macro. Here's a Text command which prompts for an attorney's initials:

```
{TEXT}1~Enter the attorney's initials: ~
```

Later in the macro you can test Variable 1 to see which attorney was selected. Or you could use the entered initials as part of a file name. Simply include the {VAR 1} notation wherever you would otherwise type the initials.

Note that the Text command will return an empty value to the variable if the user does not type anything at the prompt (that is, just presses ENTER). To check for this in a macro, use the If Exists command right after the Text command to see if the variable has any value.

Pause

The Pause command makes WordPerfect stop and wait for user input. The program may be in any state—editing a document or waiting at a prompt or menu. The cursor remains where it would normally be, and text that is entered by the user is inserted as if there were no macro running at all. When the user presses ENTER, the macro continues with its steps. The format of the Pause command is as follows:

{PAUSE}

You can also insert a Pause command into a macro while it is being defined (see "Pause for Input" earlier in this chapter).

If you wish, you can include a Bell command (see "Bell") just before the Pause command. This will alert the user that input is required. For a macro with many Pauses, though, the Bell might become irritating.

Prompt

The Prompt command allows you to place a prompt at the bottom of the screen. The format of the Prompt command is

{PROMPT}*message~*

where *message* is a message to be displayed on the screen. See "Message Strings" later in this section for more information on the possible contents of the message.

A message placed on the bottom line will remain on the screen until the screen is rewritten. This will occur whenever the text is scrolled or wrapped, or a menu is displayed. For example, you can follow the Prompt command with a Pause command, but the message may disappear. If you want the message to be displayed for a certain period of time, follow the command with a Wait command.

If you use the special codes described in the section "Message Strings" to place the message elsewhere on the screen, however, the message may remain on the screen. Unfortunately, by placing a message somewhere other than on the bottom line, you risk placing it in a location where the user needs to type. If possible, it's best to position the prompt somewhere on the screen *above* the line where the cursor will be positioned for the pause for input. To subsequently remove the prompt from the screen, include the sequence {Screen}0 in the macro to rewrite the screen.

The Prompt command can also be used to post the progress of a long macro. For example, you could increment the value of a variable with the Assign command, to keep a count of the number of times a certain loop in the macro is executed. You could then use the Prompt command to display this running count each time the loop is executed, with a message such as "Processing occurrence #{VAR 1}".

Bell

The Bell causes the computer to beep. It's useful when you want to alert the user that input is required (for example, with a Pause command), or as a signal when a lengthy process is complete (such as a large merge, or execution of the Generate command). The format of the Bell command is as follows:

{BELL}

Message Strings

The {CHAR}, {TEXT}, and {PROMPT} macro commands described in this section can all place a message on the screen. This message would normally be one line of bold text, which would appear at the bottom of the screen. However, WordPerfect gives you a lot of control over the appearance of the message.

If the message contains one line, it is placed at the bottom of the screen. If you include {Enter} key names within it, however, the message will scroll up from the bottom of the screen, with the *last* line appearing at the bottom of the screen. This capability enables you to produce with the Char or Text commands either a single-line menu at the bottom of the screen, or a multi-line menu.

By inserting special codes within the message, you can actually place text anywhere on the screen. In addition, you can control the attributes of the text. For example, you can make only certain characters appear in boldface or in reverse video. Note that since boldface is usually turned on for the whole message, you must begin with the {^ \} bold off code if you do not want the entire message to appear bold. Table 2-2 lists all of the codes you can insert into a message string. To insert the codes, either Macro Commands mode must be active or you must precede the key sequence with CTRL+V. (See the section "Using the Macro Editor" earlier in this chapter.)

Note that message strings can also include the contents of a variable. Simply include the keyname notation of the variable (such as {VAR 1}) within the message text. When the message is displayed, the current contents of the variable will be displayed in the message.

Branching

The macro commands listed in this section allow you to regulate the flow of control within a macro by identifying and then branching to named sections. You can use these functions to add tremendous power to a macro.

Label

The Label command is used to identify a location in a macro. You can then refer to that location with the Go, Call, Case, and Case Call commands. The format of the Label command is

{LABEL}*label~*

where *label* is a name for this location. You can use uppercase and lowercase letters in the label for visual distinction, but the Go, Call, Case, and Case Call commands will ignore case. You can also use spaces in the label.

You can use as many labels as you want in a macro. Generally, WordPerfect is very fast at locating a label in a macro. However, to do so it must search through the entire macro. Because of this, you may notice some improvement in performance with large macros when you place the labelled section earlier in the macro.

Another alternative for a frequently accessed routine is to use the Nest command to call an entirely different macro file (see "Nest" later in this section).

Table 2-2.   Message String Control Characters

Character	Display	Action
Cursor-positioning		
^H	{HOME}	Positions cursor to the upper-left corner of the screen.
^J	{Enter}	Positions cursor to the beginning of the next line.
^K	{DEL TO EOL}	Clears from the cursor position to the end of the current line.
^L	{DEL TO EOP}	Clears the entire screen, and then positions the cursor to the upper-left corner of the screen.
^M	{^M}	Positions cursor to beginning of the current line.
^W	{UP}	Positions cursor up one line.
^Z	{DOWN}	Positions cursor down one line.
^X	{RIGHT}	Positions cursor right one character.
^Y	{LEFT}	Positions cursor left one character.
^P	{^P}	Positions cursor to specific column and row position on the screen. This code should be followed by two characters or codes: one for the column position (usually 0-79), and another for the row position (usually 0-24), both relative to the active window. Use ASCII characters and codes to represent the positions. For example, {^A} through {^Z} would represent 1 to 26. The sequence {^P}{^A}{^A} then would position the cursor to column 1, row 1.
Display Attributes		
^R	{^R}	Reverse video on
^S	{^S}	Reverse video off
^T	{^T}	Underline on
^U	{^U}	Underline off
^]	{^]}	Bold on
^\	{^\}	Bold off
^V	{^V}	Turns on whatever attribute is specified for mnemonic menu letters in Setup. (Use ^Q to turn off.)

Table 2-2. (*continued*)   Message String Control Characters

Character	Display	Action
^N	{^N}	Turns on specific display attribute for text. Follow this code with one of the following: ^L Bold ^N Underline ^P Blink ^Q Reverse video
^O	{^O}	Turns off specific display attribute for following text. Follow this code with one of the codes listed under ^N.
^Q	{^Q}	Turns off all active display attributes.

Go

The Go command is used to branch to a location identified by a Label command within the same macro. That is, when WordPerfect encounters the Go command in a macro, it will continue execution of the macro with the first step following the Label command identified by the Go command. The format of the Go command is

{GO}*label*~

where *label* is the name of the location where you want the macro to continue execution (see the preceding section, "Label").

The Go command is the most common way of altering the flow of execution in a macro. It is similar to the GOTO command in the BASIC programming language. If you want the macro to branch to a different location in the current macro and then *return* to where it left off, use the Call command. If you have several possible locations to branch to depending on the value of a specific variable, use the Case or Case Call commands. If you want to branch to an entirely different macro, use the Nest or Chain commands, or simply include the steps to invoke a macro.

The Go command is useful for macros that repeat a sequence of steps. For example, the following macro inserts a [Pg Num:1] code after every Hard Page break in the document:

```
{Home}{Home}{Up}

{LABEL}begin~
    {Search}{HPg}{Search}
    {Format}26
    1{Enter}
    {Exit}
{GO}begin~
```

This macro begins with a command to move the cursor to the top of the document. Then a Label command identifies the beginning of the section that will be repeated. After the new page number is inserted, the Go command branches to the place where the Label command appears, repeating the loop. Notice that the repeated steps have been indented with the TAB key to make the macro more readable.

The loop in the macro will repeat until the search fails. At that point the entire macro will end. To avoid this, you could include an On Not Found exception handler before the loop. There you could specify what action to take when the search fails (see "On Not Found" later in this section). Another way to improve a macro like this would be to turn the display off, which would make its execution much faster (see "Display On/Display Off" later in this section).

Another typical use of the Go command is to branch to a specific location when a certain condition is met. For example, the following segment from a macro will check to see if Variable 1 equals "ELA," and then branch to a specific location if it is.

```
{IF}"{VAR 1}"="ELA"~
    {GO}alderman~
{END IF}
```

Call

The Call command is used to branch to another location, and then return when that routine is finished. This allows you to use a section of a macro as a *subroutine*, which can be called from different points within the macro. The format of the Call command is

{CALL}*label*~

where *label* is the name of the location where you want the macro to continue execution. When this command is encountered, the macro executes the steps following the command identified by the label. Then, when it encounters a Return, Return Cancel, Return Error, or Return Not Found command, execution will resume with the macro step following the original Call command.

You can also include a Call or Case Call command *within* a subroutine. This means that you can have multiple levels (up to 20) of *nested* routines. Each Return command returns you one level in this nesting (see the next section, "Return").

The Call command provides a useful way to execute a commonly used routine. For example, let's say you want to create a prompt which says "Press any key to continue." Rather than type in the entire Char command each time you want the message, you could create a routine that does this, and then call that routine whenever it's needed in the macro. Here's what the routine itself would look like:

```
{LABEL}anykey~
{CHAR}0~Press·any·key·to·continue~
{RETURN}
```

Whenever you wanted to display that message, you'd use the Call command:

```
{CALL}anykey~
```

Return

The Return command is used to resume execution after the steps initiated by a Call or Case Call command have been executed. If the Return command is encountered and no Call or Case Call command has been executed, the macro ends. The format of the Return command is as follows:

{RETURN}

Since you can use the Call or Case Call command from within a called routine, you can have multiple levels of nested routines. The Return command always returns you to the point just after the most recently performed Call or Case Call command. (See "Call" and "Case Call" for examples of how to use the Return command.)

Return Cancel

The Return Cancel command is used to resume execution after the steps initiated by a Call or Case Call command have been executed, and then to indicate a Cancel condition. If the Return Cancel command is encountered and no Call or Case Call command has been executed, the macro ends. The format of the Return Cancel command is as follows:

{RETURN CANCEL}

Within nested routines, the Return Cancel command always returns you to the point just after the most recently performed Call or Case Call command.

After execution resumes, following the Call or Case Call command, a Cancel condition is indicated to the macro—just as if the user had pressed the <Cancel> key. If you had previously included an On Cancel command, the command you specified would be executed (see "On Cancel" later in this section). Otherwise, macro execution would end.

Return Error

The Return Error command is used to resume execution after the steps initiated by a Call or Case Call command have been executed, and then to indicate an Error condition. If the Return Error command is encountered and no Call or Case Call command has been executed, the macro ends. The format of the Return Error command is as follows:

{RETURN ERROR}

Within nested routines, the Return Error command always returns you to the point just after the most recently performed Call or Case Call command.

After execution resumes, following the Call or Case Call command, an Error condition is indicated to the macro. If you have previously included an On Error command, the command you specify will be executed (see "On Error" later in this section). Otherwise, macro execution will end.

Return Not Found

The Return Not Found command is used to resume execution after the steps initiated by a Call or Case Call command have been executed, and then to indicate a Not Found condition. If the Return Not Found command is encountered and no Call or Case Call command has been executed, the macro ends. The format of the Return Not Found command is as follows:

{RETURN NOT FOUND}

Within nested routines, the Return Not Found command always returns you to the point just after the most recently performed Call or Case Call command.

After execution resumes, following the Call or Case Call command, a Not Found condition is indicated to the macro. If you have previously included an On Not Found command, the command you specify will be executed (see "On Not Found" later in this section). Otherwise, macro execution will end.

Conditional Testing

Several commands allow you to write macros which can make decisions about events and actions. The Assign command lets you assign a value to a variable. The remaining commands in this section allow you to perform actions based on the outcome of a comparative statement, often using a variable as part of that statement.

Assign

The Assign command is used to assign a value to one of WordPerfect's ten variables (see "Variables" earlier in this chapter). You can then use the variable in one of the conditional commands listed below, or you can insert the contents of the variable into the document or at a prompt. The format of the Assign command is

{ASSIGN}*variable~value~*

where *variable* is a single digit from 0 to 9, and *value* is the value to be assigned to the variable. For the value you can enter text, a number, or a formula. You *do not* enclose the value in quotes. A variable in its keyname notation form can be used within the value.

To reset the variable (that is, to set its value to null), simply omit a value by typing the variable number followed by two tildes. The If Exists command would then recognize the variable as nonexistent (see "If Exists" later in this chapter).

In a formula, you can have only two values. For example, you can add two numbers, but not three. You can perform the basic arithmetic operations on the two numbers by using a plus sign (+) to add the numbers, a minus sign (−) to subtract the second from the first, an asterisk (∗) to multiply them, and a slash (/) to divide the first by the second. In addition, you can perform some logical operations on the values. You can perform a logical AND on the two numbers with an ampersand (&), and a logical OR with the vertical bar (|).

In addition, you can compare two values to test for a certain condition. These comparisons will be evaluated as either true or false. If the evaluation is true, then a value of −1 is assigned to the variable. If it is false, a value of 0 is assigned. You can then use the If, Case, or Case Call commands to test the result of the comparison. (Note that you will typically use a comparative formula directly as a value in an If, Case, or Case Call command.)

To see whether two values are equal—that is, whether two strings are identical (including case), or two numeric values are the same—separate the two values with an equal sign (=). To see whether they are different (not equal), separate them with an exclamation point followed by an equal sign (!=). You can use a greater-than sign to determine whether the first value is larger than the second, and a less-than sign to see if the first value is smaller than the second.

You can also assign a value to a variable from within a macro by marking text in the document as a block, including the {Macro Commands} key name, typing **3** (for "Assign") and then a single digit for the variable number. In addition, you can use the Char, Look, and Text commands described earlier in this section to assign a value to a variable.

If/Else/Endif

The If command is used to test a condition, and then to perform different actions depending on the result of the test. Normally you specify only the actions to be performed if the test is successful; however, you can optionally specify the actions to be performed if the test fails. The format of the If command is

> {IF}*value~*
>   (Steps to be performed if test is successful)
> {END IF}

or

> {IF}*value~*
>   (Steps to be performed if test is successful)
> {ELSE}
>   (Steps to be performed if test fails)
> {END IF}

where *value* is an expression which evaluates to either a zero or non-zero value. A non-zero value (typically −1) indicates that the condition is *true*, so the steps following the If command *are* executed. A zero value indicates that the condition is *false*, so the steps following the If command are *not* executed (but steps following the Else command, if included, *are* executed).

A typical value for the If command would be a comparative statement with two variables or a variable and a string literal (see "Assign").

For example, you could compare the value of Variable 1 against the string "quit" by using the statement "{VAR 1}"="quit". You can use the same format to check whether a variable equals a specific key. For example, you could use the statement "{VAR 1}"="{Cancel}" to see if Variable 1 has the <Cancel> key as its value, which may happen after a Char or Look command. Notice that with the If command, quotation marks are required around any string or character value, even if it is a variable name or a key name.

Another common use for the If command is to test the value of the State command (see "State" later in this chapter). For example, the statement {STATE}&128 returns 128 (a non-zero value) if Block is currently active, and 0 (zero) if it is not active. You could write a macro which determines a course of action on the basis of this condition. Here's a sample macro which performs a Block Move if Block is active, or a Paragraph Move if it is not:

```
{IF}{STATE}&128~
    {Move}BM
{ELSE}
    {Move}PM
{END IF}
```

By using this conditional capability, you can write macros which adapt themselves to the current environment.

To check a single value against a list of possible values, use the Case or Case Call commands (see "Case" and "Case Call" later in this section).

To have the macro move past the Endif command before all of the steps after the If command have been executed, use the Break command.

Break

The Break command is used to break out of an If command sequence. The format of the Break command is as follows:

{BREAK}

Case

The Case command is used to compare a value (usually a variable) against a list of possible equivalent values. Each item in the list consists of a possible value and a label to identify the routine to execute. If no items in the list match the initial value, then control passes to the next step after the Case command. The Case command is commonly used to process input from a menu presented with the Char or Text commands. The format of the Case command is as follows:

{CASE}*value~case1~label1~case2~label2~...caseN~labelN~~*

where *value* is the primary value to compare against others in the list, "*case*N" is a possible equivalent value, and "*label*N" is a corresponding destination label for that value. Each case and label ends with a tilde (~), and a final tilde is required to end the Case command. It may be easier to understand the Case command if you break up and indent the items in the list using TAB and ENTER. For example, here's the Case command described above in a format that is easier to understand:

{CASE}*value~*
case1~label1~
case2~label2~
. . .
caseN~labelN~~

Here only the initial value to compare is on the first line with the Case command itself. Each case is then placed on its own line. The last case in the list has the additional tilde to end the Case command.

For the macro to branch to any one of the labels, the value of the corresponding case must exactly match the initial value. Remember that a string or character value must be enclosed in quotation marks, even if the value is a variable or a key name. Note that uppercase and lowercase letters are significant when you compare strings with the Case command. For a menu which waits for a "yes" or "no" response with a single letter, you must check for uppercase or lowercase letters.

For example, here's a segment from a macro that prompts the user to respond to a "yes" or "no" question:

```
{CHAR}1~Continue·with·the·merge·operation?·(Y/N):·~

{CASE}"{VAR 1}"~
     "Y"~yes~
     "N"~no~
     "y"~yes~
     "n"~no~
     "{Cancel}"~end~~
```

In this macro, the Case command checks Variable 1 to see if it equals a "Y," "N," "y," "n," or the <Cancel> key, and branches accordingly to named locations within the same macro (not shown here).

Case Call

The Case Call command is used to compare a value (usually a variable) against a list of possible equivalent values, and then *call* various sections of a macro as subroutines. Each item in the list consists of a possible value and a label to identify the routine to call. If no items in the list match the initial value, then control passes to the next step after the Case Call command. The Case Call command is commonly used to process input from a menu presented with the Char or Text commands. The format of the Case Call command is as follows:

{CASE CALL}*value~case1~label1~case2~label2~...*
caseN~labelN~~

or, in a format that's easier to understand:

{CASE CALL}*value~*
case1~label1~
case2~label2~

. . .
caseN~labelN~~

The Case Call command works in almost the same manner as the Case command, except that the routines identified by the labels are called instead of simply executed (see "Case" and "Call" earlier in this section). When the macro encounters a Return command (or one of its variations) in the called routine, the macro will resume with the first step after the entire Case Call command.

If Exists

The If Exists command checks whether a variable has any value. This is useful in loops that repeat a series of steps until a variable is assigned a value. The format of the If Exists command is as follows:

{IF EXISTS}*variable~*
    (Steps to be performed if variable exists)
{END IF}

or

{IF EXISTS}*variable~*
    (Steps to be performed if variable exists)
{ELSE}
    (Steps to be performed if variable does not exist)
{END IF}

When WordPerfect begins, all variables are empty, and therefore the If Exists command would return false for each of them. You can manually force a variable to be empty with the Assign command (see "Assign"). The Text command will cause a variable to be empty if the user presses ENTER without typing anything at the prompt. (You can use If Exists to see if the user typed anything or not.) The Look command will cause a variable to be empty if no keystroke has been typed when the command is executed. To perform actions only when a variable does *not* exist, use the second form of the If Exists command shown above. (See the macros in Chapter 13, "Macro Library," for examples of this technique.)

Exception Handlers

The following macro commands are used to create *exception handlers*—that is, routines which the macro will execute in the case of specific events. When a specified event occurs, no matter what steps the macro is following, the command specified with the exception handler is immediately executed. The events for which you can create an exception handler are Cancel conditions, errors of certain types, and failures of search operations.

The exception handler commands take only one command as a parameter. Typically, this is a Go or Call command to branch to a location where you have a series of steps to handle the event. Notice that the exception handler command ends with a tilde, and that usually the command you include in the handler *also* ends with a tilde. Because of this, you'll often end the entire sequence with two tildes.

On Cancel

The On Cancel command is used to create an exception handler that is performed whenever a Cancel condition exists. This usually happens when the user has pressed the <Cancel> key during execution of the macro (and the Cancel Off command has not been performed previously). A macro subroutine, however, can also cause a Cancel condition to exist by ending in a Return Cancel command. The format of the On Cancel function is

{ON CANCEL}*action~*

where *action* is one of the following commands: Go, Call, Break, Quit, Restart, Return, Return Error, or Return Not Found. Typically, you'll use the Go or Call command to transfer control to a location in the macro where the Cancel condition is dealt with. WordPerfect will know what to do when a Cancel condition occurs only if it has already performed the On Cancel command. Therefore, you must place this command *before* the section of your macro where you want condition checking to be active. Frequently, this means that the command should be near the top of the macro. If you use the Go or Call command within the On Cancel command, you can place the routine identified by the label anywhere in the macro. Only the position of the On Cancel command is significant.

For example, you might want to prevent the user from stopping a macro dead in its tracks at any point. If the user presses the <Cancel> key while a macro is executing, you may want to display a message asking for confirmation. If the Cancel is confirmed, you may then want the macro to take some steps before actually stopping (cleaning up any markers left in the text, repositioning the cursor, and so on). Here's an On Cancel command and an accompanying routine demonstrating the ability to confirm cancellation of a macro:

```
{ON CANCEL}{CALL}cancel~~

{LABEL}cancel~
{CHAR}1~Are·you·sure·you·want·to·cancel?·(Y/N):·~
{CASE}"{VAR 1}"~
     "y"~yes~
     "Y"~yes~
     "n"~no~
     "N"~no~~
{GO}cancel~

{LABEL}yes~
{QUIT}

{LABEL}no~
{RETURN}
```

In this macro segment, the On Cancel command indicates what should happen whenever a Cancel condition exists (usually when the user presses <Cancel>). The Call command branches to the location labeled "cancel" *directly from* the point in the macro where the Cancel condition was first detected (see "Call" earlier in this section). The Char command then displays a menu asking the user to confirm the cancellation of the macro (see "Char" earlier in this section). If the user confirms the cancellation, then the Quit command ends the macro. Other steps may also be performed at this point. If the user chooses not to cancel the macro, the Return command returns control to the point where the Cancel condition was first detected, resuming operation of the macro. Note that the routines shown above do not constitute an entire macro. To use these routines, you'd likely place the On Cancel command near the top of an existing macro, and the rest of the steps near the bottom.

This same type of structure can be used for any one of the three exception handler commands: On Cancel, On Error, and On Not Found. You need to include a new exception handler at any point in the macro where you want to change the actions to be performed when the condition is encountered. The same macro, for example, may contain many Search functions. To specify the actions to be taken when the search fails for any one of them, you need to include a new On Not Found command before each search.

On Error

The On Error command is used to create an exception handler which will be performed whenever an error occurs. This includes not only WordPerfect errors (such as "ERROR: Text columns can't overlap"), and DOS errors (such as "ERROR: Disk full"), but also errors which WordPerfect encounters while interpreting a macro (such as incorrect syntax for one of the commands). A macro subroutine can cause an error condition to exist by ending in the Return Error command. The format of the On Error function is

{ON ERROR}*action*~

where *action* is one of the following commands: Go, Call, Break, Quit, Restart, Return, Return Cancel, or Return Not Found. Typically, you'll use the Go or Call command to transfer control to a location in the macro where an error condition is dealt with.

WordPerfect will know what to do when an error condition occurs only if it has already performed the On Error command. Therefore, you must place this command *before* the section of your macro where you want condition checking to be active. Typically, this means that the command should be near the top of the macro.

If you use the Go or Call command within the On Error command, you can place the routine identified by the label anywhere in the macro. Only the position of the On Error command is significant.

See "On Cancel" for more discussion of exception handlers.

On Not Found

The On Not Found command is used to create an exception handler that will be performed whenever a Not Found condition occurs. This usually happens when a search (such as a Forward or Reverse Search, Word Search, or Name Search) fails. A macro subroutine can also cause a Not Found condition to exist if it ends in the Return Not Found command. The format of the On Not Found function is

{ON NOT FOUND}*action~*

where *action* is one of the following commands: Go, Call, Break, Quit, Restart, Return, Return Cancel, or Return Error. Typically, you'll use the Go or Call command to transfer control to a location in the macro where the Not Found condition is dealt with. Without an On Not Found handler, macros usually end as soon as any search fails.

WordPerfect will know what to do when a Not Found condition occurs only if it has already performed the On Not Found command. Therefore, you must place this command *before* the section of your macro where you want condition checking to be active. Typically, this means that the command should be near the top of the macro. If you use the Go or Call command within the On Not Found command, you can place the actual routine identified by the label anywhere in the macro. Only the position of the On Not Found command is significant.

See "On Cancel" for more discussion of exception handlers.

Macro File Flow Control

In addition to the ability to control the flow of a macro's steps *within the same macro* using the Go, Call, Case, and Case Call commands, WordPerfect also has several macro commands that are used to control the flow of execution of entire macros. These commands are documented below.

Chain

The Chain command is used to indicate the name of a macro that should be executed when the current macro is finished. The format of the Chain command is

{CHAIN}*file~*

where *file* is the name of the macro you want to invoke. Note that the .WPM extension is assumed, so that you do not need to include it. Normally, WordPerfect will look for the macro in the same location where it would look for macros invoked manually. That is, if you've specified a macro directory in the Setup menu (see Appendix A, "Using Setup"), WordPerfect will look in this directory. If you have not specified such a directory, it will look first in the default directory, and then in the WordPerfect system directory. If you wish, you can precede the macro name with a drive or path designation.

Note that this command does not immediately transfer control to the specified macro. If that is your goal, you should simply include the steps in the macro to invoke the second macro. To do this, you would include the second macro's ALT key designation (press CTRL+V, then include the ALT key combination assigned to the macro), or you'd include the {Macro} key name, type the macro's name, then include the {Enter} key name.

Nest

The Nest command is used to transfer control to another macro, then return when the nested macro is complete. This provides a useful way to use an entire macro as a *subroutine*, just as you can call a section of the same macro as a subroutine with the Call or Case Call commands (see "Call" and "Case Call" earlier in this section). The format of the Nest command is

{NEST}*file~*

where *file* is the name of the macro you want to nest. Note that the
.WPM extension is assumed, so that you do not need to include it.
Normally, WordPerfect will look for the macro in the same location where it would look for macros invoked manually. That is, if
you've specified a macro directory in the Setup menu (see Appendix A, "Using Setup"), it will look in this directory. If you have not
specified such a directory, it will look first in the default directory, and then in the WordPerfect system directory. If you wish,
you can precede the macro name with a drive or path designation.

You might use the Nest command for macro routines which
you frequently need to use in other macros. For example, you
could write a macro which simply waits for the next keystroke,
and stores it in Variable 1. You can easily do this with the Char
command. Char, however, uses a prompt at the bottom of the
screen, which means the cursor does not stay in its original position in the document or in a menu or prompt (see "Look" earlier in
this section). The following macro performs this function more
elegantly:

```
{LABEL}start~
{LOOK}1~
{IF EXISTS}1~
{ELSE}
     {GO}start~
{END IF}
```

You might save this macro as ONEKEY. You can invoke it
from within any other macros by using the Nest command. Here's
a sample macro which nests the ONEKEY macro:

```
{Format}Z7

{NEST}onekey~
{VAR 1}

{Exit}
```

This macro calls up the Page Number Position menu, and then
the Nest command calls the ONEKEY macro, which waits for a
single keystroke, and then returns its value in Variable 1. When
the Page Number macro continues, the value of Variable 1 (that

is, the key you pressed) is inserted. You might want to include an If or Case command at this point to test the result of the variable.

Restart

The Restart command is used to terminate the macro when the currently running subroutine is completed. The format of the Restart command is as follows:

{RESTART}

Quit

The Quit command is used to terminate all macro execution. You can place the Quit command anywhere in a macro, even within a subroutine or an If command structure. In fact, the Quit command is especially useful when a condition has been found true with an If command. The format of the Quit command is as follows:

{QUIT}

Environment Control

Several macro commands are used to control and monitor the general environment while a macro is executing.

Cancel On
Cancel Off

The Cancel On and Cancel Off commands are used to control whether WordPerfect will allow the <Cancel> key to cancel a macro. The format of the commands is as follows:

{CANCEL ON}
{CANCEL OFF}

The default option is for the Cancel key to be enabled (Cancel On). When you execute the Cancel Off command in a macro, pressing the <Cancel> key during the execution of the macro does not cancel it. During input with the Pause command, the <Cancel> key will perform its normal WordPerfect functions (cancelling menus and prompts, and Undelete).

The On Cancel command will not respond to the user pressing the <Cancel> key if the Cancel Off command has been issued.

Display On
Display Off

The Display On and Display Off commands control whether WordPerfect will update the screen while macro steps are being performed. With Display On (the default for macros created with the macro editor), you'll see all of the program's menus and prompts flash by as the macro follows its steps. With Display Off (the default for macros created "on the fly"), you'll see the message "Please wait" at the bottom of the screen while the macro is executing. The format of the commands is as follows:

{DISPLAY ON}
{DISPLAY OFF}

With Display turned off, WordPerfect rewrites the entire screen when the macro is finished. Because of this, macros which consist of just a few keystrokes (such as one which transposes two characters, or one which underlines a word) should usually have Display turned on. On the other hand, macros that perform many steps often run much slower when Display is on. For example, a macro with a repeating loop that constantly scrolls the text, marks blocks, calls up menus, and so on, will run considerably faster with Display turned off.

When you create a macro, WordPerfect inserts the Display Off command at the beginning of the macro automatically. If you want the macro steps to be visible, you can simply delete this command in the macro editor.

You can also insert the Display On and Display Off commands in a macro during macro definition. To do this, press the <Macro Commands> key (CTRL+PGUP), type **2** for "Display," and you'll see the prompt "Display execution?" at the bottom of the screen. Type **Y** to insert the Display On command, or **N** to insert the Display Off command.

State

The State command is used to determine WordPerfect's state at any given time. For example, you can determine whether the Block mode is currently active, whether the Reveal Codes screen is being displayed, or whether a merge is being performed. You can also determine whether Document 1 or 2 is being edited. The format of the State command is as follows:

{STATE}

The State command returns a number which enables you to determine the current state of the program. Each possible state is assigned a number from 1 to 1024, as shown in Table 2-3.

The numbers for all states that are currently active are added together, and the result is returned by the State command. The easiest way to determine a single state is by using the logical

Table 2-3. STATE Result Values

Value	Description
3	Active Document ({STATE}&3 returns 1 if Document 1 is active, 2 if Document 2 is active, or 3 if Document 3, used by the Sort command, is active).
4	Main editing screen is active (that is, no menu or prompt is being displayed).
8	Editing structure other than document itself is active (footnote, header, footer, or style editing screen, for example—the main editing screen might still be "active").
16	Macro definition is active (never set).
32	Macro execution is active (always set).
64	Merge is active.
128	Block is active.
256	Typeover is active.
512	Reveal Codes is active.
1024	A prompt with a Yes/No question (such as "Save Document? (Y/N)") is being displayed.

AND operator (&) with the number that represents the state. For example, the statement {STATE}&128 will be equal to 128 (non-zero, and therefore true) if the Block mode is active. It will be equal to 0 (and therefore false) if the Block mode is not active. Similarly, the statement {STATE}&512 returns 512 if Reveal Codes is active, or 0 if it is not.

Typically, you'll use the State command in an If, Case, or Case Call command. For example, you could write a simple macro which will move a block if Block mode is active, or move the current paragraph if Block mode is not active. This macro can be used in two different ways, depending on whether you've turned on Block before invoking the macro. Here's a macro that will perform this function:

```
{IF}{STATE}&128~
    {Move}BM
{ELSE}
    {Move}PM
{END IF}
```

You can use the State value 1024 to check whether a Yes/No prompt is currently being displayed. This is useful, for example, when a macro will be retrieving a document from List Files. By checking {STATE}&1024 right after the Retrieve command is issued, the macro will be able to determine whether the prompt "Retrieve into current document?" is being displayed. Similarly, when a macro saves a document, it can use the same command to determine whether the "Replace file?" prompt is being displayed. In both cases, the macro will know whether or not it is necessary to include a "Y" or "N" answer.

Macro Programming Aids

Several macro commands are helpful in the macro creation and editing process.

; (Comment)

The Comment command is used to insert comments into a macro to make it easier to understand. Comments can be helpful when you modify your own macros, and they can be invaluable to others who need to understand and modify your macros. The format of the Comment command is

{;}*comment~*

where *comment* is text which you enter as a comment. This text will be ignored by the macro as it executes. If you wish, you can make the comment several lines long. WordPerfect knows that the comment has ended only when the ending tilde is encountered. If you omit the ending tilde, all remaining macro steps (until another tilde) will be ignored as a comment.

Note that you can either put comments on their own lines, or you can append them to the end of macro steps. You may want to use the TAB key to align the comments — this makes them easier to read. (See the macros in Chapter 13, "Macro Library.")

Step On
Step Off

The Step On and Step Off commands are used to turn WordPerfect's Step Macro mode on and off. This mode allows you to execute macros one step at a time, which can make it easier to debug a complex macro. The format of the commands is as follows:

{STEP ON}
{STEP OFF}

Once a macro has encountered the Step On command, the remainder of the macro will be executed one keystroke at a time (although macro commands are executed in one step, no matter how long the name is). Each time the macro has executed a step, it displays the character or command at the bottom of the screen, and waits for you to press any key to continue. By strategically placing the Step On and Step Off commands within your macro, you can use the Step mode for only the portion of the steps where you feel you may have a problem.

Original Key

The Original Key command performs the *original* (not redefined) action of the last key pressed. (In the case of a macro executing as a redefined key, the last key pressed will usually be the redefined key itself.) Here is the format of the Original Key command:

{ORIGINAL KEY}

Timing

Two commands are used to control the timing of your macros, Speed and Wait.

Speed

The Speed command is used to control the speed at which macros are executed. The format of the command is

{SPEED}*100ths~*

where *100ths* is a number indicating the hundredths of a second to wait between each keystroke of the macro. Macros normally execute as fast as possible, with no delay between keystrokes. However, there may be cases where you need to slow down execution. For example, you may want a macro which types text on the screen to slow down so that text is displayed at a readable speed. You might use a value of 20 for this (equivalent to 2/10ths of a second).

Wait

The Wait command causes a macro to pause for a specified period of time. The format of the command is

{WAIT}*10ths~*

where *10ths* is a number indicating the tenths of a second to wait. For example, you may want to display a certain menu or help screen for a few seconds before continuing with the macro. You can also use this command to pause after displaying a message with the Prompt command.

KEYBOARD DEFINITION

WordPerfect allows you to redefine the function of most keys on the keyboard. In addition to swapping individual functions, you can also attach entire macro sequences to any key. You create and edit your modified key definitions using a Keyboard Edit menu, which uses its own key editor. This editor is almost identical to the macro editor (described in the previous section, "Editing Macros").

To begin redefining keys, you must first create a new keyboard file (or, alternatively, begin editing an existing one).

Creating a Keyboard File

To create a new keyboard file, begin by pressing the <Setup> key (SHIFT+F1), and type **6** for "Keyboard Layout." The Keyboard Layout screen will appear, as shown in Figure 2-4. Type **4** for "Create," type the desired name for the keyboard file, and press ENTER. The keyboard file name can be any valid DOS file name of up to eight characters. Do not include a filename extension, because WordPerfect will add .WPK automatically. (If a file with the name you specify already exists, you will see an error message. Choose another name.)

Once you've created the keyboard file, you'll see the Keyboard Edit menu. Now you can create, edit, and manage the key definitions within this keyboard file, as described in the sections that follow. (Alternatively, you can select an existing keyboard file from the Keyboard Layout screen, and type **5** for "Edit.")

Setup: Keyboard Layout

1 Select; 2 Delete; 3 Rename; 4 Create; 5 Edit; 6 Original; N Name search: <u>1</u>

Figure 2-4.   The Keyboard Layout screen

Creating a Key Definition

To create a key definition (that is, to redefine what a key will do when it is pressed), type **4** for "Create" from the Keyboard Edit menu. At the "Key:" prompt, press the key you wish to define. (For example, to define what actions the F1 key will perform, press F1. To define the actions the CTRL+X combination will perform, press CTRL+X.) You'll then see the Key Edit screen, which will resemble the one shown in Figure 2-5.

   Now you can modify the actions which the key you pressed will perform.

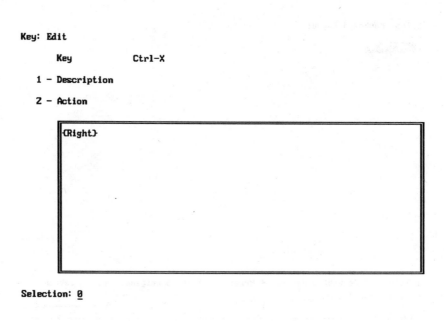

```
Key: Edit

        Key             Ctrl-X

  1 - Description

  2 - Action

   ┌─────────────────────────────────────────────────┐
   │ {Right}                                         │
   │                                                 │
   │                                                 │
   │                                                 │
   │                                                 │
   │                                                 │
   │                                                 │
   │                                                 │
   └─────────────────────────────────────────────────┘

Selection: 0
```

Figure 2-5.   The Key Edit screen

Modifying a Key's Action

When you've issued the command to create or edit a key definition
(see "Editing a Key Definition" later in this section), you'll see the
Key Edit screen. On this screen, you'll first see the name of the
key you pressed (for example, F1 for the F1 key, or Ctrl—X for
CTRL+X). Next you will see a prompt asking for a description of
the key's new purpose. To enter a description, type **1**, then enter
any description you want for the new key definition. The description can be up to 39 characters in length, and can include spaces.
Press ENTER when you are through.

   To modify the actions which the key will perform, type **2** for
"Action," and the cursor will move into the Key Editing window. If
the key you pressed has a "native" WordPerfect function (such as
Cancel for the F1 key), you'll see the name of that function in the
window. Otherwise, the key will show whatever other actions you
have previously defined for it. You can delete those key names if

you wish, and replace them with any other steps which you want the key to perform. You can specify a foreign character, for example, by using the Compose function.

You can insert other WordPerfect key names by simply pressing the appropriate keys. Currently active redefinitions are always inserted, not the original meanings. If your intent was to insert the original meaning of a key, first restore the original keyboard by pressing CTRL+6 (see "Reverting to Original Definitions"). (See Chapter 13, "Macro Library," for a method of inserting the original definition of only a single key.) To include the same key you're *currently defining* as a step in the key's definition, use the macro command {ORIGINAL KEY} (see "Macro Commands" earlier in this chapter). This inserts the original definition of the last key pressed (usually the key that is currently being redefined).

In cases where keys perform a function within the Key Editing window (such as arrow keys, the <Exit> key, and the <Cancel> keys), you can either insert a single key name by preceding the key with the CTRL+V sequence, or you can press the <Macro Define> key (CTRL+F10), which puts you into a special Macro Commands mode. In this mode, every key inserts its actual key name. Press the <Macro Define> key a second time to resume normal editing.

In addition to WordPerfect key names, you can also include normal text as well as any of the macro commands in a key's definitions. All of the macro commands are inserted (and operate) exactly as they do in macros. See "Macro Commands" earlier in this chapter for details on the use of these commands, and the section "Using the Macro Editor" for additional instructions on the use of the Macro and Key Editors.

When you're satisfied with your changes to the key definition, press the <Exit> key (F7). If you want to abort the changes you made, press the <Cancel> key (F1). WordPerfect will confirm your request. Then, press the <Exit> key to return to the Keyboard Edit screen. If you saved the changes you made to the key (or if there was an existing redefinition), you'll see it listed with the key descriptions on the screen.

When you select this keyboard file, all of the key redefinitions shown in this list will be active. (See "Selecting a Keyboard File" later in this chapter.)

Editing a Key Definition

Once you've created key definitions, you can easily edit the actions which a key will perform. To do this, begin by positioning the cursor bar onto the name of the key you want to affect. You can also press the <Search> key (F2) to find a key in the list quickly. At the "Key:" prompt, press whatever key you want to edit. The cursor bar will move to that key's description in the list. Once you've selected a key, type 1 for "Edit," and the Key Edit screen will appear.

Now you can modify the actions which the key you pressed will perform.

Retrieving and Saving Macros

Since macros and key definitions can actually perform the exact same actions, WordPerfect allows you to easily retrieve the steps of a macro into a key's definition, or save a key's definition as a separate macro file.

If you have created a macro whose actions you want to be invoked by a specific key, you can retrieve the macro into that key's definition. To do this, type 6 for "Retrieve" from the Keyboard Edit screen. At the bottom of the screen, you'll see the prompt "Key:". Press the key within whose definition you want to retrieve a macro's steps. If the key you specify has already been defined within the current keyboard file, you'll be asked to confirm the replacement. Next, a "Macro:" prompt will appear. Type the name of the macro that you want to retrieve, and press ENTER. (WordPerfect looks in the specified directory for macros and keyboard files, or in the default directory if you haven't specified one, and then in the WordPerfect system directory.) The key you specified will now appear in the list of keys. If you edit the key's definition, the macro's steps will be inserted into the Key Editing window.

You can also save the actions of any key as a macro, and thus have the steps stored in a separate file on disk. To do this, begin by positioning the cursor on the name of the key you want to affect. Then type **5** for "Save," and the "Define Macro:" prompt will appear at the bottom of the screen. Type the name of the macro to create, and press ENTER. If a macro with the name you specify already exists, you'll be asked for confirmation to replace it. Now the new macro file will contain all of the steps specified for the indicated key.

Managing Key Definitions

You can also perform some management tasks with the defined keys from the Keyboard Edit menu.

To delete a key definition that you no longer want in the keyboard file, begin by positioning the cursor bar on the desired key in the list. Then type **2** for "Delete" (or simply press the DEL key). WordPerfect will ask whether you want to delete the key redefinition. Type **Y** to confirm the deletion, or type **N** to have the key retain its redefinition.

In addition to deleting a key definition, you can also move a definition from one key to another. For example, let's say you've defined CTRL+F to perform an action, but decide that you'd rather have that same action performed by CTRL+S instead. You could move the definition directly from CTRL+F to CTRL+S.

To move a key definition, begin by positioning the cursor bar on the key in the list whose definition you want to move. Then type **3** for "Move," and you'll see the "Key:" prompt at the bottom of the screen. Press the key onto which you want to move the definition. If the new key has already been redefined in the current file, you'll see a prompt asking for confirmation to replace the definition. Type **Y** to replace the definition. Once the definition has been moved, you'll see the new key name appear in the list next to the original description. If you replaced another key's definition, it will disappear from the list.

After you've made any desired additions and modifications to the key definitions in a keyboard file, press the <Exit> key (F7) to return to the Keyboard Layout menu.

Selecting a Keyboard File

Once you've created a keyboard file, you can begin using it by
selecting it from the Keyboard Layout menu. On this menu, you'll
see listed all of the keyboard files currently defined. This will
include any you've added, as well as those which were provided
with WordPerfect. To select which file will be active (that is,
which file's definitions will be in effect), begin by positioning the
cursor bar on the desired file name. If you wish, you can also
press the <Search> key (F2), and use Name Search to find the file
you want by simply beginning to type its name. Press ENTER or
SPACE BAR to leave Name Search mode.

Once you've positioned the cursor bar to the desired file, type **1**
for "Select" (or press ENTER, as "1" is the default menu selection),
and the specified keyboard file will become active. This file will
remain active for all future WordPerfect editing sessions, until
you select another file.

Managing Keyboard Files

In addition to editing the contents of the keyboard files from the
Keyboard Edit menu, you can also perform several management
tasks with the files.

To delete an unwanted keyboard file, position the cursor bar at
the desired keyboard file, and type **2** for "Delete." A prompt will
ask for confirmation to delete the file.

To provide a new name for an existing keyboard file, begin by
positioning the cursor bar on that file. Type **3** for "Rename," type
a new name for the file, and press ENTER.

Reverting to Original
Definitions

If you want WordPerfect to use all of the original key definitions
(that is, if you don't want it not to use any of the keyboard files),
type **6** for "Original" from the Keyboard Layout screen. You'll
need to return to this screen at a subsequent point to select a key-

board file, if desired.

You can also switch (for the current editing session only) to the original key definitions by pressing CTRL+6 at any time, using the 6 key along the top row of keys on the keyboard. This is useful as an "emergency escape"—for example, if you've accidentally redefined the SHIFT+F1 sequence as something other than the <Setup> key. It's also useful when you're in the middle of performing some other function in WordPerfect and want to use the original definitions. (See the section "Original Definition Prefix Key" in Chapter 13, "Macro Library," for a method of inserting the original definition of only a single key.)

Provided Keyboard Files

WordPerfect includes several sample keyboard files. These can be found on the Conversion disk.

The ALTRNAT keyboard file moves the Help function to F1, the Cancel function to the ESC key, and the Repeat function to the F3 key. This may be more familiar to people who use other programs with this arrangement.

The ENHANCED keyboard file contains definitions for many keys on the Enhanced keyboard. These are keys which are not available for redefinition on standard keyboards. For example, the 5 key on the numeric keypad is redefined as the Home function, while the 7 key (originally the HOME key) is redefined to move the cursor to the beginning of the line.

The MACROS keyboard file contains a collection of useful predefined macros assigned to various keys. For example, there are macros to move the cursor up or down in the document by sentence or paragraph. There's also a macro that allows you to view the List Files display while creating a graphics box.

USING DOCUMENT 2

WordPerfect can work with two separate documents at once, as discussed in Chapter 1. This dual-document editing capability can be quite handy when used in conjunction with macros.

If you make an assumption that Document 2 will be available when a macro is invoked, the macro can use it as a temporary editing work space. This work space provides a perfect area either for storing gathered bits of text or for performing any other action that requires the use of an editing environment but that would disrupt the flow of text in Document 1.

You can, for instance, write a simple macro that will copy whatever line of text the cursor is on (or copy a sentence, paragraph, or other block of text), retrieve (paste) it into Document 2, and return to Document 1. If you try this, you will see that when the macro is executed, the cursor disappears for less than a second while it copies the text. It then becomes a simple matter to browse through your document, find the lines you want to collect, and execute the macro once for each line. When you are done, all of the lines you selected will be gathered in one place—Document 2.

You can also use Document 2 as a temporary holding place for a mass search operation. Say, for example, you want to write a macro that searches a document, finds all of the footnote references, and combines them into a single separate document.

There are several ways to perform this task. One good method is to create a macro that uses the Edit Footnote function for the first footnote, marks its text as a block, copies the block, exits Edit Footnote, and retrieves (pastes) it into Document 2. Then the macro returns to Document 1 and repeats the procedure with the next footnote. Switching back and forth between the two documents is instantaneous, and block copying requires a minimum of disk access, so that this is a fairly fast process.

Another example would be a block of text that you need to process in some way. You may need to perform a series of Replace operations on the block. By cutting the text from the main document and retrieving it in the alternate document, you can perform these actions without worrying about modifying the rest of the text. When the steps are complete, the macro could cut the text and retrieve it back to where it came from in the main document.

USING OTHER MACRO PROGRAMS

There are several general-purpose, *memory-resident* utilities available, such as Prokey and Superkey, that function much like WordPerfect's macros.

Most of these programs can be used with WordPerfect. However, because WordPerfect has the ability to redefine any key on the keyboard, and because the program's macro language is so powerful, you are not likely to need an external program. Usually, the only advantage these utilities would offer you over WordPerfect's own macros and keyboard definition functions is that they would work with other programs as well.

3

MERGE

WordPerfect's Merge function allows you to create one "form" document (called a *primary document*) and use it repeatedly with information that is filled in either automatically (from a list of items stored in a *secondary document*) or manually (from the keyboard).

The most common application of the Merge function is a *mailmerge* operation. In this case the primary document is a form letter, and the secondary document contains a mailing list. The Merge function will combine the two documents, generating a new letter for each person on the list. Each personalized letter can be printed as it is generated, or the Merge function can save the letters to be printed later, in one batch.

The Merge function can also be used for a variety of other tasks. You may, for example, want to have information about a book collection printed both as a series of index cards in a specific format and as a columnar report of the book titles. Using Word-Perfect's Merge function, you could maintain the actual data for all your books in a secondary file and then create several primary files that would format the data in different ways.

Most database programs design reports in a similar fashion. In fact, the Merge function is similar to a database program in many ways. You may find, after reading this chapter, that the Merge function is flexible enough to make unnecessary the purchase of an additional program for database work.

Although in its simplest form the Merge function is easy to use, it is also, in its more advanced forms, one of the most complex of WordPerfect's functions. In Chapter 1 you saw the benefits of WordPerfect's *clean screen* (that is, with no control codes shown). With the Merge function, you will notice an exception to the rule. After all, you are ready to learn the Merge function, one of the program's most advanced features; you should also be ready to bend a little in your expectation of the way WordPerfect appears on the screen.

BASIC MERGE COMPONENTS

The most basic form of the merge operation combines a single document with a list of information. To perform this task, you must create two files on disk: the primary document and the secondary document. Each of these documents has its own set of rules about the placement of text and about special *Merge codes* that will direct the merge operation.

Although it may not seem logical, it will be easier for you to understand the different layouts of the primary and secondary documents if the secondary document is discussed first.

The Secondary Document

The secondary document contains the information to be inserted into the primary document when you execute the Merge. For example, the secondary document might contain a list of names and addresses for use in a form letter merge operation. The secondary document is divided into *fields* and *records*. A field contains a single piece of information, like a name. A record contains a set of fields, like a person's name, address, phone number, date of birth, and salary. Special Merge codes separate the fields and records from one another.

You mark the end of a field by pressing the <Merge Return> key (F9), which inserts ^R and a Hard Return into the text at the cursor position. This key is identified as <Merge R> on the keyboard template.

Note: Letters preceded by a caret (^) are often referred to as if they had been entered using the CONTROL key. Thus, ^R is sometimes referred to as CONTROL R, even though in this particular case you have not pressed the CONTROL key. Do *not* enter this or any other Merge code by typing a caret followed by the single letter, since it would not be recognized by the Merge function. When marking the end of a field, you must always use the <Merge Return> key (F9).

Fields, for most purposes, are unlimited in length. They can consist of many lines, since the field ends only when the program encounters the ^R [HRt] combination. For most applications, however, fields are only one or two lines long.

Mark the end of a record by pressing the <Merge Codes> key (SHIFT+F9), and typing **E**, which inserts ^E and a Hard Page Break into the text at the cursor position. Records are also unlimited in length. They can contain as many fields as you want, but the number of fields in each record of a secondary document should always be the same.

The secondary document, like the primary document, is simply a standard WordPerfect file with some special codes inserted. Its potential size, then, like that of any other WordPerfect document, is determined by a combination of available disk space and cache memory (RAM). The number of records that can be stored in a secondary document is limited only by the total document size.

WordPerfect will internally number the fields sequentially, starting with 1 for the first field in each record. When the merge is actually executed, these numbers are used to pull information from the secondary document and place it into the primary document. Since WordPerfect will extract the information by counting the fields in each record, it is important that you keep the number of fields the same for each record. Therefore, if a field will be blank in one of the records, you still need to press the <Merge Return> key to insert a Merge Return code into that field. The field will not contain any text, but inserting the Merge Return code will keep the field numbering accurate.

Merge Practice—Creating A Secondary Document

As a simple example of a secondary document, let's create a file that contains a mailing list of only two people. Be sure the screen is clear before beginning the lesson.

1. Type **John** and press the <Merge Return> key (F9).
2. Type **Kent** and press <Merge Return>.
3. Type **Amalgamated Steel** and press <Merge Return>.
4. Type **334 Main St.** and press <Merge Return>.
5. Type **Toledo, OH 09332** and press <Merge Return>.
6. Press the <Merge Codes> key (SHIFT+F9), and type **E**.
7. Type **Jan** and press <Merge Return>.
8. Type **Frankenbaumer** and press <Merge Return>.
9. Press <Merge Return>.

   Notice that in this record, you simply press <Merge Return> for the third field, since there is no company name.
10. Type **554 Pine Ave.** and press <Merge Return>.
11. Type **Eureka, CA 94543** and press <Merge Return>.
12. Press the <Merge Codes> key, and type **E**
13. Press the <Save> key (F10).
14. Type **list** and press ENTER.

Your screen should look like the one in Figure 3-1. (Note that the ^R and ^E codes are usually the only two Merge codes that are inserted into a secondary file.)

In this secondary document, field 1 is the first name, field 2 is the last name, field 3 is the company name, field 4 is the street address, and field 5 is the city, state, and ZIP code. (You should

```
John^R
Kent^R
Amalgamated Steel^R
334 Main St.^R
Toledo, OH 09332^R
^E
=============================================================
Jan^R
Frankenbaumer^R
^R
554 Pine Ave.^R
Eureka, CA 94543^R
^E

=============================================================
-
```

Doc 1 Pg 3 Ln 1 Pos 10

Figure 3-1.   A sample secondary document

keep a written list of the fields and their corresponding field numbers whenever you create a secondary document. See the section entitled "Using Field Names" later in this chapter for an alternative to using field numbers.) You can see that if you want to specify a full name in the primary document, you will need to use both field 1 and field 2. Note that in the first record field 3 contains a company name, while in the second record field 3 is empty.

Now let's see how this data is used in the primary document.

The Primary Document

There are two ways of using WordPerfect's Merge function: the *simple method* and the *flexible method*. In this section, you will learn how to create a primary document for a simple merge. The flexible method, discussed later in the chapter, can perform some interesting tricks. However, it requires more effort and patience to implement.

Create the primary document exactly as you want the final printed document to appear. That is, type the document using WordPerfect's formatting commands (like Bold, Tab, and Center). The only difference is that you will insert one of the Merge codes into the text at each point where you want variable information to be entered. The variable information will come from either a secondary file or the keyboard. (Entering information from the keyboard during a merge operation is discussed later in this chapter, in the section "Give and Take—The Keyboard Merge.")

To insert any Merge code into the text of the primary document, press the <Merge Codes> key (SHIFT+F9). At the bottom of the screen a menu will appear that looks like this:

^C; ^D; ^E; ^F; ^G; ^N; ^O; ^P; ^Q; ^S; ^T; ^U; ^V:

This is probably the most cryptic of WordPerfect's menus. Each of the letters indicates a specific Merge function. To implement a simple merge, you need only the ^F Merge code.

^F Insert Field

This code extracts a specific numbered field from the secondary document and inserts it into the primary document at the place where the code was inserted.

Here are three things to remember about inserting the ^F Merge code into a primary document:

- You do not need to insert every field in your secondary document into your primary document.
- You do not need to insert fields in numerical order.
- You can include any field as many times as you want.

To enter the ^F Merge code after pressing the <Merge Codes> key, type **F**. WordPerfect will respond with "Field:". Type the number of the field you want to include and press ENTER. The ^F code, followed by the field number you specified and a final ^, will be inserted into the text at the cursor position. For example, to insert field 1 of the secondary document into the primary document at the cursor position, press the <Merge Codes> key

(SHIFT+F9), **F** for Field Number, **1** for field 1, and ENTER. The code ^F1^ will be inserted in the text.

When the merge is actually executed, it deletes the entire ^F code sequence and inserts the text from the specified field exactly where the sequence was located. You can place formatting commands (like Center, Underline, Flush Right, Align Tab, and so on) into the primary document before and after the ^F code sequence. The inserted text will be affected by these commands.

If, for example, you want the text from a specific field underlined in the final document, press the <Underline> key in the primary document before pressing the <Merge Codes> key. After entering the ^F code, press the <Underline> key again. The ^F code sequence will appear underlined (or marked for underlining depending on your monitor). When the primary document is merged with a secondary document, the text from that field will be underlined.

Suppressing Blank Lines

Sometimes, you need to insert a field in a primary document which may or may not contain information, depending on the record that is being merged. For example, you may have a field for company name, but not all of the people on your list are associated with a company. To avoid having a blank line in your merged document when a field is empty, simply include a question mark after the field number. For each record, merge will look to see whether or not the field is empty. If it is, the remainder of the line on which the field appears will be deleted (including the [HRt] code). Thus, the blank line will be suppressed. (You should be careful about using the question mark for a field that appears on the same line with text or other ^F Merge codes.)

For example, if the field that may or may not contain information is field 2, insert the ^F Merge code by pressing the <Merge Codes> key (SHIFT+F9), typing **F** for Field, typing **2?**, and pressing ENTER. The Merge code sequence ^F2?^ will appear at the cursor location. The Merge codes for the entire address, then, would look similar to this:

```
^F1^
^F2?^
^F3^
^F4^ ^F5^
```

```
March 15, 1988

^F1^ ^F2^
^F3?^
^F4^
^F5^

Dear ^F1^:

We are very sorry to inform you that all of the tickets for the
All-Star Spectacular at the Grenoble Theater this Friday, March
18, have been sold out.  Enclosed, please find a refund for the
deposit you left with us last July.

We regret that you will be unable to attend, as we have always
appreciated the patronage of the ^F2^ family.  Thank you for your
patience and your consideration.


Sincerely,


The Management of the Grenoble Theater
  -
                                        Doc 1 Pg 1 Ln 24 Pos 10
```

Figure 3-2.   The primary document with merge codes

When the merge is executed, only those records with information
in field 2 will have a line for the field. For records that do not have
information in field 2, merge will skip from field 1 to field 3.

Merge Practice—Creating
A Primary Document

To create a primary document that will generate form letters for
the list you made earlier, clear the screen and enter the text as
shown in Figure 3-2. To insert the $^\wedge$F Merge codes into the letter,
press the <Merge Codes> key (SHIFT+F9), type **F**, type the appropriate field number, and press ENTER. Next, save the primary
merge document by pressing the <Save> key (F10), typing **letter**,
and pressing ENTER.

Performing the Simple Merge

The process of executing the simple merge procedure is what its name indicates—simple. After creating and saving the merge documents as just described, and then clearing the screen, you press the <Merge/Sort> key (CTRL+F9), type 1 for "Merge," and enter the names of the primary and secondary documents. Then the merge begins. To stop a merge before it is complete, press the <Cancel> key (F1).

In a simple merge like this, WordPerfect combines the primary file and the secondary file to make *one big merged document*. This file will contain one copy of the primary document for each record that is found on a new page.

Make sure the screen is clear before you begin performing the merge. It is very important to do this since the on-screen document is used to generate the merged document. (Any text that is on the screen when a merge is executed will be included in the final merged document.) Follow these steps:

1. Press the <Merge/Sort> key (CTRL+F9).
2. Type 1 for "Merge."
3. At the "Primary file:" prompt, type **letter** and press ENTER.
4. At the "Secondary file:" prompt, type **list** and press ENTER.

   The screen will clear, and this message will be displayed briefly at the bottom of the screen:

   ```
   × Merging ×
   ```

5. Press HOME,HOME,UP ARROW to move to the top of the merged document. Your screen should look like the one in Figure 3-3.

The Merge function has now created a two-page document containing two versions of the primary file. Scroll through the document to see how the data from the two records in the secondary file has been incorporated into the text. Notice that the address is four lines long in the first letter but three lines long in the second

```
March 15, 1988

John Kent
Amalgamated Steel
334 Main St.
Toledo, OH 09332

Dear John:

We are very sorry to inform you that all of the tickets for the
All-Star Spectacular at the Grenoble Theater this Friday, March
18, have been sold out.  Enclosed, please find a refund for the
deposit you left with us last July.

We regret that you will be unable to attend, as we have always
appreciated the patronage of the Kent family.  Thank you for your
patience and your consideration.


Sincerely,


The Management of the Grenoble Theater

                                         Doc 1 Pg 1 Ln 1 Pos 10
```

Figure 3-3.   Merged document

letter. Also notice that the longer last name in the second record caused the last paragraph of the letter to be formatted differently from the first record. WordPerfect automatically reformats paragraphs while performing the merge operation. If you printed the document now, you would have two personalized letters.

THE FLEXIBLE MERGE

With the simple merge procedure, WordPerfect performs many functions automatically. For instance, it generates a Hard Page Break between copies of the primary document, and it moves successively to each record in the secondary document. With the flexible merge, these operations are not performed automatically. If you want a Hard Page Break inserted, you have to put it in yourself. You also need to specify when the merge should move to the next record in the secondary file.

The procedure for using WordPerfect's flexible merge is similar to that for computer programming. When you create a primary document, you are essentially writing a "program" that will lead WordPerfect through a series of instructions when the merge procedure is initiated. When you execute a merge and specify a primary document, you are "running" the program. The program places output into the merged document as it executes. This output consists of text that is entered in the primary file, fields that are requested from a secondary file, and keyboard input.

As the merge executes, it examines each character in the primary document. Text (like the body of a form letter) is passed directly into the merged document. The Merge function processes field codes (like ^F1^) by deleting the code, extracting the specified field number, and placing it in the merged document.

Beyond this, there are several Merge codes that control the merge operation, performing such actions as moving to the next record in the secondary file, or switching to a new primary or secondary document.

Flexible Merge Codes

The flexible merge is implicitly selected when you use any one of three Merge codes in the primary document: ^N, ^P, or ^S. As soon as the merge operation encounters one of them, the simple merge cycle is cancelled. Thereafter, you must use the Flexible Merge codes to manually perform the functions that are performed automatically by the simple merge.

The ^N code performs a step that is normally handled by the simple merge:

^N Next Record

This code tells the Merge function to start using the next record in the current secondary document. All subsequent ^F codes will retrieve information from this next record. When there are no more records, the merge operation ends.

The ^P code instructs the system to continue the merge operation using a new primary file. This primary file can be the same one that you specified when the merge was originally executed (which means the merge would be repeating the same steps, as with the simple merge). The new primary file can also be different from the one originally specified. In this case, the control of the merge operation is transferred to the new document. This document is then processed like the first one.

^P   Primary Document

This code specifies a new primary document for the merge to use. It is entered in Matched Pair form. The name of the primary document is entered between two ^P codes, without any spaces. For example, ^Pform.ltr^P instructs the merge to begin using the "form.ltr" primary file. If no file name is entered between the codes (that is, ^P^P), the merge will reuse the primary file currently being used.

If you can use the ^N and ^P codes to perform the same functions as the simple merge, you may wonder why you can't *always* use the simple merge. In fact, you can completely simulate the simple merge cycle using Flexible Merge codes. However, the flexible merge performs many functions that could not be performed by the simple merge.

For example, the flexible merge can suppress the Hard Page Break that the simple merge automatically inserts between copies of the primary document. With the Hard Page Break suppressed, the copies will not appear on separate pages in the final merged document. To perform this function, add these codes to the end of a primary document:

^N^P^P

These codes tell the merge to use the next record in the secondary document and then to continue the merge reusing the current primary document. When the merge encounters this string of codes at the end of a primary document, the simple merge cycle is cancelled, and no Hard Page Break is inserted. This might be useful in a number of situations.

Instead of writing form letters, you may want to see a report showing only the names of everyone on your mailing list. You want the names to appear one after the other, not on separate pages.

Clear the screen and create a short primary document consisting only of these Merge codes:

```
^F1^ ^FZ^
^N^P^P
```

Save the file with the name "report", clear the screen, and execute the merge. Use "report" as the primary file name and "list" (the file from your previous exercise) as the secondary file name. After the merge is complete, you will see the names of the two people on your list. (Naturally, with a larger mailing list you would see more names.) After a report like this is generated, you could move the cursor to the top of the document and retrieve a "report header" document that consists of a title and field names for the report.

You can make a report like this more elaborate by adding more fields separated by Tab or Tab Align codes or by adding print enhancements like Bold and Underline. (Pressing <Tab Align> and then entering the ^F Merge code for a field that contains numbers causes the numbers to line up properly in the final merged document.) You can generate some fancy columnar reports using this technique.

^S Secondary Document

This command specifies a new secondary document for the merge to use. The file name is specified exactly as with the ^P code. You must always specify a name. You might want to use the ^S code to maintain two separate secondary documents that you often use together.

Perhaps you have one secondary document that contains a list of people with IBM computers and another of people with Compaq computers. You frequently use the lists separately but occasionally need to perform a mailmerge using both lists at once. By inserting a set of ^S codes that specify the name of the second list at the end of the first list, you can perform the mail merge on both lists with the same merge instruction.

Merging to the Printer

The simple merge creates one large document that can then be saved, printed, or otherwise processed. However, if you are using a secondary file that contains a large number of records, the resulting merged document can often become too big to handle. In fact, you may simply be unable to create a document as large as the one that would be produced by the simple merge.

The solution to this problem is the flexible merge. With it, the Merge function can automatically print each copy of the primary document after it has been merged with a record from the secondary document.

To merge to the printer, use the ^T Merge code:

^T   Type (Print) Merged Document

This command will generate a Full Document Print of the merged document, and then it will clear the screen.

This code generates a print job, exactly as if you had pressed the <Print> key and typed 1 for "Full Document." This means that, as with all documents, the printer will automatically advance to the next sheet of paper (if you are using continuous paper) after the document has been printed. You do not want to use the simple merge, which would force an extra Hard Page Break between records, causing a blank piece of paper to be ejected between pages.

The ^T Merge code, then, does not invoke the flexible merge itself, but its use requires other codes that do. To avoid the extra Hard Page Break, use the ^N and ^P^P sequences to perform the actual merge loop. Use the <Merge Codes> key to place this sequence at the end of a primary document for executing a merge to the printer, as shown here:

^T^N^P^P

This code sequence prints the merged document and clears it from memory (^T), advances to the next record in the secondary file (^N), and cycles back to the beginning of the same primary file (^P^P).

Give and Take — The Keyboard Merge

There are two Merge codes that provide interaction between you and WordPerfect during the merge process. They are ^C, for "input from the Console," and ^O, for "Output to the screen."

^C   Input from the Console/Keyboard

When the system encounters this code during the actual merge operation, the merge will pause and wait for you to enter data. After entering the data, press the <Merge Return> key (F9). (Think of pressing the <Merge Return> key here as ending a field, in the same way that you would end a field in the secondary document.)

^O   Output to the Screen

The text that appears between two ^O codes will be placed at the bottom of the screen when the merge encounters the sequence. This is a Matched Pair Merge code. Most hidden codes may not be placed between the two ^O codes — for example, margin changes and centering are not allowed.

Note that you can place both these codes in either the primary or secondary document. If you want the Merge function to pause for input once for every record in the secondary file (or if there will be no secondary file), insert the code into the primary file at the appropriate location. To have it pause for only selected records, insert the code into the secondary file within the appropriate records.

The ^O and ^C codes are commonly used together. For example, you can remind yourself of the type of information to be entered from the keyboard before stopping the merge for input. To do this, use the ^O code to output a message to the screen. The ^C code requests this input:

```
^OEnter client's 1985 donation^O^C
```

When the merge encounters this sequence it will delete the ^O codes and all text between them, display the text at the bottom of the screen, and wait for input. The input will actually be placed in the document at the location of the first ^O, since everything else will be deleted during the merge.

These codes can be used to execute a fill-in-the-blanks type of operation. Perhaps you have a standard document that you use frequently. Only key information, like the client's name and dollar amounts, will change each time. You can use the keyboard merge to prompt you for these variable pieces of text. Simply enter a code sequence like the one just shown anywhere in the document that text should be entered manually during the merge.

If a ^C code appears between a set of ^G, ^P, or ^S Matched Pair codes, the text that you enter when the merge pauses will specify the macro or the primary or secondary file name, depending on which Matched Pair codes you used. (The ^G code, used to execute a macro, is described later in this chapter.)

You may choose to enter part of the file name after the ^C code—for example, the file extension—and then enter the first part of the file name (which might vary each time) when the merge pauses for input. This is useful if there are several related files from which you need to choose. For instance, let's say you've created a header primary file (containing codes which should appear at the top of the report) for several possible primary files. To have the merge prompt for one of a set of report primary files, enter a sequence like this at the bottom of the header primary file:

```
^P^C.rpt^P
```

This tells the merge that a new primary file will be specified, that it should prompt for a text string, and that it should combine that text string with ".rpt" to produce the complete file name.

If you enclose a series like this with a set of ^O codes (with a text prompt), then the prompt will appear at the bottom of the screen (instead of "Primary name:" or "Secondary name:" or "Macro:"). You will also enter the inputted text at the bottom of the screen (instead of wherever the ^C code happens to be placed in the primary document). This is the most elegant way to enter a file name during a merge.

To have the merge prompt for a new primary document at the bottom of the screen, enter this at the end of a primary document:

```
^OWhich report would you like to use? ^P^C^P^O
```

Providing this type of "custom prompt" makes the procedure easy to understand, which is especially helpful when it will be executed by another person.

When you use the ^C code in this way, you need to press only the ENTER key to continue with the merge operation. Pressing the <Merge Return> key is not required.

Other Merge Codes

Here are several other Merge codes that can be useful in the merge process:

^D   Insert Date

This code inserts the current date, as set by the computer's system clock, into the merged document. This code produces a result similar to pressing the <Date/Outline> key (SHIFT+F5) and choosing "Date Text."

^Q   Quit Merge

When the system encounters this code, the Merge function stops executing. If you place it just before the ^E code in the last record you want to process in a secondary file, it will halt the Merge function after processing the record.

^U   Update Screen

This code "rewrites" the screen, performing the same function as pressing the <Screen> key (CTRL+F3) and choosing "Rewrite." Usually, the Merge function will not display an accurate screen while the merge is being performed. The ^U code allows you to see the state of the document at a certain point in the merge.

USING FIELD NAMES

Normally, you indicate which fields to include in a primary file by using field numbers. Unfortunately, it can be difficult to remember which field numbers correspond to which fields. If you use the Notebook program from WordPerfect Corporation (see Appendix C, "WordPerfect Corporation Programs") to manage your secondary documents, you can refer to the fields using the names you specified there. However, even if you don't use Notebook, you can still use field names if you prepare the secondary document properly.

To name your fields manually, you create a *header record* in the secondary document—that is, the first record will be a special one containing the names of the fields. This record will not be included as normal data when you perform a merge operation.

To insert a header record, first retrieve the secondary document you wish to use. Then, with the cursor at the top of the document, press the <Merge Codes> key (SHIFT+F9), type **N**, and press ENTER. This inserts the ^N Merge code, which tells WordPerfect during a merge that it should go to the next record.

Then, for each field in your secondary document, press the <Bold> key (F6), type the field name, press the <Bold> key again, and press ENTER. Each field name must be bolded separately, and followed by a Hard Return. After you've entered all of the field names, and pressed ENTER for the last one, press the <Merge Return> key (F9).

Now, you must create empty fields to complete the header record. There must be as many fields in this header record as there are in each normal record in the secondary document. (You've already entered one field—the list of field names ending with ^R.) To create each additional empty field, press the <Merge Codes> key, type **N**, and press the <Merge Return> key.

Once you've entered all of the empty fields, press the <Merge Codes> key (SHIFT+F9), and type **E**. The line after the one with ^E should be the first line of your actual data. Save the document.

To use the field names in a primary file, simply enter a name at the "Field?" prompt, instead of a number. WordPerfect will insert the ^F Merge code, the field name you entered, and a caret (^). For example, to enter the Name field into a primary file, you would press the <Merge Codes> key, type **F** and then **Name**, and then press ENTER. The program will insert ^FName^ at the cursor location.

USING THE MERGE
FUNCTION WITH MACROS

Merges and macros can work together to form a powerful alliance. Each has the ability to invoke the other.

A merge can only start a macro when the merge process has come to its natural halt. However, a macro has the ability to start a merge, and then to remain dormant until the merge is complete, at which point the macro can resume performing steps. For this reason a macro can actually initiate several merge procedures in sequence.

Macros and merge procedures can both be considered languages of control. They operate in very different ways, with different strengths and weaknesses. For many purposes, macros are the best device for automating a procedure, but the Merge function does have some abilities that macros do not.

To execute a macro from within a merge, insert the ^G Merge code into a primary document.

^G   Go to (Execute) a Macro

This command specifies a macro that will be executed when the merge is complete, even if the primary document is changed during the merge with a ^P code. The macro will not execute until the merge has been completed, regardless of whether it is a simple or flexible merge or where the code is inserted in the primary document. It is a Matched Pair code.

Here is a sequence of codes that will execute a macro when a merge is complete:

```
^GALTM^G^
```

Here, the string "^GALTM^G" specifies that the ALTM.WPM macro will execute when the merge is complete. It is important to put the set of ^G codes specifying the macro name before any set of ^P codes. Otherwise, the ^G codes will never be processed — control will have passed to another primary document before the merge encounters the codes. However, once the merge has encountered a set of ^G codes with a macro name, it will remember which macro to execute after the merge, no matter which primary document is being processed. When the merge is complete, the macro will be executed (unless another set of ^G codes is encountered).

To execute a merge from within a macro, simply enter the normal steps to execute the merge while you are defining the macro. When the merge procedure begins, macro definition automatically ends. Because of this, executing a merge is always the last step of the macro definition process. (Note that you may later edit the steps of a macro so that it continues to execute during a merge operation. (See below.) You may wish to include a Pause for Input command at either the "Primary file:" or "Secondary file:" prompt (see Chapter 2, "Macros").

The Two-Step

You can have a macro executing at the same time WordPerfect is processing a merge operation. In fact, the macro starts the merge, and then remains inactive while the merge is processed. When the merge is finished, the macro resumes its steps.

This capability can be useful in a number of situations. For example, let's say you want to use a macro to perform a common mail merge operation (one that merges to the screen using the simple merge process). If you were to perform the steps in this process manually, you'd begin by clearing the screen, starting the merge function, and specifying the names of the primary and secondary documents. When the merge was complete, you'd be left with a merged document on the screen, with each letter separated by a Hard Page Break. You'd then print the entire document and clear the screen. A macro that performed this sequence for you would contain the steps to begin the merge, and perform the remaining steps after the merge was complete.

During macro definition, WordPerfect automatically turns off Macro Define when you begin a merge. However, you can edit the macro to include additional steps beyond the initiation of the merge (see "Editing Macros" in Chapter 2, "Macros").

Here's an example of the macro described above:

```
{Merge/Sort}1           {:} Start merge~
letter{Enter}           {:} Specify Primary Document~
list{Enter}             {:} Specify Secondary Document~

{:} Merge processes here~

{Print}1                {:} Print entire merged document~
{Exit}nn                {:} Clear screen~
```

MENU MAGIC

You have already seen how to use the Merge function in many ways besides the traditional combining of a single document with a list of information. Another way in which you can use the Merge function to make your life easier is to create a menu system.

You can use the menu to select from several macros that execute frequently performed word processing tasks. You can also use the menu in the middle of a mail merge operation to prompt you for a new primary or secondary file name.

You create a menu with the technique described in the "Give and Take" section of this chapter. That is, you place a prompt string, as well as a Matched Pair code like ^P, ^S, or ^G, and finally a ^C code, between two ^O codes. The ^C code is used to prompt for the file or macro name.

The only difference between a normal keyboard merge and creating a menu is that for the menu, the prompt string is several lines long. When the merge encounters a multi-line prompt string, it scrolls each line up from the bottom of the screen until it comes to the line containing the ^C code, where it stops. It is this last line that is actually used for the prompt string at the bottom of the screen. In this way, the menu choices constitute the first part of this string, and a prompt like "Enter your choice:" constitutes the final part.

Let's look at a one-line menu that asks the user a yes or no question. A different macro will be carried out depending on how the user responds to the prompt. (This general technique is also described briefly in the preceding section "Give and Take—The Keyboard Merge".)

In this example, let's assume you've created two envelope-printing macros (see Chapter 13, "Application Library," for the steps of an envelope printing macro). Both macros copy the text of an address at the cursor position, and print it at the correct location on an envelope. The difference is that one includes an "ATTN:" line that follows the address block, and the other does not. What you need in this situation is a prompt that will ask whether or not the "ATTN:" line should be included, so you'll know which macro to execute.

Begin on a blank screen, then type the following line (remember to use the correct keystrokes when entering the Merge codes):

```
^OInclude the "ATTN:" line? (Y/N): ^G^Cenv^G^O
```

Now save this file as ENV.MNU (it can be helpful to identify files that you use to create menus with a common filename extension such as .MNU). Since the entire sequence is enclosed within a pair of ^O codes, all of it will be deleted during the merge process. The ^G^Cenv^G sequence will cause WordPerfect to begin a macro when the merge is complete. The name of the macro to be executed will be derived from concatenating the text entered during the ^C merge pause with the text "env". A macro called YENV will be executed if Y is typed (uppercase or lowercase), and NENV will be executed if N is typed.

You will now need to create the macros. Create one called YENV.WPM (or rename an existing macro) that performs the envelope printing task *with* the "ATTN:" line included. Next, create one called NENV.WPM (or rename an existing macro) that does not include the "ATTN:" line. You might also create a macro called ENV.WPM that performs no steps at all (or performs some innocuous steps, such as displaying and then cancelling the Format menu) so that when the user enters nothing at all, the menu prompt will simply be cancelled, and an error message will not be displayed.

To display the menu, you would simply begin a merge using the menu file as the primary document—no secondary document will be used. One unfortunate side effect is that once the menu has been displayed, and the user has entered some information, the merge process will continue reading through the remainder of whatever document is on the screen, assuming it to be a primary file. This means that the cursor will always end up at the bottom of the document before the merge ends and the specified macro begins.

The solution to this problem is to use a macro to call up the menu. The first step of the macro would be to insert the ^Q Merge code in the current document, and then press LEFT ARROW. The ^Q Merge code ends the merge immediately, so that once the menu has been processed, the merge stops right away and begins the macro.

You might want to create a macro called ALT+E (for "envelope printing") that enters a ^Q Merge code, presses LEFT ARROW, press the <Merge/Sort> key, chooses "Merge", types **ENV.MNU** for a primary file name, and presses ENTER twice start the merge.

Another way to place a similar prompt at the bottom of the screen is to use the Char or Text macro commands (see Chapter 2, "Macros"). You would then use the IF or CASE commands to decide how to handle the response.

Let's now take a look at a full macro menu that lets you choose from several commonly performed tasks. (Use only spaces to format the menu, not the TAB key.) Clear the screen and follow these steps:

1. Press the <Merge Codes> key (SHIFT+F9) and type **O**
2. Press ENTER six times.
3. Press ESC, type **34**, and press SPACE BAR.
4. Type **Main Menu** and press ENTER.
5. Press ESC, type **34**, and press SPACE BAR.
6. Type -------- and press ENTER twice.
7. Press ESC, type **28**, and press SPACE BAR.

8. Type **1. Start mailmerge** and press ENTER twice.

9. Press ESC, type **28**, and press SPACE BAR.

10. Type **2. Document Assembly** and press ENTER twice.

11. Press ESC, type **28**, and press SPACE BAR.

12. Type **3. Print mailing labels** and press ENTER twice.

13. Press ESC, type **28**, and press SPACE BAR.

14. Type **4. Backup files** and press ENTER twice.

15. Press ESC, type **28**, and press SPACE BAR.

16. Type **5. Quit WordPerfect** and press ENTER seven times.

17. Press ESC, type **28**, and press SPACE BAR.

18. Type **Enter your choice:** and press SPACE BAR.

19. Press the <Merge Codes> key and type **G**

20. Press the <Merge Codes> key and type **C**

21. Type **menu**

22. Press the <Merge Codes> key and type **G**

23. Press the <Merge Codes> key and type **O**

Notice that "menu" appears after the ^C code but within the ^G codes. When the merge encounters this, it will execute a macro whose name starts with the number chosen from the menu and ends with "menu".

Save this primary file as "menu" and then clear the screen. To complete this menu system, define macros that perform the various functions listed on the menu, and give them names like "1menu," "2menu," and so on. As with the one-line menu previously described, you can display this menu by starting a merge, using "menu" as a primary file name.

When you've displayed the menu, your screen will look like the one in Figure 3-4. To execute a macro from the menu, you would simply type the corresponding number and press ENTER. If the macro you request has not been defined, the message "ERROR: File not found" will be displayed.

```
Main Menu
_____

1.  Start mailmerge

2.  Document Assembly

3.  Print mailing labels

4.  Backup files

5.  Quit WordPerfect




Enter your choice: _
```

Figure 3-4.   Macro menu example

As an example, "Start mailmerge" is the first choice in the menu shown above. You would want this choice to enter all the keystrokes necessary to initiate a commonly performed merge procedure (like a form letter and customer list). The macro, named "1menu," would start the merge and enter the primary and secondary file names for you. When you choose "1" from the menu, the macro 1menu is executed, starting the merge procedure.

You can also use a menu like this to select from several primary or secondary files during a merge procedure. Simply create a menu like the preceding one for macros but containing ^P or ^S codes and names of primary or secondary documents instead. Then include the entire sequence of text between the ^O codes in a primary document; when it is encountered, the menu will appear. When you choose from the menu, the merge will continue with the new primary or secondary document.

THE DUAL MERGE

With the dual merge the primary file is combined with the secondary file to create another primary or secondary file. This feature, although somewhat complicated, provides abilities that would not otherwise be possible.

Suppose you have a standard contract with four pieces of information that will change each time they are used: name, contract date, dollar amount, and location. You would use the Merge with Keyboard function discussed earlier, right? Yes, but what if the name appears 24 times in the document, the dollar amount 5 times, and the location twice. You would have to repeatedly enter the same information throughout the document. To avoid this, use the dual merge.

What you want is a merge that will prompt you for the correct entries, *creating* a secondary file that will then be merged with the contract.

The key to the dual merge is the ^V Merge code:

^V   Insert Merge Code

^V is a Matched Pair Merge code. A set of ^V codes acts as a "shield" for Merge codes that appear between them. When you execute the merge, the ^V codes are deleted, but any Merge codes that appear between them will be transferred, unprocessed, into the merged document.

Note: Most of WordPerfect's Merge codes have some logic behind their single-letter nomenclature. ^V is so named because "CTRL+V" has traditionally meant "insert control codes" in the microcomputer industry.

Now create a primary file that, as described in the example above, will generate a secondary file. (When typing the ^R code in this lesson, press <Merge Codes> and then type **R**, rather than pressing <Merge Return>; this avoids insertion of an [HRt].)

Enter this sequence of text and codes:

```
^OEnter client's name^O^C^U^R^U
^OEnter the date of the contract^O^C^U^R^U
^OEnter the dollar amount^O^C^U^R^U
^OEnter the location of the property^O^C^U^R^U
^U^^E
==============================================================================
^U
```

Save this file as "contract.inp" and then clear the screen. Execute the merge by pressing <Merge/Sort>, typing **1** for "Merge," entering **contract.inp** for the primary file, and just pressing ENTER for the secondary file. You will be prompted for each of these items. Press the <Merge Return> key to move to each new field. After you have entered all of the information, what you see will look just like a single record in a secondary file, with the ^R code at the end of every field and the ^E code at the end of the record.

Here is what happened: The Merge function first processed each set of ^O codes by displaying the text at the bottom of the screen and then deleting the text and the codes. Next it paused for you to enter the field contents. When you pressed the <Merge Return> key, the system went on to process the string "^V^R^V". The ^V codes were deleted, and the ^R code was left intact. The ^E code was also left intact when the merge encountered it at the end of the file.

You end up with a formatted record that can be saved and used as a secondary file for a merge with the contract as the primary file. In this way, the information that you entered once can be spread through the contract as many times as necessary. Simply create the contract as a primary file that has ^F codes at appropriate places to retrieve one of the four items in the file you just created, and then execute the merge. You might want to create a macro to start the first merge, then save the created secondary file, clear the screen, and start the second merge.

The functions of the Merge codes are summarized in Table 3-1.

Table 3-1.   Summary of Merge Codes

^R   *End of Field*
Marks end of field in secondary document.

^E   *End of Record*
Marks end of record in secondary document.

^F   *Insert Field*
Inserts a specific numbered field from the secondary document into the primary document.

^N   *Next Record*
Tells the Merge function to start using the next record in the current secondary document. When there are no more records, the merge operation ends.

^P   *Primary Document*
Specifies a new primary document for the Merge function to use.

^S   *Secondary Document*
Specifies a new secondary document for the Merge function to use.

^T   *Type (Print) Merged Document*
Generates a Full Text Print of the merged document and then clears the screen.

^C   *Input from the Console/Keyboard*
Pauses and waits for you to enter data. Continue with <Merge Return>.

^O   *Output to the Screen*
Places text at the bottom of the screen.

^G   *Go to (Execute) a Macro*
Specifies a macro that will be executed when the merge operation is complete.

^D   *Insert Date*
Inserts the current date, as set by the computer's system clock.

^Q   *Quit Merge*
Causes the Merge function to stop executing.

^U   *Update Screen*
Rewrites the screen.

^V   *Insert Merge Codes*
Allows Merge codes to be ignored during a merge for a dual merge.

SORTING AND SELECTING DATA

You can sort records stored in secondary documents with Word-Perfect's Sort function—for example, to print a set of mailing labels in ZIP code order. You can also select specific records from the secondary document for use in a merge operation, such as printing labels for a specific ZIP code range.

The sort/select operation also works with individual lines (like a profit and loss statement) or paragraph text (like bibliographic entries). You can sort the data based on a specific column or word in the text.

Starting the Sort/Select Operation

Unlike the merge operation, you can sort and select information that is either in memory or stored on disk. To start the procedure, clear the screen and follow these steps:

1. Press the <Retrieve> key (SHIFT+F10).

2. Type **list** and press ENTER.

   This is the secondary document that you created earlier in the chapter.

3. Press the <Merge/Sort> key (CTRL+F9).

4. Type **2** for "Sort."

   Here the program prompts you to enter the name of the file containing the information you want to sort. Note that the default response is (Screen). If you press ENTER to use the default, the document currently on screen will be used as the source for the sorting and selection process.

5. Press ENTER.

   Here the program prompts you to enter the name of a file to contain the result of the sorting and selecting process. Note that the default for this prompt is (Screen) as well. If you press ENTER to use the default, the result will be placed in the current document after the original text has been deleted. If the name of the file you specify already exists on disk, the program will ask for confirmation before continuing.

6. Press ENTER.

You will see the sort/select display on the screen, as shown in Figure 3-5.

In addition to sorting a file on disk or a document in memory, you can sort a block of text. To do this, mark the text with the <Block> key and then press the <Merge/Sort> key. The program immediately shows the sort/select display. The result of the sort/select process will replace the marked text.

The screen is divided into two parts. At the top, you can see ten lines of the current document. At the bottom is the sort/select display. At the top of this display you can see the type of sort that is currently active: Line, Paragraph, or Secondary Merge. Some parts of the display will change depending on which type of sort you select. Initially, the function will be set to "Sort by Line." Along the bottom of the screen is a menu.

If at any time during the sort/select process you need to see more of the document than the ten lines shown, type **2** for "View." The cursor will move into the document area, and you can scroll the document using any of WordPerfect's cursor positioning commands. (You cannot enter or edit the text of the document in this mode.) To return to the sort/select screen, press the <Exit> key (F7).

Now specify the type of sort/select you will need to work with the "list" file.

7. Type **7** for "Type."

This allows you to specify the type of sort/select you want.

8. Type **1** for "Merge."

The title of the sort/select display becomes "Sort Secondary Merge File."

You are now ready to begin the sort/select process.

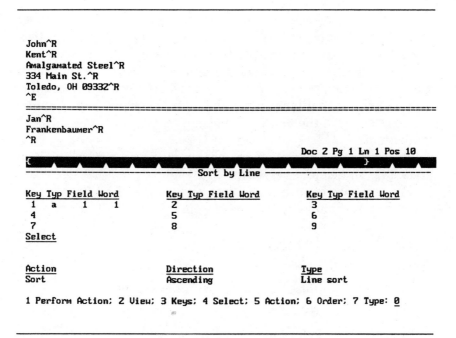

Figure 3-5.   The sort/select display

Specifying Keys

Before WordPerfect can rearrange or select records from your data, you need to tell it exactly which part of the data will be used for performing the sort or selection. You do this by specifying *keys*. A key is simply a word that has been isolated within your data. The program will first sort using the word specified with key 1; then the records that have identical words in key 1 will be sorted with key 2, and so on. You can define up to nine keys.

To specify a key, type **3** to select "Keys" from the sort/select display. The cursor will move to the middle of the display, where the key definitions are shown. You specify keys by entering four pieces of information about the data. The first is type, which is either alphanumeric (text) or numeric. Second is the field number that the word appears in. Third is the line of the field number that the word appears in (for example, the second line of a two-line address). Fourth is the position of the word within the line of the field number specified. If the number is positive, the words are counted from the left. If it is negative, the words are counted from the right. Similarly, if the line number is positive, the lines are counted from the top. If it is negative, they are counted from the bottom.

To insert a key, position the cursor with the arrow keys and press INS. To delete a key, press DEL.

For example, to specify the first key as the second field in your document, last name, follow these steps:

1. Type **3** to select "Keys" from the sort/select display.

   This moves the cursor to the definition for key 1.

2. Press ENTER to use "a" for alphanumeric type.

3. Type **2** and press ENTER.

   This specifies field 2.

4. Press ENTER to use 1 for the line number.

5. Press ENTER to use 1 for the word number.

   The cursor moves to the definition for key 2.

6. Press the <Exit> key (F7) to stop specifying keys.

Performing the Sort

To perform the sort, type **1** for "Perform Action." (To sort the records in descending order instead of ascending order, you could have typed **6** for "Order" and selected "Descending" before selecting "Perform Action.") A message will appear briefly at the bottom of the screen to show the number of records that have been examined. When the sort is done, you are returned to the document screen. Notice that the two records have reversed positions.

Specifying Selection Criteria

To perform a selection on a list of data, you use the same keys that are specified for sorting. Once you have defined these keys, you use them in a comparative statement that WordPerfect can use to determine which records will be included in the output.

When entering the selection criteria, you specify which key you are comparing by typing "key" followed immediately by the key number. For example, if you have key 1 defined as the last name (as you have done for the exercise), then you use "key1" in the selection criteria. When you choose 4 for "Select," a message at the bottom of the screen shows the allowable operators that you can use for comparative purposes in the selection criteria.

The selection criteria is entered as a logical statement. You need to first think about how you would state a request to yourself and then translate that request into a statement that WordPerfect can understand.

Perhaps you want to perform a merge using only those people whose ZIP codes are higher than 80896. First, you need to define the ZIP code as key 1. Then the statement would be translated to "key1 > 80896" or "all those records where key 1 is greater than 80896." Let's perform the steps to change key 1's definition and enter the selection criteria.

1. Press the <Merge/Sort> key (CTRL+F9).

2. Type 2 for "Sort" and press ENTER twice.

3. Type 3 for "Keys."

   Be sure the Selected Sort type is "Secondary Merge."

4. Press ENTER to use "a" for alphanumeric type.

   Even though a ZIP code consists of digits, it is usually considered alphanumeric. The numeric type should only be used with numbers that you might use to perform some mathematical function.

5. Type **4** to specify Field Number 4.

6. Press ENTER to use 1 for line number 1.

7. Type **−1** to specify the last word of the line.

   The Sort/Select function will look backward from the end of the line to locate a space when you use a negative number as the word number. The word that follows the first space it finds is used for the key.

8. Press ENTER and then <Exit>.

   Now you are ready to enter the selection criteria.

9. Type **4** for "Select."

   The cursor moves below the "Select" prompt in the middle of the sort/select display.

10. Type **key1 > 80896** and press ENTER.

When you enter selection criteria, the Action indicator changes from "Sort" to "Select and Sort." If you prefer to use the selection criteria without also sorting the data, you can press **5** for "Action" and choose "Select Only."

Performing the Selection

Be very careful when performing the selection. If you are replacing a file on disk or are working with a document on screen, you might lose some of your data by entering an incorrect selection criteria since the old text will be *replaced* by the selected text. (For example, if you had entered **key1 > 99654** as the selection criteria for this document, you would be presented with a blank screen when the selection was complete—none of the records would have matched the criteria.)

Make sure that you are not replacing the only copy of a secondary document. Also be sure that you have saved the document, if you are working with one in memory, before executing the selection.

To extract from your file all of the records whose ZIP codes are higher than 80896, simply type 1 for "Perform Action." The sort/select screen will disappear, and you will be returned to the document. Only Jan Frankenbaumer's record remains on the screen, since John does not live in the targeted area.

Advanced Selection Criteria

The selection criteria can actually be much more complex than the example just shown. There, you used only one comparative statement. However, you can join several comparative statements using special symbols in the selection criteria.

If you wanted to produce a list of clients whose ZIP codes were within the range of 46553 and 74554, for instance, you would need to combine two statements with an "and" operator. In other words, you want "all those records where key 1 is greater than 46553 *and* key 1 is less than 74554." To specify this, use the * (asterisk) for the "and" character. Parentheses are also used to make the statement more understandable. Thus, the selection criteria would be as follows: "(key1 > 46553) * (key1 < 74554)".

Another logical operator is "or." To specify "or" in the selection criteria, use the + (plus) character. If you wanted a list of people with ZIP codes of either 95446 or 94704, then the selection criteria would be "(key1 = 95446) + (key1 = 94704)".

You can use any combination of the nine keys in the selection criteria. If, for example, you have defined key 1 as the salary and key 2 as the city, you could enter the following criteria to produce a list of people who earn between $20,000 and $30,000 and live in Dayton: "((key1 >= 20000) * (key1 <= 30000)) * (key2 = Dayton)".

There is one special key that is used in selecting records. The *global key* is used to specify text that might appear anywhere within a record. This key is identified as "keyg" in the selection criteria.

Table 3-2.   Summary of Selection Criteria Operators

+ (OR)	Separates two key statements when only one or the other must be true to match
∗ (AND)	Separates two key statements when both must be true to match
=	equal to
<>	not equal to
>	greater than
<	less than
>=	greater than or equal to
<=	less than or equal to

The operators that can be used in the selection criteria are summarized in Table 3-2.

Sorting/Selecting Lines and Paragraphs

The only difference between using the sort/select feature with secondary merge files and with lines and paragraphs is in defining the keys.

When using the feature with lines, you specify keys with just a field number and a word number. You separate fields in a line with either a Tab code or an Align Tab code. The first field (column) in a line is field 1. Specify the word number in the same way as with merge files. Records are separated by a Hard or Soft Return.

With paragraphs, you specify keys with line, field, and word numbers. Specify line numbers as with merge files. Field and word numbers are specified as with lines. Records are separated by two or more Hard Returns. Use the paragraph sort to sort and select bibliographic references.

EDITING SECONDARY MERGE FILES WITH NOTEBOOK

WordPerfect Library, which is sold separately from WordPerfect, includes a program called Notebook that allows you to manipulate secondary merge files more easily. With Notebook, you can view records in the merge file either in a custom-designed screen form or in a row-and-column format. Files saved from Notebook can be used in a WordPerfect merge operation without prior translation.

For a discussion of Notebook, as well as of other programs included in WordPerfect Library, see Appendix C, "WordPerfect Corporation Programs."

4

OUTLINE AND PARAGRAPH NUMBERING

WordPerfect's Outline and Paragraph Numbering functions allow you to assign a number automatically to outline entries or individual paragraphs and larger blocks of text. (You can also use bullet characters in place of the numbers.) These functions provide two important advantages over entering numbers manually:

- If outline entries or numbered paragraphs are moved from one location in the document to another, all of the affected numbers will be recalculated instantly.

- Specific formatting required for the various *levels* of the outline or paragraphs is performed automatically. Legal documents, for example, often contain numbered parts. A section may be level 1, a paragraph level 1.1, and a subparagraph level 1.1.1. Outlines typically use a combination of Roman numerals, uppercase letters, numbers, and lowercase letters to distinguish the levels of the headings.

Figure 4-1 is an example of a three-level outline. Figure 4-2 shows a typical application of the Paragraph Numbering function in a legal document that uses three levels.

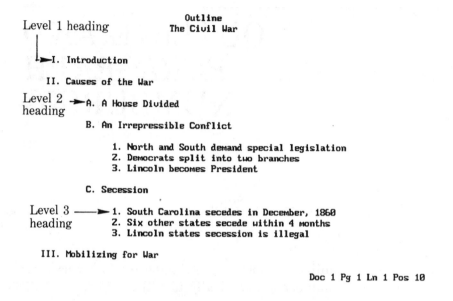

Level 1 heading

Outline
The Civil War

└─►I. Introduction

   II. Causes of the War

Level 2 ─►A. A House Divided
heading

     B. An Irrepressible Conflict

        1. North and South demand special legislation
        2. Democrats split into two branches
        3. Lincoln becomes President

     C. Secession

Level 3 ──►1. South Carolina secedes in December, 1860
heading   2. Six other states secede within 4 months
       3. Lincoln states secession is illegal

   III. Mobilizing for War

Doc 1 Pg 1 Ln 1 Pos 10

Figure 4-1.   A three-level outline

   Although the Outline and Paragraph Numbering functions can use letters, numbers, or bullets, the code that is inserted into the text when you use these functions is called a *number code,* and the number, letter, or bullet generated by the code is called a *number.*

   You can specify how a number or letter will be punctuated. For instance, a level 1 paragraph number can appear as a number followed by a period, and a level 2 paragraph number can appear as a lowercase letter followed by a parenthesis.

   You can also use the Paragraph Numbering function to number a list of items automatically. You could assign a paragraph number to each step of a tutorial (like the ones in this book) so that if they were rearranged, the program would recalculate the numbers. A simple macro can be created to insert a code number quickly.

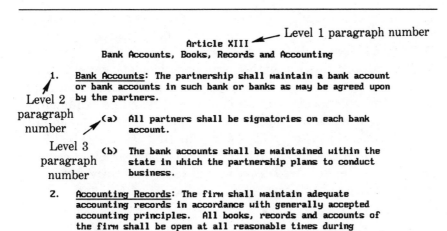

Figure 4-2.   A three-level numbered legal document

In an outline, you indicate the levels by preceding each number code with [Tab] codes. A number code entered at the left margin produces a level 1 entry, a code entered after one [Tab] produces a level 2 entry, and so on. With the Paragraph Numbering function, you can indicate the level of a number code either by inserting [Tab] codes before the number code or by specifying the level directly.

DEFINING A FORMAT

Before using either the Outline or the Paragraph Numbering function, you must specify the format that you desire for the different levels. First position the cursor anywhere in the text *preceding* the place where you want to use paragraph numbering or to begin your outline. Then press the <Date /Outline> key (SHIFT+F5), and type **6** for "Define." The Paragraph Number Definition screen is displayed. This screen is shown in Figure 4-3.

You will use this screen to specify the format for both outline and paragraph numbers. The menu shows three common number and letter punctuation combinations, and a bullet combination. Another choice lets you specify the format for each level manually. For example, if you select choice 2, your first level will be identified by a number followed by a period (1.), your second level by a lowercase letter followed by a period (a.), your third level by a lowercase Roman numeral followed by a period (i.), and so on.

Paragraph Number Definition

1 - Starting Paragraph Number   1
    (in legal style)

		Levels						
	1	2	3	4	5	6	7	8
2 - Paragraph	1.	a.	i.	(1)	(a)	(i)	1)	a)
3 - Outline	I.	A.	1.	a.	(1)	(a)	i)	a)
4 - Legal (1.1.1)	1	.1	.1	.1	.1	.1	.1	.1
5 - Bullets	•	o	–	■	⋈	+	•	x
6 - User-defined								

Current Definition   I.   A.   1.   a.   (1)   (a)   i)   a)

Number Style	Punctuation
1 - Digits	# - No punctuation
A - Upper case letters	#. - Trailing period
a - Lower case letters	#) - Trailing parenthesis
I - Upper case roman	(#) - Enclosing parentheses
i - Lower case roman	.# - All levels separated by period
Other character - Bullet	(e.g. 2.1.3.4)

Selection: 0

Figure 4-3.   The Paragraph Number Definition screen

If one of the four preset formats meets your needs, type the number of that choice.

If not, type **6**, for "User-defined." The cursor will move to the Current Definition area in the middle of the screen. You can specify the format for up to eight levels.

For each level, you enter a representative sample of the format using the characters suggested in the two lists at the bottom of the screen. Note that in addition to using a digit, letter, or roman numeral, you can also type any other character as a bullet. This option is useful with the Outline function, when you want your outline to be bulleted. You can also choose to initially create your outline using numbers or letters, and then later switch to bullets, or vice versa.

Enter your choices of number style and punctuation for the levels you want to use. You can simply press TAB or ENTER for levels that contain a default setting with which you are satisfied. If you want to go back to a level you've already set, press SHIFT + TAB. You must go through all the levels to get out of the menu, even if you won't be using all eight levels in your document.

In addition to defining the formats for numbering, you can also set a starting number on this screen. To do this, type **1** for "Starting paragraph number." This function also allows you to specify the level at which numbering will begin. This is helpful for continuing numbering in another document, or for restarting numbering within a document.

If you want numbering to start at 1 (or I for Roman numerals, A for letters), simply press ENTER. Otherwise, you can type another starting number and press ENTER. Use the Legal format (numbers with previous levels separated by periods) to specify the number, as well as the desired level. For example, to start with paragraph "3.", section "b." (Paragraph Numbering style), type **3.2** and press ENTER.

Press the <Exit> key (F7) several times to return to the document. A [Par Num Def] code is inserted in the text at the cursor position. You can restart numbering at any point in the document by positioning the cursor, and repeating the definition process.

USING THE OUTLINE AND PARAGRAPH NUMBERING FUNCTIONS

Although number codes for the Outline and Paragraph Number functions are the same, they are implemented differently.

Outline Mode

To use the Outline function, you must put WordPerfect into a special *Outline mode*. Move your cursor to the point where you want to begin typing your outline. Then press the <Date/Outline> key (SHIFT + F5), and type **4** for "Outline." At the bottom of the screen, you will see

`Outline`

The menu choice acts as a toggle. When you are finished creating your outline, press <Date/Outline> and type **4** again to turn off Outline mode.

In Outline mode, an Outline Number code is automatically inserted into your text every time you press the ENTER key (or generate a Hard Page Break). After you press ENTER (or CTRL+ENTER), the inserted outline number will be at the left margin. The Outline function generates a level 1 code at the left margin. To increase the code's level, press the TAB key. (Even though the cursor will appear after the number code, the [Tab] codes are inserted before the number code.) With each press of the TAB key, the level increases by one, and the number format changes to reflect the new level. When the number is at the desired level, you can continue with your typing. (Normally, you will precede text with an indent or a space or two.)

After typing the outline entry, press ENTER to return the cursor to the left margin for the next entry. A new outline number appears before the cursor. If you want to insert a blank line before the next outline entry, press ENTER again before typing any text. You can insert as many blank lines as you want.

Clear the screen and try this exercise to create a simple two-level outline:

1. Press the <Date/Outline> key, and type **4** for "Outline."
   "Outline" will appear at the bottom of the screen.

2. Press ENTER.
   The Roman numeral I. will appear before the cursor.

3. Press SPACE BAR and type **Introduction**

4. Press ENTER and then TAB.
   A level 2 number code, A. will appear before the cursor.

5. Press SPACE BAR and type **How are you?**

6. Press ENTER and then TAB.

7. Press SPACE BAR and type **Nice to see you again.**

8. Press ENTER and then SPACE BAR and type **Conclusion**

9. Press ENTER and then TAB.

10. Press SPACE BAR and type **See you later.**

11. Press ENTER and then TAB.

12. Press SPACE BAR and type **Goodbye.**

13. Press the <Date/Outline> key, and type **4** for "Outline."
    "Outline" will disappear from the bottom of the screen.

14. Press ENTER.

Your screen should look like the one in Figure 4-4.

To reduce the level of an outline entry (to change a level 4 heading to a level 3 heading, for instance), press the Margin Release key (SHIFT+TAB) when the cursor is to the right of an entry's number code. You can also delete one or more of the [Tab] codes which precede the number code. Start by moving the cursor onto the number code, using the Reveal Codes screen to help position the cursor. There should be at least one [Tab] code to the left of the highlighted number code. Press BACKSPACE as many times as needed to reduce the entry's level. Each time you press BACKSPACE to delete a [Tab] code, the entry is reduced one level.

When the entry is at the level you desire, press the RIGHT ARROW key to position the cursor after the number code. You will see the changed level on the screen. You can then continue with the text for the entry, if you have not already typed it.

```
      I. Introduction
         A. How are you?
         B. Nice to see you again.
     II. Conclusion
         A. See you later.
         B. Goodbye.

         _
```

Figure 4-4.   Example of a simple outline

To increase the level of an outline entry, simply insert a [Tab] code before the entry's number code. Position the cursor to just before the code and press TAB. Press RIGHT ARROW to see the changed level.

Try deleting some lines from the outline you created to see how the other entries are affected. You can insert [Tab] codes before some of the entries to see how that affects the rest of the codes.

Paragraph Numbering

Paragraph numbers, like outline entries, are each assigned a specific level. This level can be specified manually or assigned automatically.

Designating Levels Manually

If your paragraph numbers will appear in irregular locations (as in the middle of a heading) or if you will not be indenting to differentiate among the levels, you will need to specify the number's level manually. Position the cursor where you want the number to appear and press the <Date/Outline> key (SHIFT + F5). Type **5**, for "Para Num." You will be prompted for a paragraph level number. Type the desired level and press ENTER. The paragraph number will be inserted in the text at the cursor position. This process is an excellent application for a macro.

Designating Levels Automatically

If your paragraph numbers will be more structured (for example, if all level 1 paragraphs will start at the left margin and all level 2 paragraphs will be indented), you can let WordPerfect assign the paragraph number level for you. First insert the correct number of [Tab] codes for the desired level. (You indicate levels with automatic paragraph numbering just as you do in an outline: with [Tab] codes.) Then press the <Date/Outline> key, and type 5 for "Para Num." When you press ENTER, an automatic paragraph number will be inserted at the cursor position.

ALIGNING OUTLINE OR PARAGRAPH NUMBERS

You can use the Tab Align function (or right-aligned tab stop) to line up outline or paragraph numbers as shown in Figure 4-5.

Outline
The Civil War

    I.   Introduction

   II.   Causes of the War

 III.   Mobilizing for War

  IV.   The Home Fronts

   V.   Results of the War

Outline numbers are aligned at the period

Doc 1 Pg 1 Ln 15 Pos 10

Figure 4-5. Aligning outline entries

The [Algn] code inserted by these functions does not increase the level of the number code as the [Tab] code does. However, it does position the number at the next tab stop; you may need to adjust your paragraph number definition so that the format of the number codes is what you intended.

The align functions do not recognize a period in the outline or paragraph number format as an Align Character. Because of this, you must end the alignment so that you can continue with the text for the line. You press the <Indent> key (F4) to end the function, and then you use the BACKSPACE key to delete the [→Indent] code. Since you need to generate the code, even though it will be deleted, you must have a tab stop defined following the one you plan to use for alignment.

To align paragraph numbers using a right-aligned tab stop, follow these steps:

1. Set a right-aligned tab stop at the position you wish to use for alignment. Be sure to include another tab stop after this one.

2. Press the TAB key.

3. Press the <Date/Outline> key (SHIFT+F5).

4. Type 5 for "Para Num," and either press ENTER for automatic level or type a level number and press ENTER.

5. Press <Indent> key (F4) to end the alignment.

6. Press BACKSPACE to delete the extraneous [→ Indent] code.

7. Press SPACE BAR twice or the <Indent> key (F4), and enter the text.

8. Press ENTER to end the line or paragraph.

You may want to create a macro to perform steps 2 through 7.

To align outline numbers, follow these steps:

1. Set a right-aligned tab stop at the column you wish to use for alignment. Be sure to include another tab stop after this one.

2. Press the <Date/Outline> key (SHIFT+F5) and type 4 for "Outline" to turn on Outline mode.

3. Press ENTER to generate an outline number.

4. Press TAB (if necessary) until the number is one tab stop before the desired position (although its format should reflect the correct level).

5. Press LEFT ARROW to position the cursor before the number code.

6. Press the TAB key.

7. Press RIGHT ARROW to position the cursor after the number code.

8. Press the <Indent> key (F4) to end the Tab Align function.

9. Press BACKSPACE to delete the extraneous Indent code.

10. Press SPACE BAR twice or the <Indent> key (F4), and enter the text.

11. Press ENTER to end the line and insert a new outline number, or press <Date/Outline> and type 4 to turn off Outline mode.

DOCUMENT
ACCESSORIES

WordPerfect has a variety of features that can help you produce large documents. These include the ability to create

- An *index*
- A *table of contents*
- A *table of authorities*
- Up to nine separate *lists* (of tables or figures, for example)
- *Footnotes* and *endnotes*

In addition, WordPerfect has two other features that facilitate the creation of large, complex documents:

- *Master Documents*
- *Automatic References*

CREATING AN INDEX

WordPerfect can compile an index for you from text in a document. This index can include subtopics as well as main topics. WordPerfect lets you create the index either with or without page numbers.

You can decide which words to include in the index either after the document has been written or while you are writing it. If you determine that a word or phrase should be included, you need to mark it as an index entry. You can also specify the words and phrases you wish to index in a separate *concordance file*.

Marking the Text

You can use text from your document as an index entry, or you can manually enter the text. In either case, WordPerfect will insert a hidden code in your document when you create the entry. The page that the hidden code falls on determines the page number for this entry in the completed index.

Using Text from Your Document

To use text from your document, move the cursor so that it is anywhere on the word you wish included in the index. If your entry contains two or more words, mark the entry as a block using the <Block> key.

Then press the <Mark Text> key (ALT+F5) and type **3** for "Index." (Notice that the Mark Text menu varies, depending on whether you have marked the text as a block.) WordPerfect will then ask for the index *heading* and *subheading*. Before you can go on, it is necessary to understand the meaning of these two terms.

An index heading is the main reference to an index item. Each entry must have an index heading. A subheading is any one of many items included under a heading. (You do not need to specify a subheading for each entry.) For example, imagine you are creating an index for a cookbook. You might specify one heading to be *Chicken*, with subheadings for *baked*, *broiled*, and *fried*. When readers look up *Chicken* in the index, they are directed to the type of chicken that interests them. In this example, *Chicken* would be an index heading and *baked*, *broiled*, and *fried* would be subheadings. WordPerfect automatically capitalizes the index headings.

WordPerfect first suggests the text that you marked as a block (or the word that the cursor was on) as the index heading. If this is correct, press ENTER. Otherwise, edit the text or type the correct heading and press ENTER.

If you typed your own text for the heading, the text you marked on the screen will be suggested for the subheading. Press ENTER to use the suggested text.

If you pressed ENTER to accept the suggestion for the heading, then the subheading prompt will be blank. You can press ENTER if you do not need a subheading, or you can type a subheading and press ENTER.

Thus, to mark a single word as a heading for an index (without a subheading), simply position the cursor anywhere within the word, press the <Mark Text> key, type **3** for "Index," and press ENTER twice. To mark several words as a heading for an index (without a subheading), mark them as a block, press the <Mark Text> key, type **3** for "Index," and press ENTER twice.

Manually Creating Index Entries

To manually create an index entry, move the cursor to the place in your document to which you want the entry to refer. Then, press the <Mark Text> key (ALT+F5), and type **3** for "Index." Enter the heading and subheading for the entry. If the program suggests the word at the cursor location for the heading, simply type over the suggestion. Then, when it suggests the same word as a subheading, you can edit the text, type over the subheading, or press CTRL+END and then ENTER to create an index entry without a subheading.

That's all there is to marking the text. WordPerfect inserts an [Index:] hidden code immediately before the word or phrase you specified. You can view this code by pressing the <Reveal Codes> key (ALT+F3).

Notice that this method of marking text is different from the way WordPerfect marks text for may other features. Instead of placing a matched pair of hidden codes around the text (as with such functions as Bold, Underline, and Center), WordPerfect duplicates the marked text and inserts it into a hidden code. Within the code, the heading text and subheading text are separated by a semicolon.

Using a Concordance File

WordPerfect gives you the option of maintaining a concordance file, a document which contains a list of words and phrases that the program will include in a compiled index. This is especially useful for entries which appear frequently throughout the document. If you wish, you can use the concordance file in addition to marking specific entries in the text of a document.

Creating Entries

To create entries for a concordance file, start with a blank screen. Type each entry on its own line, and press ENTER. When the index is generated, WordPerfect will build an index entry for each occurrence in the document of an entry in the concordance file. Continue typing entries in this manner until you have entered all of the words and phrases you wish to include. Since the file will be saved as a normal WordPerfect document, you'll be able to retrieve and modify it at any time.

Modifying the Generated Entry

Normally, WordPerfect will use the text from the entry in the concordance file to build the entry for the index. However, you can choose to have the program use a different word or phrase for the actual entry than the one it used to match occurrences in the text. For example, you may want the words *moose, deer,* and *antelope* to all generate the index entry *Animals, four-legged.*

To do this, insert an Index code (as described in the previous section "Manually Creating Index Entries") on the same line as the entry in the concordance file, after the entry but before the Hard Return. For the example above, you would position the cursor on the line that contained *moose,* press the END key to be sure that you are at the end of the line, press the <Mark Text> key, type **3** for "Index," type **Animals** for the heading and press ENTER, and type **four-legged** for the subheading and press ENTER.

Creating Multiple Entries

If you wish, you can have one match of a word or phrase in the concordance with an occurrence in the document generate a series of index entries, instead of just one. For example, you may want occurrences of *moose* to be indexed not only in *Animals, four-legged,* but also in *Animals, hooved* and *Canada, animals.*

To do this, simply enter as many index entries as you wish at the end of the line that contains the entry in the concordance file. When the entry matches an occurrence in the document, an index entry will be generated for each index code that exists at the end of the entry's line in the concordance file.

Saving the File

When you have entered all of the entries and associated index codes you wish to include in the concordance file, save it using the <Save> key (F10). You might want to give the concordance file a name that will remind you for which document it was created. For example, you may want to adopt ".con" as a standard file extension for a concordance file, so that it can share the same file name as the document you are indexing.

Positioning the Index and Defining Its Format

Once you have specified all the words and phrases to be indexed, the next step is to indicate where you want the index to appear and how you want it to look.

Move your cursor to the position in your document where you want the index to appear. When WordPerfect generates the index, it will only process marked entries that appear before the definition code that this command produces. Therefore, you would normally position the cursor at the end of the document. When you have properly positioned the cursor, press the <Mark Text> key (ALT+F5), type **5** for "Define," and then **3** for "Define Index." Type the name of the concordance file you wish to use, and press ENTER. If you will not be using a concordance file, simply press ENTER. The Index Definition screen appears, as shown in Figure 5-1.

Now you have to decide how you want the index to look. Press the number corresponding to the format you desire.

With options 4 and 5, the page number appears flush right (at the right margin). If you change the margin settings, the page numbers move accordingly. This allows you to reformat the index easily.

After you type a number to specify the index format, you are returned to the document. A [Def Mark:Index] hidden code is placed into the text at the cursor position.

Index Definition

    1 - No Page Numbers

    2 - Page Numbers Follow Entries

    3 - (Page Numbers) Follow Entries

    4 - Flush Right Page Numbers

    5 - Flush Right Page Numbers with Leaders

Selection: 0

Figure 5-1.   The Index Definition screen

Generating the Index

After defining a format, you are ready to generate the index (the cursor can be anywhere in the document). To begin, press the <Mark Text> key (ALT+F5), and type **6** for "Generate," and then **5** for "Generate Tables, Indexes, Automatic References, etc."

Before the program begins the generation process, it will ask for confirmation that you wish to replace any previously generated tables and index with the new ones. If you wish to save one of the tables or the index, type **N** at the prompt and the generation process will abort. Copy the desired tables of index to another document and restart the generation. If you wish to replace the old ones with new versions, type **Y**.

It can take some time for the program to find all of your marked references and arrange them appropriately, especially if you are using a concordance file. As WordPerfect reads through your document, it keeps you posted on its progress by means of a *pass* and *page* counter. When the program is finished, the index appears in the document where you placed the Index Definition code.

Reformatting the Index

WordPerfect formats the index using a combination of Left Indent, Left/Right Indent, and Margin Release hidden codes, all of which depend on tab settings to position the text. Thus, it is important to set tab stops appropriately.

There are three important tab positions in an index:

- The first tab stop should always be at the left margin. This is where the heading is positioned.
- The second tab stop is where the subheading is positioned. Typically, this is set two to five characters from the left margin.
- The third tab stop is where the second and subsequent lines of both the heading and the subheading will wrap around if the entry is too long for one line. Typically, the third tab stop is set

the same distance away from the second tab stop as the second tab stop is from the left margin (and the first tab stop).

CREATING A TABLE OF CONTENTS

A table of contents is handled in a similar fashion to an index. You begin by marking the text that you want included in the table. Then you define a format and generate the table.

Marking the Text

Unlike the Index function, the Table of Contents function requires that you use the <Block> key to mark an entry. After the text has been marked as a block, press the <Mark Text> key (ALT+F5). Type **1** for "ToC" to mark the entry. WordPerfect then asks you to indicate the "ToC Level:."

There are up to five *levels* for the table of contents. A level indicates the position on the page (relative to the left margin) where the item will appear. Use level 1 for major headings and higher levels for lesser divisions within the document.

For example, level 1 might be used for chapter headings, level 2 for major divisions within chapters, and level 3 for minor divisions within the major divisions. You do not have to use all the levels.

Type a level number from 1 to 5 and press ENTER. [Mark: TOC] and [EndMark:TOC] codes are placed around the blocked text. These codes also contain the level that you specified for the entry.

Positioning the Table of Contents and Defining Its Format

When you have finished marking all of the entries for the table of contents, move your cursor to the location where you want the table to appear and press the <Mark Text> key (ALT+F5). (This location should be near the top of the document, *before* all entries marked for inclusion in the table of contents.) Type **5** for "Define," and then **1** for "Define Table of Contents." The Table of Contents Definition screen is displayed, as shown in Figure 5-2.

To change the number of levels you want in your table of contents, type **1**, then the desired level number, and press ENTER. This number should be the same as the highest-level number you used when marking text in your document for the table of contents. Make sure that you specify enough levels; if you don't, you will have to go through the definition step again. If you wish, you can define more levels than you have used (or plan to use) in your document.

To change whether or not you want the last level in wrapped format to be displayed, type **2**. The Wrapped Level option combines entries at the last level into paragraph form, with the entries separated by semicolons. Figure 5-3 shows an example on the screen of a table of contents with the last level in wrapped format. This format can save space in the table of contents and may be appropriate when the last level contains minor topics. Type **Y** if you want to use wrapped format for the last level, or type **N** if you do not.

To change the format you want for each level in the table of contents, type **3**. Then, use the UP ARROW and DOWN ARROW keys to select a level, and choose a format from the menu at the bottom of the screen. The default setting is 5, for "Flush Right Page Numbers with Leaders."

If you indicate that you want the last level of the table of contents in wrapped format, the default setting for the last level will be 3, "(Page #) follows entry." Also, when you choose a format for your last level, the Option menu will display only the first three format choices. This is because the flush right format of the last two choices is inappropriate for the paragraph format of the wrapped level. When you finish setting the formats, press the <Exit> key (F7).

When all of the options have been set, press the <Exit> key to return to the document. A [Def Mark:ToC] code is inserted in the document at the cursor position.

```
Table of Contents Definition

    1 - Number of Levels                    1

    2 - Display Last Level in               No
        Wrapped Format

    3 - Page Number Position - Level 1      Flush right with leader
                               Level 2
                               Level 3
                               Level 4
                               Level 5




Selection: 0
```

Figure 5-2.   The Table of Contents Definition screen

```
                    Table of Contents
                      The Civil War

Introduction . . . . . . . . . . . . . . . . . . . . . .      1
Causes of the War . . . . . . . . . . . . . . . . . . .      5
    A House Divided . . . . . . . . . . . . . . . . . .      6
    An Irrepressible Conflict . . . . . . . . . . . . .     10
        North and South demand special legislation;
        Democrats split into two branches; Lincoln becomes
        President
    Secession . . . . . . . . . . . . . . . . . . . . .     19
        South Carolina secedes in December, 1860; Six
        other states secede within 4 months; Lincoln
        states secession is illegal
    Mobilizing for War . . . . . . . . . . . . . . . .     32
    _                                              .




                                          Doc 1 Pg 1 Ln 16 Pos 10
```

Figure 5-3.   A table of contents with the last level wrapped

Generating the Table of Contents

Now you are ready to generate the table of contents (the cursor can be anywhere in the document). Press the <Mark Text> key, type **6** for "Generate," and then **5** for "Generate Tables, Indexes, Automatic References, etc."

As when you create an index, WordPerfect will confirm the replacement of any old tables, lists, or indexes. Type **Y** to proceed with the generation, or type **N** to abort. A counter shows the program's progress.

TABLE OF AUTHORITIES

The Table of Authorities function allows you to compile up to 16 separate tables of cases and other authorities cited in a legal brief. For example, you might want to maintain one table for cases, another for legislative material, and another for statutes. You can

---

<u>TABLE OF AUTHORITIES</u>

                                                                          <u>Page</u>

                            <u>Federal Cases</u>

<u>Cipollone v. Liggett Group, Inc.</u>,
  649 F.Supp. 664 (D.N.J. 1987) 19

<u>Cipollone v. Liggett Group, Inc.</u>,
  789 F.2d 181 (3d Cir. 1986),
    <u>cert denied</u>, ___ U.S. ___, 107 S.Ct. 907 (1987) 1, 7, 9, 10,
                                                            12, 21

<u>Fidelity Federal Savings & Loan Association v. de la Cuesta</u>,
  458 U.S. 141 (1982) 3, 8

<u>Gibbons v. Ogden</u>, 9 Wheat. 1, 211 (1824) 8

<u>Grinnell v. The American Tobacco Co.</u>, No. E-122,
  878, slip op. (Dist. Ct. Jefferson County,
  172nd Jud. Dist., Tex. May 28, 1987) 7

<u>Hillsborough County v. Automated Medical Laboratories, Inc.</u>,
                                             Doc 1 Pg 1 Ln 1 Pos 10

Figure 5-4.   An example of a table of authorities

specify a different format for each table. An example of a table of authorities is shown in Figure 5-4.

Marking Authorities

There are two distinctly different methods for marking an authority in the text. The first is for marking the first occurrence of an authority and the second is for marking subsequent occurrences. When you mark the first occurrence, you enter the text of the authority exactly as you want it to look in the finished table (the *full text*), and you also give the authority a *short form*, or nickname. Then, you use the short form to mark subsequent occurrences of the authority.

Marking the Full Text of an Authority

To mark the full text of an authority, first mark the authority as a block. The text of the authority may appear in the body of the text, or in a footnote. Then, press the <Mark Text> key (ALT+F5) and type **4** for "ToA." Type the section number in which the authority should appear, and press ENTER. For example, if this authority is a statute, and your table of statutes corresponds to Section 2, type **2** and press ENTER. The Table of Authorities Full Form screen will appear.

At the top of the screen, you will see the text of the authority you marked as a block. Edit the authority to look exactly as you want it to appear when the table is actually compiled, by adding or deleting text as necessary. You can shorten lines or add blank lines by pressing ENTER, and then indent some lines by pressing TAB or the <Indent> key at the beginning of a line. You can also create a "hanging indent" format by pressing the <Left/Right Indent> key (SHIFT+F4) and then the <Left Margin Release> key (SHIFT+TAB) at the beginning of the text. The text can be up to 30 lines long. When you are finished editing the text, press the <Exit> key (F7).

If the full text of the authority will not closely resemble any text in the document, you can choose to start with a blank screen when entering the Full Form. To do this, simply position the cursor at the place in the document where the authority should be referenced, press the <Block> key, the <Mark Text> key, and then proceed as previously explained. When you see the blank Full Form screen, type the full form of the authority, and then press the <Exit> key.

After you have entered the text for the full form, you will see the prompt "Short Form:" at the bottom of the screen. WordPerfect suggests the first 40 characters of the full form. You can either accept the suggested short form by pressing ENTER, type a new short form and press ENTER, or edit the existing short form using the cursor control keys and press ENTER. The short form will be used to mark subsequent occurrences of the same authority. It should be short enough to be easily typed, yet long and unique enough to describe the authority. Typically, the first word or two of the full form makes an appropriate short form.

After you have entered a short form for the authority, you are returned to the document. A [ToA] hidden code is placed in the text at the cursor position.

Using the Short Form

For subsequent occurrences of the same authority, you use the short form you specified when you marked the first occurrence. To do this, first position the cursor near the authority you wish to mark. Then, press the <Mark Text> key (ALT+F5), and type **4** for "ToA Short Form." WordPerfect suggests the most recently entered short form name. If this is the correct short form, you can simply press ENTER. Otherwise, type a new short form or edit the suggested one, and press ENTER.

WordPerfect will not check to make sure that you have entered a valid short form name at this time. When the table is compiled, short forms that were not matched with a full form will appear with a leading asterisk (you will also see a warning message). If this happens, you should go to the indicated page and search for the [ToA] code using Reveal Codes. Delete the code, and enter another with an accurate short form.

A short form hidden code can appear before its full form. This might happen, for example, if you move text around in your document. When the table is compiled, WordPerfect will sort through all of the short forms and full forms, regardless of their respective positions in the document.

Editing the Full Form

To edit the text of a full form you have entered, or to change its section number, first position the cursor after the full form hidden code that you wish to edit. You may want to use Reveal Codes to help you with this. You can also use the Search function to locate the [ToA:] hidden codes. (If there is no full form hidden code before the cursor position when you give the command to edit the reference, the first one in the document will be used instead.)

Press the <Mark Text> key (ALT+F5), type 5 for "Define," and type 5 for "Edit Table of Authorities Full Form." The Table of Authorities Full Form screen will appear, with the text of the appropriate authority. Edit the text as desired, and press the <Exit> key. You will be prompted for a section number for the full form, and WordPerfect will be suggesting the reference's previously entered section number. Press ENTER to leave the section number unchanged, or type a new section number and press ENTER.

Defining and Positioning the Table

The next step is to define and position the table in the document. First, position the cursor at the place in the document where you want the table to appear, normally at the top of the document. You may want to type any heading information that you want to appear before the table when it is generated. For example, if this will be a Table of Cases Cited, you may want to type that title, centered and bolded, and then press ENTER several times to leave some blank space.

When you are ready to position and define the table, press the <Mark Text> key (ALT+F5), type 5 for "Define," and type 4 for "Define Table of Authorities." Type the section number you wish to define, and press ENTER. The Table of Authorities Definition screen will appear, as shown in Figure 5-5. At this point, you can type an appropriate number to change one of the settings, and then type **Y** if you want the option, or type **N** if you do not.

The first option is whether or not you wish to have dot leaders inserted before the page references, or whether they should be flush right without dot leaders. The second option is whether to allow underlining in the compiled table. Often you will use underlining in an authority in the body of your text, but you do not want it to appear in the finished table. When you type **N** for this option, WordPerfect will automatically delete all underlining codes from the table. The last option is whether or not the authorities in the table will be separated by a blank line.

You can change any of the options, or simply leave them all at their initial settings. (You can change these initial settings using the Setup function. See Appendix A, "Using Setup.") When you

---

Definition for Table of Authorities 1

    1 - Dot Leaders   Yes

    2 - Underlining Allowed   No

    3 - Blank Line Between Authorities   Yes

Selection: 0

Figure 5-5.   The Table of Authorities Definition screen

have finished changing the options, press the <Exit> key. A [DefMark:ToA] hidden code will be inserted in the text at the cursor position.

After you have defined the format and position of the table, you may want to enter a Hard Page Break so that subsequent text will begin on a new page. Also, you should enter a New Page Number code on the first page of actual text, so that the page numbers that appear in the table are accurate.

Generating the Table of Authorities

Now you are ready to generate your tables of authority (your cursor can be positioned anywhere in the document). Press the <Mark Text> key (ALT+F5), type 6 for "Generate," and type 5 for "Generate Tables, Indexes, Automatic References, etc." WordPerfect displays a reminder that the generation process will replace any previously generated tables. If you want to retain these tables, type N and the generation process will be aborted. Otherwise, type Y (or press ENTER) to proceed with the generation.

During the generation, a pass and page counter at the bottom of the screen indicates WordPerfect's progress. A message may appear that indicates you do not have sufficient memory to complete the generation. If this happens, clear the screen in Document 2, and try to generate again.

When generation is complete, you will be returned to the document, and the new Table of Authorities will appear in the location where you placed the definition code.

CREATING LISTS

WordPerfect's List function allows you to maintain up to nine separate lists of items in a document. The first five are *custom* lists that can be used for any purpose. (For example, you may want to produce a list of all tables in a document.) The remaining four are used to generate lists of captions for figures, tables, text boxes, and user-defined boxes that you've created in your document (see Chapter 10, "Presentation Features").

For the five custom lists, the List function works in almost exactly the same fashion as the Index function. The major difference is that with the List function, you *must* mark the entries with the <Block> key.

Marking the Text

To mark an entry for a list, mark the text as a block, press the <Mark Text> key (ALT+F5), and type 2 for "List." Next, enter the number of the list to use for the selected entry (from 1 to 9). WordPerfect automatically includes captions from figures in list 6, from tables in list 7, from text boxes in list 8, and from user-defined boxes in list 9. However, you can also add your own entries to these lists using the steps described.

Positioning the List and Defining Its Format

To position the list, move the cursor to the place in your document, *before* all marked entries, where you want the list to appear. Press the <Mark Text> key, type 5 for "Define," 2 for "Define List," and then a number from 1 to 9 to designate the list number you wish to define. The List Definition screen will appear, as shown in Figure 5-6.

Type the number that corresponds to the format option you desire for the list. After you enter the number of a format, you are returned to the document.

Generating the List

After you have marked all of the entries for your lists and have located and defined a format for them, you are ready to generate the lists. The cursor can be anywhere in the document. Press the

```
        List 1 Definition

            1 - No Page Numbers

            2 - Page Numbers Follow Entries

            3 - (Page Numbers) Follow Entries

            4 - Flush Right Page Numbers

            5 - Flush Right Page Numbers with Leaders




        Selection: 0
```

Figure 5-6.   The List Definition screen

<Mark Text> key (ALT+F5), type **6** for "Generate," and then **5** for "Generate Tables, Indexes, Automatic References, etc." WordPerfect will confirm the replacement of any old tables, lists, or indexes. Type **Y** to proceed with the generation or type **N** to abort. A counter shows WordPerfect's progress as it creates your lists.

FOOTNOTES AND ENDNOTES

WordPerfect's Note function will automatically number footnotes and endnotes for you. When the document is printed, the program will place footnotes at the bottom of the page and endnotes at the end of the file. If you add or delete notes, all subsequent notes will be instantly renumbered. The Note function is flexible in that it lets you select from a variety of note options to customize the note format to your satisfaction.

Although you can customize the note format if you want, you can also create notes without doing so. All the options have default values, which can be changed from the Setup menu. (See Appendix A, "Using Setup.")

Creating Notes

Each note is automatically assigned a number that will appear in the text as a *note* reference, as well as with the note text at the bottom of the screen or end of the document. To create a note, move the cursor to the place in your document where you want the note reference to appear. Then press the <Footnote> key (CTRL+F7). Type **1** for "Footnote," or **2** for "Endnote," and then **1** for "Create." The Note Text screen will appear, as shown in Figure 5-7.

You will see the note number appearing just before the cursor. If this is the first note in the document, the number will be 1.

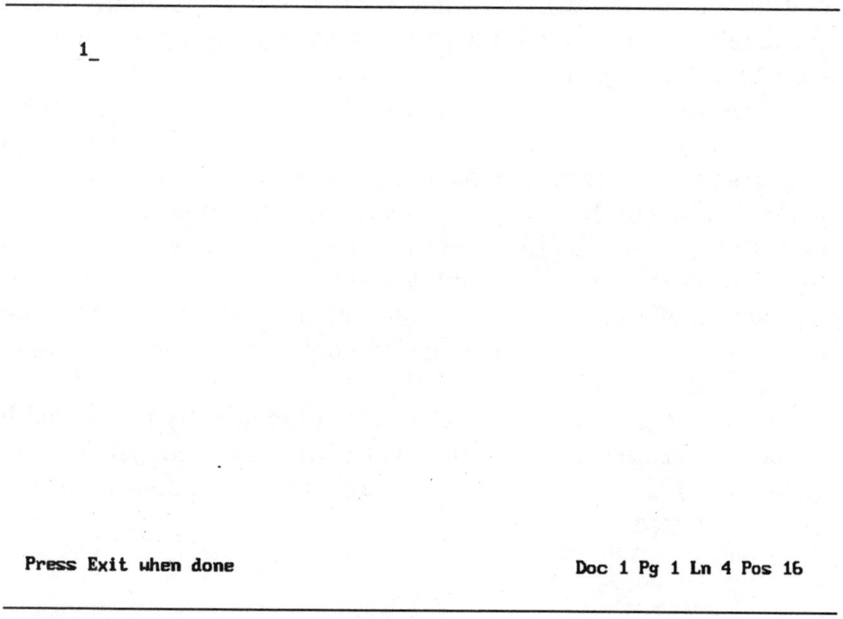

1_

Press **Exit** when done   Doc 1 Pg 1 Ln 4 Pos 16

Figure 5-7.   The Note Text screen

Otherwise, it will be the next sequential number after the number of the previous note. You can now enter the text for the note. (You may want to separate the note number from the text with a few spaces, the TAB key, or the <Indent> key (F4).)

The note number is actually a hidden code, [Note Num], that you can see by pressing <Reveal Codes>. Although the Reveal Codes function shows nothing more than the [Note Num] code, the screen shows an indent of five spaces and the number. In the printed document, the number is also superscripted. You can change the note number format with the Footnote or Endnote Options screen discussed later in this chapter—for example, to start every note with the note number, a period, and two spaces.

The text of the note can be virtually any length—up to 16,000 lines. With footnotes, WordPerfect puts as much of the text as possible onto the same page as the footnote reference. If it needs to break the note onto more than one page, WordPerfect will keep at least .5″ of the note on each page. (The amount of text to keep together can also be changed with the Note Options screen.)

While entering the text, you can use most of WordPerfect's editing and cursor-control commands. If you accidentally delete the note number, you can make a new one simply by pressing the <Footnote> key (CTRL+F7).

When you have finished entering the text of the note, press the <Exit> key (F7) to return to the document. The note reference appears in the text just before the cursor. When the document is printed, the number will be superscripted. Press the <Reveal Codes> key to see the [Footnote:] or [Endnote:] code that the Note function generated. The hidden code will display the first 50 characters of the note. To see more of it, use the Edit function described in the next section. You can delete a note by deleting its hidden code.

As you create more notes, they are automatically numbered in sequence. (Footnotes and endnotes are numbered independently of each other.) If you add or delete a note, all subsequent notes will be renumbered.

Editing Notes

Because notes are created on the special Note Text screen, you must also edit them there by using the Edit Note command. Your cursor can be anywhere in the document.

To edit a note, first press the <Footnote> key (CTRL+F7). If you want to edit a footnote, type **1**; to edit an endnote, type **2**. Then, type **2** for "Edit," and the program will ask you for a note number. (The default note number will be the number of the note following the cursor position. For example, if the cursor is located between footnotes 8 and 9, then the default footnote number will be 9.) Type the number of the note you wish to edit and press ENTER. The desired note appears on the Note Text screen. (If WordPerfect cannot find the note you requested, it will display the "* Not Found *" message.) Make any changes to the note that you need to, and then press the <Exit> key.

When you return to your document, the cursor will be placed immediately after the note's hidden code in the document. If you were to repeat the command to edit a footnote or endnote, the default note to edit would be the next one in the document. This makes it easy to edit many notes in succession or to write a macro that manipulates all the notes in a document.

Specifying a New Starting Number

At any point in a document, you can specify a new starting number for footnotes or endnotes. This can be useful if you want to reset numbering at the beginning of each chapter or if you want one document to pick up numbering where another left off. The next footnote or endnote the system encounters will be given the number you specify, and subsequent notes will then be numbered sequentially. (Note, however, that using the Master Document is a better way to manage multiple related documents. See "Master Documents" later in this chapter.)

To specify a new starting number, first position the cursor before the note you want to renumber. Press the <Footnote> key (CTRL+F7) and type **1** for "Footnote" or **2** for "Endnote," then **3** for "New Number." Type the new note number and press ENTER. All subsequent notes will be renumbered, although the notes on the current screen won't change until you move the cursor down through the notes, or until you rewrite the entire screen by pressing the <Screen> key (CTRL+F3) and type **0** for "Rewrite."

```
Footnote Options

    1 - Spacing Within Footnotes          1
              Between Footnotes           0.16"

    2 - Amount of Note to Keep Together   0.5"

    3 - Style for Number in Text          [SUPRSCPT][Note Num][suprscpt]

    4 - Style for Number in Note                    [SUPRSCPT][Note Num][suprscpt]

    5 - Footnote Numbering Method         Numbers

    6 - Start Footnote Numbers each Page  No

    7 - Line Separating Text and Footnotes  2-inch Line

    8 - Print Continued Message           No

    9 - Footnotes at Bottom of Page       Yes



    Selection: 0
```

Figure 5-8.   The Footnote Options screen

Setting Note Options

To customize the format of your footnotes and endnotes, first position the cursor before the notes that you want to change. When you have finished changing the format, WordPerfect will generate a code that will control the format of all subsequent notes. Press the <Footnote> key and type **1** for "Footnote" or **2** for "Endnote," and then **4** for "Options." The Footnote Options screen, as shown in Figure 5-8, or the Endnote Options screen, as shown in Figure 5-9, will appear.

```
Endnote Options

    1 - Spacing Within Endnotes          1
              Between Endnotes           0.16"

    2 - Amount of Endnote to Keep Together  0.5"

    3 - Style for Numbers in Text        [SUPRSCPT][Note Num][suprscpt]

    4 - Style for Numbers in Note        [Note Num].

    5 - Endnote Numbering Method         Numbers




Selection: 0
```

Figure 5-9.   The Endnote Options screen

As you can see, each of the options is assigned a default value. To change an option's value, type its number, enter the new value, and press ENTER.

The following options are available on both the Footnote Options screen and the Endnote Options screen:

1. Spacing within and between notes

   For the first option, enter a number for the line spacing within each note. This number is entered in the same way as the Line Spacing option on the Line Format menu.

   Default: 1 (Single-line spacing)

   For the second option, enter a measurement to indicate the space to be left between notes.

   Default: 0.16″

2. Amount of note to keep together

   Enter a measurement to indicate the amount of text that should be kept together if a note needs to be split across a page break. (This works like the Conditional End-of-Page command.)

   Default: 0.5″

3. Style for number in text, and

4. Style for number in note

   When you create any note entry, two strings are generated based on the settings for options 3 and 4. Option 3 specifies what will appear in the text where the note reference is made, and option 4 specifies what will appear in the note text area.

   When you want to change one of the strings, type the corresponding option number. The prompt "Replace with:" appears at the bottom of the screen. Type the string and press ENTER.

   The strings can consist of the following:

   - Text (such as spaces or characters)
   - A [Note Num] code which represents the note number
   - Any font size or appearance code

You insert codes into the string in the same way that you insert codes into a Search string. For example, to underline part of the string, press the <Underline> key (F8). To insert a Superscript command (which prints the text higher than the rest of the line), press the <Font> key (CTRL+F8), type **1** for "Size," and then **1** for "Suprscpt." A [SUPRSCPT] code appears in the string. To insert the [Note Num] code, press the <Footnote> key (CTRL+F7), type **1** for "Footnote," and **2** for "Number Code."

If you don't end a font size or appearance function by issuing the command (or pressing the key) a second time, the program will insert the end code for you at the end of the string.

Most other codes are not allowed in the strings. If you enter a code that is not allowed, it will be removed from the string when you press ENTER.

Defaults:

Footnote and Endnote in Text: "[SUPRSCPT][Note Num][suprscpt]"

Footnote in Note: " [SUPRSCPT][Note Num][suprscpt]"
Endnote in Note: "[Note Num]."

Let's say you've selected **4** from the Footnote Options screen to specify the style of the note number. If you don't want the numbers to be superscripted in the note text area at the bottom of the page, type five spaces (if you want a five-space indent), press the <Footnote> key (CTRL+F7), type **1** for "Footnote," and **2** for "Number Code," and press ENTER. You could also type a period and one or two spaces after the [Note Num] code.

Some examples of note format strings and the note formats they generate are

String	*Example*
"[Note Num]. "	"1. "
" [Note Num]:"	" 1:"
"Note #[Note Num]: "	"Note #1: "

5. Numbering method

Select whether notes will be labeled with numbers, letters, or other characters. If you select "Characters," type the character that you want the function to use. For the first note, one of the characters is used; for the second, two of them are used; for the third, three are used, and so on. You can also enter up to five different characters (that is, "*#+"). If you do, the function will use one of each character first (*, #, +), then two of each (**, ##, ++), then three (***, ###, +++), and so on. When you've entered the character(s), press ENTER.

Default: Numbers

The following options are available only on the Footnote Options screen:

6. Start footnote numbers each page

   Type **Y** for "Yes" or **N** for "No" to specify whether footnote numbering should be reset for each page. If you specify "Y," the first footnote number on each page will be "1" (if your footnotes use numbers), "a" (if your footnotes use letters), or a single character (if your footnotes use characters).

   Default: No

7. Line separating text and footnotes

   From the menu, select a format for the line that appears between the text of the document and the footnotes at the bottom of the page. You can select no line at all, a two-inch line, or a line that extends from margin to margin.

   Default: 2-inch line

8. Print continued message

   Type **Y** to print "(continued...)" at the bottom of a footnote that must be carried over to next page. The footnote number and the message "(...continued)" appear at the beginning of the footnote area on the next page. Type **N** to suppress the display of the continued messages.

   Default: No

9. Footnotes at bottom of page

   Type **Y** or **N** to specify whether blank lines should be inserted automatically to place the footnote text at the bottom of the page when the page isn't full. If you type **N**, the footnote text will immediately follow the last line of text on the page.

Default: Yes

Reformatting Notes

Note text uses the line format settings (such as margins and tab sets) that are indicated on the document's Initial Codes screen, or that are in effect at the point in the document where a note option code appears. If you go back and change these settings after you have created the note, all of the subsequent notes will be reformatted accordingly.

Endnote Placement and Generation

Normally, endnotes are automatically printed at the end of a document. If endnotes are placed within a subdocument of a master document, they are printed together with those of the other subdocuments at the end of the master document. If you wish, you can place a Hard Page Break at the end of the document so that the endnotes will begin on a new page.

To gain more control over the placement of endnotes, you can use the Endnote Placement command, which allows you to specify precisely where endnotes, should be placed in the document. In addition, it allows you to print multiple sections of endnotes. If, for example, you wanted each section in a manual to have its own list of endnotes, you would issue the Endnote Placement command after each section. You can also elect at that time to have endnote numbering restarted at 1.

Endnote Placement is especially helpful when you're using the Master Document feature. Without it, all of the endnotes from all of the subdocuments are printed together. The Endnote Placement command can be given at the end of each subdocument. Endnotes will then appear after each subdocument.

Endnote Placement

To place the endnotes in the document, begin by positioning the cursor where you want the endnotes to appear. WordPerfect will place at the cursor position all of the endnotes that appear in the document *above* this point. Press the <Footnote> key (CTRL+F7), and type **3** for "Endnote Placement."

You'll next see the prompt "Restart endnote numbering?" at the bottom of the screen. You'll most likely want to restart endnote numbering from this point forward in the document. This is provided merely as a convenience, however, because you can perform the same function later by using the New Number command on the Endnote menu. Type **Y** to have a [New End Num:1] code inserted after the Endnote Placement code, or type **N** to have the endnotes continuously numbered.

WordPerfect inserts a box which marks the location of the Endnote Placement, followed by a Hard Page Break, as shown here:

```
Endnote Placement
It is not known how much space endnotes will occupy here.
Generate to determine.
```

==

A [New End Num:1] code is also inserted if you choose to restart numbering. A message in the box indicates that the amount of space to be taken by the endnotes cannot be determined until you give the Generate command. In addition, any automatic references to the page number of an endnote will not be accurate until you perform the Generate command (see "Automatic References" later in this chapter).

The page break that WordPerfect inserts for you will cause the text following the endnotes to begin on a new page. If you want the endnotes themselves to begin on a new page, insert a page break before the Endnote Placement box.

Generating Endnotes

To find out the amount of space taken by the endnotes placed at a specific location, or to update automatic references to endnote text, you need to use the Generate command. (This is the same command used to generate an index, table of contents, table of authorities, and so on. Any tables that you've defined for the document will be updated along with the endnotes.) The cursor can be anywhere in the document.

To begin, press the <Mark Text> key, type **6** for "Generate," and then **5** for "Generate Tables, Indexes, Automatic References, etc." A prompt will appear asking for confirmation to replace all existing tables. Type **Y** to continue. A pass and page counter tracks the program's progress.

If you are using the Master Document feature, and the master document was condensed when you began the generation, you will see the prompt "Save Subdocs?" This gives you an opportunity to save the subdocuments with their updated automatic references.

When the generation is complete, you will be returned to the Document Editing screen. The Endnote Placement box now contains only the words "Endnote Placement." The code now "occupies" the space that will be taken up by the actual endnotes when you print the document. To see this, position the cursor just before the Endnote Placement code. Note the page and line numbers from the status line at the bottom of the screen. Press RIGHT ARROW to move past the code. You'll see that the status indicators reflect the amount of space to be taken by the endnotes. If you do not see a change, then there are no endnotes above this Endnote Placement code, or between this code and the previous one.

MASTER DOCUMENTS

The Master Document function allows you to manage large documents by dividing them into smaller, more manageable files on disk. Within each master document you specify the names of all of the *subdocuments* that constitute the entire work. For example, you may want to use the Master Document feature to manage the chapters of a book or manual, or any other sections of a lengthy document.

Although the documents are actually stored as separate files on disk, the Master Document feature lets you generate an index, list, table of contents, or table of authorities for the entire body of text. In addition, you can have continuous page numbering, paragraph numbering, and footnote and endnote numbering throughout the document, and you can use the Automatic Referencing feature to refer to various segments of the entire document. Finally, style definitions in the master document will override those with the same names in the subdocuments. This means, for example, that you can maintain a set of *draft* styles within each subdocument, and another set of *final* styles within the master document.

Here are the basic procedures you will follow when using the Master Document feature:

- Build the master document
- Expand the master document to generate or print
- Condense the master document to save

Building the Master Document

You can create all of your individual subdocuments either before or after you begin to build the master document. Even after you add them to the master file, you continue to load and edit them separately, as you would without the Master Document feature. In addition, you use all other features, such as the definition of headers or footers, paragraph numbering, automatic references, and so on, just as you would with a normal document.

When you're ready to build a master document, start with a blank screen. Enter any text you want to precede the first subdocument in the master document. You may, for example, want to type a title for the entire document. (You may also want to return to the top of the master document later to define a definition mark for a table of contents or a list.)

Including a Subdocument

To include a subdocument in the master document, begin by positioning the cursor at the place in the document where you want the subdocument to appear. Next, press the <Mark Text> key (ALT+F5), and type 2 for "Subdoc." At the prompt "Subdoc Filename:," type the name of the document that you want to include.

Optionally, you can include a drive or path designation before the document name. On a hard disk system, this may be very important. When you condense the document (see "Condensing the Master Document" later in this chapter), WordPerfect looks for the original subdocument file in the default directory if no pathname is specified. If it can't find the original file, it will create a new one. By omitting the name of the directory where the subdocument is located, you may cause WordPerfect to create extra copies of the document. On the other hand, if you do specify the directory name, you will not be able to move the document from that directory without deleting and re-creating the Subdocument code.

After entering the document name, press ENTER, and a Subdocument box similar to this one will appear.

```
┌──────────────────────────────────────────────────────────────┐
│ Subdoc:                                                        │
└──────────────────────────────────────────────────────────────┘
```

This box, which is displayed as [Subdoc:] in Reveal Codes, acts as a placemarker for the full text of the specified document (even if it has not yet been created). When you expand the master document, this code will be replaced with the full text of the specified subdocument, surrounded by a different set of codes marking its beginning and end. (All other subdocument codes will be similarly replaced.) When you condense the master document, the [Subdoc:] code will again appear in place of the full subdocument text.

Continue to position the cursor and follow the steps described above, inserting [Subdoc:] codes for all of the subdocuments you want to include in this master document.

You may want to precede the second and subsequent [Subdoc:] codes with a Hard Page Break (press CTRL+ENTER to insert an

[HPg] code). If you don't, the subdocument texts will appear immediately below one another.

Saving the Master Document

When you're through including all of the [Subdoc:] codes, save the master document. You may want to adopt a standard filename extension for master documents, such as .MAS.

When you see all of the [Subdoc:] boxes on the screen, without the actual subdocument texts, the master document is said to be *condensed*. When you see the start and end codes, and the actual text of the subdocuments, the master document is said to be *expanded*. Master documents are normally stored in their condensed form. In this way, the master documents remain quite small.

Expanding the Master Document

When you're ready to print the entire document, or if you need to use the Generate command to prepare a table of contents or update automatic references, you need to expand the master document. (If you give the Generate command when the master document is condensed, it will automatically expand the master document, perform the generation, then condense it again. It will also ask whether you want to save changes, such as updated automatic references, in the subdocuments. See "Generating the Master Document" later in this chapter.)

To expand a master document currently on the screen, press the <Mark Text> key (ALT+F5), type **6** for "Generate," and then **3** for "Expand Master Document." A message at the bottom of the screen will read "Expanding Master Document." When WordPerfect has finished, you will return to the Document Editing screen.

If WordPerfect is unable to locate the document specified by a subdocument code (either in the default directory or in the specified directory, if any), the program notifies you and asks whether you want to continue. Type **Y** to skip the missing document and proceed with the expansion; the [Subdoc:] code for that document will remain intact. Type **N** to abort the command; subdocuments previously processed will remain expanded.

The program inserts a [Subdoc Start:] code at the beginning of each subdocument text, and a [Subdoc End:] code at the end of each subdocument text. The [Subdoc Start:] code looks like this on the editing screen:

```
Subdoc Start:
```

The [Subdoc End:] code looks like this on the editing screen:

```
Subdoc End:
```

After you expand a master document, you can edit the text within any of the displayed subdocuments as if you were editing the subdocument alone. You can use automatic references, if you wish, with targets and references either in the same or different subdocument. (See "Automatic References" later in this chapter.)

When expanded, the combined subdocuments act exactly as if they were all stored in one file. (In fact, they really are: when expanded, the master document is as big as all of the subdocuments combined. That's why the master document is usually not saved in expanded form.) Because of this, all formatting, numbering, and option codes behave just as they would in a normal document—numbering codes will be continuous, and formatting and option codes will remain in effect until the end of the document, or until another code of the same type is encountered. If, for example, the first subdocument in a master document contains a code changing the left and right margins to 2″, that code will affect all subsequent subdocument text unless another margin code is encountered.

Because of this, you'll probably want to place all document formatting codes at the top of the master document, rather than at the top of each subdocument.

Condensing the Master Document

After you're through printing, generating, or making any editing changes to the master document, you'll want to condense it before saving it. Condensing allows you to save all of the subdocuments to their own files.

To condense a master document, press the <Mark Text> key (ALT+F5), type **6** for "Generate," and **4** for "Condense Master Document." WordPerfect responds "Save Subdocs?" at the bottom of the screen. Type **Y** to save any changes you've made to any of the subdocuments since you last expanded the master document. Type **N** to discard any changes. (Be careful that you don't lose work by typing "N" here by mistake.)

If you answered "Yes" to the prompt described above, WordPerfect proceeds to save the subdocuments under their individual names. If a document with the file name specified by a subdocument code does not exist in the default directory (or in the specified directory, if one is included), WordPerfect creates a new file. If a document already exists, the program asks whether you want to replace the original file. Type **1** for "Yes" to replace the document. If you want to save the document under a different name, type **2** for "No," then enter the new name. (WordPerfect will modify the [Subdoc:] code in the master document to reflect the new name.) Type **3** for "Replace All Remaining" to replace the remaining subdocuments without prompts.

After you've saved the subdocuments (if you chose to save them), you'll return to the Document Editing screen. All of the text of each subdocument, along with its start and end codes, will have been replaced with the original [Subdoc:] code. If you modified any of the [Subdoc:] codes or if you edited any text outside of the subdocuments, you may now want to save the master document in its condensed form.

Generating the Master Document

You are most likely to use the Master Document feature to generate an index, list, table of contents, table of authorities, or automatic references for several related documents, such as chapters of a book, or sections of a report or manual. Most often, you'll want to place the [Def Mark:] codes for the tables, lists, and index within the master document itself. A typical master document for a book might consist of a title page, a table of contents definition mark, several list definition marks, the chapter subdocument codes for all the chapters in the book, and an Index Definition code.

To generate, you should have the master document on the screen. If the document is in condensed form, WordPerfect will expand it automatically during generation.

Next, press the <Mark Text> key (ALT+F5), type **6** for "Generate," and then **5** for "Generate Tables, Indexes, Automatic References, etc." WordPerfect will warn you that existing tables and indexes will be replaced. Type **Y** to continue, or type **N** to abort the generation. While the master document is being generated, a pass and page counter keeps track of the program's progress.

If the document was condensed when you began the generation, the program will display the prompt "Update Subdocs?" Type **Y** to have the program update the subdocuments with any changes the generation process may have made. For example, automatic references will have been modified in the documents. WordPerfect briefly displays the message "Condensing subdocuments," then you are returned to the Document Editing screen.

Hiding and Displaying
Subdocument Codes

The [Subdoc:], [Subdoc Start:], and [Subdoc End:] codes are normally displayed in single-line boxes that resemble document comment boxes. You can choose to suppress their display by using the Setup function (see Appendix A, "Using Setup").

To display or suppress document comments, press the <Setup> key (SHIFT+F1), type **3** for "Display," and then **3** for "Display Document Comments." Type **Y** if you want the subdocument codes to be displayed (along with document comments), or **N** to suppress the display. Press the <Exit> key (F7) to return to the Document Editing screen. This change is permanently made for all future WordPerfect editing sessions, until you change the setting again.

Remember that the codes themselves can always be viewed by means of the Reveal Codes function.

AUTOMATIC REFERENCES

WordPerfect's Automatic Reference feature allows you to insert cross-references within your documents. For example, you may want to include the reference "...(see Figure 21, page 54)" within the body of your document. By using the Automatic Reference feature, you can have the "21" and "54" linked directly to the actual number of the figure to which you're referring, and to the page number it's on. If as a result of editing changes that figure ends up with a different number, or on a different page, the reference can be updated automatically.

The reference itself can be any one of the following:

- Page number
- Paragraph number
- Footnote number
- Endnote number
- Figure, table, Text box, or user-defined box number

When you create a reference, you mark not only the point where the reference number should appear, but also the exact location of the *target*. The type of reference number displayed (page number, paragraph number, and so on) is identified within the reference code. However, the target to use (which page, paragraph, and so on) is identified by the precise location of the target code.

Note that several references can use the same target code. (That is, the target code itself has no specific "type," like the reference code.) For instance, in the example "...(see Figure 21, page 54)", both the "21" and the "54" have the same target, which is the figure itself. The reference number, however, is different: for "21," it's the figure number; for "54," it's the page number on which the target code (next to the figure) is located.

You can also have several targets for the same reference. That is, you may want to create a reference to two different pages, as in: "(See the discussion of Pit Bull Psychology, pages 5, 53.)". In this case, you may have the same target code in two places, on pages 5 and 53. A single reference code after the word "pages" produces the numbers for each page on which the target code is found, with each number separated by a comma and a space.

Marking References and Targets

Typically, you'll create the reference and mark the target at the same time (when you're ready to insert the reference). However, you also have the option of creating a reference without marking the target. In addition, you can identify a target at any time for future references.

Marking Both

Before you create the reference and mark the target, you should type any preliminary text, such as "See figure" and a space. References can be placed anywhere you type normal text, such as within footnotes, endnotes, headers, footers, graphics box captions, and within a Text box. When you've positioned the cursor at the place you want the reference to appear, press the <Mark Text> key (ALT+F5), type **1** for "Auto Ref," and **3** for "Mark Both Reference and Target." A menu will appear asking you to select the type of reference, as shown in Figure 5-10.

Type the number that represents the reference you want to create. (If you type **5**, you'll see an additional menu that allows you to choose from several possible graphics box types.) You will return to the Document Editing screen, and a message that tells you to select the target will appear at the bottom of the screen.

If you typed **1** for "Page Number," position the cursor on the relevant page. You'll typically select this option to refer to text

---

```
Tie Reference to:

     1 - Page Number

     2 - Paragraph/Outline Number

     3 - Footnote Number

     4 - Endnote Number

     5 - Graphics Box Number

After selecting a reference type, go to the location of the item you want to
reference in your document and press Enter to mark it as the "target".




Selection: 0
```

Figure 5-10.   Automatic Reference screen

that is not marked with a paragraph number, but you can use this option to identify the page number of any element in the document. For example, you could put the cursor next to a [Figure] code if you want to refer to the page on which the figure appears. Similarly, you could put the cursor in the text of an endnote to refer to the page on which that endnote will appear once it is generated (see "Footnotes and Endnotes" earlier in this chapter).

If you typed 2 for "Paragraph/Outline Number," position the cursor within the paragraph you want to refer to. Normally, you should put the cursor just after the [Par Num:] code (it cannot appear before the code). You can put it anywhere in the body of the paragraph, but you'll risk it being accidentally deleted or moved.

If you typed 3 for "Footnote Number" or 4 for "Endnote Number," you should edit the note to which you want to refer, which positions the cursor within the note text. To do this, press the <Footnote> key (CTRL+F7), type **1** for "Footnote" or **2** for "Endnote," and then **2** for "Edit." Type the number of the desired note, and press ENTER. You can also position the cursor to just after the [Footnote:] or [Endnote:] code in the document, although it is more safely placed within the footnote itself.

If you typed **5** for "Graphics Box Number," and then subsequently selected one of the graphics box options, position the cursor to *just after* the appropriate [Figure], [Table], [Text Box], or [Usr Box] code.

After you've positioned the cursor in the correct location for the type of reference you selected, press ENTER to mark the location. The prompt "Target Name:" appears at the bottom of the screen. Here, you must enter a unique name for the reference that will be used to form a connection between the reference and the target. The name can be up to 31 characters long, and can include spaces. (WordPerfect ignores the case of the name that you enter; it always converts it to uppercase.) When you've typed the name, press ENTER.

WordPerfect inserts a [Target()] code where you positioned your cursor for the target location, and a [Ref():] code in the cursor's former location. The appropriate reference number should appear in the document where the [Ref():] code is placed. If a question mark (?) appears instead, this means you didn't position the cursor at a location appropriate for the type of reference selected. Check the location of the [Target()] code, and move it if necessary. (You can do this easily by deleting the code, and by using Undelete to place it somewhere else.) Then, use the Generate command to update the reference.

Marking Reference Only

There are some occasions when you want to mark only the reference, without identifying the target location. This would be the case when you're making a second reference to the same target, in which case you could simply refer to the original target by name. Another possibility would be that you have not yet created the object or location to which you want to refer, or, that you're using the Master Document feature, but the reference is to an object in another subdocument.

In any case, begin with the cursor at the place where you want the reference to appear. Then, press the <Mark Text> key, type **1** for "Auto Ref," and **1** for "Mark Reference." Select the type of reference from the list provided (if you type **5**, select the type of graphics box from the following menu). Next, type the name of the target, and press ENTER. If you are making a reference to a target for which you've already created a reference, use the same target name. (The most recently used name is the suggested response.) If you're making a reference to an object or section of text that you have not yet created, make up a target name for it. A [Ref():] code is inserted in the document.

WordPerfect always inserts a question mark in place of the reference number when you mark only the reference. Use the Generate command to update the reference (see "Generating Automatic References" later in this chapter).

If your goal is to create a second reference to the same target, you can do this by using the procedure described earlier in "Marking Both." When you position the cursor at the target, however, carefully place the cursor just to the right of the original [Target:] code before pressing ENTER (use Reveal Codes to be sure of the placement). WordPerfect will thus realize that you want to refer to the same target and it will not create another target code (and it will not ask you for a new target name). One advantage of this method is that the reference number will be shown accurately right away, without the need to use the Generate command.

Marking Target Only

There may also be occasions when you only need to identify the target, without creating a reference. You might want to do this when you know that you will be referring to an object or section of text later, or when you're creating a reference with more than one target.

To mark the target only, begin by positioning the cursor at the correct location for the type of reference you plan to make (see the preceding descriptions). Then, press the <Mark Text> key (ALT+ F5) and type **1** for "Auto Ref," and **2** for "Mark Target." Enter a name for the target, and press ENTER. A [Target()] code is inserted at the cursor position.

Generating Automatic References

As you create each reference, WordPerfect attempts to display an accurate number for the target. However, this is not always possible—you may, for example, have marked some references without directly specifying a target. In addition, although the references are likely to change as you edit your document, the numbers do not automatically adjust to the new positions of the target. You'll need to update the automatic references before you print the document.

To update all of the references in a document, you must use the Generate command. (This is the same command used to generate an index, table of contents, table of authorities, and so on. Any of the tables that you've defined in this document will be updated along with the automatic references.) The cursor can be anywhere in the document.

If you're using the Master Document feature (see "Master Documents" earlier in this chapter), you should have the master document on the screen. When you generate, WordPerfect will expand the master document if necessary. Automatic references throughout the subdocuments will act as if the master document was one whole document.

To begin the generation, press the <Mark Text> key, type **6** for "Generate," and then **5** for "Generate Tables, Indexes, Automatic References, etc." A prompt will appear asking for confirmation to replace all existing tables. Type **Y** to continue. A pass and page counter tracks the program's progress.

If you are using the Master Document feature, and the master document was condensed when you began the generation, you will see the prompt "Save Subdocs?" This gives you an opportunity to save the subdocuments with their automatic references updated.

When the generation is complete, you will be returned to the Document Editing screen. All references should now appear updated. If any reference has a question mark in place of a number, use Reveal Codes to determine whether the target name was entered correctly. If it was, check that the target code was placed in an appropriate location (see "Marking Both," earlier in this chapter). Give the Generate command again once you've made any necessary corrections.

6

OFFICE FEATURES

WordPerfect has several functions that are intended for general office environments, although some of them are useful in other situations as well. These are

- Document Summary
- Comments
- Line Numbering
- Document Compare

The Document Summary function allows you to specify some summary information about each document, such as the subject, author, typist, and a general description of the document. The Comments function allows you to insert comments in the body of your text that will not print, and will not affect the layout of your document. The Line Numbering function will place line numbers along the left edge of the paper when the document is printed. It is useful both for legal documents that must be printed in this format, and for any document where line numbers would provide a useful reference to the material, such as for a draft. The Document Compare function will compare two versions of the same document and mark the differences between the two.

This chapter will discuss each of these features.

219

DOCUMENT SUMMARY

You can use the Document Summary function in two ways. You can choose to manually enter Document Summary items for individual documents. Or you can choose to have WordPerfect automatically prompt you for the Document Summary information the first time any file is saved. In either case, you will be able to edit the Document Summary information at any time.

You can use the Word Search function to search for documents based on the Summary information (see Appendix B, "Using Word Search").

Automatic Operation

To invoke the automatic feature of the Document Summary function, you need to use the Setup menu. Press the <Setup> key (SHIFT+F1), type **5** for "Initial Settings," and then **3** for "Document Summary." Finally, type **1** for "Create on Save/Exit," and type **Y**. (You can also use this screen to specify the text the program will use to identify the subject of a document. See Appendix A, "Using Setup.") Press the <Exit> key to return to the Document Editing screen. From now on, each time you press the <Save> key, or press the <Exit> key and type **Y** for "Save Document (Y/N)?", the Document Summary screen will automatically appear.

Manual Operation

To manually insert Document Summary information, the cursor can be positioned anywhere within the document. Press the <Format> key (SHIFT+F8), type **3** for "Document," and **5** for "Summary." The Document Summary screen will appear.

Document Summary Contents

If you have previously named the current document (that is, you retrieved a file, or you created a file and subsequently saved it), its filename along with its full pathname appears as the first entry on the Document Summary screen. This information is not actually stored with the Document Summary in the document. For example, if the file is copied to another directory on your hard disk, or saved with a different name, the information on the Document Summary screen will change appropriately.

The second item on the Document Summary screen is Date of Creation. This date is automatically inserted for you when you first save the document, based on the current date stored in the computer's memory. In order for this to be accurate, you must be sure the date is correctly set whenever you start your computer.

For each remaining item on the screen you must type the appropriate number to modify its entry.

First, you can enter a more descriptive file name of up to 39 characters. The entry that follows allows you to specify the subject of the document (or the account to which it refers).

The subsequent items on the screen are the names of the Author and the Typist of the document. These items are commonly used in an office environment where the person entering the document is typically not the same person who wrote the text. Type the name of the author of the document and press ENTER, then type the name of the typist and press ENTER. You can enter up to 39 characters in each of these fields.

The last item on the screen is a box for any comments about the document. This is a useful way to remind yourself about the contents of a file. For example, you may have several versions of the same document. While these might be difficult to tell apart by simply scrolling through them, the Document Summary could be used to describe the differences. WordPerfect initially sets the comments of each document to the first 400 characters or so of the document's text. Line endings are indicated by a semicolon and a space.

As you enter Comment text, the words will automatically wrap to the next line when you reach the end of each line. You can use the ENTER key to end a line, or to make blank lines, and you can use most of WordPerfect's cursor controls. You can also use bold and underline to spruce up the text. You can enter up to 780 characters of Comments text.

When you are finished entering Comments, press the <Exit> key (F7). Press the <Exit> key a second time, and you will be returned to the document.

One of the most useful aspects of the Document Summary function is that it can help you when you're looking for a particular document. When you use the Look function from the List Files display, the full contents of the summary information are displayed at the top of the document.

Editing the Document Summary

To edit the contents of the Document Summary, press the <Format> key (SHIFT+F8), type **3** for "Document," and **5** for "Summary." The previously created Summary will appear on the screen. Enter the appropriate number of the section you wish to edit. Press the <Exit> key when you are finished editing.

COMMENTS

You can place nonprinting comments anywhere in a document, even in the middle of a line. A comment can be useful to remind yourself to rewrite some text, or to mark the location of a sequence of hidden codes.

Comments do not appear when you print the document; they only appear on the screen. If you wish, you can choose to suppress the screen display of comments as well. In this case, the only way you will know that comments have been used in a document is by using the Reveal Codes function.

Inserting Comments

To insert a comment into the text, position the cursor where you want the comment to appear. Then, press the <Text In/Out> key (CTRL+F5), type **5** for "Comment," and then **1** for "Create." Next, type the text of the comment. When you reach the end of a line, the text will automatically wrap to the next line. Use the ENTER key to end a line, or generate blank lines. You can use most of WordPerfect's cursor controls, as well as bold and underline. You can enter up to 1024 characters in a single comment. When you are finished entering text, press the <Exit> key (F7). A [Comment] hidden code will be inserted in your text.

If you have set WordPerfect to display Comments (see the section "Displaying and Hiding Comments" below), the comment text you entered will appear at the cursor position, surrounded by a double-line box. If you inserted the comment when the cursor was in the middle of a line, you will notice that the cursor is now located in the correct column, underneath the comment. Although the Comment breaks up the text on the line, WordPerfect keeps track of the column and line position, and simply picks up where it left off after the comment. You can continue to use the RIGHT ARROW and LEFT ARROW keys, as well as the <Word Right> and <Word Left> keys to position the cursor on the line.

Editing Comments

To edit the contents of a comment, position the cursor anywhere after the comment you wish to edit, press the <Text In/Out> key, type 5 for "Comment," and then 2 for "Edit." The Comment text will appear on the screen. Edit the text and press the <Exit> key when you are finished. Your cursor will be positioned directly after the Comment you edited.

If there is no comment before the cursor when you issue the Edit Comment command, you will edit the first comment in the document. If there are no comments in the document, WordPerfect will respond "∗ Not Found ∗."

Displaying and
Hiding Comments

You can choose whether or not Comments will be visible on the screen. To do this, press the <Setup> key (SHIFT+F1), type **3** for

"Display," and **3** for "Display Document Comments." Now, type **Y** to display Comments, or type **N** to hide them. Comments are retained as [Comment] codes in the text even when they are not shown. You can choose to hide or display them at any time.

LINE NUMBERING

WordPerfect has a function that will place line numbers along the left edge of the text when a document is printed. This is a common need for many legal documents. In addition, it is a useful feature anytime you want to number the lines in a document. For example, if a document is being reviewed by several people, or is being edited on paper by one person and on screen by another, line numbers provide an easy way to locate specific text.

Using Line Numbering

First, position the cursor at the place in your document where you want line numbering to begin. Be sure the cursor is at the beginning of a line—otherwise, line numbering will begin with the following line. Press the <Format> key (SHIFT+F8), type **1** for "Line," and **5** for "Line Numbering." Type **Y** to begin line numbering and the Line Numbering screen will appear. You can now change any of the other parameters on this screen from their initial values.

The first option is whether or not WordPerfect will include blank lines (made by pressing the ENTER key) when counting the lines in the document. The second is the increment with which the program will place the numbers. For example, a common incremental setting of 5 would cause WordPerfect to place a number every five lines.

You can also specify how far from the left edge of the paper the line numbers should appear. You specify this using the current units of measure (initially inches). The initial value for this is 6/10 of an inch.

You can then specify a starting number for the line numbers (initially set to 1). Lastly, you can specify whether or not line numbering should restart at the beginning of each page. If you choose not to, line numbering will continue through the entire numbered area. You may need to adjust the position of the line numbers to allow enough room for larger numbers.

When you are finished changing the parameters, press the <Exit> key to return to the document. A [Ln Num:On] hidden code will be inserted into the text at the cursor position.

You can use the Print View function (see Chapter 1, "Basics Refresher") to see how the line numbers will appear when the document is printed.

Text within footnotes and endnotes are included in the line numbering, but not text within headers and footers.

Ending Line Numbering

If you want line numbering to end before the end of the document, first position the cursor at the place where you want numbering to end. Be sure you position the cursor at the beginning of a line—otherwise, line numbering will end on the following line. Press the <Format> key (SHIFT+F8), type **1** for "Line," and **5** for "Line Numbering." Type **N** to end line numbering. Then press the <Exit> key to return to the document. A [Ln Num:Off] hidden code will be inserted in the text.

DOCUMENT COMPARE

WordPerfect can compare two versions of the same document to determine the differences between the two. This is useful if, for example, you are collaborating with another person on the creation of a document. After receiving your initial version of the document, your collaborator can proceed to make any necessary changes to it. When you receive a copy of the revised document on disk, you can use the Document Compare function to determine what changes have been made.

Inserted text is marked for *redlining* (printed in a different font, or with a vertical *change bar* in the margin). Deleted text is struck out (a line appears running through the text).

Comparing Documents

To compare documents, you need to load one of the versions onto the screen. Typically, this will be the most recently changed of the two versions you want to compare. (Be sure you have saved the document before starting, since the comparison process will modify the current document.) Also, be sure you know the name (and path designation, if necessary) of the document to use for comparison (called the "other" document).

To begin, press the <Mark Text> key (ALT+F5), and type **6** for "Generate," and then **2** for "Compare Screen and Disk Documents and Add Redline and Strikeout." Next, you will be prompted for the name of the document with which you want to compare the one currently on screen. The current document's path and filename are suggested. Type the name of the document (or edit the suggested response), and press ENTER.

A counter at the bottom of the screen tracks the program's progress as it compares the screen version of the document with the one stored on disk. When the comparison is finished, you will be returned to the document's screen. You will see the changes marked in the on-screen document.

The smallest unit WordPerfect will mark as added or deleted is a phrase. That is, even if you change just a single letter in a word, the program still marks the entire phrase. It uses commas and other punctuation marks to determine the boundaries of a phrase. If the sentence does not appear to contain more than one phrase, the entire sentence is marked.

Text that has been added to the on-screen document (which does *not* appear in the disk document) is marked for redlining. Text that has been deleted from the on-screen document (which *does* appear in the disk document) is marked for strikeout.

If WordPerfect is able to determine that a section of text (such as a sentence or paragraph of text or more) has been moved from one location to another in the document, the phrase "THE FOL-LOWING TEXT WAS MOVED" is inserted before the moved text, and the phrase "THE PRECEDING TEXT WAS MOVED" appears after the moved text. (Note that there's no way for Word-Perfect to know the original location of the text.) These two phrases are each preceded by a Hard Return, to allow them to stand out from the normal text. In addition, each phrase is marked for strikeout, so that when you choose to remove struck-out text, the phrases will be deleted.

Incorporating Changes

Once you've compared two documents, you may need to decide which changes you want to leave intact, and which you want to modify. You can use the Reveal Codes function to individually remove strikeout codes ([STKOUT] and [stkout]) from text that you do not want deleted. And you can manually delete text that has been marked for redlining, indicating that it was added to the current document.

Once you've made such manual changes, you can have Word-Perfect automatically remove all remaining redline codes and delete all text marked for strikeout. To do this, begin by pressing the <Mark Text> key (ALT+F5), type **6** for "Generate", and then type **1** for "Remove Redline Markings and Strikeout Text from Document." Type **Y** to confirm the command. You're now left with the updated document on-screen.

7

STYLES

The Styles function in WordPerfect provides one of the program's most powerful and flexible tools for preparing and reformatting documents.

The Styles function enables you to create a description, or *style*, for each of the various elements in your document. Styles have common names, such as "Level 1 Heading" or "Indented Quotation." For each style, you insert the hidden codes that are to precede the actual text in that element, and then (optionally) those that are to follow the text.

After creating the styles, you apply them to the text. You can do this while you're typing the text or after the document has been created (although it's more convenient to do it "on the fly"). Once you've created and applied the styles, you can easily go back and change their definitions by modifying the codes that precede and follow each element's text. If, for example, you decide you want your first-level headings to appear in italics rather than boldface, you simply change the codes in the style. All of your headings will change instantly.

Styles can be used to simplify the process of creating template documents. By preparing a set of styles, you can hide long sequences of hidden codes from less proficient WordPerfect users (and reduce the risk of accidental deletion). In addition, you can maintain consistency of formats within a group of users, such as all the users in an office.

THE NATURE OF STYLES

Using styles involves two essential actions: creating them, and applying them.

When you create styles, they become attached to the current document. The next time you retrieve the document, the same styles will be available. In addition, you can easily retrieve one document's styles into another. You may want to exploit this capability by maintaining empty documents that contain only style definitions. You can then use those styles for any other document. When you retrieve styles into a document that already contains some styles with the same names, the *retrieved* styles will overwrite the *resident* styles.

When you apply a style, hidden codes are inserted in the document which identify the style by a unique name of up to 11 characters. When you retrieve styles from another document, and the styles you retrieve overwrite the ones that were resident, the new styles will affect the styled text. Thus, you can efficiently reformat entire documents by simply maintaining more than one set of like-named styles. You might, for example, maintain a "draft" set of styles, and a "final" set of styles. You could even create a macro (or redefine a key) to quickly switch between them (see Chapter 2, "Macros").

CREATING STYLES

To create a style, you normally begin with the document on screen within which you want to apply the style. (If you wish, you can mark as a block an example of the format you want for the style. See "Creating Styles by Example" later in this chapter.) Then, you press the <Style> key (ALT+F8), and the Styles screen will appear, as shown in Figure 7-1. Next, type **3** for "Create" and you'll see the Style Edit screen, as shown in Figure 7-2. From this screen you can modify any of the attributes of the new style (as later described). When you're through modifying its attributes, press the <Exit> key (F7) to return to the Styles menu.

Name

To change the name of the style, type **1** for "Name." The name
that you specify must be unique for this document. You can enter
up to 11 characters, including uppercase and lowercase letters,
spaces, and punctuation. This name is the one that will appear in
the document's Reveal Codes when you later apply the style.

When you've entered the name, press ENTER. If a style with
this name already exists for the current document, the name you
have entered will disappear, and you'll have to enter another one.

Styles

   Name   **Type Description**

1 On; 2 Off; 3 Create; 4 Edit; 5 Delete; 6 Save; 7 Retrieve; 8 Update: 4

Figure 7-1.   The Styles screen

```
Styles: Edit
     1 - Name
     2 - Type          Paired
     3 - Description
     4 - Codes
     5 - Enter          HRt




Selection: 0
```

Figure 7-2.   The Style Edit screen

Type

Next, you can change the type of the style. A *paired* style (the default choice) is one that will have codes that begin the style as well as codes that end the style. A paired style is similar in nature to a matched pair of hidden codes, such as those used for underlined or boldface text.

For example, you might want to create a style for a heading which you want to appear in boldface, followed by two Hard Returns. To do this, you would need a [Bold] code and two [HRt] codes to end the style. You would use a paired style to begin and end this format.

An *open* style is one which will have codes that simply set a format a certain way. For example, you may want to have an open style that begins each major section of a document. In this style you would include codes for page numbering, headers, and so on. In this case, you don't require a style that will begin and end, but rather one that simply begins. For such a format you would use an open style.

To change the type of the style, type **2** for "Type," then type **1** for "Paired" or **2** for "Open." Choice 5 on this screen, "Enter," will appear only for Paired styles.

Description

You can next type **3** for "Description" to enter a longer description of the style than the Name option will allow. The description is not required to be unique, and can contain up to 54 characters, including uppercase and lowercase letters, spaces, and punctuation. Press ENTER when you've finished typing the description.

The description will appear in the list of styles on the Styles screen, but it will not be displayed anywhere in the document. You may want to use the description to provide a long name such as "Level One Heading" or "Emphasized Text."

Codes

Codes are the most important attribute of a style. To modify the codes that will be used by a style, type **4** for "Codes." A blank document screen will appear, with the Reveal Codes function active. Enter the codes for the style, as described below for the two types of styles. When you're through, press the <Exit> key (F7), and you'll return to the Style Edit screen.

For both types of styles you can include not only formatting codes, but other codes and text as well. For example, you might want to include a Paragraph Number code or Table of Contents Marking codes. You may also want to include punctuation marks or other text.

Paired Style

If you select a Paired Style, a comment will appear on the screen. If you currently have Comments displayed (see Appendix A, "Using Setup"), the comment box will read "Place Style On Codes above, and Style Off Codes below." You should treat the [Comment] code displayed on the Reveal Codes portion of the screen as if it were the text between the begin (or Style On) codes and the end (or Style Off) codes. For example, if you wanted the text to appear in bold, you would mark the [Comment] code as a block, and press the <Bold> key.

When you use this type of style in a document (see "Applying Styles" later in this chapter), all of the codes that appear before the [Comment] code will be in effect at the location of the [Style On:] code. All of the codes that appear after the [Comment] code will be in effect at the location of the [Style Off:] code.

Most formatting codes only need to be inserted before the [Comment] code. This is because any formats you invoke (such as underlining, or a new font), are automatically reset when you turn a style off. For example, let's say you have a style that includes a [Font:] code that switches to a Times Roman font. If your current font before you insert the [Style On:] code is Courier, then the [Style Off:] code will automatically switch back to Courier.

Open Style

If you select an Open Style, you'll see a blank screen. Enter any series of codes that you want the style to invoke. When you later turn on the style in the document, an [Open Style:] code is inserted. This code will have the effect of inserting any series of codes you enter on this screen.

Unlike a Paired Style, an Open Style has no [Style Off:] code. Any formatting codes included in its definition will remain in effect from the point in the document where you turn it on to the end of the document, or until other codes of the same types (or styles that contain such codes) are encountered.

For example, you may want to use an Open Style to begin major new sections in a document. You might want each section to begin with a [Pg Num:1] code to reset page numbering, and a [Suppress:PgNum] code to prevent a page number from appearing on the first page.

Enter Action

To modify the action WordPerfect will take when you press ENTER after turning on a Paired Style, type 5 for "Enter." To have WordPerfect insert an [HRt] code (as it normally would), type **1**. To have it automatically turn off the active style, type **2**. To have it automatically turn off the active style, and then turn it back on again, type **3**.

For styles that apply to small sections of text, such as headings, titles, or emphasized text, you'll probably want to choose option 2. This will enable you to turn on the style, type the text, and press ENTER to end the style.

For styles that you plan to use several times in a row, such as multiple paragraphs within an indented quotation, or even for normal paragraphs, you may want to use option 3. (You can always turn off a Paired Style by pressing RIGHT ARROW to move the cursor past the [Style Off:] code.)

CREATING STYLES BY EXAMPLE

An alternative to defining a style by manually inserting all of the codes is to use codes from the document itself. To do this, begin by marking as a block an example of the format you want, making sure that you include in the block any relevant formatting codes. Then proceed to create a style as described earlier. When you type 4 for "Codes" from the Style Edit menu, you'll see that WordPerfect has already inserted codes for you, which it has extracted from the marked block.

While examining the marked block, the program will ignore any text. If you are creating a Paired Style, WordPerfect will attempt to locate a series of starting codes followed by a passage of text, which is in turn followed by a series of ending codes. If it identifies this pattern, it will replace the text in the block with the [Comment] code. This way, the starting codes will appear before the [Comment], and the ending codes after it.

Let's say, for example, that you have formatted a heading in your document which looks like the following line on the Reveal Codes screen:

```
[Cntr][BOLD]Introduction[bold][C/A/Flrt][HRt]
[HRt]
█
```

Notice that the heading is followed by two Hard Returns, one to end the line, and another to insert a blank line. To create a Heading style from this example, you would begin with the Reveal Codes cursor highlight on the [Cntr] code. Then, you'd press the <Block> key, DOWN ARROW, and then RIGHT ARROW. The Reveal Codes screen should now display the following:

```
[Block][Cntr][BOLD]Introduction[bold][C/A/Flrt][HRt]
[HRt]
█
```

Now that you've marked the example as a block, press the <Style> key (ALT+F8), and type **3** for "Create." Next, type **1** for "Name," type **Heading** and press ENTER to indicate the name of the style. Then type **4** for "Codes," and the Reveal Codes screen will display the following:

```
[Cntr][BOLD][Comment][bold][C/A/Flrt][HRt]
[HRt]
```

You can see that WordPerfect has substituted the [Comment] code for the word "Introduction" in the marked block. (Remember that the [Comment] code represents the text that will be formatted when you apply the style.) Press the <Exit> key to return to the Style Edit screen. (At this point you could also modify other options.) Press the <Exit> key twice more to return to the document. You've now created a style by using an example format from the document.

APPLYING STYLES

You apply a style in basically the same way that you apply most format options in WordPerfect: by positioning the cursor or marking a block of text, and then issuing the command.

Open Styles

For an Open Style, you begin by positioning the cursor where you want the style to take effect. You then press the <Style> key (ALT+F8) and use the cursor keys to locate the style you want. (You can optionally press the <Search> key (F2) or type **N** for "Name Search," and then locate the style by simply typing the first few letters of its name. Press ENTER to leave Name Search.) Next, type **1** for "On," and you'll be returned to the document. An [Open Style:] code, which contains the style's name, will have been inserted in the document at the cursor position.

Paired Styles

You can apply a Paired Style either to text that you're about to type, or to text that already exists in the document.

For text that you're about to type, begin by positioning the cursor at the point where you want to type the text. Press the <Style> key (ALT+F8), and use the cursor keys to locate the style you want to apply. (You can optionally press the <Search> key (F2), and then use Name Search to locate the style by simply typing the first few letters of its name. Press ENTER to leave Name Search.) Next, type **1** for "On," and you'll be returned to the document.

WordPerfect inserts into the document [Style On:] and [Style Off:] codes that contain the name of the style. The cursor is placed between them, so that any text you type will be affected by the style. If you've so specified on the Style Edit menu, pressing ENTER can indicate that the style should be turned off (the cursor moves past the [Style Off:] code), or that the style should be turned off and then back on again (the cursor moves past the [Style Off:] code, and a new set of codes is inserted, with the cursor once again positioned between them). See "Enter Action" earlier in this chapter.

You can also manually turn off a style. Press the <Style> key (ALT+F8), and you'll see that the cursor bar is already placed on the style that is currently turned on. Type **2** for "Off," and you'll be returned to the document. The cursor will have moved past the [Style Off:] code.

For text that already exists in the document, begin by marking the text as a block. Then, press the <Style> key (ALT+F8), and use the cursor keys to locate the style you want to apply. (You can optionally use Name Search as described previously in this section.) Next, type **1** for "On," and you'll be returned to the document. The [Style On:] code will be placed at the beginning of the text marked as a block, and the [Style Off:] code will be placed at the end.

Style Codes

The codes that the program inserts when you apply a style ([Style On:] and [Style Off:] for a Paired Style, and [Open Style:] for an Open Style), actually represent the codes that make up the definition of the style. WordPerfect treats the codes exactly as if the actual codes in the style's definition were inserted in their place.

Normally, the style codes will display only the name of the style that they invoke. However, there is a way you can "peek" at the codes represented by the style codes without actually editing the style. To do this, first be sure that you are in Reveal Codes. Then position the cursor highlight onto one of the style codes. You'll see that the code expands to display all of the codes that are represented by the Style code. When you move the cursor highlight away from the Style code, it is restored to its normal, abbreviated form.

If you delete one of a matched pair of [Style On:] and [Style Off:] codes, its counterpart will also be automatically deleted.

EDITING STYLES

To edit the definition of a style, press the <Style> key (ALT+F8), and use the cursor keys to locate the style you want to edit. (You can optionally press the <Search> key (F2) or type **N** for "Name Search," and then locate the style by typing the first few letters of its name. Press ENTER to leave Name Search.) Next, type **4** for "Edit," and the Edit Style screen will appear. You can modify any of the options shown, as described in "Creating Styles" earlier in this chapter.

If you change an Open Style to a Paired Style, all of the codes included in the style's definition will appear *before* the [Comment] code. If you change a Paired Style to an Open Style, the codes that appear before the [Comment] code are retained, but the codes that appear after the [Comment] code are lost.

When you're through modifying the style options, press the <Exit> key to return to the Styles menu, and then press the <Exit> key again to return to the document.

When you modify the codes of a style, WordPerfect automatically reformats the entire document so that the text will reflect the changes you've made to the style. In this way, you can quickly and easily modify the format of an entire document.

MANAGING STYLES

WordPerfect has several functions for managing styles. You can delete unwanted styles, and you can save and retrieve a group of styles.

Deleting Styles

To delete a style, press the <Style> key (ALT+F8), and use the cursor keys to locate the style you want to delete. (You can optionally press the <Search> key (F2) and then use Name Search to locate the style by simxply typing the first few letters of its name. Press ENTER to leave Name Search.) Next, type **5** for "Delete" (or simply press DEL), and you'll see the prompt "Delete Style? (Y/N)" at the bottom of the screen. Type **Y** to confirm the deletion, or type **N** to abort the deletion. If you confirm the deletion, the style will be removed from the list.

Saving Styles

Styles are stored along with WordPerfect documents. However, you can easily create *empty* WordPerfect documents to be used solely for the storage of style definitions. You can then retrieve those styles into any other document. In addition, the ability to save styles provides a way to "clone" the format of an existing document.

To save the styles in the current document within a new empty document, begin by pressing the <Style> key (ALT+F8). Then, type **6** for "Save," and type a name for the empty document that will contain the styles. (You can optionally include a drive or path specification.) Press ENTER. If a document with the name you have specified already exists on disk, a prompt will appear asking for confirmation that you want to replace the existing document with a new, empty one. Type **Y** to confirm the replacement, or **N** to specify a new name. Once the document has been saved, press the <Exit> key to return to the Document Editing screen.

The current document's styles will be saved in a new, empty WordPerfect document. If you were to clear the screen and retrieve that document, the editing screen would be blank. However, the Styles menu for that document would display the styles you saved.

Retrieving Styles

You can easily retrieve the styles stored within one document into another. This makes it convenient for several documents to share the same styles. In addition, this capability permits you to switch a document between two or more different sets of styles.

To retrieve styles into a document, begin by pressing the <Style> key (ALT+F8). Then, type **7** for "Retrieve," and type the name of the document containing the styles that you want to copy into the current document. (You can optionally include a drive or path specification.) Press ENTER and WordPerfect will retrieve the styles from the specified document.

WordPerfect retrieves styles in much the same way that it retrieves documents. That is, the retrieved styles are *combined* with the styles already in the current document (those listed on the Styles screen). If you do not want to combine the styles, you will need to delete all of the defined styles individually (see the earlier section "Deleting Styles").

If one of the retrieved styles has the same name as one already resident, the *retrieved* style overwrites the *resident* style. Before WordPerfect actually overwrites any styles, it will display a prompt "Style(s) already exist. Replace? (Y/N)." Type **Y** to replace any styles with retrieved ones of the same name. Or, type **N** to prevent the replacement, but still retrieve any uniquely named styles.

STYLE LIBRARY FILE

WordPerfect allows you to maintain a Style Library File containing a set of styles that can be easily copied into new documents you create. This allows you to conveniently maintain a standard set of styles that all documents will share. If you later modify the styles in the Style Library File, you can individually update your documents so that they will use the new style definitions.

Creating the Style Library File

To create the Style Library File, begin with a blank screen. Create any styles that you want to be able to copy to new documents. (You can also retrieve the styles from another document. See "Retrieving Styles" in this chapter.) Next, save the Style Library File with either the Save option on the Styles menu or with the <Save> key. You may want to give files that contain only style definitions (such as the Style Library File) a unique extension such as .STY.

Specifying the Style Library File

To specify the location of the Style Library File, use the Setup function (see Appendix A, "Using Setup" for details). To begin, press the <Setup> key (SHIFT+F1). Type **7** for "Location of Auxiliary Files," and then **6** for "Style Library Filename." Now type the name of the document to be used as the Style Library File. The file you specify need not already exist.

You can optionally include a drive or path specification before the file name. If you omit one, WordPerfect assumes that the file is to be stored in the current default directory. For example, if the \WP\DOCS directory is the default directory when you start the Setup function, and you enter the file name STYLES at the "Style Library File" prompt, WordPerfect will from then on consider the \WP\DOCS\STYLES document to be the Style Library File.

After typing the name of the Style Library File, press ENTER. Press the <Exit> key (F7) to return to the document editing screen.

From now on, when you press the <Style> key in a document which has no previously defined styles, the program automatically copies the styles from the specified Style Library File into the current document.

Updating the Style Library

Once you've created and begun using a Style Library File, most of your documents will contain the styles from this file. However, you may subsequently edit the styles in the Style Library File. When you do this, you may want to update any document that has used the styles from the Style Library File, so that the document will use the new style definitions.

To do this, begin with the document you want to update on the screen. Press the <Style> key (ALT+F8), and type 8 for "Update." WordPerfect retrieves the styles from the Style Library File, replacing the old definitions. You'll need to repeat these steps for each document you want to update.

PRACTICE WITH STYLES

Let's try working with a document that uses a style. Make sure the screen is clear. Then follow these steps to create and supply a style:

1. Press the <Style> key (ALT+F8), and the Styles screen will appear.

   First, we'll create a "Heading" style for the document that is boldfaced, centered, and followed by one blank line.

2. Type **3** for "Create," and the Style Edit screen will appear.

3. Type **1** for "Name," type **Heading**, and press ENTER.

4. Type **3** for "Description," type **Major Section Heading**, and press ENTER.

5. Type **4** for "Codes," and you'll see a blank screen in Reveal Codes.

6. Press the <Center> key (SHIFT+F6) to center the line.

7. Press the <Bold> key (F6) to mark the heading for bold text.

8. Press RIGHT ARROW to move the cursor past the [Comment] code.

9. Press ENTER once to end the line, and then press ENTER again to leave a blank line after the heading.

   Now that the style has been properly formatted, we're ready to return to the Style Edit screen.

10. Press the <Exit> key (F7).

11. Type **5** for "Enter," and then **2** for "Off."

    This step modifies the style so that when you press ENTER after typing the Heading text, the style will be turned off automatically.

12. Press the <Exit> key (F7) to return to the Styles screen.

13. Type **1** for "On" to turn on the Heading style. You will be returned to the document editing screen.

14. Type **Introduction** and press ENTER.

    Notice that the heading you just typed appears centered, and in bold text. By pressing ENTER, you turned off the style. The cursor is now placed one blank line below the heading.

15. Press the <Reveal Codes> key (ALT+F3) to display the Reveal Codes screen.

    You can see that a [Style On:Heading] code appears at the beginning of the text you typed, and a [Style Off:Heading] appears at its end. The [Style Off:] code contains the two Hard Returns that end the heading line and leave a blank line (that's why no [HRt] codes are visible on the Reveal Codes screen).

Now that you've created and applied the first style, let's continue by typing text, and using the style again. Follow these steps:

1. Type the following text:

   This report will cover those aspects of the events which transpired last April that involve such parties as may otherwise have been engaged, regardless of their respective positions as pertaining to guilt or innocence.

2. Press ENTER to end the paragraph, and then press ENTER again to leave a blank line.

3. Press the <Style> key, and type **1** to turn on the "Heading" style.

4. Type **Event Summary** and press ENTER.

5. Type the following text:

   Below, you'll find summaries of all events pertaining to this report. Each one is a shortened version of another, longer document.

6. Press ENTER to end the paragraph.

Now, let's modify the Heading style's definition. Follow these steps:

1. Press the <Style> key, and type **4** for "Edit" to modify the definition of the Heading style.
2. Type **4** for "Codes," and the style's codes will be displayed.
3. Press RIGHT ARROW to position the cursor highlight onto the [BOLD] code, and press DEL to delete the code.
4. Press the <Underline> key (F8).
5. Press the <Exit> key three times to return to the Document Editing screen.

You can see that when you changed the Heading style definition, both headings changed their format. Your screen should look like the one in Figure 7-3.

<u>Introduction</u>

This report will cover those aspects of the events which transpired last April that involve such parties as may otherwise have been engaged, regardless of their respective positions as pertaining to guilt or innocence.

<u>Transpired Events</u>

Below, you'll find summaries of all events pertaining to this report. Each one is a shortened version of another, longer document.

—

Doc 1 Pg 1 Ln 13 Pos 10

Figure 7-3.   Sample document using a style for a heading

USING STYLES WITH MACROS

Once you've created a series of styles that you plan to use frequently, you may want to create macros (or redefine keys) to turn the styles on.

When you do this, be careful that the macro contains the right keystrokes to positively select the correct style. You would not want to use the arrow keys for this, because the number of styles might change between the time you define the macro and the time you use it. The best way to select a specific style is to use the Name Search function. From the Styles screen, press the <Search> key (F2), and type the *full name* of the style. Then press ENTER to leave Name Search. Now you've positively selected the style.

Another use for a macro or a redefined key would be to retrieve a set of styles from another document.

8

TEXT COLUMNS

WordPerfect can arrange your text into columns, up to twenty-four across a page. There are two basic types of columns you can produce

- Newspaper-style columns, which allow you to have text that continues from the bottom of one column to the top of the next.
- Parallel columns, which allow you to have columns of text that are always aligned along their top edge, whether the columns contain short side-by-side entries, or long entries that span several pages.

NEWSPAPER-STYLE COLUMNS

Use newspaper-style columns when you want to have continuous columns with text that "snakes" from one column to the other. That is, text will flow from the top of the first column to the bottom of the page, then to the top of the next column, then to the bottom of the page, and so on. When you have filled the last column on the page, text will continue on the first column of the following page. (You can also end a column at any point with the <Hard Column> key, as you will see later in this chapter.) You can right justify each of the columns independently, giving the final document a professional appearance. Figure 8-1 shows an example of a document on the screen formatted with newspaper-style columns.

PARALLEL COLUMNS

There are two different ways to use WordPerfect's Parallel Columns function. If you want two or more columns of text to always begin in the same place, but have the ability to continue for several pages if necessary (such as with screenplays), you would use normal parallel columns. If you want small amounts of text ("entries") to appear side-by-side on a page (such as in an address list, or a feature and benefit chart), you would use parallel columns with block protection. Block protection prevents any

---

There is a distribution for a mutual fund.

The records of all those transactions where the client has purchased shares in the fund must be updated as to the current distribution amounts.

The current distribution amount is added to the distributions-to-date amount for each transaction.

Also, all those mutual fund transactions that specifiy a client request for reinvestment of shares distributed must maintain the amount of the current reinvestment as well as the share price and number of

shares involved as of the transaction date. The number of shares reinvested is added to the reinvested shares-to-date amount.

A client purchases shares in a mutual fund.

Operator is prompted for client name, mutual fund name, date and amount of investment, the original share price, and whether the client has requested reinvestment of distributions for this transaction.

The Client DBMS will then calculate the number of shares purchased based on the investment amount and the original price per share.

Col 2 Doc 1 Pg 1 Ln 24 Pos 45

Figure 8-1.   Newspaper-style columns

of the entries in each group of entries from extending onto a subsequent page. Instead, the entire group is moved to the next page.

Parallel columns with block protection can also be useful for
tables where one column consists of many lines—for example, in
a list of personal information on clients in which one of the entries
consists of a four-line address, but in which each other entry is
only one line long.

Without the Parallel Columns function, you would have to
create documents with side-by-side text by using the TAB key to
separate the columns, like this:

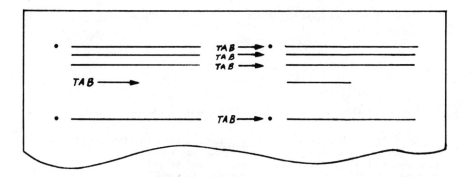

This method makes it nearly impossible to reformat the text, since
the column entries are not treated as separate and distinct sections of text.

With the Parallel Columns function, however, each entry is an
independent section of text and will be formatted separately from
the other columns on the page, as illustrated below:

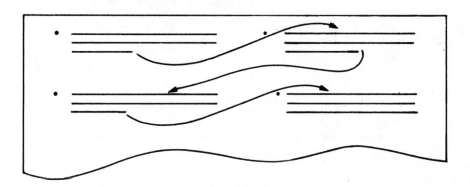

When text is edited, deleted, or inserted, it reformats only within its column. Figure 8-2 shows an example of a document on the screen with parallel columns. For this example you would probably choose parallel columns with block protection.

USING COLUMNS

To use newspaper-style or parallel columns, you must follow these steps:

1. Set your left and right margins to leave enough room for all the columns.

Columns: The Column function allows you to format text into columns that will be displayed on screen as well as on the printed output.

Indexing: You can mark individual words or phrases to be included in an index.

Undelete: Three levels of deleted text are stored in memory and can be "recovered".

Thesaurus: With the Thesaurus function you can ask WordPerfect to look up synonyms for any word.

Shell: You can temporarily exit WordPerfect and perform any DOS command without having to save and re-load your document.

Word Search: You can use the Word Search function to search through the files on your disk to find a particular word or phrase.

Col 1 Doc 1 Pg 1 Ln 19 Pos 10

Figure 8-2.   Parallel columns

2. Define the column layout, including the number of columns to be used.

3. Turn on Column mode.

4. Enter the text.

5. Turn off Column mode.

DEFINING THE FORMAT

Before you can use columns in your document, you need to define the column layout. This step tells WordPerfect how many columns you will use, which type they are, and where they will be placed on the page.

To define column formats, position the cursor at the place in your document where you want columns to begin. If you want WordPerfect to calculate the column margin settings for you, set the left and right margins first. The left margin setting will control the position of the left edge of the far-left column, and the right margin setting will control the position of the right edge of the far-right column. Make sure your margins leave enough room to accommodate all your columns. During the column definition in the next step, margin settings for the individual columns will be specified.

Press the <Math/Columns> key (ALT+F7) and type **4** for "Column def." The Text Column Definition screen is displayed, as shown in Figure 8-3. Default options are provided for each of the prompts shown. You can either accept them all (for two evenly spaced newspaper-style columns a half-inch apart), or type the number of any option to change it.

The first prompt allows you to choose the type of columns you want. To change it, type **1** for "Type," then type **1** for newspaper-style columns, **2** for normal parallel columns, or **3** for parallel columns with block protection. The screen will reflect your choice.

Next, you can specify how many columns you want across the page. The default option is two columns. To change this, type **2** for "Number of Columns," type the number of columns desired (from 2 to 24), and press ENTER.

```
Text Column Definition

     1 - Type                          Newspaper

     2 - Number of Columns             2

     3 - Distance Between Columns

     4 - Margins

     Column   Left    Right    Column   Left    Right
        1:    1"      4"          13:
        2:    4.5"    7.5"        14:
        3:                        15:
        4:                        16:
        5:                        17:
        6:                        18:
        7:                        19:
        8:                        20:
        9:                        21:
       10:                        22:
       11:                        23:
       12:                        24:

Selection: 0
```

Figure 8-3.   The Text Column Definition screen

You then specify the distance WordPerfect should leave between each column. By changing this value, WordPerfect will be able to calculate the exact column margins. However, you can simply adjust the column margins manually and ignore this option.

To calculate the column margins, WordPerfect first figured the total amount of horizontal space available between the left and right margins that were current when you entered the Text Column Definition screen. Then, taking into account the number of columns specified, it subtracted the amount of space to be left between columns. It divided the remaining distance by the total number of columns to determine each column's width, and calculated the margin settings for each column.

If you want to modify the column margins that WordPerfect has calculated for you, type **4** for "Margins." Enter the positions of the left and right margin for each column you've specified. To leave a margin setting as is, simply press ENTER. When you've pressed ENTER for the last column, the cursor will return to the menu. You can also press the <Exit> key (F7) at any time to return to the menu.

Once you have set the options for the columns, press the <Exit> key, and you'll be returned to the Math/Columns menu. A [Col Def:] code will have been inserted into the text at the cursor position. Any columns of text that follow the code will use the format you entered, until the system encounters another such code.

CREATING COLUMNS

After defining the column format, you create the columns by entering WordPerfect's Column mode.

Entering Column Mode

To enter Column mode, press the <Math/Columns> key (ALT+F7), and type **3**. (If you've just defined columns, you'll already be at the Math/Columns menu and you can simply type **3**.) Unlike some other WordPerfect modes (such as the Typeover or Outline mode), entering Column mode places a hidden code [Col On] into the text at the cursor position. To stop using columns, press the <Math/Columns> key and type **3** again. A hidden code [Col Off] is placed in the text. When the cursor is located anywhere between a [Col On] code and a [Col Off] code, WordPerfect will be in Column mode. When you move the cursor out of this area, WordPerfect will not be in Column mode.

When WordPerfect is in Column mode, the indicator line at the bottom of the screen includes a "Col" reference, like this:

Col 1 Doc 1 Pg 1 Ln 1 Pos 10

This indicates that the program is ready to use columns.

Once you have defined the column format, you can go in and out of Column mode as often as you like without having to redefine the format each time. For example, you can create a headline that stretches across several columns. You can use any combination of column text and normal text within a single document or page.

Continuing To the Next Column

When you are in Column mode, the <Hard Page Break> key (CTRL+ENTER) becomes the <Hard Column> key and is used to force the beginning of a new column. The key sequence produces slightly different results depending on which type of column you are using.

Parallel Columns

If you are using parallel columns, press the <Hard Column> key to create a new entry in the next column. When you have entered text in the last column, the new entry starts again at the left margin. What actually happens is that Column mode is temporarily turned off, returning the cursor to the beginning of the next line. A Hard Return is inserted, separating your entries with a blank line, and Column mode is turned back on. (If you're using parallel columns with block protection, WordPerfect also inserts Block Protection codes at this point.) You can then type the next group of entries.

If you've just typed the last entry in a group of entries, and you *do not* want to begin a new group of entries with the <Hard Column> key —that is, you want to return to normal text— simply turn Column mode off by pressing the <Math/Columns> key (ALT+F7) and typing 3.

When Column mode is turned off and back on with the Hard Column sequence, one blank line is always inserted below the last line of the longest entry in the previous group. For example, say you are working with three columns. Your first entry is 6 lines long, your second entry is 12 lines long, and your third entry is 4 lines long. If you press the <Hard Column> key, the cursor will appear two lines below the second entry, which is 12 lines long.

Newspaper-style Columns

With newspaper-style columns, text continues in the next column when it reaches the bottom of the page. Pressing the <Hard Column> key (CTRL+ENTER), however, forces the column to end before it normally would, just as this key forces the *page* to end before it normally would when you are not using columns. Text then continues in the next defined column to the right. If you are in the last column when you press the <Hard Column> key, the function generates a Hard Page Break, and the text continues with the first column of the next page.

When you turn off Column mode, the cursor is placed below the bottom line of the columns at the left margin. You can then type text without columns within the current left and right margins. When you want to begin typing text in columns again, turn Column mode back on.

Cursor Control in Column Mode

Most of WordPerfect's cursor-control functions work in the usual way when in Column mode. However, some will be confined to the current column. For example, pressing the END key will move the cursor to the end of the line *within the current column.*

To move the cursor to the next column, press the <Go to> key (CTRL+HOME), and then press RIGHT ARROW. To move the cursor to the previous column, press the <Go to> key, and then press LEFT ARROW.

To move the cursor to the last column, press the <Go to> key, press the HOME key, and then press the RIGHT ARROW key. To move the cursor to the first column, press the <Go to> key, press the HOME key, and then press the LEFT ARROW key.

SOME PRACTICE EXAMPLES

Here are some examples to give you practice using parallel and newspaper-style columns.

Parallel Columns

Make sure the screen is clear. Then follow this exercise first to define the column format for two parallel columns a half-inch apart and then to produce a document with parallel columns in the format you have defined.

1. Make sure your margins are set for one inch on both the left and the right.

   Note: Your screen will only match the illustrations shown here if you have a 10-pitch font selected as your default font. See Chapter 11, "Using Printers."

2. Press the <Math/Columns> key (ALT+F7).

3. Type **4** for "Column def."

   You will see the Text Column Definition screen.

4. Type **1** for "Type."

5. Type **3** for "Parallel with block protect."

6. Press the <Exit> key (F7).

7. Type **3** to turn on Column mode.

   You will see the "Col 1" indicator at the bottom of the screen.

8. Type * and press the <Indent> key (F4).

9. Type the following text:

All of the text that follows will, in fact, be completely contained within the first column.

10. Press the <Hard Column> key (CTRL+ENTER).

    The cursor moves to the top of the next column, which starts at position 4.5″, creating a new entry.

11. Type * and press the <Indent> key.

12. Type the following text:

    This text will appear in the second column, right next to the text we typed for the first column.

The screen will look like the one in Figure 8-4.

```
*   All of the text that          *   This text will appear in
    follows will, in fact, be         the second column, right
    completely contained             next to the text we typed
    within the first column.         for the first column._
```

Col 2 Doc 1 Pg 1 Ln 4 Pos 71

Figure 8-4.   Creating parallel columns

13. Press the <Hard Column> key.

14. Type * and press the <Indent> key.

15. Type the following text:

   This is the first entry of the second group of entries on this page.

16. Press ENTER twice and then press the <Indent> key.

17. Type the following text:

   This is a second paragraph that is also a part of the first entry of the second group of entries.

18. Press the <Hard Column> key.

19. Type * and press the <Indent> key.

20. Type the following text:

   This is the second entry in the second group.

21. Press the <Hard Column> key.

   The screen will look like the one in Figure 8-5.

Newspaper-style Columns

Clear the screen, and then follow these steps to produce a document using newspaper-style columns:

1. Press the <Math/Columns> key (ALT+F7) and type **4** for "Column def."

2. Press the <Exit> key (F7) to accept all default options.

3. Type **3** to turn on Column mode.

   Now that you have defined the column format and turned on Column mode, you are ready to enter the column text. To reduce the amount of text you will need to type, you will first reduce the page length to two inches by increasing the bottom margin to nine inches.

4. Press the <Format> key (SHIFT+F8).

All of the text that follows will, in fact, be completely contained within the first column.

This text will appear in the second column, right next to the text we typed for the first column.

This is the first entry of the second group of entries on this page.

This is the second entry in the second group.

This is the second paragraph that is also a part of the first entry of the second group of entries.

Col 1 Doc 1 Pg 1 Ln 16 Pos 10

Figure 8-5. Creating parallel columns with several groups of entries

5. Type **2** for "Page," and **5** for "Margins."
6. Press ENTER to leave the top margin, type **9**, and press ENTER for the bottom margin.
7. Press the <Exit> key (F7) to clear the menu.
8. Type the following text:

   Also, all those mutual fund transactions that specify a client request for reinvestment of shares distributed must maintain the amount of the current reinvestment as well as the share price and number of shares involved as of the transaction date.

   Notice that when you reach the end of a page (which is very short for this example) the text automatically continues at the top of the second column.

9. Press HOME, HOME, UP ARROW, which will position the cursor on the first letter in the word "Also" at the top of the first column on the first page. (Use Reveal Codes to see that the cursor is positioned after the hidden codes.)

10. Type the following text:

     The number of shares reinvested is added to the reinvested shares-to-date amount.

11. Press SPACE BAR twice to separate the sentences and press DOWN ARROW once to reformat the text.

The screen will look like the one in Figure 8-6.

```
The number of shares              specify a client request for
reinvested is added to the        reinvestment of shares
reinvested shares-to-date         distributed must maintain the
amount.  Also, all those          amount of the current
mutual fund transactions that     reinvestments as well as the
```
```
share price and number of
shares involved as of the
transaction date.
```

Col 1 Doc 1 Pg 1 Ln 5 Pos 19

Figure 8-6.   Creating newspaper-style columns

Notice how the text from the second column "snaked" to the first column of the second page.

LIMITATIONS OF THE COLUMN FUNCTION

Many of WordPerfect's functions can be used when you work in Column mode. For example, the Tabs, Align Tabs, Flush Right, and Center functions all work normally within the confines of the current column.

However, there are some functions that cannot be used when you are in Column mode. These include the following:

- Footnotes (Endnotes work fine, however)
- Margin changes
- New column format definitions (turn Column mode off before defining a new column format)
- The Sort function

When you press the <Move> key (CTRL+F4) while marking a block of text, choice 2 is "Tabular Column." This *does not* refer to the multiple columns discussed in this chapter. Rather, it refers to columns that you separate by pressing the TAB key. You should not use this command with parallel or newspaper-style columns. You can, however, use the normal commands (Move Sentence, Move Paragraph, Move Page, or Block Move) to move text within, between, into, and out of columns.

9

MATH

Although WordPerfect's Math function lacks the sophistication of a spreadsheet program, it can nonetheless perform many types of calculation on numbers within a document. With this function, you can total and subtotal columns; you can even create simple mathematic formulas that add, subtract, multiply, and divide the numbers in the columns.

For example, WordPerfect can calculate a billing statement for you. The program can total current and past services, subtract payments received, and present a grand total for the payment due. An example of a statement of this type is shown on the screen in Figure 9-1. The Math function can also be used to calculate totals of sales figures that you have arranged in columns.

THE MATH PROCESS

To use the Math function, you follow these basic steps:

1. Set tab stops for the columns you plan to use.
2. Define your *math columns*.
3. Turn on Math mode.
4. Enter text and numbers into the *math area*.

5. Calculate the *math area*.

6. Turn off Math mode.

You can have as many math areas as you want in your document. Simply repeat the steps listed above for each math area that you want to define. If the tab settings and math columns have been previously established in your document, you can skip the first two steps.

There are two ways the Math function can calculate numbers for you: down columns and across lines. You enter special *math operators* to calculate different types of totals down individual columns, and you enter *formulas* to compute totals and to perform other calculations across individual lines.

```
                       Law Offices of
                  Jablonski and Kurtweiler

CURRENT SERVICES

Client meeting, Jones - 6/2/84           65.00
Telephone - 3/4/84                       34.00
Telephone - 5/2/84                       23.00

Total Current Services                  122.00+

PAST SERVICES

Court Appearance - 1/4/84                87.00
Telephone - 2/12/84                      23.00

Total Past Services                     110.00+


TOTAL SERVICES RENDERED                 232.00=
PAYMENTS RECEIVED                     T-110.00

TOTAL AMOUNT DUE                        122.00×
  -
                          Doc 1 Pg 1 Ln 24 Pos 10
```

Figure 9-1.   Example of a math document

PREPARING TO USE THE MATH FUNCTION

Before you can actually start using the Math function, you must set tab stops to position the math columns, create and define the columns in the column definition process, and then turn on Math mode.

Setting Tabs

The tab stops you set determine the position and width of your math columns. If you later want to reposition the math columns, you can change the tab stops by inserting a new [Tab Set:] code after the old one.

Set your tab stops where you want the decimal points in each column to be aligned. If you will not be using decimal points in your numbers, set the tab stops where you want to right align the numbers. You need to make sure that the tab stops you set leave enough room for the numbers that the Math function will calculate. If you do not, the results of the calculations will not be accurate, since the numbers will overlap.

The first math column (column A) will have its numbers aligned at the first tab stop you define. You cannot use numbers entered at the left margin (before pressing TAB) in your calculations. However, you can enter *labels* at the left margin for lines that contain numbers in math columns to the right.

Note: To keep track of the column positions when you use the Math function, use the Window function to show a ruler at the bottom of the screen. The ruler will always display the current tab settings. To use a ruler, press the <Screen> key (CTRL+F3), type **1** for "Window," type **23**, and press ENTER.

After you have positioned your columns, you may want to type text at the top of each one to label it. For example, you may want to type "Sales" at the top of a column containing sales figures or

"Price" at the top of a column containing prices. You should type in these labels after setting tabs but *before* turning on Math mode because some keys work differently when you are in Math mode.

Defining Math Columns

After you have set the tab stops you plan to use (and entered any necessary column labels), you need to define the Math columns. The Math column definition process allows you to specify whether each column will contain numbers or text. You also specify how many digits you want to the right of the decimal point in numbers calculated by the Math function, as well as whether negative numbers should be preceded by a minus sign or enclosed in parentheses. If you will be calculating across lines, as described later in the chapter, you also enter the formulas you plan to use.

The default settings for the Math column definition are for all columns to contain numbers, for calculated numbers to contain two digits to the right of the decimal point, and for negative numbers to be enclosed in parentheses. If these defaults are satisfactory and you do not plan to calculate across lines, you can skip the entire definition process and proceed with turning on Math mode as described in the next section.

To define the Math columns, move the cursor to where you want the math area to begin (making sure it is after any column labels), press the <Math/Columns> key (ALT+F7), and type 2 for "Math Def." The Math Definition screen appears, as shown in Figure 9-2.

You can have up to 24 math columns, each identified with a single letter from A to X. Across the top of the screen are the letters that indicate the individual columns. Below each letter are settings for that particular column. You need to change the settings only for those columns you intend to use, and only for those that differ from the default settings. While the Math Definition screen is displayed, you can freely move the cursor to any setting using the arrow keys.

```
Math Definition          Use arrow keys to position cursor

Columns                  A B C D E F G H I J K L M N O P Q R S T U V W X

Type                     2 2 2 2 2 2 2 2 2 2 2 2 2 2 2 2 2 2 2 2 2 2 2 2

Negative Numbers         ( ( ( ( ( ( ( ( ( ( ( ( ( ( ( ( ( ( ( ( ( ( ( (

Number of Digits to      2 2 2 2 2 2 2 2 2 2 2 2 2 2 2 2 2 2 2 2 2 2 2 2
  the Right (0-4)

Calculation      1
   Formulas      2
                 3
                 4

Type of Column:
      0 = Calculation    1 = Text     2 = Numeric    3 = Total

Negative Numbers
      ( = Parentheses (50.00)         - = Minus Sign  -50.00


Press Exit when done
```

Figure 9-1.   Math Definition screen

Note: While working with the Math function, you may find it difficult to keep track of how you have defined each column. To help you with this, keep a written copy of the column definitions handy.

When you are finished entering your math column definition, press the <Exit> key (F7). You will return to the Math/Columns menu, ready to turn on Math mode as described in the next section. A [Math Def:] hidden code that contains the settings you just specified will have been inserted into the text at the cursor position.

Each of the settings on the Math Definition screen is described in detail in the following sections.

Setting Column Type

The first setting is for the column type, which you choose from a menu at the bottom of the screen.

Formulas perform addition and other calculations across lines, instead of down columns. Type **0** (for a Calculation column) if the column will contain a formula. The cursor will move to the middle of the screen, where you can enter the formula for the column. You can have only four Calculation columns per math area. (See "Calculating Across Lines" later in this chapter for a discussion of formulas.)

Type **1** to define a Text column if you will have a label or other text in the middle of a math area. For example, you may want to produce a table of sales figures with salespeople's initials in the fourth column. Specifying a Text column will prevent the column's entries from being included in any totals or formulas, even if you enter a number into the column. (WordPerfect will not, however, prevent you from entering, in a Calculation column, a formula containing a reference to a Text column. When the formula is calculated, it will treat the text in the column as having a value of zero.) Specifying a column as a Text column also tells WordPerfect to treat any characters you later type in that column as ordinary characters rather than as special math operators.

Type **2** (for a Numeric column) if the column will contain numbers. You can also place *math operators* in a numeric column to perform subtotals, totals, and grand totals. These operators are displayed on the screen but are not printed.

Type **3** (for a Total column) if the column will contain *offset totals*. This special type of total is derived from the numbers that are in the column to the *left* of the Total column, instead of from the Total column itself. Offset totals are frequently used in accounting reports.

Setting Negative Number Format

Next you select the format you want for negative numbers resulting from calculations. You can choose to have the numbers either enclosed in parentheses (the default) or preceded by a minus sign. Type a minus sign to change the format from the default setting.

Setting the Number of Digits After the Decimal

The last setting on the Math Definition screen allows you to select the number of digits you want after the decimal point in all calculations for each column. You can type any number from 0 to 4. Note that the Math function will format only the numbers that are calculated, not numbers that you enter. However, for consistency, you can enter numbers in the same format as the format you specify here for calculated numbers.

Turning Math Mode On and Off

After defining your columns, you enter Math mode to create a *math area* in your document. While in Math mode, you enter the text and numbers in the columns you previously defined. After pressing <Exit> to end Math column definition, type **1** for "Math On" to turn on Math mode. If you skipped the definition process, you will first need to press the <Math/Columns> key (ALT+F7). The following message appears at the bottom of the screen:

Math

A hidden code, [Math On], is inserted into the document at the cursor position.

After you have entered the text and numbers for this math area (as described in the next section), you will press the <Math/Columns> key (ALT+F7) and type **1** for "Math off." The "Math" message will disappear from the screen, and a hidden code, [Math Off], will be inserted into the document. Each math area is defined by these two hidden codes. When the cursor is positioned between them, you will see the "Math" message displayed at the bottom of the screen, indicating that Math mode is on.

USING THE MATH FUNCTION

After following the steps described in the previous section, you enter text, numbers, and math operators into the math area, and then you calculate the results.

Entering Text, Numbers, and Operators

Press the TAB key to move the cursor to the first Math column you want to use. If the column you tab to is defined as a Numeric, Calculation, or Total column, the TAB key will *automatically* perform the Tab Align function (and you will see the "Align Char = ." message at the bottom of the screen). That is because these columns usually contain numbers with decimal points that need to be aligned. The TAB key will function normally (that is, it will left align your text) when you tab to a Text column.

After positioning the cursor at the column you wish to use, enter the number, math operator, or text that you want to appear in the column. (Math operators are described in the section "Calculating Down Columns" later in this chapter.) Then, press TAB to move to the next column, or press ENTER to end the line.

If the column you tab to is a Calculation column, you will see an exclamation point (!) after you tab to the column. This indicates that the result of a formula will be placed at this point when the math area is calculated. (Since the Math function automatically performs the Tab Align function when you tab to a Calculation column, the decimal point of the result will be aligned at the column's tab position.) To continue, press the TAB key to move to the next column, or press ENTER to end the line. If you do not wish a result to be placed at this position, simply press BACK-SPACE to erase the ! before continuing. You can separate the lines in the math area by any number of blank lines, if you wish.

Calculating a Math Area

When you want WordPerfect to calculate the numbers in a math area, you use the Calculate command. Make sure that the cursor is positioned within the math area (the "Math" message should be displayed at the bottom of the screen). Then press the <Math/Columns> key (ALT+F7) and type **2** for "Calculate." All formulas and totals in the current math area will be updated.

Subtotal, Total, and Grand Total operators will only add numbers that are within the math area in which the operators are located. For example, a Subtotal operator will not include in its result numbers that were entered in a previous math area.

If WordPerfect cannot evaluate one of your formulas, it will produce "??" in place of a result. Check the formula by positioning the cursor immediately after the [Math Def:] code you generated earlier and repeating the Math column definition process.

CALCULATING DOWN COLUMNS

The characters +, =, *, t, T, and N all function as math operators when entered in Math mode. The operators are not printed, even though they appear on the screen. Because these characters function differently from the way they usually do (you can tell they are different because they are bold and appear in square brackets on the Reveal Codes screen), you cannot enter them into a normal document and then later add the [Math Def:] and [Math On] codes. You must enter the operators while Math mode is turned on, or WordPerfect will not recognize them as math operators.

To insert one of the operators, you simply type the character, instead of or with a number, in a column. You can precede any math operator with a dollar sign or other symbol that you want to appear in front of the number when it is calculated.

Math Operators

Here are the math operators you can use and the function each performs

> **+ Subtotal** This character adds all of the numbers above it that are in the same column. If you place the character in the document after another Subtotal operator, it will add all the numbers that appear *after* that operator.

> **= Total** This character adds all of the subtotals above it that are in the same column. If you place the character in the document after another Total operator, then it will add all the subtotals that appear *after* that operator.

Name	Sales
John	54,000
Mary	23,500
Julie	62,750
Frank	87,250
George	23,000
Paul	140,750
Mellissa	40,500
Ringo	35,250
Steve	125,000
Dale	96,500
Total:	+
−	

Math   Doc 1 Pg 1 Ln 15 Pos 10

Figure 9-3. Example of a math document with a Subtotal operator

* Grand Total   This character adds all of the totals above it that are in the same column. If you place the character in the document after another Grand Total operator, it will add all the totals that appear after that operator.

Figure 9-3 shows an example of a column of figures on the screen with a Subtotal operator at the bottom.

When you place one of these operators in a column that has been defined as a Total column (see "Setting Column Type" earlier in this chapter), the operator will perform its function on numbers and totals that appear in the column to its left, creating an offset total. This allows subtotals, totals, and grand totals to be broken out from the columns of numbers that they are adding. An example of an offset total is shown in Figure 9-4.

Name	Sales
John	54,000
Mary	23,500
Julie	62,750
Frank	87,250
George	23,000
Paul	140,750
Mellissa	40,500
Ringo	35,250
Steve	125,000
Dale	96,500

Total Sales ------------>   688,500+

‒

Figure 9-4.   Example of a math document with an offset total

If there are no totals of the proper type in the previous column, then the function will work normally with numbers and totals from within the same column. For example, let's say you have a document with numbers in the third column, like the one shown in Figure 9-5.

In the fourth column (which you have defined as a Total column), you have periodic subtotals of the numbers in the third column. At the end of the report, you want a total of all the subtotals in the fourth column. You can simply place the = operator in the fourth column; since there are no subtotals in the third column, it will add up the subtotals in the fourth column as it would if the column were not defined as a Total column.

	Text Column	Numeric Column	Totals Column
	↓	↓	↓
<u>Name</u>	<u>Dept</u>	<u>Salary</u>	
John	ACCT	54,000	
Mary	ACCT	23,500	
Julie	ACCT	62,750	
Frank	ACCT	87,250	
	Sub-Total:		227,500+
George	PERS	23,000	
Paul	PERS	140,750	
Mellissa	PERS	40,500	
Ringo	PERS	35,250	
	Sub-Total:		239,500+
Steve	DATA	125,000	
Dale	DATA	96,500	
Jim	DATA	235,500	
Fred	DATA	165,000	
	Sub-Total:		622,000+
	SALARY TOTAL:		1,089,000=

Math   Doc 1 Pg 1 Ln 22 Pos 10

Figure 9-5. Example of a math document with an offset column for totals

Forced Total Operators

There are three other math operators that you can place in a Math column. You place the first two before a number to force the Math function to treat the number *as if it were a calculated subtotal or total*. The last is used to force a negative value.

t Subtotal Number   When you type this character before a number in a Math column, the number is treated as if it had been calculated as a subtotal by the Math function. It will then be included in any subsequent total calculations.

T Total Number   When you type this character before a number in a Math column, the number is treated as if it had been calculated as a total by the Math function. It will then be included in any subsequent grand total calculations.

N Negative Number   When you type this character before a number or math operator in a Math column, the number (or result) is considered a negative value in subsequent subtotals, totals, and grand totals.

SOME PRACTICE EXAMPLES

Follow these steps to create a simple document that uses some of these special math operators. Make sure the screen is clear.

1. Press the <Screen> key (CTRL+F3) and type **1** for "Window."

2. Type **23** and press ENTER.

   This sets the size of the current window to 23 lines, causing a ruler to appear at the bottom of the screen. The ruler is useful when you are using the Math function, since it displays the current tab settings.

3. Press the <Format> key (SHIFT+F8), type **1** for "Line Format," and **8** for "Tab Set."

4. Press the <Delete End-Of-Line> key (CTRL+END).

5. Type **3.5** and press ENTER.

6. Type **4.5**, press ENTER, and then press the <Exit> key (F7) twice.

   This sets tab stops at 3.5″ and 4.5″ for two Math columns. The ruler will reflect the two tab stops you have defined.

7. Press the <Tab Align> key (CTRL+F6).

8. Press the <Underline> key (F8), type **Sales**, press the <Underline> key again, and press ENTER twice.

9. Press the <Math/Columns> key (ALT+F7) and type **2** for "Math def."

   For this exercise, column A needs to be defined as a Numeric column. Since this is the default setting, you can skip the entry.

10. Press RIGHT ARROW.

11. Type **3** to define column B as a total column.

12. Press DOWN ARROW twice, then press LEFT ARROW twice.

13. Type **0** and then **0** again to set a format of zero decimal places for calculated numbers in both columns.

14. Press the <Exit> key.

15. Type **1** to turn on Math mode.

    You will see the message "Math" appear at the bottom of the screen. Now you are ready to enter labels and numbers in the math area.

16. Press the <Bold> key (F6), type **S.F. Office**, press the <Bold> key, and then press ENTER.

17. Type **John**, press TAB, type **54,000**, and press ENTER.

18. Type **Mary**, press TAB, type **23,500**, and press ENTER.

19. Type **Julie**, press TAB, type **62,750**, and press ENTER twice.

20. Type **Total**, press TAB, type + (a plus sign), and press ENTER twice.

    The plus sign indicates that you want the Math function to subtotal the numbers in the column above. Your screen will look like the one shown in Figure 9-6.

21. Press the <Math/Columns> key (ALT+F7).

```
                    Sales

S.F. Office
John            54,000
Mary            23,500
Julie           62,750

Total               +


  _
```

Math   Doc 1 Pg 1 Ln 10 Pos 10

Figure 9-6.   Example of a math document with Subtotal operator

Notice that choice 2 is "Math Def" when you are not in Math mode but "Calculate" when you are in Math mode. You must be in Math mode (when the cursor is in a math area) to perform calculations.

22. Type **2** for "Calculate."

The screen will look like the one shown in Figure 9-7.

That's all there is to using the Math function to add a column of numbers. This example used the Subtotal operator; the next example uses the Total operator to add two subtotals. With the text from the previous exercise still on the screen, follow these steps:

                    <u>Sales</u>

S.F. Office
John   54,000
Mary   23,500
Julie   62,750

Total   140,250+

        —

Math   Doc 1 Pg 1 Ln 10 Pos 10

Figure 9-7.　Example of a math document with a calculated Subtotal operator

1. Using the same procedure as in the previous exercise, enter the following text and numbers directly under the previous text:

```
L.A. Office
Bill            65,000
Frank           32,000
Linda           12,250

Total                +
```

Your screen should look like the one shown in Figure 9-8.

2. After typing + in the last line, press ENTER twice, press the <Bold> key, type **WEST COAST:**, and press the <Bold> key again.

```
                Sales

S.F. Office
Julie           62,750
John            54,000
Mary            23,500

Total          140,250+

L.A. Office
Bill            65,000
Frank           32,000
Linda           12,250

Total                +_
```

Math   Doc 1 Pg 1 Ln 15 Pos 36

Figure 9-8.   Example of a math document with two Subtotal operators

3. Press TAB and type = (an equal sign).

The equal sign indicates that you want the Math function to total the two subtotals that appear above it.

4. Press ENTER twice.

5. Press the <Math/Columns> key, and type 2 for "Calculate."

Your screen should look like the one shown in Figure 9-9.

This example used the Total operator to add two subtotals. The next exercise will use the Grand Total operator to add two totals.

Although you could place the Grand Total operator in the same column as the Total operators, in this exercise you will place it in the next column to the right, creating an offset total. This makes the number more noticeable. The number will calculate properly,

```
Total            140,250+

L.A. Office
Bill             65,000
Frank            32,000
Linda            12,256

Total            109,250+

WEST COAST:      249,500=

-
```

Math   Doc 1 Pg 1 Ln 19 Pos 10

Figure 9-9.   Example of a math document with a Total operator

since you defined column B (the second column) as a Total column.

1. Following the same steps as in the first exercise, enter the following text and numbers below the previous text:

```
N.Y. Office
Rachelle          87,000
Alphonzo          54,250
Jim               31,000

Total:                +

Boston Office
Skippy            92,500
Biff              42,250
Muffy             39,750

Total:                +

EAST COAST:           =
```

Your screen should look like the one shown in Figure 9-10.

2. After typing = in the last line, press ENTER three times, press the <Bold> key, type **TOTAL COMPANY SALES:**, and press the <Bold> key again.

3. Press the TAB key *twice* and type *

4. Press ENTER.

5. Press the <Math/Columns> key and type **2** for "Calculate."

The number 596,250 will appear as the grand total for all of the sales figures you entered. The next exercise uses the Total Number operator to enter a sales total that is not actually calculated by the Math function.

1. Move the cursor to the line below the line that starts "EAST COAST."

2. Press ENTER, press the <Bold> key, type **EUROPE:**, and press the <Bold> key again.

3. Press the TAB key and type **T154,000**

4. Press ENTER.

```
Bill             65,000
Frank            32,000
Linda            12,250

Total           109,250+

WEST COAST:     249,500=


N.Y. Office
Rachelle         87,000
Alphonzo         54,250
Jim              31,000

Total:                +

Boston Office
Skippy           92,500
Biff             42,250
Muffy            39,750

Total:                +

EAST COAST:          =_
Math
                                    Doc 1 Pg 1 Ln 34 Pos 36
```

Figure 9-10.   Example of a math document with two Total operators

5. Press the <Math/Columns> key and type **2** for "Calculate."

Notice that the "Total Company Sales" now reflects the sales from the European Division.

CALCULATING ACROSS LINES

The math operators described in the previous section total numbers only down columns. To total numbers and perform other calculations across lines, WordPerfect uses math formulas that you enter during the Math column definition process. When you enter a formula for a column, it applies to every line in that column. You cannot use different formulas for individual lines in a single column without turning off Math mode and redefining the Math columns.

You can use formulas to calculate tax and commission amounts, as well as averages and totals of numbers (or other totals) on the same line.

Using Formulas

To use a formula for a column entry in a line, type **0** for the column type on the Math Definition screen. (See "Defining Math Columns" earlier in this chapter.) The cursor will move to the middle of the screen, where you enter the formula. You can enter formulas for up to four columns in each math area.

Formulas can contain numbers, letters identifying other column entries on the same line, and common math operators. You cannot use values from other lines in a formula. (The math operators used in a formula are different from the math operators used to subtotal, total, and grand total columns of numbers.) Column letters can be either uppercase or lowercase. Here is a list of math operators you can use in a formula:

Operator	Function
+	Addition
−	Subtraction
*	Multiplication
/	Division

Math formulas are usually calculated from left to right. You can use parentheses to affect the order of calculation, but you cannot *nest* them. That is, you cannot use a set of parentheses within another set. The numbers and operators in parentheses are evaluated before the rest of the formula.

To enter a negative number into a formula, type a minus sign (−) and then the number. To use a positive column value as a negative number, or vice versa, type a minus sign (−) and then the column letter.

Following are some examples of formulas and their results. Let's assume that in one line, column A contains the number 350 and, in the same line, column B contains the number 52.

Column C Formula	Result
A*.03	10.50
2+A*.5	176.00
2+(A*.5)	177.00
A/B	6.73
−A−5	(355.00)

Special Formula Operators

Several special operators are used by themselves as the entire formula. These special operators must be entered without any numbers, column letters, or other math operators. They perform functions on numbers or totals across lines. Here is a list of the special operators you can use, as well as which function each operator performs:

+ **Line Total—Numeric Columns**   When this character is entered by itself as a formula, the result will be the total of all the numbers on each line that appear in Numeric columns (whether calculated or entered).

= **Line Total—Total Columns**   When this character is entered by itself as a formula, the result will be the total of all the numbers on each line that appear in Total columns (whether calculated or entered).

+/ **Line Average—Numeric Columns**   When these characters are entered by themselves as a formula, the result will be the average of all the numbers on each line that appear in Numeric columns (whether calculated or entered).

=/ **Line Average—Total Columns**   When these characters are entered by themselves as a formula, the result will be the average of all the numbers on each line that are in Total columns (whether calculated or entered).

SOME PRACTICE EXAMPLES

Follow these steps to create a math document that calculates across lines using formulas. Make sure the screen is clear.

1. Press the <Format> key (SHIFT+F8), type **1** for "Line Format," and **8** for "Tab Set."

2. Press the <Delete End-Of-Line> key (CTRL+END).

3. Type **3.5** and press ENTER.

4. Type **4.5** and press ENTER.

5. Type **5.5**, press ENTER, and then press the <Exit> key (F7) twice.

   This sets tab stops at 3.5, 4.5, and 5.5 inches, for three Math columns.

6. Press TAB, and then press the <Center> key (SHIFT+F6).

   This will center the text over the tab stop.

7. Type **Cost**, press TAB, and press the <Center> key.

8. Type **Markup**, press TAB, and press the <Center> key.

9. Type **Price** and press ENTER twice.

10. Press the <Math/Columns> key (ALT+F7) and type **2** for "Math Def."

11. Press RIGHT ARROW to accept the default setting (Numeric column) for column A.

12. Type **0** to define column B as a Calculation column.

13. Type **A*.3** and press ENTER.

14. Type **0** to define column C as a Calculation column.

15. Type **A+B** and press ENTER.

16. Press the <Exit> key.

17. Type **1** to turn on Math mode.

18. Type **Rubber Gloves**, press TAB, type **23.65**, press TAB twice, and press ENTER.

19. Type **Rubber Cement**, press TAB, type **4.32**, press TAB twice, and press ENTER.

20. Type **Rubber Ball**, press TAB, type **6.32**, press TAB twice, and press ENTER.

The screen should look like the one shown in Figure 9-11.

	Cost	Markup	Price
Rubber Gloves	23.65	!	!
Rubber Cement	4.32	!	!
Rubber Ball	6.32	!	!

—

Math   Doc 1 Pg 1 Ln 6 Pos 10

Figure 9-11.   Example of a math document with formulas

21. Press the <Math/Columns> key (ALT+F7) and type **2** for "Calculate."

22. Press the <Math/Columns> key and type **1** for "Math Off."

The screen should look like the one shown in Figure 9-12.

Follow these steps to create a document that uses one of the special math operators. Make sure the screen is clear.

1. Press the <Format> key (SHIFT+F8), type **1** for "Line Format," and **8** for "Tab Set."

	Cost	Markup	Price
Rubber Gloves	23.65	7.10!	30.75!
Rubber Cement	4.32	1.30!	5.62!
Rubber Ball	6.32	1.90!	8.22!

Math   Doc 1 Pg 1 Ln 6 Pos 10

Figure 9-12.   Example of a math document with calculated formulas

2. Press the <Delete End-Of-Line> key (CTRL+END).

3. Type **2.5** and press ENTER.

4. Type **3.5** and press ENTER.

5. Type **4.5** and press ENTER.

6. Type **5.5**, press ENTER, and then press the <Exit> key (F7) twice.

   This sets tab stops at 2.5″, 3.5″, 4.5″, and 5.5″ for four math columns.

7. Press the <Tab Align> key (CTRL+F6) and type **Jan**

   The Tab Align function will right align your column labels.

	Jan	Feb	Mar	Aug
Harry	87	45	23	52!
George	45	98	23	55!
Britt	12	9	12	11!
Total	144+	152+	58+	118!

Math   Doc 1 Pg 1 Ln 8 Pos 10

Figure 9-13. Example of a math document with a special operator

8. Press the <Tab Align> key and type **Feb**

9. Press the <Tab Align> key and type **Mar**

10. Press the <Tab Align> key and type **Avg**

11. Press ENTER twice.

12. Press the <Math/Columns> key and type **2** for "Math Def."

13. Press RIGHT ARROW three times to accept the default settings for columns A, B, and C.

14. Type **0** to define column D as a Calculation column.

15. Type **+/** and press ENTER.

    This formula will produce the average of the numbers on each line.

16. Press DOWN ARROW twice and press LEFT ARROW four times.

17. Type **0** four times to set all four columns for no decimal places.

18. Press the <Exit> key (F7).

19. Type **1** for "Math on."

20. Type **Harry**, press TAB, type **87**, press TAB, type **45**, press TAB, type **23**, press TAB, and press ENTER.

21. Type **George**, press TAB, type **45**, press TAB, type **98**, press TAB, type **23**, press TAB, and press ENTER.

22. Type **Britt**, press TAB, type **12**, press TAB, type **9**, press TAB, type **12**, press TAB, and press ENTER twice.

23. Type **Total**, press TAB, type **+**, press TAB, type **+**, press TAB, type **+**, press TAB, and press ENTER.

24. Press the <Math/Columns> key and type **2** for "Calculate."

25. Press the <Math/Columns> key and type **1** for "Math Off."

The Math function calculates the average sales level for each salesperson, totals each month's sales, then calculates the average sales level for all of the months. The screen should look like the one shown in Figure 9-13.

10

PRESENTATION FEATURES

WordPerfect has several presentation features you can use to enhance the appearance of your documents. These features enable you to

- Insert graphic images
- Create text boxes
- Draw special lines (or *rules*)
- Shade specific areas

WordPerfect's graphics boxes allow you to insert graphic images from a wide variety of graphic programs and to insert boxes which contain text (such as pull-quotes in a newsletter, or some other independent section of text). The Line function allows you to draw special vertical or horizontal lines (also called *rules*), or to shade areas on a page.

In Figure 10-1, you can see a sample document created using some of these features.

Atop Mount Solana, on 355 acres of serene redwood forest and meadows overlooking all of Solana Bay, **Mount Solana Center** offers a uniquely beautiful, warmly supportive setting for retreat workshops and conferences. High quality facilities and services are provided at remarkably affordable prices.

Near Mount Solana County Park off Highway 19, 10 miles from Solanaville and 22 miles from the ocean, **Mount Solana Center** is both secluded and readily accessible to cosmopolitan services.

Recreational facilities include volleyball and basketball courts, a playing field, a lake for boating and swimming, and miles of hiking and jogging trails. Massage and herbal steambath sessions also are available.

Package plans include delicious, high quality vegetarian meals. Varied menus are designed in cooperation with your coordinator to insure greatest satisfaction in every detail.

Figure 10-1.   Sample document created with presentation features

GRAPHICS BOXES

WordPerfect's graphics boxes allow you to define a specific rectangular area on the page that can contain either text or a graphic image (it can also remain empty). Normal text will automatically wrap around the box, although you can prevent this.

WordPerfect has four different *graphics box types:* Figure, Table, Text, and User-defined. All of them operate in exactly the same way. That is, any one of them can contain a graphic image or text. The different box types simply serve as categories and allow you to determine the format of each type separately.

Although the different box types are almost identical, there are some differences in their default options (which you can easily change). For example, the borders for Figures are preset to single lines, Tables and Text boxes are set with no borders on the sides and with thick lines at the top and bottom, and User-defined boxes have no borders at all. Text boxes have a default ten percent gray shading. For descriptions of these options, see "Changing Graphics Box Options" later in this chapter.

You may want to use the Figure box type for graphic images, the Table box type for tables, and the Text box type for quotes in a newsletter or for any other type of independent text that you want to enclose in a box. However, you're free to use the three pre-named box types, as well as the User-defined box type, in any way you like. You can use the List function to generate caption lists for the different box types. (See Chapter 5, "Document Accessories.")

Creating Graphics Boxes

The first thing you have to decide when you create a graphics box is whether its position should be relative to a character, paragraph, or page.

If you want the box to be treated like any other single character within a line, begin by positioning the cursor at the place within the line where you want the box to appear. If you want the box to be associated with a specific paragraph (and move along with the paragraph as you edit the text), position the cursor anywhere within the paragraph. If you want the box to be placed in a specific location on a page, position the cursor on that page (usually at the top).

Once you've positioned the cursor at the appropriate location, press the <Graphics> key (ALT+F9). A menu allowing you to select a graphics box type will appear. Type a number from 1 to 4

```
Definition: Figure

    1 - Filename

    2 - Caption

    3 - Type                    Paragraph

    4 - Vertical Position       0"

    5 - Horizontal Position     Right

    6 - Size                    3.25" wide x 3.25" (high)

    7 - Wrap Text Around Box    Yes

    8 - Edit




Selection: 0
```

Figure 10-2.   The Graphics Box Definition screen

to indicate the box type you want, and then type **1** for "Create." The Graphics Box Definition screen will appear, as shown in Figure 10-2. (The screen shown is for Figures, but the same screen is also displayed for the other graphics box types.)

On this screen, specify the contents and format of the graphics box (as will be described later). When you're through modifying the options, press the <Exit> key (F7), and a [Figure:], [Table:], [Text Box:], or [Usr Box:] code is inserted in the document. (To abort the process and to avoid inserting a code, press the <Cancel> key instead.) If you chose to have the box associated with a paragraph, then the code is placed at the beginnin of the current paragraph. (WordPerfect looks backwards for the last [HRt] or [HPg] code to locate the beginning of the paragraph.)

Filename

To place a graphic image or WordPerfect document into the graphics box, type **1** for "Filename." (The WordPerfect document must be a small amount of text—less than a page in length. To enter text directly into the graphics box, use the Edit command. See "Edit" later in this chapter.) At the prompt "Enter filename:", type the name of the graphics file or document you want to retrieve. If you wish, you can precede the file name with a drive or path specification. Otherwise the program assumes the file will be located in the default directory. When you've typed the file name, press ENTER. WordPerfect looks for, and then examines, the file you specified.

If you have previously placed a graphic image on some text in this box, you'll see a message asking whether you want to replace the current contents of the box with the specified file. Type **Y** to confirm the replacement, or type **N** to abort the command. (To place more than one image in the same location on the page, create separate graphics boxes with the same location.)

If the file is a graphics file, and is in a format recognized by the program as one it supports, you'll see a message at the bottom of the screen indicating that the file is being loaded. Once this is accomplished, you'll see its name appear next to the "Filename" prompt, followed by the notation "(Graphic)" .

If the file you specified is a WordPerfect document, the name of the document will appear next to the "Filename" prompt, followed by the notation "(Text)".

To place the contents of the WordPerfect Shell Clipboard into the graphics box (if you started WordPerfect from the Shell menu), press the <Shell> key (CTRL+F1) at the "Enter filename:" prompt, and then type **Y** at the "Retrieve contents from clipboard?" prompt.

To clear the contents of a box, press CTRL+END at the "Enter filename:" prompt, press ENTER, and then type **Y** at the "Clear contents?" prompt.

Caption

Although graphics boxes do not initially have captions, you can easily add them. You can specify a different location for the captions (relative to the box itself) for the four different graphics box types (see "Changing Graphics Box Options" later in this chapter). The captions will move along with the graphics boxes as they are resized or repositioned on the page.

To add a caption to a graphics box, type **2** for "Caption." You'll see the Caption Text screen, which has margins set to correspond to the size and placement of the graphics box. To the left of the cursor you'll see the style for the caption title as it was set with the Options command. For Figure graphics boxes it is set initially to "Figure" plus the number of the figure. For Table graphics boxes it is set to "Table" plus the Roman numeral of the table. For Text box and User-defined graphics boxes it is set to the number of the box alone. The style is shown in Reveal codes as [Box Num].

You can add any text that you like to the caption. For example, you may want to type a space or a comma, and then a description of a graphic image, or the title of a table. If you accidentally delete the [Box Num] code, you can insert a new one by pressing the <Graphics> key (ALT+F9). You may also want to insert some codes into the caption. For example, you may want to use a *style* to format the text of the caption (see Chapter 7, "Styles"). Or you may want to insert an Automatic Reference target code, so that you can refer to the graphics box elsewhere in the document.

When you're through editing the caption, press the <Exit> key to return to the Graphics Box Definition screen.

Type

You can choose whether a graphics box will be a character, paragraph, or page type box.

Character type boxes can be placed anywhere on a line. They are treated like individual characters and are displayed on the Document Editing screen as solid blocks. (Unlike Paragraph and Page type boxes, you can place Character type boxes within footnotes and endnotes.)

You normally use a Character type box for small graphic images that you want to appear in-line with other text. For example, you may have drawn a picture of a pointing hand, which you want to use like a bullet character in a list. By creating a very small Character type box for the hand, you can place it anywhere in the text as a bullet character.

When you create a Character type box, a hidden code is placed at the cursor position. Because the box is treated like any other character, WordPerfect will adjust the height of a line to accommodate the size of the graphics box. Using the Vertical Position command described in the next section, you can choose whether the box is aligned along the top, bottom, or middle of the line. If you want the line height to remain constant, set it to a fixed value (see "Line Spacing" in Chapter 1, "Basics Refresher").

Paragraph type boxes move along with the paragraph in which they're placed. If you later edit your document so that you move a paragraph in which you've placed a Paragraph type box, the graphics will move along with the paragraph. You would use this type of graphics box when the contents of the box are specifically related to the text in a paragraph.

The code generated when you create a Paragraph type box is placed at the beginning of the paragraph. You should always leave any Paragraph type box codes at the beginning of the paragraph, so that WordPerfect can properly format the text in the paragraph.

Page type boxes appear in a specific location on a page. When you create a Page type box, the resulting code is placed at the current cursor position. However, if you want text on the page to automatically wrap around the graphics box (see "Wrap Text Around Box" later in this chapter), you must place the cursor before this text *before* creating the graphics box. If you don't, the box will be moved to the next page. If you want the box to begin on the first line of a page, you must place the cursor at the beginning of the page before creating the box.

You should use Page type boxes when the content of the boxes is related to a general section of text, as opposed to a single paragraph. They're also useful when you want more control over the layout of the page.

To change the type of the graphics box, type **3** for "Type," then type **1** for "Paragraph," **2** for "Page," or **3** for "Character." The Vertical Position and Horizontal Position options will adjust to reflect your choice.

Vertical Position

To affect the position of the graphics box vertically on the page, type **4** for "Vertical Position."

If you have indicated that you want this to be a Character

graphics box, you'll be given the option of aligning the text surrounding the graphics box with the top, center, or bottom border of the box. Type **1** for "Top of box" if you want the top edge of the text to be aligned with the top border of the graphics box (the default setting). Type **2** for "Center of box" if you want the text to be centered between the top and bottom borders of the box. Type **3** for "Bottom of box" if you want the bottom edge of the text to be aligned with the bottom border of the box. "Top," "Center," or "Bottom" will appear next to the Vertical Position option after you've made your choice.

If you've indicated that you want this to be a Paragraph graphics box, you need to enter a measurement indicating the vertical distance from the top of the paragraph to the top border of the graphics box. To have text wrap around the graphics box as closely as possible, you should enter this measurement in multiples of the current line height.

This option is set initially to the distance measured from the top of the paragraph to the line on which the cursor is currently resting. If you want the top of the graphics box to be aligned with the beginning of the paragraph, enter **0″**. If you want two lines of the paragraph to appear before the graphics box, and your current line height is 0.16″, you would type **.32**. Once you've entered the measurement, press ENTER.

If there isn't enough room for the graphics box at the bottom of the page, the box will move up in the paragraph. To specify the minimum distance you want to maintain between the top of the paragraph and the graphics box, use the Graphics Box Options command (see "Changing Graphics Box Options" later in this chapter).

If you've indicated that you want this to be a Page type box, you'll see a menu which provides some options for the vertical position of the box. Type **1** for "Full Page" if you want the graphics box to fill the entire page. The size of the box (see "Size" in a later section) will be adjusted to conform to the current page margins. Type **2** for "Top" if you want the top border of the graphics box to be aligned at the top margin of the page. Type **3** for "Center" to have the graphics box centered vertically on the page, between the top and bottom margins. Type **4** for "Bottom" to have the bottom border of the graphics box align with the bottom margin on the page (above any specified footnotes or footers).

To specify a vertical location on the page, type **5** for "Set Position." Next, type a measurement to indicate the distance from the top edge of the paper to the top border of the graphics box. Press ENTER when you've typed the measurement.

Horizontal Position

To affect the horizontal position of the graphics box, type **5** for "Horizontal Position." You can only specify the horizontal position of a paragraph or Page type box. A Character type box, however, is treated like any other character, so its horizontal position is determined by the formatting of the text.

If you've indicated that you want a Paragraph type box, you'll see a menu which allows you to specify the horizontal location of the graphics box. Type **1** for "Left" to align the left border of the graphics box on the left margin. Type **2** for "Right" to position the graphics box against the right margin. Type **3** for "Center" to center the graphics box between the left and right margins. To stretch the graphics box from the left margin to the right margin, type **4** for "Both Left & Right." The size of the graphics box (see "Size" in the next section) will be adjusted accordingly.

If you've indicated that you want this to be a Page graphics box, you'll see a menu which allows you to select the position of the graphics box relative to the left and right margins, the defined text columns, or to a specific horizontal position.

To set the horizontal position relative to the current left and right margins, type **1** for "Margins," and you'll see another menu appear. Type **1** for "Left" to align the left border of the graphics box on the left margin. Type **2** for "Right" to position the graphics box against the right margin. Type **3** for "Center" to center the graphics box between the left and right margins. To stretch the graphics box from the left margin to the right margin, type **4** for "Both Left & Right." The size of the graphics box (see "Size" in the next section) will be adjusted to conform to the selected position.

To set the horizontal position of the graphics box relative to the defined text columns (see Chapter 8, "Text Columns"), type **2** for "Columns." (The cursor should have been placed within the defined column area.) Next, type the number of the column where you want the graphics box. If the graphics box is to be placed between two columns, type the first column number, followed by a hyphen, and then the second column number. For example, to position the graphics box between the first and second columns, type **1-2**. (The columns you specify need not be contiguous. You can, for instance, place a graphics box between the first and third columns, in which case it will span the second column.)

After you indicate the column numbers, a menu appears, allowing you to choose the position of the graphics box relative to the columns you've selected. Type **1** for "Left" to align the left border of the graphics box on the left margin of the first column. Type **2** for "Right" to position the graphics box against the right margin of the last column. Type **3** for "Center" to center the graphics box between the left margin of the first column and the right margin of the last column. To stretch the graphics box from the left margin of the first column to the right margin of the last column, type **4** for "Both Left & Right." The size of the graphics box (see "Size" in the next section) will adjust to conform to the selected position.

To specify a particular horizontal position on the page for the graphics box, type **3** for "Set Position." You then need to enter a measurement indicating the distance from the left edge of the paper to the left border of the graphics box. Press ENTER when you've finished.

Size

To control the size of the graphics box, type **6** for "Size." You would usually enter only the desired width or height of the graphics box, and let WordPerfect calculate the other dimension, based on the original proportions of the box. You can, however, set both the height and width of the box. You can also change the size of a graphics box by changing its position on the page. For example, if you choose to have a graphics box extend from the left to the right margin (see the preceding section, "Horizontal Position"), the width of the graphics box will be set to the distance between the margins, and the height will be recalculated based on the new width.

When a graphics box contains text rather than a graphic image, the height of the box grows and shrinks according to the amount of text it contains. The width, however, will remain the same unless you change it. If you wish, you can manually set the height of the graphics box. The box will then not adjust to the amount of text, but will remain fixed. To return the box to automatic height calculation, reset its width.

To specify the width of the graphics box (the distance between the left and right borders of the box), type **1** for "Width (auto height)." Type a measurement to indicate the desired width of the box, and press ENTER. WordPerfect calculates the appropriate height for the graphics box based on the previous proportions of the box.

To specify the height of the graphics box (the distance between top and bottom borders), type **2** for "Height (auto width)." Then, type a measurement to indicate the desired height of the box, and press ENTER. WordPerfect calculates the appropriate height for the graphics box based on the previous proportions of the box.

To specify both the width and height of the graphics box, type **3** for "Both Width & Height." Type a measurement to indicate the desired width of the box, and press ENTER. Then, type a measurement to indicate the desired height of the box, and press ENTER.

Wrap Text Around Box

You can choose whether or not WordPerfect should automatically wrap text around the graphics box. Only text which *follows* the graphics box hidden code can be wrapped around the box. This is why it's best to put Page type box hidden codes at the beginning of the page.

WordPerfect initially sets all graphics boxes so that text will wrap around them. To change the setting, type **7** for "Wrap Text Around Box." Type **Y** to have text wrap around the graphics box, or type **N** to prevent text wrapping.

When text is not wrapped around a graphics box, WordPerfect will print the box and the text in the same location on the page.

You may want to do this to achieve a tighter wrap effect. For example, you may want the lines in a paragraph to wrap around the graphic image itself, rather than around the rectangular border which surrounds the image. You could do this by manually inserting Hard Returns in the text where you want the text to wrap. Note that this will make the text much more difficult to reformat.

To affect the amount of blank space that WordPerfect will leave between the text and the borders of the graphics box, use the Options command (see "Changing Graphics Box Options" in a later section). Note that WordPerfect allows text wrapping for a maximum of 20 graphics boxes per page.

Edit

To alter the contents of the graphics box, type 8 for "Edit." For empty graphics boxes, or ones in which you've already entered some text or loaded a document (see the earlier section "Filename"), you'll see a blank document editing screen. For graphics boxes in which you've placed a graphic image, you'll see the Graphics Edit screen.

For graphics boxes which contain text, you can type or edit the text that will appear in the graphics box. WordPerfect automatically adjusts the left and right margins on the document editing screen to conform to the current width of the graphics box. Although the program will allow you to enter up to a page of text, only text that can be contained within the confines of the graphics box will be displayed. If you wish, you can use WordPerfect formatting and positioning commands to format the text.

To rotate the text within the graphics box, press the <Graphics> key (ALT+F9). A menu at the bottom of the screen allows you to choose a rotation. The default is 0 degrees, which indicates a graphics box that is oriented with the rest of the text on the page. Type a number from one to four to indicate the rotation you want. WordPerfect will then adjust the margins, if necessary, to account for the new rotation. (Note that your printer must support rotated text to use this option. Some printers will not allow rotated text to appear on the same page with normal text.)

When you've finished entering or editing the text, press the <Exit> key. To adjust the amount of space left between the borders of the graphics box and the text within it, use the Options command (see "Changing Graphics Box Options").

For graphics boxes which contain a graphic image, you'll see a representation of the image on your screen. (If you don't have a graphics monitor, WordPerfect uses characters to build a rough representation of the image.) With the image displayed, you can manipulate the graphic image in several ways (see the next section "Editing Graphic Images"). When you've completed the changes, press the <Exit> key to return to the Graphics Box Definition screen.

Editing Graphic Images

Once you've placed a graphic image within a graphics box using the "Filename" choice on the Graphics Box Definition screen, you can use the "Edit" choice to manipulate the graphic image. When you do so, you'll see the Graphics Edit screen appear, as shown in Figure 10-3.

Rotating and Mirroring Images

To rotate the image within the graphics box, you can use either the Rotate command or its keyboard equivalents.

To specify the precise rotation of the image or to mirror (flip) the image, type **3** for "Rotate." Next, type the number of degrees which you want to rotate the graphic, and press ENTER. (Simply press ENTER if your goal is to mirror the image.) Note that the rotation you specify is not relative to the image's current rotation. A rotation of zero degrees always means that the image is oriented with the rest of the text on the page.

After specifying the rotation, WordPerfect asks whether you want to mirror the image. Type **Y** to mirror the image, or type **N** to leave it in its normal state. Note that this command does not work as a toggle. An image is either mirrored or not. If you choose to mirror an image and then change your mind you invoke the

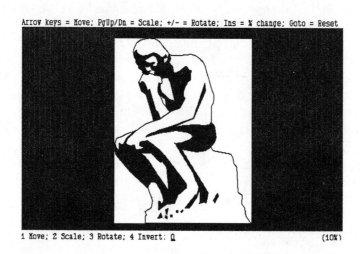

Figure 10-3.   Graphics image on the Graphics Edit screen

command again and choose "No," rather than choosing to mirror the image again. After you respond to the Mirror prompt, you'll see the image displayed with the rotation and mirroring you specified.

You can also change the rotation of the image using keyboard equivalents. Press the gray plus (+) key (usually located at the far right side of the keyboard) to increase the rotation, and press the gray minus (−) key to decrease the rotation. These keys use the current increment value, so each key press will initially affect the rotation by ten percent of 360 degrees, or 36 degrees.

Note that you can only rotate object-type line drawing graphic images. Paint-type *bitmap* images can be mirrored, but not rotated. Figure 10-4 shows an image rotated 180 degrees. Figure 10-5 shows the same rotated image mirrored.

Scaling (Zooming) Images

You can easily change the scale of an image relative to its original size, allowing you to "zoom" the image in and out. For example,

Figure 10-4.   Graphics image rotated 180 degrees

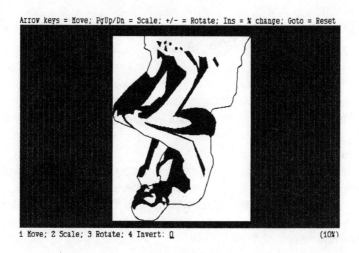

Figure 10-5.   Graphics image rotated 180 degrees and mirrored

you may only want a portion of an image to be displayed in the graphics box. Or you may want the image to be smaller while the graphics box itself remains the same size. There are two ways to change the scale of an image: by using the Scale command, or by using key equivalents.

To specify a precise scale for the image, type **2** for "Scale." You'll then be prompted for a "Scale X:" value, and then for a "Scale Y:" value. The first one specifies the scale for the X-axis of the image (from left to right), and the second for the Y-axis (from top to bottom). A scale of 100 represents the image in its original form. A scale of 200 would represent the image scaled twice as big as the original size of the image. A scale of 50 would represent the image scaled to half its original size. The scale can range from 1 to 999. Type the value you want for the X-axis, press ENTER, then type the value you want for the Y-axis, and press ENTER. The image will be redrawn to the specified scale.

You can also use key equivalents to simultaneously change the scale for both the X-axis and the Y-axis (maintaining the proportions of the image). To increase the scale of the image (zoom in), press PGUP. To decrease the scale of the image (zoom out), press PGDN. These keys use the current increment value (described later), so each key press will initially affect the scale by ten percent of the 100 scale, or a value of 10.

Figure 10-6 shows an image scaled to half its original size (a scale value of 50 for both X and Y).

Moving Images

You can easily reposition the graphic image within the borders of the graphics box. You can do this either by using the Move command to specify a distance and a direction to move the image, or you can use key equivalents.

When moving images, you need to think in terms of moving the "frame" shown on the Graphics Edit screen over the image, rather than moving the image itself within the frame. Apparent movement of the image, as discussed in this section, is actually a result of the movement of this frame.

To specify the distance and direction to move the image, type **1**

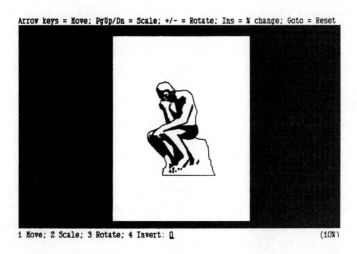

Arrow keys = Move; PgUp/Dn = Scale; +/- = Rotate; Ins = % change; Goto = Reset

1 Move; 2 Scale; 3 Rotate; 4 Invert: Q   (10%)

Figure 10-6.   Graphics image scaled to half its normal size

for "Move." At the "Horizontal:" prompt, which appears next, type a measurement to indicate the distance you want the image to be moved horizontally. A positive value will move the image to the left, and a negative value will move it to the right. Press ENTER when you've typed the value. At the "Vertical:" prompt, which appears next, type a measurement to indicate the distance you want the image to be moved vertically. A positive value will move it down, and a negative value will move it up. Press ENTER when you've typed the value. The image will be redrawn in the new location.

You can also use key equivalents to move the image (or rather, the frame over the image). To move the frame to the right (and therefore the image to the left), press RIGHT ARROW; to move it to the left (and the image to the right) press LEFT ARROW; to move it down (and the image up) press DOWN ARROW; and to move the frame up (and the image down) press UP ARROW. (Remember: think about moving the frame, and not the image itself.) These keys use the current increment value, so each key press would initially affect the location of the frame/image by ten percent of its corresponding width or height. For a graphics box which is three inches wide, pressing the LEFT ARROW key once would move the frame 0.3 inches to the left (a −0.3 inch horizontal movement).

Inverting Images

You may find that some bitmap graphic images are inverted—for example, white on a black background, as opposed to black on a white background. You can use the Invert command to invert (reverse) the image, if necessary.

To invert the image, type **4** for "Invert," or press the <Switch> key (SHIFT+F3). If the graphic you've loaded is a bitmap image, it will be redrawn in an inverted form (every white dot becomes black, and every black dot becomes white).

This option will only work with paint-type bitmap images. You cannot invert images imported from HPGL files, .PIC files, CGM metafiles, or any other object-based line drawings.

Changing the Increment Value

Several of the editing keys used on the Graphics Edit screen use the increment indicator shown in the lower right-hand corner of the screen. This is initially set to ten percent. The rotation keys, for example, will rotate the image in increments of ten percent of 360 degrees, or 36 degrees. To change the increment, press the INS key to toggle the value between 1, 5, 10, or 25 percent.

Saving Graphics Files

When you load a graphic image into WordPerfect, the program automatically converts it to its own internal format. This may take some time, depending on the type of graphic image being converted. If you wish, you can save a graphic image which has been loaded and converted in a separate file that is already in WordPerfect's internal format (indicated by a .WPG filename extension). This way, loading the graphic image will be much faster in the future, since no conversion will be necessary.

To do this, begin with the desired image on the Graphics Edit screen. Then, press the <Save> key (F10), and the prompt "Graphics file to be saved:" is displayed at the bottom of the screen. You can see that the suggested filename is the image's original one, but with a .WPG extension. Type a new name for the image and press ENTER, or simply press ENTER to take the suggested name. You can also precede the filename with a drive or path designation (otherwise, the graphic image is stored in the default directory).

Editing Graphics Boxes

To modify the contents or format of a graphics box, begin with the cursor anywhere in the document (you can optionally place the cursor before the code of the box you want to edit). Press the <Graphics> key (ALT+F9), and type the number indicating the *box type* of the graphics box you want to edit. At the next prompt, type the *number* of the graphics box that you want to edit. This number is displayed in the hidden code for the graphics box. The default number is that of the next graphics box in sequence of the type you requested. This is why you may find it convenient to start with the cursor placed just before the code of the graphics box that you want to edit.

When you've specified the number you want, press ENTER, and the Graphics Box Definition screen will appear. You can now proceed to change any of the options (as described earlier in "Creating Graphics Boxes"). When you've finished making changes, press the <Exit> key to return to the Document Editing screen.

If you want to change the box type of the graphics box without changing any of its options, press the <Graphics> key (ALT+F9) when the Graphics Box Definition screen is displayed. From the menu presented, select a new box type for the graphics box. After you've made your selection, the title of the screen will change to reflect your choice. The box will now conform to the options set for the new box type, and will be renumbered according to the current sequence of the new box type in the document.

If you don't want a graphics box to appear in a document, simply delete its hidden code using the Reveal Codes function. You can also use the Undelete function to recover a graphics box should you delete it by accident. To copy or move the box, mark the appropriate code (or its surrounding text) as a block, and then use the <Move> key to copy or move the block.

Changing Graphics Box Options

To change the options for any one of the four different box types of graphics boxes, begin by positioning the cursor where you want the new options to take effect. If you want to affect all of the graphics boxes in a document of a given box type, you should position the cursor at the top of the document.

When you've positioned the cursor, press the <Graphics> key (ALT+F9), and type a number indicating the box type of the graphics box whose options you want to modify. Then type **4** for "Options," and the Graphics Box Options screen will appear, as shown in Figure 10-7. (The screen shown is for Figures, but the screens corresponding to other box types are similar.)

You can now change any of the options you want, as further described. When you've completed making changes, press the <Exit> key to return to the Document Editing screen. A [Fig Opt], [Tab Opt], [Txt Opt], or [Usr Opt] code is inserted in the document at the cursor position (if you made any changes). This code will affect all subsequent graphics boxes of a specified box type.

Border Style

You can choose whether to place a border around graphics boxes of a given box type, while specifying the style of the border. To change the settings for borders, type **1** for "Border Style." Select from the menu displayed the type of border you want for each of the four sides of the graphics boxes. Type **1** for no border, or a number from 2 to 7 indicating the type of border desired, as shown here:

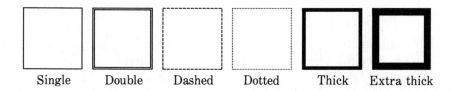

You can press ENTER if you want to leave any choice unchanged. WordPerfect indicates the selection you've made for each side when you type the number.

Figure graphics boxes are preset for single lines on all sides. Table and Text Box graphics boxes are preset for no border on the left and right sides, and for thick lines at the top and bottom. User-defined boxes are preset for no borders at all.

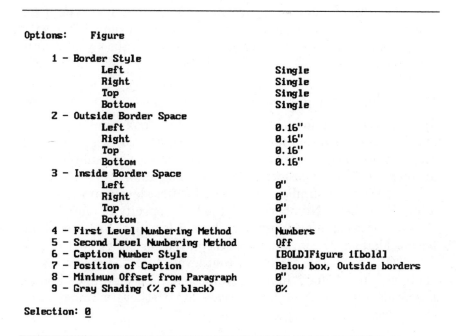

Figure 10-7.   Graphics Box Options screen

Outside Border Space

This option allows you to specify the amount of blank space Word-Perfect should leave outside the borders (that is, between the border and the document text). Initially, this is set to 0.16″ for all sides of all graphics box types. To change the setting, type **2** for "Outside Border Space," and then enter a measurement for each side of the graphics box. Press ENTER for any values you want to leave alone.

Inside Border Space

This option allows you to specify the amount of blank space Word-Perfect should leave inside the borders (that is, between the border and the contents of the graphics box, whether text or image). Initially, this is set to 0″ for all sides of all graphics box types. This means that the text or graphic image in the box would appear right up against the border. To change this, type **3** for "Inside Border Space," and then enter a measurement for each side of the graphics box. Press ENTER for any values you want to leave alone.

Numbering Method

You can choose a format for the graphics box number, which appears in the caption for each box. In fact, you can choose two separate formats: one for the first-level graphics box number, and another for the second-level graphics box number.

To specify the numbering method for first-level numbers, type **4** for "First Level Numbering Method." To specify the numbering method for second-level numbers, type **5** for "Second Level Numbering Method." From the menu displayed for either choice, type **1** for "Off" to disable the use of that level, **2** for "Numbers," **3** for "Letters," or **4** for "Roman Numerals." Letters and Roman numerals are displayed in uppercase for first-level numbers, and in lowercase for second-level numbers.

Caption Number Style

This option allows you to specify precisely what will appear at the location of the [Box Num] code, which is inserted automatically into the caption of each box. You can include text, appearance codes and other font attributes, and the number of the graphics box.

To change the caption number style, type **6** for "Caption Number Style." Type the desired style, and press ENTER. The new style will appear next to the prompt on the screen.

Type **1** at the position in the style where you want to place the first-level number for the graphics box. Type **2** at the position where you want to place the second-level number. (The formats for these numbers are set with options 4 and 5 on this screen. See the preceding section, "Numbering Method.")

The default style for Figure graphics boxes is "Figure," followed by a blank space and the first-level box number. The default style for Table graphics boxes produces "Table," followed by a blank space and the first-level box number. The default style for Text Box and User-defined graphics boxes produces the box number alone. All of these default styles are in boldface.

Position of Caption

If you choose to use a caption with a graphics box, you can control its placement with this function.

To change the caption's location, type **7** for "Position of Caption." From the menu displayed, type **1** to place the caption below the graphics box, or **2** to place the caption above the graphics box. From the next menu displayed, type **1** to place the caption outside the border of the box, or **2** to place it inside the border. Your choice will be displayed next to the prompt on the screen.

Minimum Offset from Paragraph

When you create a Paragraph graphics box (see "Creating Graphics Boxes"), you can specify a vertical distance from the top of the paragraph to the top of the graphics box. If necessary, however, WordPerfect will move the image higher in the paragraph if it would otherwise extend below the bottom margin of the page.

The "Minimum Offset from Paragraph" option allows you to specify the minimum distance that should be maintained between the top of the paragraph and the top of the graphics box. If there isn't enough room for the graphics box on the page, taking this minimum distance into account, the box is moved to the next page.

The initial setting for this option is 0″ for all types of graphics boxes. This means that graphics boxes might get pushed all the way up to the top of the paragraph, regardless of the vertical position set with the options for the boxes.

Gray Shading

You can use this option to add gray shading (also called a *screen*) to graphics boxes. For example, you may want all of your Figure graphics boxes to have a fifteen percent shading (measured in degrees of blackness). Note that you will see gray shading only if your printer supports it. Here's an example of ten levels of gray shading (10% to 100%) from a PostScript laser printer:

To specify the level of gray shading, type **9** for "Gray Shading." Type a number (from 0 to 100) representing the desired level. A value of 0 indicates no gray shading. For printers with variable gray shading, a value of 100 indicates total blackness. If your printer supports only one level of gray shading, however, you should enter a value of 100 to use that level. Press ENTER when you've typed the desired level. The program adds the percent sign for you, if you omitted it.

Figure, Table, and User-defined graphics boxes are initially set for no gray shading (zero percent). Text-box graphics boxes, however, are initially set for ten percent gray shading.

Specifying a Graphics Box Number

You can choose to restart numbering for any type of graphics box, at any point in a document. To do so, begin by positioning the cursor where you want the new number to take effect. Then press the <Graphics> key (ALT+F9), and type a number indicating the type of graphics box you want to affect. Next, type **3** for "New Number," type the desired starting number, and press ENTER. A [New Fig Num:], [New Tab Num:], [New Txt Num:], or [New Usr Num:] code is inserted in the document at the cursor position.

If you're using two levels of numbering, you can specify both the first level and the second level numbers. For example, you can enter "IV-1" to specify a level 1 number of 4 (using Roman numerals), and a level 2 number of 1.

LINES

You can use the Lines function to draw lines and to shade areas on a page. Vertical lines can appear alongside your document's margins, between text columns, or at any other specific location. Horizontal lines appear at the location in the document where you give the command, and can stretch from the left to right margin, or be of any specific length. You can adjust the width of either type of line. By increasing the width of a line, you can use the Lines function to shade specific areas on a page.

Once a line has been created, you cannot edit its format or position. If you need to modify the line, you'll need to delete its [HLine:] or [VLine:] hidden code and create a new line. You might examine the hidden code before deleting it, so you can note its settings.

Creating Horizontal Lines

To create a horizontal line, begin by positioning the cursor on the text line on which you want the line to appear. Press the <Graphics> key (ALT+F9), and type **5** for "Line," and then **1** for "Horizontal." The Horizontal Line Definition screen will appear, as shown in Figure 10-8. You can now set the options for the line. When you're through, press the <Exit> key (F7), and you'll be returned to the document editing screen. An [HLine:] hidden code

```
Graphics: Horizontal Line

      1 - Horizontal Position            Left & Right

      2 - Length of Line

      3 - Width of Line                  0.01"

      4 - Gray Shading (% of black)      100%




      Selection: 0
```

Figure 10-8.   Horizontal Line Definition screen

is inserted into the document at the cursor position. You'll see the line the next time you print or view the document.

Horizontal Position

To change the horizontal placement of the line across the page, type **1** for "Horizontal Position." Next, type **1** to have the line appear flush against the current left margin, **2** to have it flush against the right margin, or **3** to have it centered between the left and right margins. Set the length of the line with the Length of Line option, as described in the next section.

Type **4** if you want the line to extend between the left and right margins. Because the length of the line varies according to the distance between the current margins in the document, the Length of Line option will be disabled when you make this selection.

To specify a horizontal location for the beginning of the line, type 5 for "Set Position." Then type a measurement to indicate the distance from the left edge of the paper to the beginning of the line. The initial setting for this will be the current position of the cursor on the line. Press ENTER when you've typed a measurement.

Length of Line

To adjust the length of the line, type 2 for "Length of Line." (Note that this option is not available when you have the Horizontal Position option set for "Left & Right.") Now, type a measurement to indicate the desired line length, and press ENTER. The default setting is for the line to extend from the position you specified with the Horizontal Position option to the current right margin.

Width of Line

You can use this option to control the width of the line. Initially, this is set to 0.01 inches for a very thin line. You can, however, make as thick a line as you like, as long as it will fit on the current page.

To change this option, type 3 for "Width of Line." Type a measurement to indicate the line width (the distance from the top edge to the bottom edge of the line). For example, to create a line that is a half-inch thick, type **0.5″**. Press ENTER when you've typed the measurement.

Gray Shading

To draw the line using gray shading (as opposed to the line appearing black), type 4 for "Gray Shading." Type a number (from 0 to 100) representing the degree of shading. A value of 0 indicates no gray shading and a value of 100 indicates total blackness. Press ENTER when you've typed the level. The program adds the percent sign, if you've omitted it.

Creating Vertical Lines

To create a vertical line, begin by positioning the cursor anywhere on the relevant page. Then, press the <Graphics> key (ALT+F9),

and type 5 for "Line," and then 2 for "Vertical." The Vertical Line
screen will appear, as shown in Figure 10-9. You can now set the
options for the line. Press the <Exit> key (F7), and you'll be
returned to the Document Editing screen. A [VLine:] hidden code
is inserted in the document at the cursor position. You'll see this
line the next time you print or view the document.

Horizontal Position

To change the horizontal placement of the line, type 1 for "Horizontal Position." To place the line along the left margin, type 1 for
"Left" (this is the initial setting). To place it along the right margin, type 2 for "Right."

If you're using text columns (see Chapter 8, "Text Columns"),
you can choose to place the vertical line between two columns. To

```
Graphics: Vertical Line

     1 - Horizontal Position          Left Margin

     2 - Vertical Position            Full Page

     3 - Length of Line

     4 - Width of Line                0.01"

     5 - Gray Shading (% of black)    100%




     Selection: 0
```

Figure 10-9.   Vertical Line Definition screen

do this, type **3** for "Between Columns." At the next prompt, type the number of the column (counting from the left) that you want left of the line. For example, if you wanted to place a line between columns 1 and 2, you'd type **1** to place the line to the right of column 1. Press ENTER when you've typed the column number.

To set a specific horizontal position for the line, type **4** for "Set Position." Then type a measurement to indicate the distance from the left edge of the paper to the left edge of the line. The initial setting for this will be the current position of the cursor on the line. Press ENTER when you've typed a measurement.

Vertical Position

This option is used to specify the vertical starting point for the line. To set this option, type **2** for "Vertical Position."

Type **1** for "Full Page" if you want the line to extend from the top margin to the bottom margin (this is the initial setting). If you choose this option, the Length of Line options will be disabled.

Type **2** for "Top" if you want the top end of the line to align at the top margin of the page. Type **3** for "Center" to vertically center the line between the top and bottom margins. Type **4** for "Bottom" to have the bottom end of the line align with the bottom margin on the page (above any specified footnotes or footers).

To set an explicit vertical location on the page, type **5** for "Set Position." Next, type a measurement to indicate the distance from the top edge of the paper to the top end of the line. Press ENTER when you've typed the measurement.

Length of Line

To adjust the length of the line, type **3** for "Length of Line." (Note that this option is not available when you have the Vertical Position option set for "Full Page.") Now, type a measurement to indicate the line length you want, and press ENTER. It will initially be set to extend from the position you specified with the Horizontal Position option to the current bottom margin.

Width of Line

You can use this option to control the width of the line. Initially, it is set to 0.01 inch—a very thin line. However, you can make the line as thick as you want, as long as it will fit on the current page.

To change this option, type **4** for "Width of Line," and type a measurement to indicate the width of the line (the distance from the left edge to the right edge of the line). For example, to create a line that is a half-inch thick, type **0.5″**. Then press ENTER.

Gray Shading

To draw the line using gray shading (as opposed to the line appearing black), type **5** for "Gray Shading." Then type a number (from 0 to 100) representing the desired level of gray shading. A value of 0 indicates no gray shading and a value of 100 indicates total blackness. Press ENTER when you've typed the level. The program adds the percent sign for you, if you omitted it.

Shading Areas

You can use a thick vertical line to create shaded areas (or *screens*). You might want to do this to highlight a specific portion of text, such as an important article in a newsletter.

To do this, begin by positioning the cursor anywhere on the page on which you want the shaded area to appear. Then, press the <Graphics> key (ALT+F9), type **5** for "Line," and then **2** for "Vertical Line." The Vertical Line Definition screen will appear.

To create the shaded area, you'll use the first four options on the screen to indicate its location and size. You can then specify the degree of shading with the last option. You can think of the first two options ("Horizontal Position" and "Vertical Position") as the X and Y coordinates on the page for the upper-left corner of the desired shaded area. The third option, "Length of Line" will determine the depth of the area, and the fourth option, "Width of Line" will determine its width.

To begin, type **1** for "Horizontal position," then **4** for "Set Position." Now, type a measurement indicating the distance you want from the left edge of the paper to the left edge of the shaded area, and press ENTER.

Next, type **2** for "Vertical Position," and then **5** for "Set Position." Type a measurement to indicate the desired distance from the top edge of the paper to the top edge of the shaded area, and press ENTER.

Then type **3** for "Length of Line," and a measurement indicating the desired depth of the shaded area—that is, its size from top to bottom. Press ENTER when you've entered the measurement.

Finally, type **4** for "Width of Line," and a measurement indicating the desired width of the shaded area—that is, its size from left to right. Then press ENTER.

Once you've specified the location and size of the shaded area, you can use the last option to indicate the degree of shading. Type **5** for "Gray Shading," and type a number (from 0 to 100) representing the level of shading. A value of 100 indicates total blackness. Press ENTER when you've typed the desired level. The program adds the percent sign for you, if you omitted it.

Practice with Shaded Areas

To place a ten percent shaded area on the bottom three inches of a letter-size page (within standard one-inch margins), begin with a blank screen, and follow these steps:

1. Press the <Graphics> key (ALT+F9).
2. Type **5** for "Line," and then **2** for "Vertical Line."
3. Type **1** for "Horizontal Position," and then **4** for "Set Position."
4. Type **1″** (for one inch from the left edge of the paper), and press ENTER.
5. Type **2** for "Vertical Position," and then **5** for "Set Position."

You then need to calculate where the top of the shaded area should be placed. Given a letter-sized page (8 1/2″ by 11″) with one-inch margins, there would be nine vertical inches of printable area on the page. If the last four are taken up by the three inches of shaded area and a one-inch bottom margin, then the shaded area will start seven inches from the top edge of the paper.

6. Type **7″** (for seven inches) and press ENTER.
7. Type **3** for "Length of Line," then type **3″** (to set the depth of the shaded area to three inches), and press ENTER.

8. Type **4** for "Width of Line," then type **6.5″** (to set the width of the shaded area to six-and-one-half inches), and press ENTER.

9. Type **5** for "Gray Shading," then type **10** (for ten percent shading), and press ENTER.

10. Press the <Exit> key to return to the Document Editing screen.

A [Vline:1″,7″,3″,6.5″,10%] hidden code is inserted in the document. The next time you view or print the document you'll see the shaded area.

11

USING PRINTERS

Printers are often a source of frustration to computer users. In fact, printers sometimes seem to have minds of their own. Text mysteriously does not print in boldface (although it appears as boldface on the screen), lines are not centered, and paper and mailing labels get jammed behind the platen.

The first step in reducing printer anxiety is to configure your software properly to work with your printer. This chapter leads you through that process and then helps you find ways to use your printer's various capabilities. The chapter first teaches you how to install your printer; then it shows you how to change fonts and attributes within a document. Finally, it describes how to select forms and send special codes to the printer.

WordPerfect supports a wide variety of printers. In the process of installing those which you will be using on your system, you will indicate which ports you will have them connected to, and other details such as available fonts and forms.

INSTALLING PRINTERS

WordPerfect's printer definitions are initially stored in files with an .ALL filename extension on the Printer Disks. When you follow the steps described in this section to install your printer, you'll create a smaller Printer Definition file which contains only the required information for your own printer. This file will have a .PRS filename extension, and will be stored on the WordPerfect System Disk #2 on a floppy disk system, or in the WordPerfect program directory on a hard disk. (If you've specified a directory for printer files with the Location of Auxiliary Files option in the Setup command, .PRS files will be stored in this location.)

To install printers in WordPerfect, you need to know three things:

- The name and model of each printer you have (or for which you want to prepare documents).
- The interface ports your printer(s) will use, such as LPT1: for the first parallel port on your system or COM1: for the first serial port. Most printers are parallel, but if yours is serial, you will also need to know the printer's baud rate and other communication parameters.
- The types of paper feed your printer(s) will use (for example, sheet feeder bins, continuous fanfold, hand-fed, and so on).

In addition, you may also need to specify:

- In the case of a laser printer, the built-in, cartridge, and downloadable fonts which you plan to use.
- A location on your disk where you plan to store downloadable fonts.
- A desired Initial Font for documents prepared with each printer.

Starting the Installation Process

To begin the printer installation process, press the <Print> key (SHIFT+F7), and you'll see the Print screen as shown in Figure 11-1. Normally, the name of the currently selected printer is

---

```
Print

    1 - Full Document
    2 - Page
    3 - Document on Disk
    4 - Control Printer
    5 - Type Through
    6 - View Document
    7 - Initialize Printer

Options

    S - Select Printer
    B - Binding                0"
    N - Number of Copies       1
    G - Graphics Quality       Medium
    T - Text Quality           High




Selection: 0
```

Figure 11-1.   The Print screen

shown next to the "Select Printer" prompt. When you first install WordPerfect, however, no printer is selected, so this area will be blank. As long as no printer is selected, you will not be able to print or view a document. In addition, you will not be able to perform any printer-specific actions, such as changing the Base Font.

To install a printer, start by typing S for "Select Printer." You'll then see the Select Printer screen, as shown in Figure 11-2. This screen shows all of the printer definitions that you've previously selected. You'll want this screen to show a definition for each of the printers on which you plan to print any of your documents—regardless of whether the printers will actually be attached to your computer. If this is the first time you've performed the printer selection process, however, you won't see any definitions on this screen.

Print: Select Printer

1 Select; 2 Additional Printers; 3 Edit; 4 Copy; 5 Delete; 6 Help: <u>1</u>

Figure 11-2. The Select Printer screen

Adding Definitions

To add printer definitions to this screen, type **2** for "Additional Printers." WordPerfect now looks on the disk for the .ALL printer files which are originally located on the program's Printer Disks. (The program looks in the directory specified with the Location of Files option in Setup. If no directory is specified with this option, it looks in the WordPerfect program directory.) If you copied the .ALL files from the Printer Disks onto your hard disk, you'll see a list of printer names.

   If you didn't copy the files, you'll see a message indicating that the printer files were not found. From this screen, you can choose to view either the .PRS files already installed on your disk, or the .ALL files on the Printer Disks. To choose from the .PRS files, type **4** for "List Printer Files," and you'll see all of the currently available .PRS files. Initially, you'll see only the STANDARD.PRS file. Select a .PRS file to use and press ENTER, or press the <Exit> key (F7) to return to the Additional Printers screen.

To see the .ALL files on the Printer Disks, begin by inserting one of them into an available disk drive. (Usually, this will be drive A on a hard disk system, and drive B on a floppy disk system.) Then type 2 for "Other Disk," and type a drive letter followed by a colon indicating the location of the Printer Disk. Press ENTER, and you'll see a list of printer names corresponding to definitions contained within the .ALL file on the disk you inserted. Now locate the name of your printer in the list, using the arrow keys. If you do not see the desired printer definition, replace the Printer Disk with another Printer Disk, and repeat the Other Disk command.

Selecting a Definition

Once you've located the name of the desired printer definition (whether on the list of installed .PRS files, or on the list of definitions in an .ALL file), type 1 for "Select," or simply press ENTER.

If you selected a printer definition from an .ALL file, you'll see the prompt "Printer filename:" at the bottom of the screen. The suggested response will be the default file name for the printer you've selected. Normally, you will accept the suggested file name. However, you can also edit the file name or type a new one. (Do not specify an extension for the file. WordPerfect will add a .PRS extension to the file name automatically.) The file will be stored in the directory specified with the Location of Files option in the Setup command. When you're through, press ENTER.

You'll next see the Help screen for the printer you've selected. If no help is available for the printer, you'll see the message "No help available." If you selected a printer definition from an .ALL file, you'll see the message "Updating font" at the bottom of the screen. After you're finished reading the information (if any), and the program is through updating fonts, you can press the <Exit> key (F7). You'll see the Edit Printer screen (like the one shown in Figure 11-3), which allows you to edit the options for the specified printer definition.

```
Select Printer: Edit

            Filename                    HPLASEII.PRS

       1 - Name                         HP LaserJet Series II

       2 - Port                         LPT1:

       3 - Sheet Feeder                 None

       4 - Forms

       5 - Cartridges and Fonts

       6 - Initial Font                 Courier 10 pitch (PC-8)

       7 - Path for Downloadable
           Fonts and Printer
           Command Files




   Selection: 0
```

Figure 11-3.   The Edit Printer screen

Editing Printer Options

On the Edit Printer screen, you can modify the settings for a specific printer definition. The default choices appear next to the options on this screen (as described in this section).

When you've set all the options you want on the Edit Printer screen, press the <Exit> key (F7), and you'll return to the Select Printer screen. The new printer definition will appear on this screen. You can now make this the currently selected printer (as described in the section "Selecting a Printer Definition").

Name

To change the name of the printer definition, type **1** for "Name." Next, type a name for the printer (or edit the existing one). The name can contain up to 36 characters. It can contain spaces, and both uppercase and lowercase letters. Press ENTER when you've finished entering the name.

Port

To specify the port to which the printer is attached, type **2** for "Port." Initially, this is set to LPT1: (primary parallel port), the most common setting. Type a number from 1 to 8 to indicate the destination of output for this printer. (Option 8 allows you to send output to a disk file. See "Printing to Disk.")

If you enter a number that corresponds to a serial port (4 through 7), you'll see the Serial Port Settings screen, as shown in Figure 11-4. On this screen, you can specify five additional serial port settings: baud rate, parity, number of stop bits, character length (number of data bits), and whether XON/XOFF handshaking should be used. If you do not know these settings, you should either consult your printer manual or contact your dealer. The most common baud rate settings are 1200 and 9600. The most common combinations for the next three options are either "Even," 1 and 7, or "None," 1 and 8. When you're through with this screen, press the <Exit> key to return to the Edit Printer screen. You'll see the settings you specified appear next to the "Port" option on the screen.

Sheet Feeder

If your printer uses a sheet feeder or has multiple paper trays, you can include a sheet feeder definition in the current Printer Definition file. To do this, type **3** for "Sheet Feeders." WordPerfect will look for the .ALL file used to create the printer definition that you are currently editing. If it cannot find the file, it displays a message indicating this. If this occurs, insert the Printer Disk containing the correct .ALL file into the available disk drive, type the drive letter followed by a colon, and press ENTER.

You'll see a list of sheet feeder definitions. When you've located the correct definition, type **1** for "Select" (or press ENTER). The Help screen for the sheet feeder will appear. Next, press the

---

```
Select Printer: COM Port

    1 - Baud                       9600

    2 - Parity                     None

    3 - Stop Bits (1 or 2)         1

    4 - Character Length (7 or 8)  8

    5 - XON/XOFF                   No




Selection: 0
```

Figure 11-4.   The Serial Port Settings screen

<Exit> key (F7), and you'll return to the Edit Printer screen. The name of the sheet feeder you selected will be displayed on the screen next to the Sheet Feeder option.

Forms

To specify the forms available to the printers, type **4** for "Forms." Modify the form list as desired, and then press the <Exit> key when you're through. (See "Selecting Forms.")

Cartridges and Fonts

To specify the fonts available to the printer, type **5** for "Cartridges and Fonts." Modify the font list as desired, and press the <Exit> key when you're through. (See "Selecting Fonts.")

Initial Font

To change the Initial Font for the printer definition, type **6** for "Initial Font." You'll see a list of all the available fonts for the current printer. Position the cursor bar on the name of the desired font (or type **N** for Name Search to locate the name by typing the first few letters of its name). When you've located the font, select it by typing **1** for "Select" (or by pressing ENTER). You'll return to the Edit Printer screen, and the name of the font you specified will appear next to the Initial Font option.

The Initial Font you specify will be the one used initially for all documents you create while this definition is selected (see the section "Selecting a Printer Definition"). You can override the Initial Font for any document using the Initial Font option on the Format Document screen. In addition, you can change the Base Font at any point in a document.

Path for Downloadable Fonts

If your printer uses downloadable fonts, or if you plan to send command files to the printer, you can specify a location for these files. To do this, type **7** for "Path for Downloadable Fonts and Printer Command Files." Next, type a drive letter and colon or a path specification to indicate where you plan to store these files for the printer definition. If you do not specify a location, Word-Perfect will assume that these files will be located on the Word-Perfect System Disk #2, or in the WordPerfect program directory on the hard disk. Press ENTER when you've typed the location.

Selecting Forms

On the Edit Printer screen, choice 4 is used to specify the forms available for use on the printer. Use this feature to indicate where various types of paper are normally stored or how they are inserted into the printer. For example, a laser printer may have a paper tray for letter-size paper, and a manual feed slot for individual sheets and envelopes. You can also indicate the orientation of the text paper, portrait (right side up), or landscape (sideways), if your printer has that capability. Finally, you can specify the size of the form, whether it is always present, and whether to offset the text by a specific distance.

After typing **4** for "Forms," you'll see a Forms Selection screen like the one shown in Figure 11-5. On this screen, all of the defined forms for the printer are shown. You can add, edit, or delete these forms using the commands described in this section. When you're through selecting forms, press the <Exit> key (F7) to return to the Edit Printer screen.

To add a form, type **1** for "Add" (or press the INS key), and the Form Type screen will appear, as shown in Figure 11-6. Select the type of paper for the form from the choices provided. Choice 8, "[ALL OTHERS]" is used to define the location for forms that are requested in a document but not defined. Next, you'll see a screen displaying information about the form you just added, like the one shown in Figure 11-7. You can now modify the options for the form as described below. (Note that the screen for the "[ALL

```
Select Printer: Forms
                                   Orient Init           Offset
Form type              Size        P L    Pres Location  Top    Side

Envelope               4" x 9.5"   N Y     Y   Manual    0"     0"
Standard               8.5" x 11"  Y Y     Y   Contin    0"     0"
[ALL OTHERS]           Width ≤ 8.5"        N   Manual    0"     0"
```

If the requested form is not available, then printing stops and WordPerfect waits for a form to be inserted in the ALL OTHERS location. If the requested form is larger than the ALL OTHERS form, the width is set to the maximum width.

1 Add: 2 Delete: 3 Edit: 3

Figure 11-5.   The Forms Selection screen

```
Select Printer: Form Type

        1 - Standard

        2 - Bond

        3 - Letterhead

        4 - Labels

        5 - Envelope

        6 - Transparency

        7 - Cardstock

        8 - [ALL OTHERS]

        9 - Other




Selection: 1
```

Figure 11-6.   The Form Type screen

OTHERS]" form has no option for orientation, and has only a Maximum Width option, rather than a Size option.)

To edit a form, begin by positioning the cursor bar at the desired form on the Forms Selection screen. (If you wish, you can use the Name Search function to locate the form by pressing the <Search> key (F2), typing the first few letters of the form's name, and then pressing ENTER.) When you've located the desired form, type **3** for "Edit." The Form Information screen will appear (see Figure 11-7). You can now modify the options as with the Add option.

To delete a form, position the cursor bar at the desired form (or use the Name Search function). Then type **2** for "Delete" (or press the DEL key). You'll see a message which asks "Delete Form?" Type **Y** to delete the form, or **N** to abort the command.

```
Select Printer: Forms

           Filename              HPLASEII.PRS

           Form Type             Standard

    1 - Form Size                8.5" x 11"

    2 - Orientation              Portrait, Landscape

    3 - Initially Present        Yes

    4 - Location                 Continuous

    5 - Page Offsets - Top       0"
                      Side       0"




Selection: 0
```

Figure 11-7.   The Form Information screen

When you're through modifying the options for a form after adding or choosing to edit one, you can return to the Edit Printer screen by pressing the <Exit> key (F7). The options for a form are described in the following section.

Form Type

This option is specified when you add a form, and it cannot be changed. If you made a mistake and specified the wrong form type, you'll need to delete the form and create a new one.

Form Size

To modify the size of the form, type **1** for "Form Size," and you'll see the Form Size screen as shown in Figure 11-8. The first size listed for each choice reflects the side of the paper that is *inserted*

```
Select Printer: Form Size
                              Inserted
                              Edge

      1 - Standard            8.5"   x   11"

      2 - Standard Wide       11"    x   8.5"

      3 - Legal               8.5"   x   14"

      4 - Legal Wide          14"    x   8.5"

      5 - Envelope            9.5"   x   4"

      6 - Half Sheet          5.5"   x   8.5"

      7 - US Government       8"     x   11"

      8 - A4                  210mm  x   297mm

      9 - A4 Wide             297mm  x   210mm

      0 - Other

Selection: 1
```

Figure 11-8.   The Form Size screen

into the printer. For example, this may be the top edge of standard letter-size paper, or the right edge of an envelope. If you do not see the desired size of the form on the list, type **O** for "Other," then type a measurement to indicate the width of the form and press ENTER, then type a measurement to indicate the length of the form and press ENTER. (For example, an envelope form for a laser printer would be defined as 4″ wide and 9.5″ long.) You'll return to the Form Information screen, and the size you requested will be shown next to the Form Size option.

Orientation

The Orientation option allows you to specify whether the text on the form will be printed parallel to the inserted edge of the paper (portrait), or perpendicular to the inserted edge (landscape). This option is typically used with laser printers, which can easily rotate text. Some laser printers require specific landscape fonts before you can print in a landscape orientation (see the section "Selecting Fonts").

To change the orientation of the form, type **2** for "Orientation," then type **1** for "Portrait," **2** for "Landscape," or **3** for "Both." (Select "Both" only if your printer is capable of printing text in both portrait and landscape orientations on the same page.)

Initially Present

Use this option to specify whether the form will be available each time a print job begins, or whether WordPerfect should stop at the point in the document where the form is requested, and wait for you to make the form available. For example, you may need to insert a different type of paper into a sheet feeder bin, or insert a different paper cassette into a laser printer. If you specify that the form is not initially present, then WordPerfect will stop printing when it encounters the Form Change code in a document. You'll need to go to the Control Printer screen and use the Go command to restart printing after you've made the form available. If you want the printer to handle the pause (such as for an envelope on a laser printer), indicate that the form is initially present.

To specify whether the form is initially present or not, type **3** for "Initially Present," and then type **Y** or **N**.

Location

You use this option to specify where the form will be located on the printer. For example, you may have several bins on a sheet feeder, you may need to insert pages one at a time, or the pages may be fed continuously.

To specify the location of the form, type **4** for "Location," then type **1** for "Continuous" if the paper is fed continuously by the printer (as is fanfold paper on a dot matrix or daisywheel printer, or paper from a cassette on a laser printer). If the form is in a specific bin on a sheet feeder (and you've selected a sheet feeder on the Edit Printer screen), type **2** for "Bin Number," then type the number of the bin, and press ENTER. Finally, if you need to insert the pages one at a time (as you might with letterhead pages on a dot matrix printer or envelopes on a laser printer), type 3 for "Manual." The choice you select will appear on the screen next to the Location option.

Note that you can indicate that hand-fed forms for laser printers (such as envelopes) can be defined as "Manual." If you want the printer to receive explicit instructions on the type of form to be used (to accommodate a display prompt on the printer, for example), you can define a laser printer as using a sheet feeder (even if you aren't actually using one), and then specify manual feed by indicating a bin number. Refer to the Help screen for the sheet feeder you've selected to determine which bin number is used for this purpose.

Page Offsets

The last option on this screen allows you to specify page offsets for the form. This option lets you compensate for forms that are aligned in the printer differently from standard forms. For example, you may have to roll a hand-fed form into your printer farther than continuous paper (so that the top edge is placed under the platen). Or your sheet feeder might be located in the center of the platen rather than on the left side. You can specify an offset for either the top edge, the left edge, or both. You can specify both positive and negative offsets. Page offsets enable WordPerfect to accurately use the margin settings for documents with all forms, regardless of their position in the printer.

To change the offsets for the form, type 5 for "Page Offsets." Type a measurement to indicate the distance to allow for the top edge of the paper, and press ENTER. Next, type a measurement to indicate the distance to allow for the left edge of the paper, and press ENTER.

Entering a positive offset for the top edge means that you have to position the top edge of the paper the distance specified *above* the printhead. WordPerfect will avoid leaving the normal amount of space at the top of the page to compensate for the distance already advanced down the page. Entering a negative offset for the top edge means that you have to position the top edge of the paper the distance specified *below* the printhead. WordPerfect will leave more than the normal amount of space at the top of the page to compensate for the additional distance to be advanced.

Entering a positive offset for the left edge means that you have to position the left edge of the paper the distance specified to the *right* of the printhead. WordPerfect will move farther across the page to leave more space on the left edge of the paper. Entering a negative offset for the left edge means that you have to position the left edge of the paper the distance specified to the *left* of the printhead. WordPerfect will move a shorter distance across the page to compensate for the distance already advanced.

Selecting Fonts

On the Edit Printer screen, selection 5 specifies which font resources are available to your printer *besides* those fonts which are built-in. You may, for example, have a printer that uses downloadable (sometimes called *soft fonts*) or font cartridges.

To select fonts for the printer, type **5** for "Cartridges and Fonts." If the printer you're defining does not have any cartridges or fonts, you'll see a message to this effect. Otherwise, you'll see a Cartridges and Fonts screen similar to the one shown in Figure 11-9.

Note that WordPerfect must have access to the same .ALL printer file that you used to create the printer definition. If you've left the disk in the disk drive, or if the files are on your hard disk, you can proceed normally. Otherwise, you'll see a message asking for the Printer Disk. Insert the *same* Printer Disk you used to create the definition, type the drive letter followed by a colon, and press ENTER.

This screen lists the printer's available font resources. The first column shows the name of each font type, such as "Cartridge Fonts" or "Downloadable Fonts." The second column describes the font resources available to the printer in a quantifiable form, such as memory for fonts or slots for font cartridges. The third column

Select Printer: Cartridges and Fonts

Font Category	Resource	Quantity
Cartridge Fonts	Font Cartridge Slot	2
Soft Fonts	Memory available for fonts	350 K

1 Select Fonts; 2 Change Quantity; N Name search: 1

Figure 11-9.   The Cartridges and Fonts screen

indicates the quantity of the resource that the printer can accommodate— for example, the amount of memory or the number of slots.

On this screen, you can specify which fonts will be available from each resource or modify the available quantity of any resource. These actions are described in the following sections. When you have completed modifying the printer's resources, press the <Exit> key to return to the Edit Printer screen. When you do this, WordPerfect updates the fonts in the Printer Definition file, and calculates correct fonts for Automatic Font Changes (see "Using Fonts" later in this chapter).

Changing Resource Quantity

To modify the quantity of an available font resource on your printer, begin by positioning the cursor on the resource you want to affect. Then type **2** for "Change Quantity." At the "Quantity:" prompt, type the desired quantity for the resource, and press

ENTER. WordPerfect displays the new quantity on the resource's line.

For downloadable fonts, the resource you will quantify is the amount of RAM in the printer, which affects the number of fonts that can be downloaded at any one time. (Note that your printer may have other limitations on the number of fonts that can be printed on a page. The Help provided for the printer definition should detail any such limitations.) The default setting for this option will be the amount of RAM normally provided with the printer. If you've upgraded your printer's memory, you need to tell WordPerfect you have more room for fonts by increasing this number. For example, if you've increased your memory to one megabyte, you would enter 1000 (for 1000K) for the quantity of RAM available.

For cartridge fonts, the resource you're quantifying is the number of slots on your printer which can hold a font cartridge. Normally, this will be one, but there are some printers that have two or more available slots.

The quantity you enter for a resource will limit the fonts you can select for the resource. For example, WordPerfect limits the number of downloadable fonts you can select to the number that can be downloaded into the printer at any one time. Similarly, you can select only the number of font cartridges that can be present in the printer at any one time. In this way WordPerfect prevents you from creating a document which you would not be able to print.

However, there may be times when you want to override this protection. For instance, you may have more font cartridges than you can insert into the printer at one time, or more downloadable fonts than can fit into the printer's memory at one time. Normally, this would mean that you have to create more than one printer definition (by using the Copy command on the Select Printer menu). If you wish to take the responsibility upon yourself to avoid creating documents with too many fonts, you can fool WordPerfect into thinking you have a more capable printer than you actually have. In this way, all of the fonts you own will be available to you at any time (although in the case of cartridge fonts, you must be sure not to request fonts from an unavailable cartridge in a document).

For example, you may want to change the quantity of memory in your printer to 2000, even though it actually contains much less. This would allow you to select many more downloadable fonts for the definition.

Selecting Fonts for a Resource

To specify which fonts will be available for a resource (for instance, which cartridges will be put into a font cartridge slot, or which downloadable fonts you have), begin by positioning the cursor bar on the resource that you want to modify. Then type **1** for "Select Fonts," and you'll see the Font Selection screen. For downloadable (or *soft*) fonts, the screen will resemble the one shown in Figure 11-10. For cartridge fonts, the screen will resemble the one shown in Figure 11-11.

Now you can identify which fonts you have available for this printer definition. In the upper-right corner of the screen, you can see that WordPerfect is keeping track of the total quantity of the resource that is available, as well as what remains after you've

```
Select Printer: Cartridges and Fonts

                                    Total Quantity:    350 K
                                Available Quantity:    350 K

Soft Fonts                                          Quantity Used

 (AC) Helu 06pt                                        8 K
 (AC) Helu 06pt (Land)                                 8 K
 (AC) Helu 06pt Bold                                   8 K
 (AC) Helu 06pt Bold (Land)                            8 K
 (AC) Helu 06pt Italic                                 8 K
 (AC) Helu 06pt Italic (Land)                          8 K
 (AC) Helu 08pt                                        9 K
 (AC) Helu 08pt (Land)                                 9 K
 (AC) Helu 08pt Bold                                  11 K
 (AC) Helu 08pt Bold (Land)                           11 K
 (AC) Helu 08pt Italic                                10 K
 (AC) Helu 08pt Italic (Land)                         10 K
 (AC) Helu 10pt                                       13 K
 (AC) Helu 10pt (Land)                                13 K
 (AC) Helu 10pt Bold                                  13 K

Mark Fonts:   × Present when print job begins        Press Exit to save
              + Can be loaded during print job     Press Cancel to cancel_
```

Figure 11-10.   The Downloadable (Soft) Font Selection screen

```
Select Printer: Cartridges and Fonts

                                          Total Quantity:     2
                                      Available Quantity:     2

Cartridge Fonts                                              Quantity Used

   A Cartridge                                                    1
   B Cartridge                                                    1
   C Cartridge                                                    1
   D Cartridge                                                    1
   E Cartridge                                                    1
   F Cartridge                                                    1
   G Cartridge                                                    1
   H Cartridge                                                    1
   J Cartridge                                                    1
   K Cartridge                                                    1
   L Cartridge                                                    1
   M Cartridge                                                    1
   N Cartridge                                                    1
   P Cartridge                                                    1
   Q Cartridge                                                    1

Mark Fonts:  × Present when print job begins          Press Exit to save
                                                      Press Cancel to cancel_
```

Figure 11-11.   The Cartridge Font Selection screen

selected the desired fonts. As you begin to select fonts, the available quantity will decrease.

Mark with an asterisk (*) those fonts which will be "present" in the printer when you start a print job. For font cartridges, this means that the cartridge will be inserted in the printer. For downloadable fonts, this means that you will have already downloaded the fonts to the printer before you issue a print job. To do this, select the "Initialize Printer" command from the Print screen.

For downloadable fonts, mark with a plus sign (+) those fonts which can be downloaded during a print job. This tells WordPerfect that it must download the fonts to the printer while printing. To make room for more fonts, some printers allow these fonts to be unloaded when they are no longer needed. (Note that you must use the plus sign on the top row of keys on the keyboard.)

For daisywheel printers, mark with an asterisk the print wheel that you plan normally to leave in the printer. Also mark that and all other print wheels with a plus sign to indicate that these wheels can be loaded and unloaded during a print job.

To remove a mark that you have placed on a font, position the cursor bar on the font and press the DEL key. As you continue to mark fonts, you'll see the available memory decrease. When you are through marking fonts, or when you run out of available memory, press the <Exit> key to return to the Cartridges and Fonts screen.

Printing to Disk

On the Edit Printer screen, choice 2 allows you to specify the destination for output. Normally, this will be either a parallel or serial port. However, you can also direct output to a disk file instead of to a printer. To do this, type 8 for "Other," and at the "Device or Filename" prompt, type the file name that you want to use for the output.

The file that will be created when you generate a print job using this printer definition will contain all of the special control codes for the printer, even though you are only storing the output in a file at this point. You can later send this file to a printer by entering this line at the DOS prompt:

```
COPY filename device_name
```

where "filename" is the name you just specified and "device_name" is the port that the printer is attached to (for example, LPT1: for a parallel port or COM1: for a serial port).

Printing to disk is useful if you are writing documents at one location and planning to print them at another location. Normally, you would have to take the WordPerfect system disks with you and hope that the hardware setup is compatible with your copy of the program. With the print-to-disk feature, you could format and output the document to disk and then simply take the formatted file with you to the system that has the printer. Just make sure that the document is formatted for the correct printer definition when you generate the print job.

SELECTING A PRINTER DEFINITION

Every document is formatted for a specific printer definition. The name of the .PRS Printer Definition file for which a document is formatted is saved on disk with the document. In this way, WordPerfect is able to keep track of the correct fonts and forms for the printer, and therefore will know how to format the document. If you select a different printer definition for a document, WordPerfect will make its "best guess" to match up your font and form selections with those in the new printer definition. If you later select the original printer definition, all of the originally selected fonts and forms will be restored.

If you delete a Printer Definition file that you've used to format your documents, or if you bring a document to another computer which does not have the .PRS file you used, WordPerfect will display an error message when you retrieve the document. The message will indicate that the .PRS file that was selected the last time the document was saved could not be found. A message will then be displayed indicating that the document is being formatted for the default printer. The printer that was selected when you asked to retrieve the document will temporarily become the document's selected printer, and all fonts and forms will be modified to conform to the new printer definition. If you then save the document, this definition will permanently become its selected definition.

To change the selected printer for a document, first be sure that you have retrieved the document. Then press the <Print> key (SHIFT+F7). On the Print screen, you'll see the name of the currently selected printer appear next to the "Select Printer" prompt. To change it, type **S** for "Select Printer," and the Printer Selection screen will be displayed. (If the printer definition you want is not displayed on this screen, you'll need to add it. See the section "Installing Printers" earlier in this chapter.) Now position the cursor bar at the desired printer definition, and type 1 for "Select" (or press ENTER). WordPerfect returns to the Print screen, and the name of the printer you selected appears next to the "Select Printer" prompt. Press the <Exit> key (F7) to return to the Document Editing screen. The document has now been formatted for the newly selected printer definition.

If you wish, you can perform this selection only for the purpose of printing the document. If you simply clear the screen (without saving the document) after printing, you will not record the change in the printer selection for the document. If you do this, make sure that you've saved the document first.

USING FONTS

You can control the appearance of the text in your document through a number of functions all located on the <Font> key (CTRL+F8). These include

- A *Base Font*, chosen from the list of available fonts for the current printer definition
- Appearance attributes, such as boldface, underline, and italics
- Size changes
- Color

Appearance, size, and color attributes all modify the Base Font in some way. Most of these are referred to as *Automatic Font Changes*, because they select a different font related to the current Base Font. For example, if you're using a Times Roman font, and you format some text to appear in italics, WordPerfect will automatically switch to the Times Roman Italic font (which is actually a separate font). If you were later to change the Base Font for the document (or for a section of a document), all of the automatic font changes you made would conform to the newly selected Base

Font. Because of this, it's always preferable to use the automatic font changes to change the appearance of the text (even though you often could choose a different Base Font to achieve the same effect).

To see all of the supported appearance, size, and color features available on your printer, retrieve and print the file PRINTER.TST, which is located on the Conversion Disk.

There are three different places where you can specify a font: as a default for a printer definition, as a default in Format Document for a specific document, and at any point in the document's text. These operate in a hierarchical fashion: the default for a printer definition affects what the default will be in Format Document for all documents *created* with that definition selected; and the default in Format Document specifies the Base Font in the document until it is changed in the text.

Printer Definition Initial Font

The Printer Definition Initial Font selection affects all documents that are *created* while that definition is selected. As long as the screen is clear, changes you make to the currently selected printer definition's Initial Font will affect the Initial Font for the current document (which is as yet empty). But as soon as you begin typing, you "lock in" the Initial Font of the selected printer definition for the current document. Further changes to the printer definition's Initial Font will not affect the Initial Font of the document (and will not affect any documents that you've already created).

To change the Initial Font for a printer definition, you need to be at the Edit Printer screen. To get there, begin by pressing the <Print> key (SHIFT+F7). Then type **S** for "Select Printer," position the cursor bar on the name of the printer whose definition you want to affect, and type **3** for "Edit." Now type **6** for "Initial Font," and an Initial Font Selection screen will appear similar to the one shown in Figure 11-12. Next, position the cursor bar on the font that you want to define as the Initial Font. If you wish, you can type **N** or press the <Search> key (F2) to use Name

```
Select Printer: Initial Font

* Courier 10 pitch (PC-8)
  Courier 10 pitch (Roman-8)
  Courier Bold 10 pitch (PC-8)
  Courier Bold 10 pitch (Roman-8)
  Helv 08pt (Z1A)
  Helv 10pt (Z1A)
  Helv 10pt Bold (Z1A)
  Helv 10pt Italic (Z1A)
  Helv 12pt (Z1A)
  Helv 12pt Bold (Z1A)
  Helv 12pt Italic (Z1A)
  Helv 14pt Bold (Z1A)
  Line Printer 16.66 pitch (PC-8)
  Line Printer 16.66 pitch (Roman-8)
  Solid Line Draw 10 pitch
  Solid Line Draw 12 pitch
  Tms Rmn 08pt (Z1A)
  Tms Rmn 10pt (Z1A)
  Tms Rmn 10pt Bold (Z1A)
  Tms Rmn 10pt Italic (Z1A)
  Tms Rmn 12pt (Z1A)

1 Select; N Name search: 1
```

Figure 11-12.   The Initial Font Selection screen

Search mode to locate the desired font; type the first few letters of the font name, and press ENTER to leave Name Search.

When you've located the font you want, press ENTER to select it. If you're using a printer which has scaleable fonts (such as a PostScript printer), you'll be asked for a point size for the font (the default choice is 10 points). Type a number representing the desired point size, and press ENTER. The font you selected will now appear next to the "Initial Font" option on the Edit Printer screen. Press the <Exit> key several times to return to the Document Editing screen.

Now that you've selected an Initial Font for the printer definition, WordPerfect will make that font the Initial Font for each document you create with this definition selected.

Document Initial Font

The Document Initial Font controls the font that will be used for the document's text until a [Font:] code is encountered in the document (see "Changing the Base Font"). In addition, the Document Initial Font affects footnotes, headers, footers, and page numbers in the document.

The Document Initial Font is first set to the Initial Font for the printer definition selected when the document is created. To change the Document Initial Font, begin by pressing the <Format> key (SHIFT+F8). The cursor can be anywhere in the document. Type 3 for "Document," and then 3 for "Initial Font," and you'll see the Document Initial Font screen. Next, position the cursor bar on the font that you want for the Initial Font. If you wish, you can type N or press the <Search> key (F2) to use Name Search mode to locate the desired font; type the first few letters of the font name, and press ENTER to leave Name Search.

When you've located the font you want, press ENTER to select it. If you're using a printer which has scaleable fonts (such as a PostScript printer), you'll be asked for a point size for the font (the default choice is 10 points). Type a number representing the desired point size, and press ENTER. The font you selected will now appear next to the "Initial Font" option on the Format Document screen. Press the <Exit> key to return to the Document Editing screen.

The Document Initial Font affects not only the text in the body of the document, but also other elements such as footnotes, headers, footers, and page numbering. For elements which may have *options* defined for them in the document (such as footnote options), the elements will use the Document Initial Font unless you've inserted a code for options in the document (such as a [Ftn Opt] code for footnotes). If you have inserted a code, then all of the related elements from that point forward will use whatever Base Font was in effect at that location. Headers and footers (which have no options) always use the Base Font and appearance attributes that are in effect when their codes are encountered.

For any of these elements, you can always override the Base Font by inserting a [Font:] code *within* one of the elements, such as within an individual footnote.

Changing the Base Font

To switch to a new Base Font at any point in the body of a document (or anywhere else you are editing text, such as in a header, footnote, figure caption, and so on), begin by positioning the cursor where you want the new font to take effect. Then press the <Font> key (CTRL+F8), and type **4** for "Base Font," and the Base Font Selection screen will appear. Next, position the cursor bar on the desired Base Font. If you wish, you can type **N** or press the <Search> key (F2) to use the Name Search mode to locate the desired font; type the first few letters of the font name, and press ENTER to leave Name Search.

When you've located the font you want, press ENTER to select it. If you're using a printer which has scaleable fonts (such as a PostScript printer), you'll be asked for a point size for the font (the default choice is 10 points). Type a number representing the desired point size, and press ENTER. You'll be returned to the Document Editing screen, and a [Font:] code will be inserted into the document at the cursor position.

Size and Appearance Attributes

In addition to changing the Base Font in a document, you can also use the Size and Appearance commands to change *variations* on the current Base Font. The actual appearance of the text will vary depending on the current Base Font. You could easily change the Base Font in a document, and all of the size and appearance codes would then reflect the new Base Font.

All Size and Appearance commands insert Matched Pair hidden codes. This means you can use them in one of two ways. To modify text that you're about to type, press the <Font> key (CTRL+F8), type **1** for "Size" or **2** for "Appearance," select the desired attribute, type the text, and then issue the same command again. (You can also use the Normal command on the Font menu to return to the Base Font at any point, turning off any active Size and Appearance codes.) To modify text that already exists in the document, begin by marking the text as a block, then press the <Font> key, type **1** for "Size" or **2** for "Appearance," and select the desired attribute. WordPerfect inserts the attribute's starting and ending codes for you.

Size Attributes

The size menu contains options for printing characters superscripted or subscripted, as well as in a variety of sizes. Superscripted characters appear one-third line higher than the rest of the characters on the line. Subscripted characters appear one-third line lower. The size options range from Fine to Extra Large. Not all of the size options may be implemented for your printer.

For printers which have scaleable fonts (such as PostScript printers), the size attributes on the Size menu are calculated based on a given ratio to the size of the Base Font. For example, let's assume you are using an 11-point Base Font. In this case, Fine would produce 6-point text (about 55% of Normal), Small would be 8 points (about 73% of normal), Large would be 14 points (about 127% of Normal), Very Large would be 18 points (about 164% of Normal), and Extra Large would be 24 points (about 218% of Normal).

Appearance Attributes

The Appearance menu includes boldface and underline functions (which you can also access with the <Bold> and <Underline> keys), as well as other special print attributes, such as italics and outlining. Some of these may cause your printer to automatically switch to a new font. Others, such as underlining, will simply modify the current font.

Color Text

To change the color of the text (if you have a printer which supports color printing), begin by positioning the cursor at the place in the document where you want the new color to take effect. Then press the <Font> key (CTRL+F8), and type 5 for "Print Color," and the Print Color screen will appear, as shown in Figure 11-13. You can now choose any one of the colors shown by typing the indicated letter, or you can type O for "Other," and enter your own percentages for a mixture of the base colors red, green, and blue.

When you've made your choice, press the <Exit> key to return

```
Print Color

                        Primary Color Mixture
                        Red      Green      Blue

        1 - Black        0%        0%        0%
        2 - White      100%      100%      100%
        3 - Red         67%        0%        0%
        4 - Green        0%       67%        0%
        5 - Blue         0%        0%       67%
        6 - Yellow      67%       67%        0%
        7 - Magenta     67%        0%       67%
        8 - Cyan         0%       67%       67%
        9 - Orange      67%       25%        0%
        A - Gray        50%       50%       50%
        N - Brown       67%       33%        0%
        0 - Other

        Current Color    0%        0%        0%




Selection: 0
```

Figure 11-13.   The Print Color screen

to the Document Editing screen. A [Color:] code is inserted in the document at the cursor position. From that point forward in the document, the chosen color will be in effect, until another [Color:] code is encountered.

To switch back to normal text, repeat the command described above, choosing "Black" as the color. The text appears in the specified color only when you print the document. There is no way to have the text appear in the selected color on the screen (you can only affect colors on the screen for all of the text—see Appendix A, "Using Setup").

CHANGING FORMS AND PAPER SIZES

WordPerfect allows you to work with various sizes and types of paper, envelopes, and other material on which you want to print.

Printer definitions contain definitions of the *forms* available for a given printer. You can add any additional forms you may need (see "Installing Printers" earlier in this chapter).

When you perform the Page Size/Type command, WordPerfect checks your request against the available forms for the currently selected printer. If it finds a match, it uses that form. If it cannot find a match, the program attempts to use the form defined as "[ALL OTHERS]," if there is one defined. Finally, it will try to find the closest match to the requested paper size and type among the defined forms.

To request a different form in a document, begin by positioning the cursor at the place in the document where you want to begin using the form (usually at the top of a page). Then press the <Format> key (SHIFT+F8), type 2 for "Page," and then 8 for "Paper Size/Type." You'll see the Paper Size screen, as shown in

```
Format: Paper Size

     1 - Standard              (8.5" x 11")

     2 - Standard Landscape    (11" x 8.5")

     3 - Legal                 (8.5" x 14")

     4 - Legal Landscape       (14" x 8.5")

     5 - Envelope              (9.5" x 4")

     6 - Half Sheet            (5.5" x 8.5")

     7 - US Government         (8" x 11")

     8 - A4                    (210mm x 297mm)

     9 - A4 Landscape          (297mm x 210mm)

     0 - Other


Selection: 0
```

Figure 11-14.   The Paper Size screen

Figure 11-14. Select the size of the paper you want to use by typing the appropriate number. If none of the choices corresponds to the size you want, type **O** for "Other," type a measurement to indicate a width and press ENTER, and then type a measurement to indicate a length and press ENTER.

Next, you'll see the Paper Type screen, as shown in Figure 11-15. Select the type of paper you want to use by typing the appropriate number. If none of the choices corresponds to the type you want, type **O** for "Other," and the Other Forms screen will appear. On this screen, you can position the cursor bar on the name of one of the "Other" forms that have been defined for this printer definition. When you've selected the correct form, press ENTER. If you want to specify a form that does not appear on this list (because you plan to add it later, or because you plan to use the document with a different printer definition file at a later time), type **2** for

---

```
Format: Paper Type

    1 - Standard

    2 - Bond

    3 - Letterhead

    4 - Labels

    5 - Envelope

    6 - Transparency

    7 - Cardstock

    8 - Other




Selection: 0
```

Figure 11-15.   The Paper Type screen

"Other," type the name of a form, and press ENTER.

When you've returned to the Format Page screen, you'll see the result of your form selection. If WordPerfect found a perfect match between your request and a defined form, you'll see the size and name of the defined form. If it was not able to find a match, you'll see an asterisk next to the paper size and/or the paper type. If you have an "[ALL OTHERS]" form defined, then that form's location is used, and the Maximum Width you specified will be imposed on the size you entered. If you later add the appropriate form, WordPerfect will adjust this request to reflect the new form, showing the correct name and removing the asterisks.

To return to the Document Editing screen, press the <Exit> key (F7). A [Paper Sz/Typ:] code is inserted into the text at the cursor position.

SENDING PRINTER CODES

WordPerfect sends most control codes to the printer automatically, usually in response to a formatting command that you inserted into your text. However, you can manually send control codes at any point in the document. This allows you to use printer functions that do not correspond to WordPerfect functions. (Note that WordPerfect usually supports all of a printer's features. Be sure you've checked to see whether a built-in function will perform the action you're seeking.)

To manually send control codes, you must first find out the ASCII control codes that the printer uses to initiate the desired function. (See "Interacting with ASCII Files" in Chapter 8, "Integration with Other Products," for a description of the ASCII character set.) These codes are usually listed in the printer's manual. The codes can be shown in many ways, but a code that represents an alphanumeric character is usually shown as the character itself, while a control code is usually indicated either by its ASCII control code number or by a description of the code.

For example, you may want to have your printer use ultra-condensed (very small) print, and there is no WordPerfect font set up to use this type style. Upon looking in your printer manual, you will find that the command to initiate this print style is "ESCAPE Q." You might also see a notation that the control code ESCAPE is assigned to ASCII code 27. (Most printer code sequences start with the ESCAPE control code. This code basically tells the printer: "Look out, here comes a special function." The characters that follow the ESCAPE indicate which function to initiate.) Because Q is a printable character, it is unnecessary to use its ASCII code. Therefore, to use this function you will need to send the printer an ASCII code 27, followed by the letter Q. (Since uppercase letters have different ASCII codes from lowercase letters, it is very important that you type the *exact* letter indicated in the manual.)

Sending a Code

To send the code sequence to the printer from within a document, first move the cursor to the point where you want the new style to start. Then press the <Format> key (SHIFT+F8), type **4** for "Other," **6** for "Printer Functions," and **2** for "Printer Command." From the menu, type **1** for "Command," and you'll see a "Command:" prompt. At this point, you can enter any *printable* character simply by typing it. To enter a control code, you must enter its ASCII code surrounded by angle brackets (less-than and greater-than signs).

To enter the example for ultra-condensed print, type <27> (this sends the ASCII control code 27, which is ESCAPE), followed by **Q**. When you have entered the codes, press ENTER. Press the <Exit> key (F7) to return to the Document Editing screen. You can use Reveal Codes to see that the function inserted a [Ptr Cmnd:] hidden code at the cursor position that contains the codes you entered. When the program encounters this hidden code while printing, the printer codes will be sent to the printer just as you entered them.

Sending Many Codes

Some printers require long strings of codes to invoke various features. Also, some dot matrix printers allow you to transfer a *custom character set* into the printer's memory. (This allows you to create your own special characters.) This process also requires long strings of control codes to be sent to the printer.

You can create a file on disk that contains these code sequences and have WordPerfect send them to the printer for you. You can create this file using a program written in BASIC or with a text editor. To have WordPerfect send the file, first move the cursor to the place in your document where you want the program to send the file. Then press the <Format> key (SHIFT+F8), type **4** for "Other," **6** for "Printer Functions," and **2** for "Printer Command." From the menu, type **2** for file, type the file name (including any drive letter or path specification necessary), and press ENTER. Press the <Exit> key to return to the Document Editing screen. A hidden code is placed in the text at the cursor position.

You can use Reveal Codes to see the code. You will see that the [Ptr Cmnd:] Code contains the name of the file you specified. When WordPerfect encounters this code during printing, the control codes in the specified file will be sent to the printer.

12

INTEGRATION WITH OTHER PRODUCTS

WordPerfect is well equipped to interact with files from other programs. It can read and write ASCII text files directly and can translate other types of files to and from WordPerfect format. With WordPerfect, you can also write macros to aid in file translation.

This chapter will discuss each program individually, describing the best procedures for transferring files to and from WordPerfect for each one. Some information will be duplicated in the various sections, but each section will describe the entire procedure necessary for the transfer.

In this chapter, the term *importing a file* means transferring a file from another program into WordPerfect format. The term *exporting a file* means transferring a WordPerfect file to another program.

The material in this chapter may seem somewhat technical to you. However, you will always be provided with explicit directions for making the integration between WordPerfect and the program you are working with.

DEALING WITH ASCII FILES

What is an ASCII file? ASCII stands for American Standard Code for Information Interchange. This code was established as a standard means of communication between computers, as well as between computers and peripherals such as printers.

In the ASCII environment, each character (letter, number, or punctuation mark) is identified by a number, called the character's *ASCII code*. ASCII codes 1 through 31 are considered *control codes*. Instead of producing characters, these codes usually control a function, such as clearing the screen or positioning the cursor. Many of the control codes were originally intended for use with line printers (like daisy wheel printers).

As originally defined, the ASCII codes range from 0 to 127. However, most computers have an extended ASCII character set that contains 256 characters and control codes. In the IBM Extended Character Set, the extra 128 codes consist of graphics characters, foreign letters, and special symbols. Some programs use these extra codes to designate formatting commands.

The terms "ASCII file" and "DOS text file" refer to files that contain very few, if any, control codes and no codes at all higher than the original 128. Therefore, ASCII files consist primarily of ASCII codes 32 through 127. Since most word processing programs insert control codes to add formatting commands like bold-facing and underlining, files produced by these programs are not considered ASCII files.

The most rudimentary method of transferring a document from another word processor into WordPerfect is to convert it first to an ASCII file from within the other program and then to retrieve it into WordPerfect using the Text In/Out function. Use this method only when no other transfer method is available. Since the ASCII file will not contain any control codes, all formatting will usually be lost with this method.

When you receive data by modem, it is commonly stored on disk in an ASCII file. You can use WordPerfect to edit the file by importing it with the Text In/Out function.

To see WordPerfect's functions for dealing with ASCII files, press the <Text In/Out> key (CTRL+F5) and the Text In/Out menu will appear. Menu choices 1 and 3 are used to import and export ASCII files.

Importing ASCII Files

To retrieve an ASCII file, type **1** for "DOS Text" from the Text In/Out menu. There are basically two types of ASCII files, those in a "streaming" format, which have Hard Returns only at the end of each paragraph, and those with a Hard Return at the end of every line. In WordPerfect, you have two choices for retrieving ASCII files: direct, or with Hard Return conversion. Retrieve streaming ASCII files directly with choice 2 from the menu. ASCII files with a Hard Return at the end of every line can either be retrieved directly (with choice 2) or with Hard Return conversion (choice 3).

Retrieving ASCII Files Directly

You should retrieve streaming ASCII files directly—as they require no converting—as well as spreadsheet or database "print-to-disk" reports, program files, or other files with non-paragraph form text. If a file was formatted with longer lines than WordPerfect's default margins allow, the program will insert Soft Returns in the text. In this case, you must widen WordPerfect's margins to accommodate the ASCII file.

To retrieve an ASCII file directly, type **2** for "Retrieve" from the DOS Text menu, type the name of the ASCII file, and press ENTER. (Alternatively, you can use the List Files function, highlight the file you want to retrieve, and then type **5** for "Text In." The ASCII file will be inserted at the cursor position.)

Retrieving ASCII Files
with Hard Return Conversion

You should retrieve ASCII files, which contain paragraph-form text, and are not in the streaming format, with Hard Return Conversion (option 3 from the DOS Text menu). This function converts Hard Returns to Soft Returns, so that WordPerfect will be able to reformat the text when you begin editing, or when you use margins, tabs, indents, or other formatting functions.

Hard Returns are converted to Soft Returns using these guidelines:

- Any occurrence of two Hard Returns in a row are left intact. This is usually an indication of the end of a paragraph and a following blank line, so the Hard Returns are not converted.

- An occurrence of a Hard Return that falls within the Hyphenation Hot Zone is converted to a Soft Return. The Hot Zone is initially set to extend from 10% of the line length to the left of the right margin to 4% of line length to the right of the right margin. So, any Hard Returns which are located near the end of a line will be converted.

By following these rules, WordPerfect will normally convert all of the unnecessary Hard Returns. However, it may miss some of them, or convert ones that shouldn't be converted. Look out for these problems as you edit the file. If you are in doubt, check the Reveal Codes screen to see if a line ends with a Soft or Hard Return. You may also need to change the margin settings to reflect the format of the ASCII file *before* retrieving the files.

Tab Settings

ASCII files sometimes contain tab codes. A tab code is one of the few control codes that are included in an ASCII file. A tab code (ASCII code 9) is considered a control code because it is assigned to one of the first 32 codes of the ASCII character set.

You know that you can change the tab settings in your documents at any time, but in the ASCII environment, tabs are usually 8 spaces apart. Because of this, you might want to set a tab stop every 8 spaces (or every 0.8″) in the WordPerfect document so that the text will be formatted correctly.

Use the incremental method of specifying tab stops to place them 0.8″ apart. (See the section "Line Formatting" in Chapter 1 for a discussion of setting tabs with the incremental method.)

Editing ASCII Files

If you frequently work with ASCII files which are formatted with a particular line length or with tabs set for every 0.8″ you might want to create a macro that inserts these codes for you. This way, you can execute the macro before retrieving the ASCII file, and the file will be formatted correctly.

P-Edit (a *program editor* that comes with WordPerfect Library) is a better tool for working with large ASCII files than is WordPerfect. Most importantly, it will retrieve and save them much faster than WordPerfect, since it does not have to take the time to format the text within margins and pages. For a description of WordPerfect Library, see Appendix C, "WordPerfect Corporation Programs."

Exporting ASCII Files

You can save any WordPerfect document as an ASCII file, either in a DOS Text format with a Hard Return at the end of every line, or in a Generic Word Processing "streaming" format with a Hard Return only at the end of each paragraph.

Many positioning functions will be converted to spaces to "fill" the area that would normally be blank on the WordPerfect screen. For example, centered lines will have spaces inserted in place of the Center code, so that the line *looks* centered. In the same way, other codes are converted to simulate the effect they produce on the WordPerfect screen.

Saving in DOS Text Format

This format is very useful for creating documents which you plan to send as messages through remote bulletin boards and electronic mail services. It is also used for saving DOS files such as batch files, or program files.

Tabs are converted to spaces with this function and a Hard Return is placed at the end of every line. This means the text will look correctly formatted, no matter how it is viewed, or with which word processing program. However, it also means that the format cannot be easily changed, as it could be if the tabs were left intact. To create a file with the tab codes intact, use the Generic Word Processing format.

To save a file in the DOS Text format, type **1** from the Text In/Out menu, and then **1** for "Save." Type the name of the file, and press ENTER.

Saving in Generic Word Processing Format

This format is used to save a WordPerfect document in a form that will be most easily readable by another word processing program. If you cannot find a direct conversion between WordPerfect and another program (see the next section, "Using Convert"), this is the best way to transfer the file.

In this format, Hard Returns are placed only at the end of each paragraph, instead of at the end of each line. In this way, the word processing program that will import the file will be able to easily reformat the text.

In addition, [Tab] codes and Hard Page Breaks are retained. Many other formatting functions, however, are converted to spaces.

To save a document in the Generic Word Processing format, type **4** for "Save Generic" from the Text In/Out menu. Enter the desired name for the file, and press ENTER.

Hard Return Codes

Each Hard Return used in the file formats described actually consists of two ASCII codes: a code 13 (which is a carriage return) and a code 10 (which is a line feed). The reason that two codes are used for this simple function dates back to the early days of teletype printers. For the purposes of this book, it is sufficient to say that this is considered standard for ASCII files in the MS-DOS environment.

In some situations, one of the two codes may not be needed. For example, programs on the Apple Macintosh use only a code 13 (carriage return) at the end of each paragraph. If you retrieve a file that you have saved as an ASCII file from WordPerfect into a Macintosh word processing program, you will see a small box (indicating an unprintable character) at the beginning of every line. This character is the code 10 (line feed) that is found after each code 13. (Note that you can easily transfer documents between WordPerfect for the PC and WordPerfect for the Macintosh.)

Following is a BASIC program that removes line feeds from a text file. (To use the program to remove carriage returns instead of line feeds, change the "13" in line 130 to "10".)

```
10  CLEAR:CLS:KEY OFF
20  PRINT "Program to strip LF's from text files":PRINT
30  PRINT "Hit RETURN to quit":PRINT
40  INPUT "Input file name";INF$
50  IF INF$="" THEN 200
60  INPUT "Output file name";OUTF$
70  OPEN "i",1,INF$
80  OPEN "o",2,OUTF$
90  LNFL=LOF(1)
100 CLS
110 LINE INPUT#1,LIN$
120 IF EOF(1) THEN 190
125 IF LEN(LIN$)=255 THEN PRINT#2,LIN$;:GOTO 140
130 PRINT#2,LIN$;CHR$(13);
140 POSFL=POSFL+LEN(LIN$)+2
150 DONE=INT(POSFL/LNFL*100)
160 DONE$=RIGHT$(STR$(DONE),LEN(STR$(DONE))-1)
170 LOCATE 1,1:PRINT "Processing file: ";
        INF$;" - ";DONE$;"% complete."
180 GOTO 110
190 CLOSE:GOTO 10
200 CLOSE
```

USING CONVERT

Convert is a general conversion utility that is distributed on the WordPerfect Conversion Disk. It provides a way to share files with a variety of other major programs.

Although the program you want to communicate with may not appear on Convert's menu, you can frequently find a format to act as an intermediary. That is, the program you want to communicate with may have a conversion utility of its own that has on its menu a choice that also appears on Convert's menu. You could then transfer the file from WordPerfect format to the intermediary format and then from the intermediary format to the format of the program you want to work with.

Convert works with two types of files: document files and database files. With document files, the program translates as many of the formatting codes as it can from one file format to another. With database files, the program mainly arranges the data in different ways, with a variety of field and record delimiters. (A delimiter is a character or set of characters that marks the end of a field or record.)

Document Files

Here are the types of document files that Convert can work with:

WordPerfect   This is the standard WordPerfect 5.0 format.

Revisable-Form-Text (DCA)   This is a format that IBM established as a standard for transferring documents between different word processing systems on IBM mainframe computers and microcomputers. While you may never have an opportunity to use an IBM mainframe, this format can often be a good intermediary link between two programs, since it retains such formatting commands as margin changes and underlining. Many major word processing programs have recently added the DCA to those formats they can translate to and from.

Final-Form-Text (also DCA)   This format is used for documents that are final, printable (as opposed to revision) form. It is not commonly used by microcomputers.

Navy DIF   This is a special version of DIF (Data Interchange Format) that was developed and is mainly used by the Navy as a standard format for transferring documents between various word processing systems. If you are in the Navy, you probably already know everything you need to about this format; if you are not in the Navy, you probably still know everything you need to about this format.

WordStar   Use this format for transferring files between WordPerfect and WordStar. Although almost all word processing programs can translate to and from this format, it is *not* the best one to use as an intermediary between two programs. This is because WordStar itself has many intrinsic limitations that manifest themselves in your document files. For example, when you press the TAB key in WordStar, the program inserts spaces instead of a tab code. Therefore, when you translate a file to WordStar, all tabs are translated to the appropriate number of spaces. This makes it more difficult to reformat the document after you have imported it into another program like WordPerfect.

MultiMate   Use this format for standard MultiMate documents, which have a .DOC extension.

Seven-bit transfer format   WordPerfect files contain a variety of control codes that are only understood by WordPerfect. If you were to view these files with another program, or from DOS with the Type command, you would see these codes as a lot of unintelligible graphics characters. In simple terms, these codes use 8 bits, which means that their ASCII codes are higher than 127. All normal, readable characters (like letters, numbers, and punctuation marks) use 7 bits, which means their ASCII codes are all lower than 127.

In order to transfer a document with 8-bit control codes over a telephone modem, you would need to use a communications program that has a file transfer protocol (the most common one is called XMODEM). However, you can transfer 7-bit files without this protocol. The Seven-bit transfer format provides a way to translate a WordPerfect document temporarily into a 7-bit file so that it can be sent by modem without a transfer protocol. After the file has been received, it can be translated back to the original WordPerfect format with *all* control codes intact. The Seven-bit transfer format is not very frequently used because most communication programs provide a file transfer protocol. Obviously, this is the best way to transfer WordPerfect documents, because they do not have to be converted at all.

WordPerfect 4.2   Documents created with WordPerfect 4.2 are converted automatically when you retrieve them into 5.0. However, this process can be time consuming. If you have a large number of 4.2 documents, you can use this option to convert them all at once.

ASCII Text   This format is used by WordPerfect when you save a document with the "DOS Text" command on the <Text In/Out> key (CTRL+F5). All WordPerfect codes are removed, and each line ends with a Hard Return. (Note that you must save the file with the Fast Save option turned off to ensure that the format of the resulting text file is correct.)

Database Files

The Convert program also translates database files to and from WordPerfect's secondary merge format. (See the section "Secondary Merge Files" in Chapter 3, "Merge," for a description of the secondary merge file format.) This capability allows data that is stored and manipulated in a database program to be transferred to WordPerfect for mail merge purposes. You can also transfer data in a secondary file to a database or spreadsheet program for high-power manipulation.

Here are the types of database files that Convert can work with:

WordPerfect Secondary Merge   This is a WordPerfect document with fields of data that end with a ^R [HRt] sequence and that records that end with a ^E [HPg] sequence. Documents in this format can be used by WordPerfect's Merge function to create form letters and other merged documents.

Mail Merge   This is a format that can be customized according to the type of input document you have. When you choose this format, the program will ask you for a *field delimiter*, a *record delimiter*, and any characters that should be stripped from the file. The most common format for this type of file is a comma as a field delimiter and a Hard Return as a record delimiter.

WordStar MailMerge files use this format, and most databases and programming languages can output a file into the Mail Merge format. In fact, it is among the most common of data formats for microcomputers.

When entering the characters that separate fields and records, and that should be stripped from the file, you can either enter the characters directly or enter their ASCII codes between curly brackets. For example, to indicate that records end with a Hard Return you would type {**13**}{**10**}, since these ASCII codes produce a Hard Return. Sometimes the data file will have quotation marks around text fields. These quotation marks are an example of characters that you would have Convert strip out for you.

Spreadsheet DIF   DIF (Data Interchange Format) is a format that was developed by VisiCorp for transferring data between the pioneer spreadsheet VisiCalc and other VisiCorp products. It has since become a common format for transferring any data formatted into rows and columns.

You can use the DIF format for transferring data between WordPerfect and popular spreadsheet programs such as Lotus

1-2-3 and between WordPerfect and many database programs. It can also be useful in situations where database files cannot be translated into Mail Merge format. One disadvantage of this method is that a database or spreadsheet program often includes data in the file that is unnecessary in WordPerfect, such as field titles. To rectify this situation, retrieve the converted file into WordPerfect and delete the first record, which contains the field names.

Running Convert

To run Convert, you must be in DOS and not in WordPerfect.

On a floppy-based system, insert the Conversion Disk in drive A and the disk with the files you want to convert in drive B. Type **b:** and press ENTER to make drive B the default drive. Then type **a:convert** and press ENTER to run the conversion program.

On a hard disk system, the Convert program should be loaded into your WordPerfect directory. If you are running DOS Version 2.XX, make the WordPerfect directory your default directory. Then, type **convert** and press ENTER. If you are running DOS Version 3.XX, make your current directory the one that contains the files you want to convert. Then type the name of your WordPerfect directory followed by "convert" and press ENTER. For example, you would type **\wp\convert** and press ENTER if your WordPerfect directory were named \wp.

After you have entered the command to run Convert, the program will prompt you for an input file name and an output file name.These file names cannot be the same. If you are running DOS Version 2.XX on a hard disk, you will need to precede the file name with a directory path (for example, \wp\data\input.fil). The program will then prompt you for the input file's format type, as shown in Figure 12-1.

The type of input file you select will determine the type of output file that will be created. If you type 1 for an input type (WordPerfect's document format), you will be presented with a list

```
Name of Input File? input.fil
Name of Output File? output.fil


1 WordPerfect to another format
2 Revisable-Form-Text (IBM DCA Format) to WordPerfect
3 Navy DIF Standard to WordPerfect
4 WordStar 3.3 to WordPerfect
5 MultiMate 3.22 to WordPerfect
6 Seven-Bit Transfer Format to WordPerfect
7 WordPerfect 4.2 to WordPerfect 5.0
8 Mail Merge to WordPerfect Secondary Merge
9 WordPerfect Secondary Merge to Spreadsheet DIF
A Spreadsheet DIF to WordPerfect Secondary Merge

Enter number of Conversion desired _
```

Figure 12-1.   Convert program input choices

```
Name of Input File? input.fil
Name of Output File? output.fil


1 Revisable-Form-Text (IBM DCA Format)
2 Final-Form-Text (IBM DCA Format)
3 Navy DIF Standard
4 WordStar 3.3
5 MultiMate 3.22
6 Seven-Bit Transfer Format
7 ASCII text file

Enter number of output file format desired _
```

Figure 12-2.   Convert program document output choices

of the other document formats from which to choose an output file type, as shown in Figure 12-2.

If you type a number between 2 and 6 as the input type (the other document formats), the program will automatically convert the output file to normal WordPerfect document format.

If you type 8 or A for an input type (Mail Merge or Spreadsheet DIF), the program will automatically make the output file a secondary merge document. For choice 8 (Mail Merge), the program will prompt you for the characters that are used to separate fields in the file, the characters that are used to separate records in the file, and any characters that you would like to strip from the file. For any of these, you can simply type the character, or you can enter its ASCII code between curly brackets. For example, you would type {13}{10} for the record delimiter if each record ends with a Hard Return (carriage return + line feed).

If you type 9 for an input type (secondary merge), the program will generate a DIF file as the output.

Unfortunately, the fact that these selections are made automatically means that the Convert program cannot be used to translate between formats (for example, from WordPerfect Secondary Merge to Mail Merge). However, a macro can help you effect such transfers. See Chapter 13, "Macro Library," for some macros that can help with converting files.

You can also run the Convert program from the DOS prompt by including all of the necessary information, such as file names and conversion types, after the program name. The format of the command is

```
CONVERT infile outfile #1 #2 field_delim record_delim delete_chars
```

where *infile* is the name (and pathname if necessary) of the document to be converted, *outfile* is the name of the newly converted document, *#1* is a number from the list that represents the input format, and *#2* is a number for the output format (if the input format is WordPerfect). If the input file is in Mail Merge format, *field_delim* and *record_delim* are the delimiters for fields and records and *delete_chars* are the characters to remove from the file (entered as described earlier).

You can also use the DOS wildcards ? and * in the file names. Characters that the wildcards replace in the input file name will be used in the output file name. If, for instance, * .LTR is used for the input file name, and * .LT5 is used for the output file name, then all files with a .LTR extension will be converted into files with a .LT5 extension, using the same names. Similarly, you can simultaneously convert a group of files by specifying a different location for the output files. For example, the command

```
CONVERT \wp\ltr\*.* \wp50\ltr\*.* 7
```

would convert all WordPerfect 4.2 documents in the \WP\LTR directory into WordPerfect 5.0 documents with the same names in the \WP50\LTR directory.

SIDEKICK

SideKick, from Borland International, is a popular RAM-resident program that provides instant access to several useful functions. (A RAM-resident program loads once when you turn on your computer and then remains "resident" in memory. The program can then be called up instantly while you are running another program.) One of the most important of SideKick's functions is its Notepad, which is essentially a limited word processing program.

SideKick is especially useful for taking notes while running other programs. You might be working on a spreadsheet or even typing a letter in WordPerfect when you suddenly want to type a note to yourself. In this way, SideKick can be a useful adjunct to WordPerfect. Typically, you would type text into SideKick on the spur of the moment and then transfer it into WordPerfect for editing, formatting, and embellishment.

Importing SideKick Files

SideKick produces standard ASCII files; therefore to retrieve a file that was created in SideKick into WordPerfect, use the Text

In function described in "Dealing with ASCII Files" earlier in this chapter.

If you will be using SideKick and WordPerfect together on a frequent basis, it helps to have a strategy in mind when you create your SideKick files. Text transfer will be easier if you limit what you type into SideKick. Enter just simple paragraphs that are separated with one space; leave any fancy formatting until you are editing the text in WordPerfect. This ensures that you will not have a lot of work fixing up the file after you import it into WordPerfect.

SideKick, like WordStar and many other programs, does not generate a [Tab] code when you press the TAB key. Instead, it inserts spaces to fill the area between the cursor position when you press the TAB key and the place the cursor ends up. Also, SideKick does not paginate its text, so it has no equivalent to a Hard Page Break. Because of this, SideKick files usually do not contain any control codes at all.

Exporting Files to SideKick

To save a WordPerfect document in a format that can be read by SideKick, simply use the "Saving a DOS Text File" function as described in "Dealing with ASCII Files" earlier in this chapter.

You may want to be able to view part of a WordPerfect document while running another program. Saving the document as an ASCII file and then retrieving it into SideKick allows you to view it from within any program.

NOTEBOOK

Notebook is a simple file management program that helps you work with WordPerfect's secondary merge files. It comes as part of a collection of programs called WordPerfect Library. Notebook retrieves and saves secondary merge files directly—there is no need to first translate them with the Convert program. Notebook allows you to view your data either in a row-and-column format (like a spreadsheet) or in a record format (like a traditional data-base program).

When you save a file from Notebook, it is saved as a normal WordPerfect secondary merge document that can then be used in a merge operation. Notebook inserts a *header record* into the file with special information about your data. You can retrieve this file into WordPerfect like any other secondary file.

Notebook Header Record

When you load into WordPerfect a file saved by Notebook, you will see that the first record contains a variety of settings for the file, like field names, sizes, and placements within the record format, as well as the record format layout itself as shown in Figure 12-3.

```
           ^N
01 First 1,13,1,23,
02 Last 1,25,1,51,D
03 Address 3,13,3,45,
04 City, ST 5,13,5,32,
05 Zip 5,40,5,49,
06 No. 9,13,9,15,D
07 Comments 7,18,9,51,
^R
^N
1,12 0,1 2,12 0,1 3,26 0,1 4,26 0,1 5,12 0,1 6,12 0,1
^R
^N
```

Name:	
Address:	
City, ST:	Zip:
Comments:	
No:	

Doc 1 Pg 1 Ln 1 Pos 10

Figure 12-3.   Example of a record layout

This is the special header record that Notebook inserted. The first thing that appears in each field of this record is the Merge code ^N. You will recall from Chapter 3 that the ^N code indicates to the Merge function that it should move to the next record. In this way, the Merge function never tries to merge the data that is in this header document; it will advance to the second record whenever a field is requested from the first record. In essence, it is a record that WordPerfect will ignore when merging but that contains vital data for Notebook.

Header Record Fields

The header record is divided into fields, just as a normal record is. Each field contains a different type of information that Notebook needs to keep track of the data. (^R Merge code marks the end of each field, as in normal records.) The following is a list of the first four fields in the header record and the type of data each contains. Notebook will add more fields at the end of the header record if it needs to, so that the record has as many fields as the first record of data in the file.

Field 1: *Field names and definitions*
The field names appear in boldface. You may only edit the names of the fields. Be careful not to delete the Bold codes, which Notebook uses to mark the beginning and end of each actual field name.

Field 2: *Notebook display definition*
This one-line field contains settings that Notebook uses to place the fields in the list display. Do not edit this field.

Field 3: *Record layout background text*
This field contains the record layout that Notebook will use when you enter and edit data. You can edit this layout in any way, but typically it makes more sense to use Notebook's Record Display Setup function.

Field 4: *Date format definition*

Although you can edit this field from WordPerfect, it doesn't make much sense to do so. Use the Date Format function in Notebook to change it if you need to.

Using Notebook Secondary Files with WordPerfect

If you want to use WordPerfect's Sort and Select functions to manipulate data in a Notebook secondary document, you need to take steps to ensure that you do not accidentally alter the header record. You can either define all of your data *except* for the header record as a block, or you can use the Move function to temporarily remove the header record and then "copy" it into a safe place. The former method is faster if you will be performing the Sort/Select function once or twice, but the latter method makes more sense if you will be using the function several times.

To use the block definition method, follow these steps:

1. Retrieve the file into WordPerfect.

2. Define the second and subsequent records as a block: Move the cursor to the beginning of the second record (the first record of actual data), turn Block on by pressing the <Block> key (ALT+F4), and move the cursor to the bottom of the document.

3. Start the Sort/Select function by pressing the <Merge/Sort> key (CTRL+F9).

To use the Move method, follow these steps:

1. Retrieve the file into WordPerfect.

2. Define the entire header record as a block: Move the cursor to the top of the document, press the <Block> key (ALT+F4), press the <Search> key (F2), press the <Merge Codes> key (SHIFT+F9), type **E**, and then press ESC. Press RIGHT ARROW once.

3. Use the Move function to remove the record from the document: Press the <Move> key (CTRL+F4) and type **1** for "Block," and **1** for "Move."

4. Press the <Switch> key (SHIFT+F3) to switch to Document 2.

5. Retrieve the header record by pressing ENTER.

6. Press the <Switch> key to switch back to Document 1.

7. Perform the desired Sort/Select function.

8. Move to the top of the document and "paste" the header record back: Press the <Move> key and type **4** for "Retrieve" and **1** for "Block."

If you can no longer retrieve the header (because you used the Move or Copy function again), you can get a copy of the header from the one you placed in Document 2.

By taking one of these precautions, you avoid repositioning or removing the header record during a sort or select procedure. Always make sure that the header record is not unintentionally disturbed when you are editing a Notebook secondary document with WordPerfect.

INCORPORATING REPORTS

Many spreadsheet and database management programs, such as Lotus 1-2-3 and dBASE III, have the ability to "print to disk." This means that these programs can save their files in an ASCII format that you can import directly into WordPerfect. Because of this feature, it is possible to use WordPerfect to format and print reports generated by these programs. The principles and techniques described in this section deal with Lotus 1-2-3 and dBASE III, but they can also be applied to many other programs.

First, let's define what is meant by "print to disk." Normally, when you print a Lotus or dBASE III file, the information goes directly to the printer. Sometimes it is what you see on the screen and at other times it has been formatted by the program's report mechanisms. With both programs (and with many others), it is also possible to send the output to a file on the disk, rather than to the printer. The images that would normally appear on paper are instead written to a standard ASCII file that can then be imported into WordPerfect for editing or included as part of a larger report.

There are a number of reasons you might want to do this. One is to overcome the limitations associated with the original program's print functions. You might, for instance, want to use WordPerfect's print enhancements, such as boldface and underlining, or some of WordPerfect's many format options.

Another, and perhaps more important, reason to import such files is so that they can be used as part of larger WordPerfect documents. Imagine that you are writing a 100-page report and need to include several spreadsheets as part of the report. You could, of course, retype the data in WordPerfect. Another alternative would be to print the spreadsheet using Lotus 1-2-3 and hand-insert it into the WordPerfect report after it is printed. This is not only inconvenient, it also might throw off the page breaks and page numbering of the WordPerfect document.

A better alternative is to use the ability of 1-2-3 or dBASE to "print to disk" and import that file directly into the WordPerfect report. Then you can use WordPerfect to enhance the report and ensure that all of your page numbers, headers, and other formatting standards are used for your entire document—including data generated by the other program.

In the following sections you will see how to print to disk in both 1-2-3 and dBASE. It is assumed that you already know how to use the programs. Even if you do not use one of those programs, the spreadsheet and database management programs you do use probably have similar capacities to generate ASCII print files.

Lotus 1-2-3

To print a report to disk in 1-2-3, follow the same basic steps that you would use to print it on paper. By specifying that you want the output to go to a file instead of to the printer, you create a file that can be incorporated into a WordPerfect document.

Printing to a File

The command to print a 1-2-3 file is /P. The default sends the output to the printer, but if you select "File" (by moving the cursor to the right and pressing ENTER or by typing an F), any cells that you print will be output to a file instead of to the printer. The program asks you to enter your "print file name" and displays any other "print files" that already exist on the disk. Lotus 1-2-3, by default, adds the extension .PRN to the end of any file name you give. (With 1-2-3 Release 2, you can override that default by including your own extension on the file name or by adding a period to the end of the file name to indicate that there is no extension.)

On a hard disk system, 1-2-3 will save the print file in the 1-2-3 default data directory. To override this default in 1-2-3 Release 2, press ESC twice and replace the suggested data directory with any other directory, including one normally used to store Word-Perfect files. With 1-2-3 Release 1A, you will need to issue the /File Directory command before issuing the /Print File command in order to change the default directory. If there is already a file with the name you choose, 1-2-3 will ask if you wish to replace that file.

Once this is done, 1-2-3's normal print menu is displayed. As you generally do when printing in 1-2-3, first select Range to indicate the range (or portion) of the worksheet you wish to print.

Specifying Unformatted Printing

When 1-2-3 prints to disk, it does so exactly as it prints to paper. It provides the same default margins, including margins on the top and bottom of the page. When 1-2-3 comes to what it thinks is a new page, it indicates a page break by inserting blank lines. When you tell it to "go," it creates an ASCII file with the same spacing as would normally appear when you use the printer. This formatting can create problems when you import the file into WordPerfect. Therefore, you want the 1-2-3 print file to be totally *unformatted* so that WordPerfect can provide the page breaks, margins, and other necessary formatting.

To create an unformatted print file, type **O** for "Options"; then type **O** again for "Other." This brings up another menu from which you type **U** for "Unformatted."

At this juncture you type **Q** for "Quit" to return to 1-2-3's main print menu and then type **G** for "Go" to print the file to disk. When this is done, you must type **Q** for "Quit," as this completes the printing and closes the file.

Checking the File Before
Leaving Lotus 1-2-3

There is a way to see what the file will look like prior to leaving 1-2-3. This is done with the program's File Import command.

First, you clear the worksheet by typing **/WEY**. Then you type **/FI** for "File Import" followed by **T** for "Text" and then the name of the print file you just created. You can also highlight the file name and simply press ENTER. (If you are using 1-2-3 Release 2 and you overrode either the .PRN extension or the directory for storing the file, you may have to designate the path, file name, or extension.)

Once you select the file name, the file will load into 1-2-3, and what you see on your screen is exactly what you will see when you later retrieve the file into WordPerfect.

dBASE III

To print to disk in dBASE III, use the Report command. After you have made a database active with the Use command, type

```
REPORT FORM reportname TO FILE filename
```

at the dot prompt to save a report as a file, where "reportname" is the name of a report form you have previously defined and "filename" is the name of a file that will contain the printed report. Precede the file name with a path specification if you wish to store the file in a directory other than the current directory. If you do not specify an extension with the file name, dBASE adds .TXT to the end of the name you provide.

If, for example, you type **REPORT FORM cshflow TO FILE report**, dBASE will generate a file called REPORT.TXT in the default directory that contains the dBASE III report called CSHFLOW.

Importing Reports into WordPerfect

Once you have created an ASCII print file, the next step is to exit 1-2-3 or dBASE III and enter WordPerfect so that you can retrieve the file.

First, move to the location within your WordPerfect file where you want the report to appear. If you are not sure where you want it to be placed, you can position the cursor anywhere and move the report later.

Next you need to reset the margins to leave enough room for the width of the report. Usually this means setting the margins to 0″ on both sides, at least to start with. If you have printed a report wider than 6.5″, and you don't reset the WordPerfect margins, the lines from the 1-2-3 or dBASE III print file will not fit within WordPerfect's default margins. This would result in text being wrapped around and not being very readable.

The next step is to press the <Text In/Out> key (CTRL+F5); then type **1** for "DOS Text," and type **2** to retrieve the file. Type the file name and press ENTER. (Remember that for 1-2-3 files, unless you designated a dot or another extension, the file will end in .PRN. For dBASE III, the file will end in .TXT. And, unless you designated a directory, the file will reside on the data directory that was active at the time the file was saved.)

After you enter the file name, the report will appear on your screen at the cursor location in the current document.

CONVERTING dBASE AND 1-2-3 DATA TO SECONDARY MERGE FILES

In the previous discussion you saw how 1-2-3 and dBASE print files could be integrated into WordPerfect reports. It is also possible to use data from either of the programs to create a WordPerfect secondary merge file. This enables you to take advantage of the data entry, edit, and search capabilities of dBASE or 1-2-3 while also using the merge capacity of WordPerfect. Just as with the print files, the principles here apply to other spreadsheet and database management programs.

Lotus 1-2-3, dBASE III, and many other programs can translate their files into one or more standard file structures that can be converted by WordPerfect's Convert utility into a WordPerfect secondary merge file. dBASE can create files that WordPerfect's Convert utility translates as Mail Merge files. Lotus can translate worksheet files into DIF files that can in turn be converted into secondary merge files by WordPerfect's Convert program.

Converting either a dBASE or a 1-2-3 data file into a Word-Perfect secondary merge file is a two-step process, the first step in dBASE or 1-2-3, and the second with WordPerfect's Convert program.

Lotus 1-2-3

To convert a 1-2-3 file, you must first make sure that the information you want to convert (usually a database) starts in the upper-left corner of the spreadsheet (cell A1). This reduces the amount of excess data that would otherwise be carried through the conversion process. You might want to save a separate copy of your worksheet for conversion purposes so that you can maintain the worksheet in its original layout for use within 1-2-3.

After you have prepared the worksheet, use Lotus's Translate program (available from the Lotus Access menu) to translate your spreadsheet into a DIF file. Then use WordPerfect's Convert program to convert the DIF file into a secondary merge file. (See "Using Convert" in this chapter for a description of the Convert program.) After conversion, you may need to retrieve the resulting file into WordPerfect and manually delete the first few records of the data, depending on the condition of your original worksheet.

dBASE III

To convert a dBASE III file, you use dBASE's Copy command to convert the dBASE file into a standard data file. This is done by typing

```
COPY TO filename DELIMITED
```

at the dBASE dot prompt, where "filename" is the name of the file that will contain the data. You can precede the file name with a path specification if you wish to store the file in a directory other than the current directory. If you do not specify an extension with the file name, dBASE adds .TXT to the end of the name you provide.

You can now use the Convert program to translate the file into a WordPerfect secondary merge file. (See "Using Convert" for general instructions on running Convert.)

When you run Convert, specify "Mail Merge" as the input file type. The program will then prompt you for three things: the field delimiter, the record delimiter, and any characters that should be stripped (removed) from the resulting file. The dBASE III file is formatted with character fields surrounded by quotes, fields separated by commas, and a Hard Return (ASCII code 13 *and* code 10) after each record. Therefore, at the prompt for a "field delimiter," type a comma (,) and press ENTER. At the prompt for a "record delimiter," type {13}{10} and press ENTER. At the prompt for characters to be stripped, type a quotation mark (") and press ENTER. The file will be properly translated.

dBASE III's Copy command outputs date fields with the four digits of the year, followed immediately by the two digits of the month, and then by the two digits of the day. For example, the date May 2, 1963, would be output as 19630502. Because this would not be very meaningful in a WordPerfect merged document, you might want to convert this date to a more standard format. (See Chapter 13, "Macro Library," for a macro that can perform this function.)

Multiple WordPerfects

Several popular utilities, such as WordPerfect Shell (See Appendix C, "WordPerfect Corporation Programs") and DESQ view, allow you to run two or more copies of the same program at the same time. As you know, WordPerfect can normally edit up to two documents at a time. With one of these utilities, however, you can extend that limit by running more than one copy of WordPerfect. Each copy is then capable of handling up to two files. WordPerfect is such a large program, however, that you would need a substantial amount of Expanded memory to do this.

The other problem with running more than one copy of WordPerfect is that you must watch out for the overflow files that WordPerfect creates while it is editing. WordPerfect automatically deletes these files when you exit normally. If you open a second copy of WordPerfect, the overflow files created by the first copy are going to be present. When you open WordPerfect a second time, the program asks, "Are other copies of WordPerfect currently running?" Type **Y**, and the message "Directory in use. New WP Dictionary:" is displayed. Type any directory name other than the WordPerfect system directory, and press ENTER. By using a directory different from the one currently in use, you can run as many copies of WordPerfect as you have directories and memory.

13

MACRO LIBRARY

This chapter contains a collection of useful macro applications, ranging from simple one-command macros to detailed procedures that employ advanced macro language commands.

Many of WordPerfect's features are implemented with long sequences of keystrokes or key combinations that can be difficult to find. You can use macros like the ones in this chapter to facilitate the use of frequently called functions and less frequently used advanced features.

You can also use WordPerfect's macros to create routines that perform specific tasks. You can, for example, create macros that generate letters, translate files, or scroll two documents simultaneously.

Note: Before using the macros in this chapter, you should work through Chapter 2, "Macros," unless you have had substantial previous experience using WordPerfect's macros.

ENTERING THE MACRO STEPS

The lines of each sample macro are numbered, and explanations of important lines are found in the paragraphs that follow the listings. This allows you to understand the logic well enough to duplicate the procedures in your own macros. Aside from the line numbers, the macros are listed exactly as they will appear in WordPerfect's internal macro editor.

The process of creating one of these macros typically begins by getting to the Macro Editor screen. If you want the macro to be named, or invoked with an ALT-letter combination, follow these steps:

- Press the <Macro Def> key (CTRL+F10).
- Type the name and press ENTER, or simply press the ALT key combination you want to use.
- Press the <Macro Def> key again to end definition.
- Press the <Macro Def> key again.
- Type the *same* name or key combination.
- At the prompt type **2** for "Edit."

If you want to assign the listed macro to a key, follow these steps:

- Press the <Setup> key (SHIFT+F1).
- Type **6** for "Keyboard Layout."
- Position the cursor bar at the desired keyboard file, and type **5** for "Edit."
- Type **4** for "Create."
- At the "Key:" prompt, press the key you want to use.

Once you've completed one of these two procedures, you'll see the macro/key editor on the screen. If you wish, you can type **1** to enter a description of the macro. (Press ENTER when you're finished.) When you're ready to insert the steps of the macro, type **2** for "Action." If you're defining a macro that you created with the steps shown above, you'll see a {DISPLAY OFF} command inserted for you at the beginning of the macro. You'll probably want to delete this command before continuing.

Refer to Chapter 2, "Macros," for a description of how to enter steps into a macro in the editor. For many of the macros, you may want to use the Macro Commands mode to insert the steps. Spaces in the macro listing are indicated by small centered dots (as they appear on the screen in the macro editor).

Comments are commonly placed to the right of the macro steps in the listings. Macro comments always begin with a semi-colon within curly braces ({;}), and end with a tilde (~). Insert the beginning code by pressing the <Macro Commands> key (CTRL+ PGUP), typing ; (a semi-colon), and pressing ENTER. Including the comments is optional; you may want to omit them to speed entry of the steps, but they may be helpful if you plan to modify the macro later. *Always remember to include the tilde at the end of the comment.*

Any names provided for the macros in this chapter are merely suggestions. Since you are likely to have a unique collection of macros that you use on a regular basis, you may want to invent your own names to avoid conflicts with other macros. In general, you should use ALT key macros and redefined keys for features that you use frequently, and named macros for features that you use only occasionally.

You might also want to create macros with names like DRAW, DATE, and SPELL, which invoke functions suggested by their names. Even though you may not save on keystrokes with this method, you might find it helpful, because you won't have to remember or look up the individual keystrokes.

IMPLEMENTING WORDPERFECT FEATURES

Below are some examples of ways that you can use macros to make common WordPerfect tasks simpler. You should be able to construct your own time-saving procedures using these examples as a guide.

Copying, Moving, and Deleting Text

A common way to copy, move, or delete text is to use the Move function, perhaps first marking the text as a block. This, however, may require quite a few keystrokes. A shortcut is to redefine some keys, such as CTRL+C, CTRL+M, and CTRL+D to perform the same steps. By using the macro command language's {STATE} command to determine whether a block has been marked when the key is pressed, you can affect either the block or the current paragraph.

Below are the steps for copying, moving, and deleting macros. Use the Keyboard Layout function to assign these steps to the respective keys.

```
  CTRL+C:

1 │ {IF}{STATE}&128~
2 │     {Move}12
3 │ {ELSE}
4 │     {Move}22
5 │ {END IF}


  CTRL+M:

1 │ {IF}{STATE}&128~
2 │     {Move}11
3 │ {ELSE}
4 │     {Move}21
5 │ {END IF}


  CTRL+D:

1 │ {IF}{STATE}&128~
2 │     {Move}13
3 │ {ELSE}
4 │     {Move}23
5 │ {END IF}
```

In these macros, line 1 uses the {IF} command to check the current value of State. Checking State against 128 tells the macro whether Block mode is currently active. If it is, the phrase {STATE}&128 returns a true result, so the step on line 2 is executed. This line presses the <Move> key, selects a block, and then proceeds to copy, move, or delete it. If Block mode is not active, then the step on line 4 is executed. This line presses the <Move> key, selects a paragraph, and then proceeds to copy, move, or delete it.

After executing the copy and move macros, you would position the cursor where you want the text to be placed, and press ENTER.

Mark a Line

You may want to mark an entire line as a block—for example, to underline a title or mark text for a table of contents. A simple macro can make the process quick and easy. Naming the macro ALT+L will remind you that it marks a line.

```
1 | {Home}{Home}{Home}{Left}        {;}Move·to·beginning·of·line~
2 | {Block}                         {;}Turn·on·block~
3 | {End}                           {;}Move·to·end·of·line~
```

Save and Resume

It is important that you save your document frequently to minimize the risk of losing text. You can use an ALT key macro (for example, ALT+S) to simplify the saving process.

```
{Save}{Enter}y
```

Printer Commands

You can automate many common printer commands with macros. For example, you can have the ALT+P macro start a print job:

```
{Print}1
```

Then you can have another macro, ALT+G, send a "Go" to restart the printer after a printer pause:

```
{Print}44{Exit}              {;}Send·printer·a·"Go"~
```

If you're using hand-fed forms, you need to perform two steps to start printing a document: generate a print job, and send the first "Go" (assuming that you have already loaded the first sheet of paper). In this case, you might want your ALT+P macro to perform both of these steps. You would then use the ALT+G macro to continue the print job for each page.

Everyone who uses a word processor has had the experience of wanting to abort a printout in midstream. WordPerfect has a set of commands for stopping the printer, but the time you need them most is when you are least likely to remember the sequence. You can use a Stop macro to stop the printer and cancel a print job entirely:

```
1 | {Print}45                    {;}Stop·printer~
2 | c{Enter}                      {;}Cancel·current·print·job~
3 | g{Exit}                       {;}Send·printer·a·"Go"~
```

Purge Hidden Codes

Sometimes WordPerfect's hidden codes can pose a problem when you are trying to reformat a document. For example, you cannot change the margins for the entire document if you have scattered [L/R Mar:] codes throughout the document. Other examples of codes which can cause formatting problems include Line Spacing and Tab Setting codes.

One solution is to maintain a series of macros that will purge a document of specified hidden codes. That is, they will delete *all* of the specified codes found in the current document. You can then reformat the entire document with just one hidden code.

For example, let's say that you have a document in which you have inserted several different margin settings. You decide to reformat the entire document with margins of 1.5 inches on the left and right. You can make a macro like this one to purge the document of [L/R Mar:] codes:

```
1 | {;}Purge·[L/R·Mar:]·codes~
2 | {;}Copyright·(c)·1988,·by·Eric·Alderman~
3 |
4 | {Home}{Home}{Home}{Up}                    {;}Go·to·top·of·document~
5 | {Replace}n{Format}16{Search}{Search}      {;}Replace·codes·with
6 |                                            nothing~
7 | {Home}{Home}{Home}{Up}                    {;}Go·to·top·of·document~
```

Now you can reformat all of the text by inserting a new [L/R Mar:] code at the top of the document.

You can make a more comprehensive macro by including a menu which prompts for common format settings, and then purges the selected one from the document. Here's a macro that will do this:

```
 1 | {;}Purges selected hidden code~
 2 | {;}Copyright·(c)·1988,·Eric·Alderman~
 3 |
 4 | {CHAR}0~{^]}Purge:·1{^\}·[L/R·Mar];·{^]}2{^\}·[Tab·Set];·{^]}3{^\}·
 5 | [Ln·Spacing]:·{^]}0{^\}{Left}~
 6 |
 7 | {DISPLAY OFF}
 8 | {CASE}{VAR 0}~          {;}Check·response,·branch·accordingly~
 9 |      1~lrmar~
10 |      2~tab~
11 |      3~space~
12 |      ~
13 | {QUIT}                  {;}If·no·valid·responses,·quit·macro~
14 |
15 | {LABEL}lrmar~           {;}Put·keystrokes·for·L/R·Mar·into·Var·1~
16 | {ASSIGN}1~{Format}16~
17 | {ASSIGN}2~Left/Right·Margin~
18 | {GO}continue~
19 |
20 | {LABEL}tab~             {;}Put·keystrokes·for·Tab·Set·into·Var·1~
21 | {ASSIGN}1~{Format}17~
22 | {ASSIGN}2~Tab·Setting~
23 | {GO}continue~
24 |
25 | {LABEL}space~           {;}Put·keystrokes·for·Line·Spacing·into·Var·1~
26 | {ASSIGN}1~{Format}153~
27 | {ASSIGN}2~Line·Spacing~
28 | {GO}continue~
29 |
30 | {LABEL}continue~        {;}Perform·actual·purging~
31 | {Home}{Home}{Home}{Up}
32 | {PROMPT}{^\}Now·purging·all·{^]}{VAR 2}{^\}·codes...~
33 |
34 | {Replace}n{VAR 1}{Search}{Search}        {;}Perform·replace
35 |                                          using·keys·in·Var·1~
36 | {Home}{Home}{Up}
```

Line 4 of this macro uses the {CHAR} command to display at the bottom of the screen a menu that closely resembles WordPerfect's standard format for menus. Notice that the {^]} and {^\} codes have been used to make the menu numbers appear in boldface. (You insert these codes by pressing either CTRL+] or CTRL+\.) A default choice of "0" is entered and then the {Left} code causes the cursor to rest under the "0".

Lines 8-12 use the {CASE} command, which checks the entered character against a list of possibilities, branching to an appropriate location if it finds a match. If no match is found, the macro ends with the {QUIT} command on line 13.

On lines 15-18, 20-23, and 25-28, the actual keystrokes needed to insert the appropriate hidden code into the search string are put into Variable 1. The text description of the code is put into Variable 2. The {GO} command is then used to branch to the continuation of the macro.

The remaining steps, starting with line 30, constitute the main section of the macro. First, the cursor is moved to the top of the document. Then the {PROMPT} command on line 32 displays a message indicating which code is being purged. Boldface text is turned off at the beginning of the line. Variable 2 (which contains the text description of the code) is included in the message in boldface text. Finally, the Replace function is invoked on line 34, using the keystrokes in Variable 1 to insert the correct code into the search string.

One modification you might make in this macro would allow it to support mnemonic letters, in addition to numbers, for the menu commands. To do this, replace lines 4-12 with the following steps:

```
 4   {CHAR}0~{^]}Purge:·1{^\}·[L/R·{^V}M{^Q}ar];·{^]}2{^\}·[{^V}T{^Q}ab·
 5   Set];·{^]}3{^\}·[Ln·{^V}S{^Q}pacing]:·{^]}0{^\}{Left}~
 6
 7   {DISPLAY OFF}
 8   {CASE}{VAR 0}~              {;}Check·response,·branch·accordingly~
 9       1~lrmar~m~lrmar~M~lrmar~
10       2~tab~t~tab~T~tab~
11       3~space~s~space~S~space~
12       ~
```

Notice that the {CHAR} command must now check not only for numbers, but for letters in both uppercase and lowercase as well.

Generating a Table of Contents

There are several keystrokes involved in the generation of a table of contents, but here again you can automate the process with a macro. Here's one which generates the table, and then removes underlining and boldface codes:

```
 1 | {;}Table of contents generation~
 2 | {;}Copyright (c) 1988, Eric Alderman~
 3 |
 4 | {DISPLAY OFF}
 5 | {Mark Text}65{Enter}                        {;}Generate·TOC~
 6 |
 7 | {Home}{Home}{Home}{Up}                      {;}Go·to·top·of·document~
 8 | {Search}{Mark Text}51{Search}               {;}Search·for·beg.·of·TOC~
 9 | {Block}
10 | {Search}{Mark Text}52{Search}               {;}Block·to·end·of·TOC~
11 | {Replace}n{Underline}{Search}{Search}       {;}Purge·all·[UND]·codes~
12 |
13 | {Home}{Home}{Home}{Up}                      {;}Go·to·top·of·document~
14 | {Search}{Mark Text}51{Search}               {;}Search·for·beg.·of·TOC~
15 | {Block}
16 | {Search}{Mark Text}52{Search}               {;}Block·to·end·of·TOC~
17 | {Replace}n{Bold}{Search}{Search}            {;}Purge·all·[BOLD]·codes~
18 |
19 | {Home}{Home}{Home}{Up}                      {;}Go·to·top·of·document~
```

This macro removes any [UND] and [BOLD] codes from the entries in the table of contents, because titles are commonly underlined or boldfaced in the text, but not in the table of contents. This step can be omitted if you want these enhancements in the table of contents, or if they are not used in the document. You can use the same process to strip any other unwanted codes from the table of contents.

The macro generates the table of contents with the step on line 5. Lines 7-11 remove all [UND] codes from the table, and lines 13-17 remove all the [BOLD] codes.

WINDOWS

WordPerfect's Window function allows you to view two separate documents on the screen simultaneously. (See "Windows" in Chapter 1, "Basics Refresher," for a description of the Window function.) Although you can create many different combinations of window sizes, you will probably use only a few different configurations. Macros can set up your most common window layouts with a single keystroke. You can also use macros to help scroll text in the windows.

Single Document Split-Screen

Basically, there are two distinct uses for windows in word processing programs:

- To view two separate documents simultaneously
- To view two sections of the same document simultaneously

Because WordPerfect's windows are essentially an extension of the dual-document editing feature, they do not provide the latter capability. While you *can* have the same document loaded into two windows, you *cannot* have the program automatically incorporate changes made to one into the other. Each window's document is treated as a completely separate, unrelated file.

However, you can achieve the same result by using the macro described next. This macro copies the entire contents of Document 1 into Document 2, and then returns to Document 1. Document 1 is then used as the "work document" and Document 2 as the "view document." Changes are made only to the work document and never to the view document. Whenever a sufficient number of changes have been made, you can use the same macro to update the view document.

```
 1 | {;}Duplicate·document·in·second·window~
 2 | {;}Copyright·(c)·1988·by·Eric·Alderman~
 3 |
 4 | {DISPLAY OFF}
 5 | {Home}{Home}{Home}{Up}        {;}Go·to·top·of·document~
 6 | {Block}                       {;}Block·to·end·of·document~
 7 | {Home}{Home}{Down}
 8 | {Move}12                      {;}Copy·block~
 9 | {Switch}                      {;}Switch·to·other·document~
10 | {Exit}nn                      {;}Clear·screen~
11 | {Enter}                       {;}Retrieve·text~
12 | {Switch}                      {;}Switch·back·to·first·document~
13 | {Home}{Home}{Home}{Up}        {;}Go·to·top·of·document~
```

To use the macro, follow this sequence of steps:

1. Split the screen manually (or with one of the window setup macros in this chapter).

2. Use the macro to copy Document 1 to Document 2.

3. Proceed editing the text in Document 1, switching back and forth as necessary to scroll Document 2.

4. When a significant number of changes have been made in Document 1, use the macro to update Document 2.

Miscellaneous Window Controls

You can create several macros that are useful for window control. Here are two that enable you to alter the current window size:

```
1 | {;}Make·current·window·half-size~
2 | {Screen}1
3 | 11{Enter}
```

```
1 | {;}Make·current·window·full-size~
2 | {Screen}1
3 | 24{Enter}
```

You might also want to define a macro named ALT+S (or attached to CTRL+S) which switches between Document 1 and Document 2. Although this function normally takes only one key (SHIFT+F3), ALT+S or CTRL+S might be easier to remember.

Another set of window scrolling macros allows you to scroll Document 2 up and down while keeping the cursor in Document 1. This can be useful if, for example, you are writing a document in Document 1 but need to refer to another document in Document 2. While keeping your place visually on the screen, you can scroll through your second document to find the desired text. Here are the macros:

```
1 | {;}Scroll·other·window·up~
2 | {Switch}{Screen Up}{Switch}
```

```
1 | {;}Scroll·other·window·down~
2 | {Switch}{Screen Down}{Switch}
```

FILE CONVERSIONS

WordPerfect's Convert program can perform many types of file translation. (See "Using Convert" in Chapter 12, "Integration with Other Products" for a description of the Convert program.) The use of macros in the Convert program provides an easy way for you to customize your translation routines.

The following sections present several macros that will convert a document into a different format. If you follow the steps in each macro, you should be able to understand the logic well enough to create routines to fit your own needs.

Tab Regeneration

A file with [Tab] codes is much easier to reformat in WordPerfect than a file in which indentation has been achieved with spaces. You can easily reposition columns that have been formatted with tabs by setting new tab stops. Also, you can copy and move columns separated by tabs with the Move Tabular Column function. Columns formatted with spaces will not appear properly aligned when printed in a proportionally spaced font.

Some ASCII files and documents that have been imported from other word processing programs, however, contain spaces where [Tab] codes would be more appropriate. You can use the next macro to replace these spaces with [Tab] codes.

A common use for this macro would be to aid in the conversion of WordStar files, because WordStar has no code designating a Tab function. (When the Tab or Center Line command is used in WordStar, spaces are simply inserted to indent the text. The Convert program has no way to recognize these spaces as a Tab or Center Line command.) Another typical use would be for reports printed to disk from other programs, such as Lotus 1-2-3 and dBASE. These reports will also be formatted with spaces instead of Tabs.

The macro works best if you know (or can deduce) the tab stop interval that was used when the file was created. WordStar's default ruler has tab stops set five spaces apart. The macro first replaces all occurrences of the specified number of spaces with a [Tab] code. Then it strips excess spaces after the [Tab] codes to make the file easier to edit. Here is the macro:

```
 1 | {;}Spaces·to·tabs~
 2 | {;}Copyright·(c)·1988,·by·Eric·Alderman~
 3 |
 4 | {DISPLAY OFF}
 5 | {TEXT}0~Minimum·number·of·spaces·between·columns:·5{Left}~
 6 |
 7 | {IF EXISTS}0~                        {;}If·no·value·entered·for·Variable·1~
 8 | {ELSE}
 9 |     {ASSIGN}0~5~                     {;}Then·put·5·into·Variable·1~
10 | {END IF}
11 |
12 | {Replace}n                          {;}Begin·Replace·function~
13 |
14 | {LABEL}spaceloop~                    {;}Set·beginning·of·loop~
15 | ·                                   {;}Type·a·SPACE~
16 | {ASSIGN}0~{VAR 0}-1~                 {;}Decrement·Variable·1·counter~
17 | {IF}{VAR 0}>0~                       {;}If·it's·still·greater·than·0~
18 |     {GO}spaceloop~                   {;}Go·back·for·another·SPACE~
19 | {END IF}
20 |
21 | {Search}{Tab}{Search}               {;}End·Replace·function~
22 |
23 | {Home}{Home}{Home}{Up}
24 | {Replace}n{Tab}{Tab}{Search}{Tab}{Search}   {;}Replace·all
25 |                                      occurrences·of·two
26 |                                      TAB's·with·one~
27 | {Home}{Home}{Home}{Up}
28 |
29 | {ON NOT FOUND}{GO}done~~             {;}Set·up·Not·Found·exception·handler~
30 |
31 | {LABEL}loop~                         {;}Begin·loop~
32 | {Search}{Tab}·{Search}               {;}Look·for·a·TAB·followed·by·a·SPACE~
33 | {Backspace}                          {;}Delete·the·SPACE~
34 | {Left}                               {;}Move·to·the·left·of·the·TAB~
35 | {GO}loop~                            {;}Repeat·the·loop·(until·search·fails)~
36 |
37 | {LABEL}done~                         {;}Routine·executed·when·search·fails~
38 | {Home}{Home}{Home}{Up}               {;}Return·to·top·of·document~
```

Line 5 of the macro prompts the user for the number of spaces to use as a minimum distance between columns. A default response of "5" is specified. Lines 7-10 check to see if the user pressed ENTER to accept the default. After the Replace function is started on line 12, the "spaceloop" routine on lines 14-19 types the requested number of spaces. Line 24 replaces all occurrences of two consecutive [Tab] codes with one [Tab] code. Line 29 sets up a location to branch to when the next search fails. Lines 31-35 contain a looping routine which searches for each occurrence of a

[Tab] code followed by a space, and then deletes the space. When the search fails, the macro branches to line 37 (as determined by line 29), which moves the cursor to the top of the document.

This macro is not completely reliable. For example, there may be times when there are not enough spaces between the position where the TAB key was pressed in the original document and the position of the next tab stop for the spaces to be found by the Replace function. However, the macro should be able to do most of the work, leaving you to perform a minor tune-up rather than a major overhaul.

Secondary Merge to Mail Merge

WordPerfect's Convert program can convert files from a Mail Merge format (commas between fields and a Hard Return after each record) into a secondary merge format. However, it cannot convert files in the other direction—from a secondary merge format to a mailmerge format. You can use a macro to perform this translation.

In the secondary merge document, each field ends with an ^R [HRt] sequence, and each record ends with either an ^E [HPg] sequence (for files created with WordPerfect 5.0) or an ^E [HRt] sequence (for files created with prior versions of WordPerfect). In the Mail Merge format, each field ends with a comma (except for the last field) and is usually enclosed in quotes. Each record ends with a Hard Return.

Here is a sample secondary merge record:

```
John D. Franken^R
766 Maple St.^R
San Francisco^R
CA^R
95463^R
^E
```

Here is the same record in Mail Merge format:

```
"John D. Franken","766 Maple St.","San Francisco","CA","95463"
```

Double quotes are necessary for *text* fields because some will contain a comma, which would incorrectly signal the end of the field. By enclosing fields in double quotes, you ensure that each is considered as a single field, regardless of internal commas.

Do not, however, place double quotes around a *numeric* field. (A numeric field is one that contains numbers that you might use for calculation. A salary, for example, is a numeric field, whereas a ZIP code is not.) The macro that follows will place double quotes around every field in the secondary merge file; if the file contains any numeric fields, you will need to remove them with a macro like the subsequent one.

Depending on the program into which you will be importing the mailmerge file, *date* fields may require special formatting and may also need the double quotes removed.

Here is the macro listing:

```
 1 | {;}Secondary·file·to·mailmerge·format~
 2 | {;}Copyright·(c)·1988,·by·Eric·Alderman~
 3 |
 4 | {Home}{Home}{Home}{Up}
 5 | {Replace}n{Merge R}{Enter}{Search}","{Search}
 6 |
 7 | {Home}{Home}{Home}{Up}
 8 | {Replace}n{Merge Codes}e{Enter}{Search}{Merge Codes}e{HPg}{Search}
 9 |
10 | {Home}{Home}{Home}{Up}
11 | {Replace}n,"{Merge Codes}e{HPg}{Search}{Enter}"{Search}
12 |
13 | {Del}
14 | {Home}{Home}{Home}{Up}
15 | "
16 |
17 | {Text In/Out}3{Del to EOL}
```

Lines 4, 7, and 10 of the macro move the cursor to the top of the document in preparation for each Replace command.

Line 5 replaces all of the ^R [HRt] field merge codes with a double quote (to end the previous field), a comma (to separate the fields), and another double quote (to begin the next field).

Line 8 replaces any ^E [HRt] sequences with ^E [HPg]. This ensures that all records end the same way, so that the next step will be able to locate all of the field endings.

Line 11 takes off the comma and double quote that step 3 erroneously placed at the end of each line (record), as well as the ^E and [HPg] that were originally at the end of each record.

These codes are all replaced with an [HRt] code and then a double quote to begin the first field of the next record.

The last problem with the file is addressed in lines 13 and 15. Because there is no first field after the last record, line 13 deletes the extra double quote generated by line 5, and because there is no [HRt] before the first record, step 15 adds a double quote to begin its first field.

Line 17 invokes the Save Generic command, and then deletes the suggested file name. The macro ends at this prompt.

Mail Merge Numeric Field Conversion

If you have any numeric fields in your newly created mail merge file, you will need to remove the double quotes from those fields in every record. To do this, use a macro to search for the comma delimiter as many times as necessary to get to the beginning of the numeric field, delete the leading double quote, search for the next comma, delete the trailing double quote, and then repeat the steps.

For example, let's assume that you have a file created with the previous macro that has records formatted like this:

```
"John Hawkins","Marketing","54000","Single"
```

In this case, the record consists of three text fields (name, division, and marital status) and one numeric field (salary). The numeric field is the third one in the record. You would want to remove the quotes from this record.

The macro listed below first asks which fields in the file should have their quotes removed. Then, it stores the answer, and processes the file. Here's the macro:

```
1   {;}Mailmerge·numeric·field·conversion~
2   {;}Copyright·(c)·1988,·by·Eric·Alderman~
3
4   {DISPLAY OFF}
5   {TEXT}0~{^\}Numeric·field·number(s)·(e.g.·{^]}3{^\}·or·{^]}2,5,8{^\}
6   )·:·~
7
```

```
 8 | {IF EXISTS}0~                         {;}If·no·value·entered·at·prompt~
 9 | {ELSE}
10 |     {QUIT}                            {;}Then·quit~
11 | {END IF}
12 |
13 | {ASSIGN}0~,{VAR 0}~                   {;}Put·a·comma·in·front·of·Variable·0~
14 | {Home}{Home}{Home}{Up}
15 | {HPg}{Up}                             {;}Insert·HPg·at·top·of·document~
16 | {VAR 0}                               {;}Insert·field·selections~
17 |
18 | {LABEL}sel_loop~                      {;}Beginning·of·selection·loop~
19 |
20 | {ON NOT FOUND}{GO}done~~              {;}Setup·handler·for·no·more·selections~
21 |
22 | {Search Left},{Search}               {;}Look·backwards·for·next·selection~
23 | {Block}{End}{Macro Commands}30        {;}Assign·selection·to·Var·0~
24 | {Search Left}{Search Left}            {;}Go·back·to·comma~
25 | {Del to EOL}{Backspace}               {;}Delete·comma·and·selection~
26 | {Search}{HPg}{Search}                 {;}Advance·to·beg.·of·document~
27 |
28 | {ASSIGN}0~{VAR 0}-1~                  {;}Subtract·1·from·Variable·0~
29 |
30 | {LABEL}rec_loop~                      {;}Beginning·of·record·loop~
31 | {ASSIGN}1~{VAR 0}~                    {;}Transfer·selection·number·to·Var·1~
32 | {ON NOT FOUND}{GO}next_sel~~          {;}Setup·branch·for·no·more·recs~
33 | {Search}"{Search}                     {;}Get·past·first·quote·(for·field·1)~
34 |
35 | {LABEL}field_loop~                    {;}Beginning·of·field·loop~
36 | {IF}{VAR 1}>0~                        {;}If·not·through·advancing·fields~
37 |     {Search}","{Search}               {;}Search·for·next·delimiter~
38 |     {ASSIGN}1~{VAR 1}-1~              {;}Decrement·counter~
39 |     {GO}field_loop~                   {;}Repeat·steps·until·sel.·found~
40 | {END IF}
41 |
42 | {Backspace}                           {;}Delete·first·quote~
43 | {Search}"{Search}                     {;}Advance·to·next·quote~
44 | {Backspace}                           {;}Delete·it·to
45 | {Search}{Enter}{Search}               {;}Advance·to·beginning·of·next·record~
46 |
47 | {GO}rec_loop~                         {;}Repeat·record·loop·steps~
48 |
49 | {LABEL}next_sel~                      {;}When·through·with·this·selection~
50 | {Home}{Home}{Home}{Up}                {;}Go·to·top·of·document~
51 | {End}                                 {;}Move·to·the·end·of·the·sel.·list~
52 | {GO}sel_loop~                         {;}Go·back·to·top·to·find·next·sel.~
53 |
54 | {LABEL}done~                          {;}When·finished~
55 | {Home}{Home}{Home}{Up}                {;}Go·back·to·top~
56 | {Move}ad                              {;}Delete·selection·page~
```

Lines 8-11 check to see if the user entered anything at the prompt. If not, the macro ends. Line 13 inserts a comma in front of the selection entered (so that each selection number is preceded by a comma). A new page is created, and the selections are inserted on that page. Then lines 22-26 read the next selection number, starting from the end of the list. Once assigned to a variable, the selection number and its preceding comma are deleted.

Next, the variable containing the selected field number is reduced by one. That's because the variable needs to reflect the number of times the cursor must advance to the next field delimiter. (Because the cursor starts at the beginning of field 1, it would not need to advance at all to process field 1, it would need to advance only once to process field 2, and so on.)

Line 31 transfers the value of Variable 0 to Variable 1. Variable 1 can then be used as a counter for each record, and Variable 0 will retain the selection while the entire file is processed. Line 32 sets up a branch for when the search on line 33 fails (because there are no more records).

Lines 35-40 advance the cursor through the record until the selected field is located. As long as the counter is greater than 0, line 37 searches for the next field delimiter. Each time, Variable 1 is reduced in value by 1. When the correct field is located, lines 42-45 remove the quotes, and advance to the next record. Line 47 begins the record loop again for the next record.

When the search for another record fails on line 33, lines 49-52 are executed, which return the cursor to the top of the document, move the cursor to the end of the selection line, and start the procedure over again from line 18.

Finally, when the search for a comma fails on line 22, the branch set up on line 20 is executed, and the macro continues with lines 54-56. These move the cursor to the top of the document, then delete the selection page.

dBASE III Date Conversion

As mentioned in Chapter 12, "Integration with Other Products," when you output dBASE III data to an ASCII delimited (mail merge) file, dBASE formats dates like this:

`YYYYMMDD`

where "YYYY" is the year, "MM" is the month, and "DD" is the day.

For example, here is a record created with the dBASE Copy To command that contains a text field (name), a date field (birthdate), and a numeric field (salary):

`"Frank Sarconi",19541021,34000`

The record contains the information that Frank Sarconi was born on October 21, 1954. After WordPerfect's Convert program is used to translate the mailmerge format file into the secondary merge format, the same record will look like this:

```
Frank Sarconi^R
19541021^R
34000^E
```

You can write a macro that will go through a file with records in this format and convert the dates to a more readable form. The macro uses the Undelete function to quickly reposition the numbers of the date. Here's the macro listing:

```
 1 | {;}DBASE·III·date·field·conversion~
 2 | {;}Copyright·(c)·1988,·by·Eric·Alderman~
 3 |
 4 | {DISPLAY OFF}
 5 | {TEXT}0~{^\}Date·field·number:·~       {;}Ask·for·field·number~
 6 |
 7 | {IF EXISTS}0~                          {;}If·no·value·entered·at·prompt~
 8 | {ELSE}
 9 |     {QUIT}                             {;}Then·quit~
10 | {END IF}
11 |
12 | {Home}{Home}{Home}{Up}                 {;}Go·to·top·of·document~
13 | {ASSIGN}0~{VAR 0}-1~                    {;}Subtract·1·from·Variable·0~
14 |
15 | {LABEL}rec_loop~                        {;}Beginning·of·record·loop~
16 | {ASSIGN}1~{VAR 0}~                      {;}Transfer·field·number·to·Var·1~
17 | {ON NOT FOUND}{GO}done~~                {;}Setup·branch·for·no·more·recs~
18 | {Search}{Merge R}{Search}              {;}Check·whether·another·rec·exists~
19 | {Goto}{Goto}                           {;}Go·back·to·beginning·of·record~
20 |
21 | {LABEL}field_loop~                      {;}Beginning·of·field·loop~
22 | {IF}{VAR 1}>0~                          {;}If·not·through·advancing·fields~
23 |     {Search}{Merge R}{Enter}{Search}      {;}Search·for·next·field~
24 |     {ASSIGN}1~{VAR 1}-1~                {;}Decrement·counter~
25 |     {GO}field_loop~                     {;}Repeat·steps·until·field·is·found~
26 | {END IF}
27 |
28 | {Del}{Del}{Del}{Del}                    {;}Delete·year~
29 | {Right}{Right}                          {;}Move·past·month~
30 | /                                       {;}Slash·between·month·and·day~
31 | {Right}{Right}                          {;}Move·past·day~
32 | /                                       {;}Slash·after·day~
33 | {Cancel}1                               {;}Undelete·year~
34 | {Left}{Left}                            {;}Move·to·left·of·last·two·digits~
35 | {Backspace}{Backspace}                  {;}Delete·"19"·in·year~
36 | {Search}{Merge Codes}e{Search}           {;}Search·for·^E·end·of·record~
37 | {Right}                                 {;}Move·past·[HRt]·or·[HPg]~
38 |
39 | {GO}rec_loop~                           {;}Repeat·record·loop·steps~
40 |
41 | {LABEL}done~                            {;}When·finished~
42 | {Home}{Home}{Home}{Up}                  {;}Go·to·top·of·document~
```

Line 5 prompts the user for the number of the field which contains the date. Lines 7-10 will end the macro if the user presses just ENTER at the prompt. Line 17 sets up a branch for the search on line 18. If no ^R merge code is found, then the process is over, and the macro branches to the "done" routine. Line 19 returns the cursor to where it was before the search, at the beginning of the record.

Lines 21-26 advance the cursor to the selected field (see "Mailmerge Numeric Field Conversion" for a description of a similar routine). Once the correct field is found, line 28 deletes the four digits of the year. Lines 29-32 insert the two slashes, line 33 restores the four digits of the year at the cursor position, and line 35 deletes the "19" in the year.

Line 39 repeats the procedure on all of the records until the search on line 18 fails (no more records are located). When the macro has completed execution, the records should be formatted like this one:

```
Frank Sarconi^R
10/21/54^R
34000^E
```

Formatting Articles for Newspapers and Magazines

Many newspaper and magazine publishers have in-house news editing systems that interface with typesetting computers. These systems usually have a stringent set of rules dictating the format of your text, whether it is submitted on disk or via telephone modem. You can have a macro properly format a WordPerfect document to prepare it for these systems.

You can use similar macros to format WordPerfect documents for a variety of other systems. For example, many commercial typesetters will now accept a file directly from your word processor (normally as an ASCII file). This file is then edited by the typesetter to include the many formatting commands that the typesetting computer uses to produce your text. You can have WordPerfect perform much of this formatting and avoid editing charges.

The macros listed next were written by one of the authors, who submits articles to a major newspaper that uses the SII System 55 news editing system. This system requires that quoted items start with two double quotes and end with two single quotes. (This is because, unlike computers, typesetting systems use different characters for opening quotation marks and for ending quotation marks.) This system also expects paragraphs to be separated with a less-than symbol, a Hard Return, and then a three-space indent for the next paragraph, rather than with a blank line (that is, two Hard Returns).

The following macro performs these format changes. (Be sure to save your document before executing the macro, in case something goes wrong.) When the macro is done, look over your document to make sure that the quotes were translated properly. If you did not include a closing double quote somewhere, it will throw off the macro's Search commands and you will have to reload the original document and try again.

After you are satisfied that the quotes were translated properly, enter a file name and press ENTER. You could then exit WordPerfect and run a communications program to send the file by modem to the publication. See the following section, "Automatic Control Transfer," for a description of how to fully automate this process.

Here's the macro listing:

```
 1│ {;}Translate·quotes·for·magazine/newspaper·submission~
 2│ {;}Copyright·(c)·1988,·by·Lawrence·J.·Magid·and·Eric·Alderman~
 3│
 4│ {DISPLAY OFF}
 5│ {Home}{Home}{Home}{Up}              {;}Go·to·top·of·document~
 6│ {ON NOT FOUND}{GO}hrt~~             {;}Setup·branch·for·no·more·quotes~
 7│
 8│ {LABEL}quote~                       {;}Beginning·of·Quote·loop~
 9│ {Search}"{Search}                   {;}Search·for·first·quote~
10│ "                                   {;}Insert·another·quote~
11│ {Search}"{Search}                   {;}Search·for·second·in·quote·pair~
12│ {Backspace}''                       {;}Delete·it,·insert·2·single·quotes~
13│ {GO}quote~                          {;}Repeat·until·search·fails~
14│
15│ {LABEL}hrt~                         {;}Beginning·of·HRt·routine~
16│ {Home}{Home}{Home}{Up}             {;}Go·to·top·of·document~
17│ {Replace}n{Enter}{Enter}{Search}
18│    {Enter}{Search}                  {;}Replace·two·HRt's·with·one~
19│ {Home}{Home}{Home}{Up}             {;}Go·to·top·of·document~
20│ {Replace}n{Enter}{Search}
21│    <{Enter}···{Search}              {;}Replace·paragraph·ends~
22│
23│ {DISPLAY ON}
24│ {Home}{Home}{Home}{Up}             {;}Go·to·top·of·document~
25│ {Text In/Out}11{Del to EOL}         {;}DOS·Save,·clear·filename~
```

Line 6 sets up a branch to the "HRt" routine when no more quotes can be found. Lines 8-13 search for pairs of double quotes, and replace them with two double quotes and two single quotes. When the search on line 9 fails, the "HRt" routine on line 15 is executed. Lines 15-21 first replace all occurrences of two Hard Returns in a row with one, and then replace the Hard Returns with a less-than sign, a Hard Return, and then three spaces for a first-line indentation. Finally, line 24 moves the cursor to the top of the document, and line 25 invokes the DOS TEXT SAVE command, then clears the suggested file name. The macro ends at the Save prompt, waiting for a file name. If you want to scroll through the document to check the formatting, you can simply press the <Cancel> key (F1).

Normally, you will have already saved the original WordPerfect document, which you can later retrieve and edit. Therefore, you do not need to keep the formatted ASCII file that you send to the publication. To make things simple, you can use the same file name whenever you send a document, replacing the original text each time with the new document.

Automatic Control Transfer

You can use WordPerfect macros and DOS batch files to automate the steps of sending documents via modem. In fact, you could use the concept described here to automate a variety of other tasks. Note that this advanced procedure assumes that you have a hard disk and that you know how to write a DOS batch file.

As an example, let's assume that you have WordPerfect loaded on your hard disk in the \WP directory, that you store your documents in a directory called \WP\DATA, and that you use Pro-Comm as your communications program, loaded in the \PRO-COMM directory. Let's also assume that you store batch files in the root directory (or in a directory you've placed in the DOS PATH).

This procedure uses the DOS batch file command IF EXIST to test whether the file SEND.ASC exists in your data directory when you exit WordPerfect. If it does, ProComm will be executed (so you can transfer your document), and then you are returned to WordPerfect. If it doesn't, you exit to DOS as usual.

Assuming that your regular batch file looks like this:

```
cd \wp\data
\wp\wp
cd \
```

here is a batch file that performs the control transfer procedure to
ProComm and back:

```
cd \wp\data
if exist send.asc del send.asc
\wp\wp
if exist send.asc goto send
goto end
:send
cd \procomm
procomm
cd \
wpgo
:end
cd \
```

Create this batch file in your root directory and give it the name
WPGO.BAT. Use it whenever you want to run WordPerfect. Note
that you can use a different name, as long as you change the self-
referential line in the batch file (third from the last) accordingly.

Here is a line-by-line explanation of this batch file listing:

cd \wp \data   Changes the current directory to your data directory so that files will automatically be stored there from within
WordPerfect.

if exist send.asc del send.asc   Checks to see if the document
SEND.ASC exists in the data directory, and deletes it if it does.

\wp \wp   Executes WordPerfect, which is loaded in the \WP
directory. This method is only possible with DOS 3.XX. With
DOS 2.XX, this line should read simply "wp". While in WordPerfect, you would use the macro described in the previous section to
create the file SEND.ASC.

if exist send.asc goto send   Executes when you exit from
WordPerfect, it checks for the existence of SEND.ASC (created

by the macro in the previous section). If it exists, the batch file branches to :SEND. If it does not exist, it continues with the next step.

goto end If the file SEND.ASC does not exist, the batch file branches to :END and exits WordPerfect normally.

:send Marks this as the start of the SEND routine.

cd \procomm Changes the default directory to the \PRO-COMM directory. (This can be the directory of whatever communications program you are using.) If your communications program does not support subdirectories, you could first use COPY to put a copy of the file SEND.ASC into the proper directory. Just be sure to delete the file after you exit the communications program.

procomm Executes the program ProComm (or any designated communications program). You would then dial a number and transfer the document. Some communications programs can be programmed to perform certain tasks, much like WordPerfect's macros. This capability would permit you to send your document automatically.

**cd ** Changes the default directory to the root directory.

wpgo Starts this batch file over again, which will delete the SEND.ASC file and return you to WordPerfect.

:end Marks this as the start of the END routine, which ends the batch file.

**cd ** Changes the default directory to the root directory.

To use this procedure, you need to add the following steps to the macro listed listed in the earlier section, "Formatting Articles for Newspapers and Magazines". (Be sure to delete line 25 from the macro before entering these steps.)

```
25 | {CHAR}0~Continue·with·save·and·exit?·(Y/N):·Y{Left}~
26 |
27 | {CASE}{VAR 0}~                    {;}If·response·is·Y·then·go·to·OK~
28 |     {Enter}~ok~y~ok~Y~ok~
29 |       ~
30 | {QUIT}                           {;}Otherwise,·quit~
31 |
32 | {LABEL}ok~
33 | {Text In/Out}11                  {;}Save·DOS·Text~
34 | SEND.ASC{Enter}                  {;}as·SEND.ASC~
35 | {IF}{STATE}&1024~                {;}If·at·"Replace?"·prompt,·type·Y~
36 |     y                            {;}Just·in·case~
37 | {END IF}
38 | {Exit}ny                         {;}Exit·WordPerfect~
```

Now follow these steps:

1. Write your document.
2. Execute the macro described previously, if it is necessary to save SEND.ASC.

The macro formats and saves the file as SEND.ASC. Then it exits WordPerfect, and the WPGO.BAT batch file, which you used to start the program, picks up where it left off. It checks for the existence of the file SEND.ASC, and when it finds the file, it executes your communications program.

3. Dial the phone number and transfer the SEND.ASC file.
4. Exit the communications program.

After you exit the communications program, the batch file again picks up where it left off. It restarts itself, deleting the SEND. ASC file and running WordPerfect. You can then continue with your work.

OFFICE AUTOMATION

WordPerfect's macros can be used to automate a variety of repetitive office tasks.

Letter Generation

There are several possible approaches to automating the letter writing process. For example, you could write a macro that simply inserts the current date, and then skips down to the correct line for you to begin typing the address. Or you might write a more complex macro which builds a header that will appear on the second and subsequent pages of the letter. This macro might also prompt you for the name of the recipient, to be placed in the header and at the beginning of the inside address. Or you might want to create a macro which selects a recipient from among the names and addresses stored in a secondary file, and then automatically inserts that person's name and address at the top of the page.

In this section, two letter writing solutions will be described.

Building a Letter

You can easily write a macro that builds the format of your letters. Since letter writing is such a common word processing task for many people (and a primary one for some), the time gained by the use of a macro to automate the process can become quite significant. Everyone has a preference as to the best format for a letter, so you may need to modify the macro provided here to match your own needs. Here is the macro listing:

```
 1 | {;}Building·a·Letter~
 2 | {;}Copyright·(c)·1988,·by·Eric·Alderman~
 3 |
 4 | {DISPLAY OFF}
 5 | {TEXT}0~Enter·the·name·of·the·recipient:·~
 6 |
 7 | {IF EXISTS}0~                {;}If·no·value·entered~
 8 | {ELSE}
 9 |     {QUIT}                   {;}Then·quit~
10 | {END IF}
11 |
12 | {Format}2312                 {;}Build·Header·A,·every·page~
13 |     {VAR 0}{Enter}           {;}Insert·recipient's·name~
14 |     {Date/Outline}1{Enter}   {;}Insert·the·current·date~
15 |     Page·{^B}{Enter}         {;}Insert·the·page·number~
16 |     {Exit}                   {;}Exit·the·Header·screen~
17 | 95Y{Exit}                    {;}Suppress·Header·A·on·this·page~
18 | {Cancel}                     {;}Return·to·Format·screen~
19 |
20 | 18                           {;}Set·tabs~
```

```
21  {Del to EOL}                 {;}Clear·tab·stops~
22  4"{Enter}                    {;}Set·one·tab·stop·at·4"~
23  {Exit}                       {;}Exit·Tab·Settings·area~
24  {Cancel}                     {;}Return·to·Format·screen~
25
26  412                          {;}Advance·past·letterhead~
27  1"{Enter}                    {;}Advance·1"~
28  {Exit}                       {;}Return·to·document~
29
30  {Tab}
31  {Date/Outline}1              {;}Insert·current·date~
32  {Enter}{Enter}{Enter}        {;}Return·down·for·inside·address~
33  {VAR 0}{Enter}               {;}Insert·recipient's·name~
```

Line 5 prompts for the name of the recipient, to be used in the header and in the inside address of the letter. Lines 7-10 check to see if anything was typed at the prompt; if not, the macro quits. Lines 12-18 build Header A, which includes the recipient's name, the current date, and the page number, each on separate lines. The header is suppressed for the first page, so that it appears only on the second and subsequent pages of the letter (a typical format for business correspondence).

Lines 20-24 set a single tab stop in the middle of the page, at 4 inches from the left edge. Lines 26-28 advance the cursor down one inch, to get beyond any letterhead information at the top of the page. (You may need to adjust or omit this step for your own letterhead. You may also want to create a graphic box at the top of the page for your own printed letterhead.)

Lines 30-33 enter the date at the first tab stop, skip a few lines, and insert the recipient's name. When the macro is through executing, you can continue by typing the inside address and then the body of the letter.

Using a Secondary File

You can have WordPerfect automatically add a name and address to a letter for you. By combining macros with the Merge function, you can create a procedure that will take a name and address at the cursor location and place this information into a merge document for a letter.

The following macro assumes that your names and addresses are stored in a secondary merge file with the data entered as follows:

Syntax:

```
Fname^R
Lname^R
Address^R
City, ST^R
Zip^R
^E
```

Example:

```
Frank^R
Henderson^R
435 Maple Corner^R
Guerneville, CA^R
95446^R
^E
```

If you have a secondary merge document that is not formatted like this, you will need to modify the primary document and the macro to work properly with your format. You might want to experiment with a record formatted like the preceding one before making the modifications.

Here is the macro listing:

```
 1 | {;}Create·a·letter·from·address·record~
 2 | {;}Copyright·(c)·1988,·by·Eric·Alderman~
 3 |
 4 | {DISPLAY OFF}
 5 | {Home}{Home}{Home}{Left}              {;}Go·to·left·edge·of·line~
 6 | {Block}
 7 | {Search}{^E}{Search}
 8 | {Right}                               {;}Block·to·end·of·record~
 9 | {Save}letter.add{Enter}               {;}Save·record·as·a·file~
10 |
11 | {IF}{STATE}&1024~                      {;}If·file·exists,·replace~
12 |       Y
13 | {END IF}
14 |
15 | {Exit}nn                              {;}Clear·screen~
16 |
17 | {Merge/Sort}1                         {;}Start·merge~
18 | letter.fmt{Enter}
19 | letter.add{Enter}
```

Lines 5-9 mark the record at the cursor position as a block, and then save the block as a file. Lines 11-13 confirm the replacement if the file already exists. Line 15 clears the screen, and lines 17-19 execute the merge.

This procedure requires a primary document in order to create the letter. Although you can modify the format in any way, begin by creating a letter like the one shown in Figure 13-1. Remember to use the <Merge Codes> key to insert the merge codes (see Chapter 3, "Merge"). Save the document as LETTER. FMT.

To use this procedure, first retrieve the secondary document that contains your names and addresses, and then find the name of the person (using the Search function if necessary) to whom you want to send a letter. Execute the macro, which clears the screen and inserts the current date, the person's name and address, and "Dear *fname*," at the top of the file. You can then write the text of the letter.

```
                                    ^D



^F1^ ^F2^
^F3^
^F4^ ^F5^

Dear ^F1^:


   _
```

Doc 1 Pg 1 Ln 10 Pos 10

Figure 13-1.   The letter format document—LETTER.FMT

One modification you might make to this macro would cause it to mark the name from the inside address as a block, and then use that text to create a header like the one described in the previous section. Here are the additional steps you will need to do this:

```
20
21   {Home}{Home}{Home}{Up}           {;}Go·to·top·of·document~
22   {End}{Word Right}                {;}Move·to·name~
23   {Block}{End}
24   {Move}12                         {;}Copy·name~
25   {Home}{Home}{Home}{Up}           {;}Go·to·top·of·document~
26
27   {Format}2312                     {;}Build·Header·A,·every·page~
28      {Enter}                       {;}Retrieve·name~
29      {End}{Enter}
30      {Date/Outline}1{Enter}        {;}Insert·the·current·date~
31      Page·{^B}{Enter}              {;}Insert·the·page·number~
32      {Exit}                        {;}Exit·the·header·screen~
33   95Y{Exit}                        {;}Suppress·Header·A·on·this·page~
34   {Exit}                           {;}Return·to·the·document~
35
36   {Home}{Home}{Down}               {;}Go·to·bottom·of·document~
```

Printing Envelopes

You can write a macro that will automatically print on an envelope an address taken from a letter. Typically, you will use a macro like this after you've finished writing a letter. Here's the macro listing:

```
 1   {;}Print·address·at·cursor·on·envelope~
 2   {;}Copyright·(c)·1988,·by·Eric·Alderman~
 3
 4   {DISPLAY OFF}
 5   {Block}                          {;}Mark·block·to·2·HRt's~
 6   {Search}{Enter}{Enter}{Search}
 7   {Move}12                         {;}Copy·block~
 8   {Home}{Home}{Home}{Up}           {;}Go·to·top·of·document~
 9   {HPg}                            {;}Insert·page·break~
10   {Up}
11   {Enter}                          {;}Retrieve·text·onto·new·page~
12
13   {Format}2855                     {;}Change·to·envelope·Page·Type~
14   5
15   2"{Enter}.5"{Enter}              {;}Set·Top·Mar·to·2",·Bot·to·.5"~
16   {Cancel}                         {;}Return·to·Format·screen~
17
18   17                               {;}Set·left·margin·to·3.75"~
19   3.75"{Enter}{Enter}
20   {Exit}                           {;}Return·to·document~
21
22   {Print}2                         {;}Print·the·page~
23   {Move}33                         {;}Delete·the·page~
```

Lines 5-7 mark the address as a block (using two Hard Returns to mark the end), and then copy the block. Lines 8-11 create a new page at the top of the document, and then insert the copied name and address on this page.

Line 13 inserts a [Paper Sz/Typ:] code to format the page for an envelope. Note that you must have an Envelope form type defined for your printer for this code to be recognized. (See Chapter 11, "Using Printers," for a description of this process.)

Line 15 sets a two-inch top margin and a half-inch bottom margin, and lines 18-20 set a left margin of 3.75 inches. This should place the name and address properly on the envelope. You may need to adjust these values, however, to match your own printer, envelopes, and format preferences.

Line 22 prints the envelope page, and line 23 deletes the page.

Letter Archive

Another useful office automation tool is the Letter Archive macro, which maintains a daily archive document containing all the letters you write in a day. Each letter is separated by a Hard Page Break. The biggest advantage to this type of system is that it enables you to avoid having to come up with a unique file name for every letter you write.

Here's the macro listing:

```
 1 | {;}Letter·archive·procedure~
 2 | {;}Copyright·(c)·1988,·by·Lawrence·J.·Magid·and·Eric·Alderman~
 3 |
 4 | {DISPLAY OFF}
 5 | {Home}{Home}{Home}{Up}             {;}Move·to·top·of·document~
 6 | {HPg}                              {;}Insert·a·page·break~
 7 | {Up}
 8 |
 9 | {Date/Outline}3                    {;}Change·date·format·to·MMDD~
10 | %2%1{Enter}
11 | 1                                  {;}Insert·date·in·MMDD·form~
12 | {Block}{Home}{Left}
13 | {Macro Commands}30                 {;}Put·date·into·Variable·0~
14 | {Del to EOL}                       {;}Delete·date~
15 |
16 | {Block}                            {;}Mark·entire·document·as·a·block~
17 | {Home}{Home}{Down}
18 | {Move}14
19 | {VAR 0}arc.ltr{Enter}              {;}Append·document·to·dated·file~
20 |
```

```
21 | {Home}{Home}{Home}{Up}      {;}Go·to·top·of·document~
22 | {Del}                       {;}Delete·page·break~
23 |
24 | {Date/Outline}3
25 | 3·1,·4{Enter}               {;}Reset·date·format·to·normal~
26 | {Exit}                      {;}Return·to·document~
```

Lines 5-7 insert a page break at the top of the document. Lines 9-10 change the Date format to MMDD, and line 11 inserts the current date in that format. Lines 12-13 then put that date into Variable 0, so that it can be used later for the file name. Line 14 deletes the date from the document.

Lines 16-19 append the entire document, including the page break at the beginning, to the daily archive document. The file name for the document is derived from combining the current date, inserted with the {VAR 0} statement, and "arc.ltr". So, for example, the file 0502ARC.LTR would be created on May 2. (Of course, you'll have a problem in a year, when the date will be the same. You may want to use a longer format which includes the year, although you must limit the file name to 8 characters. You probably should be storing your documents somewhere else at that point in any case.)

Lines 21-22 move the cursor to the top of the document, then delete the page break. Lines 24-26 restore the normal Date format. You may want to modify line 25 if you've changed the default Date format in Setup.

Document Assembly

The WordPerfect workbook describes how to use the Merge function to perform a *document assembly* operation. (Document assembly means that you build a document using any combination of standard paragraphs, along with customized text.) You can use a macro to create an easier and more flexible document assembly procedure.

To begin with, you need to create a document that will contain all of your standard paragraphs. Follow the steps below to create this document. Make sure the screen is clear.

Paragraphs should be numbered sequentially, so that you will later be able to print out this document for easy reference. You can use any sort of numbering system that you want for the paragraphs, although Arabic numbers are used in this procedure. (Do not use the Paragraph Numbering function, however.)

Follow these steps to create a few sample paragraphs.

1. Type **1.** and press the <Left Indent> key (F4).
2. Type

   Now we are entering the text for the first paragraph. We could be typing some legal terms for this sample, but they would be hard to type. This should give us the idea.

3. Press ENTER twice.
4. Type **2.** and press the <Left Indent> key.
5. Type

   Here we are typing the second paragraph. Again, we must let our minds roam free while we conjure up nonsense to type for the second paragraph.

6. Press ENTER twice.
7. Type **3.** and press the <Left Indent> key.
8. Type

   Already we find ourselves typing the third paragraph. It seems hard to believe that just a few minutes ago, we hadn't even started typing the first paragraph.

9. Press ENTER twice.

If you like, go ahead and type a few more paragraphs like these. Be sure to start each paragraph with a number, a period, and the <Left Indent> function. Be sure to end each paragraph by pressing ENTER twice.

When you are finished, save the document as PARA.STD and clear the screen. Here's the macro listing:

```
1│ {;}Document·assembly·macro~
2│ {;}Copyright·(c)·1988,·by·Eric·Alderman~
3│
```

```
 4 | {DISPLAY OFF}
 5 | {Switch}
 6 | {List Files}para.std{Enter}
 7 | {Down}1                          {;}Retrieve·PARA.STD·into·other·doc~
 8 |
 9 | {IF}{STATE}&1024~                {;}If·at·"Retrieve·into...?"·prompt~
10 |     {GO}abort~                   {;}Then·abort~
11 | {END IF}
12 |
13 | {LABEL}begin~
14 | {TEXT}0~{^\}Paragraph·number·({^]}Enter{^\}·to·quit):·~
15 |
16 | {IF EXISTS}0~                    {;}If·no·value·entered·at·prompt~
17 | {ELSE}
18 |     {GO}end~                     {;}Then·go·to·end~
19 | {END IF}
20 |
21 | {ON NOT FOUND}{GO}notfound~~     {;}Setup·branch·for·no·such·num~
22 | {Search}{VAR 0}.{Indent}{Search} {;}Search·for·para·request~
23 |
24 | {Block}{Enter}                   {;}Mark·paragraph·as·block~
25 | {Move}12                         {;}Copy·block~
26 | {Home}{Home}{Up}                 {;}Go·to·top·(for·next·round)~
27 | {Switch}                         {;}Switch·back·to·working·doc~
28 | {Enter}                          {;}Retrieve·text~
29 | {Search}{Enter}{Search}          {;}Search·for·end·of·paragraph~
30 | {Enter}                          {;}Insert·additional·HRt~
31 |
32 | {DISPLAY ON}                     {;}Update·screen~
33 | {DISPLAY OFF}
34 | {Switch}                         {;}Switch·back·to·PARA.STD~
35 |
36 | {GO}begin~                       {;}Go·back·for·next·para~
37 |
38 | {LABEL}abort~                    {;}If·at·"Retrieve·into...?"~
39 | {Cancel}{Cancel}                 {;}Cancel·prompt,·then·List·Files~
40 | {Switch}                         {;}Switch·back·to·working·doc~
41 | {CHAR}0~ERROR:··{^\}Other·document·not·empty---·press·any·key~
42 | {QUIT}                           {;}Display·error·and·quit~
43 |
44 | {LABEL}end~                      {;}If·no·value·entered·at·prompt~
45 | {Exit}nn                         {;}Clear·screen~
46 | {Switch}                         {;}Switch·back·to·working·doc~
47 | {QUIT}                           {;}Quit~
48 |
49 | {LABEL}notfound~                 {;}If·requested·para·not·found~
50 | {CHAR}1~{^\}Could·not·locate·Paragraph·{^]}{VAR 0}{^\}·---press·any·
51 | key~
52 | {GO}begin~                       {;}Display·message,·start·over~
```

Lines 5-7 retrieve the PARA.STD document into the inactive document (usually Document 2). The List Files function is used rather than the <Retrieve> key, so that the "Retrieve into current document?" prompt will be displayed if there is currently text in the document. Then, using the {STATE} command, the macro senses whether a yes/no question is active directly after the command to retrieve has been issued. Lines 9-11 check for the prompt. If you plan to store the PARA.STD file in a specific directory, you can precede the file name with an appropriate path specification.

Line 14 produces a prompt asking for the paragraph number. Lines 16-19 check whether the user has simply pressed ENTER, indicating the end of the macro.

Line 21 sets up a branch in case the requested paragraph number is not found. Line 22 searches for the requested paragraph number. It includes a period and the [→Indent] code, to ensure that a number within a paragraph is not mistakenly found. Lines 24-30 copy the located paragraph, and retrieve it into the working document.

Lines 32-33 update the screen, and line 34 switches back to the PARA.STD document. Line 36 starts the process over again.

Lines 38-42 are executed when the test of {STATE} on line 9 indicates that the "Retrieve into current document?" prompt is being displayed. These steps cancel the prompt, cancel List Files, switch back to the working document, and display a message.

Lines 44-47 are executed when no value is entered at the prompt on line 14, indicating the end of the macro. The steps clear the screen, and switch back to the working document.

Finally, lines 49-52 are executed when the requested paragraph number is not found. A message is displayed indicating the problem, and then the process starts over.

To use the document assembly macros, start with both documents blank. Then begin to type your document. When you want to insert a standard paragraph from the PARA.STD file, invoke the previously listed macro. The macro prompts you for a paragraph number. You type the number of the paragraph you want (keep a printed copy of the PARA.STD document for reference), and press ENTER. The paragraph is inserted into your document. Continue to enter paragraph numbers for other paragraphs you want to insert at the cursor position. When you are finished, simply press ENTER, and you are returned to the document.

To add, delete, and edit the standard paragraphs, simply retrieve the PARA.STD document, make the desired changes, and re-save the document. (You can also use the Paragraph Sort function to reorder the paragraphs.) Be sure to start each paragraph with a number (or some other unique code), and to end each paragraph by pressing ENTER twice.

WORDSTAR KEY SEQUENCES

Prior to using WordPerfect, one of the authors used WordStar as his primary word processing program. He switched to WordPerfect because of its many additional features, yet remained wedded to WordStar's keyboard interface. (WordStar uses CTRL keys for most functions, including moving around the document.) Without debating the wisdom of the WordStar interface, it is clear that it is very popular, not only among current and former WordStar users, but among many users of dBASE II, dBASE III, and other programs that use the WordStar cursor control diamond (CTRL+E for UP ARROW, CTRL+X for DOWN ARROW, CTRL+S for LEFT ARROW, and CTRL+D for RIGHT ARROW), as well as other key sequences.

Admittedly, this interface is a throwback to the days when many computers had no arrow keys (WordStar, first published in 1979, worked on old Apple II systems and on all CP/M machines), but the interface has merit because it is possible for touch typists to move the cursor around the screen without having to move their hands off the home row of keys or their eyes off the screen.

To emulate the WordStar key sequences, use WordPerfect's Keyboard Layout function described in Chapter 2, "Macros." With this function, you can redefine the CTRL key combinations (such as the cursor diamond) to perform the desired function. Some of them will require more than a simple remapping of functions. For example, WordStar's CTRL+Y sequence deletes the entire line on which the cursor is resting. Since WordPerfect does not have an identical command, you'll need to simulate it by defining the CTRL+Y key to perform a HOME, HOME, HOME, LEFT ARROW, and then a CTRL+END (for a Delete to End-of-Line).

Some of WordStar's commands require a sequence of two keystrokes in a row to perform a function. For example, CTRL+QS moves the cursor to the beginning of the line, and CTRL+QD moves it to the end. To implement these functions requires considerably more effort, because you'll need to redefine the first key to include a loop which waits for a second key.

For example, Table 13-1 shows a partial list of functions which can be performed in WordStar starting with the CTRL+Q sequence. Here are the macro steps (which you would insert into the definition of CTRL+Q) which will emulate these commands:

```
 1   {;}Emulate·Wordstar·CTRL+Q·prefix·command~
 2   {;}Copyright·(c)·1988,·by·Eric·Alderman~
 3
 4   {ASSIGN}0~~
 5
 6   {LABEL}lookloop~
 7   {LOOK}0~
 8   {IF EXISTS}0~
 9   {ELSE}
10       {GO}lookloop~
11   {END IF}
12
13   {CASE}{ORIGINAL KEY}~
14       s~qs~S~qs~{^S}~qs~
15       d~qd~D~qd~{^D}~qd~
16       r~qr~R~qr~{^R}~qr~
17       c~qc~C~qc~{^C}~qc~
18       p~qp~P~qp~{^P}~qp~
19       f~qf~F~qf~{^F}~qf~
20       a~qa~A~qa~{^A}~qa~
21       y~qy~Y~qy~{Left}~qy~
22       ~
23   {QUIT}
24
25   {LABEL}qs~
26   {Home}{Left}
27   {QUIT}
28
29   {LABEL}qd~
30   {Home}{Right}
31   {QUIT}
32
33   {LABEL}qr~
34   {Home}{Home}{Home}{Up}
35   {QUIT}
36
37   {LABEL}qc~
38   {Home}{Home}{Down}
39   {QUIT}
40
41   {LABEL}qp~
42   {Goto}{Goto}
43   {QUIT}
44
45   {LABEL}qf~
46   {Search}
47   {QUIT}
48
49   {LABEL}qa~
50   {Replace}
51   {QUIT}
52
53   {LABEL}qy~
54   {Del to EOL}
55   {QUIT}
```

Table 13-1.   WordStar CTRL+Q Key Sequences

Key Sequence	Action
CTRL+QS	Left edge of screen
CTRL+QD	Right edge of screen
CTRL+QR	Top of document
CTRL+QC	Bottom of document
CTRL+QP	Previous cursor location
CTRL+QF	Find (Search) for text
CTRL+QA	Find/Replace text
CTRL+QY	Delete to end of line

Although you may not want to emulate *all* of WordStar's commands using a macro program, you can produce the important ones.

USEFUL KEY REDEFINITIONS

WordPerfect's Keyboard Layout function provides you with considerable flexibility in modifying the program's operation. Several suggestions for key redefinitions, which you may find useful, follow.

Supercharging DEL and INS

Since WordPerfect has such a powerful Undelete function, the prompt which confirms the deletion of a block of text when you press the DEL or BACKSPACE key is really unnecessary. You can speed up your editing by defining the DEL or BACKSPACE keys to perform these macro steps:

```
1 | {IF}{STATE}&128~
2 |     {ORIGINAL KEY}y
3 | {ELSE}
4 |     {ORIGINAL KEY}
5 | {END IF}
```

In this way, the keys will always know when a block is being defined. If one is, then the confirmation response is typed in for you. If not, the keys perform their usual actions.

If you rarely use Typeover mode, you may also want to redefine the INS key. For example, you may want to define the key to undelete the last deletion. Here are the steps:

```
{Cancel}1
```

With the INS key redefined in this way, you can easily delete a block with the DEL key, and then quickly reinsert it by pressing INS. This makes it easy to move small sections of text. (Note that using the INS key like this would make the Typeover mode unavailable, unless you defined another key to perform that function. Another option would be to use the Original Definition Prefix key described below when you want to use Typeover mode.)

Temporary Reveal Codes

Many WordPerfect 4.2 users have become accustomed to pressing the SPACE BAR to exit the Reveal Codes function. (Because you could not enter or edit text in 4.2 with the Reveal Codes screen active, most keys would actually cause you to exit the function.) While the ability to enter and edit text and to perform formatting commands while using Reveal Codes is a nice added feature in WordPerfect 5.0, it is possible to bring back the SPACE BAR exit.

To allow the SPACE BAR to exit Reveal Codes, define the SPACE BAR key to perform these steps:

```
1 | {IF}{STATE}&8~
2 |     ·    {;}space~
3 | {ELSE}
4 |     {IF}{STATE}&512~
5 |         {Reveal Codes}
6 |     {ELSE}
7 |         ·
8 |     {END IF}
9 | {END IF}
```

Now whenever you use the Reveal Codes function, pressing SPACE BAR will exit the function. The disadvantage of using this method is that you will not be able to type text with spaces while in Reveal Codes. You will, however, be able to move the cursor, delete text, and perform all formatting commands.

Original Definition
Prefix Key

There are times when you may want to use the original definition for a specific key, as opposed to a new definition you may have assigned to it. One option would be to press CTRL+6 before pressing the key, which returns all keys on the keyboard to their original definitions. However, after performing this command, you would have to call up the Keyboard Layout screen with the Setup function to restore the selection of your keyboard redefinition file, thereby enabling your key redefinitions.

A better solution would be to redefine a key so that its function is to wait for the next key pressed, and then perform the action originally defined for that key. Here are the macro steps which will do this:

```
 1  {;}Original·Definition·Prefix·Key~
 2  {;}Copyright·(c)·1988,·by·Eric·Alderman~
 3
 4  {CANCEL OFF}                {;}Disable·<Cancel>·key~
 5  {ASSIGN}0~~                 {;}Empty·Variable·0~
 6
 7  {LABEL}loop~                {;}Set·beginning·of·loop~
 8  {LOOK}0~                    {;}Check·for·entered·key~
 9  {IF EXISTS}0~               {;}If·one·was·entered~
10     {ORIGINAL KEY}           {;}Then·perform·its·original·action~
11  {ELSE}
12     {GO}loop~                {;}Otherwise,·check·again~
13  {END IF}
```

This macro uses the Original Key command to insert the original definition of the last key pressed. The Cancel Off command allows the original definition of the <Cancel> key to be inserted. (Otherwise, pressing <Cancel> would end the macro.) To implement this macro, you should enter its steps into the definition of an available key that is easily accessible. For example, on many keyboards the ` key (the accent grave) is conveniently located.

To try out the Original Definition Prefix key, begin by pressing the key you redefined with the steps previously listed. Next, press any redefined key (even the Prefix key itself), and you'll see that the *original* action of that key is performed, not its redefined action. However, after the action is performed, your redefinitions are still in effect for that key and for all other keys on the keyboard.

A

USING SETUP

WordPerfect's Setup function is used to configure the program in various ways. For example, you can initiate timed backups, modify your default format settings, change the attributes of your display, and redefine the functions of the keys on the keyboard.

To access the Setup function, press the <Setup> key (SHIFT+F1), and the Setup menu will appear as shown in Figure A-1. Proceed to modify the options shown as described in the following section. As you navigate through the various menus in the Setup function, you can usually use the <Cancel> key (F1) to back up one level to a previous menu, and the <Exit> key (F7) to return directly to the document. Except where noted, the settings you change in Setup take immediate effect when you return to the document, and will remain in effect for all future editing sessions. Most options are stored in a file called WP{WP}.SET.

BACKUP

To modify the backup options, type **1** for "Backup," and the backup options screen will appear as shown in Figure A-2. There are two different backup options, timed backup and original backup.

```
Setup

     1 - Backup

     2 - Cursor Speed              30 cps

     3 - Display

     4 - Fast Save (unformatted)   No

     5 - Initial Settings

     6 - Keyboard Layout

     7 - Location of Auxiliary Files

     8 - Units of Measure




Selection: 0
```

Figure A-1.   The Setup menu

The timed backup makes a backup copy of the current document at a regular, pre-determined interval. On this screen, you can specify whether or not you want timed backup, and at what interval. You can specify any number of minutes as an interval. However, it should be short enough so that you're not likely to lose a great deal of data. Too short an interval, however, can be annoying, because WordPerfect will write to the disk whenever it does a backup.

The timed backup files, called WP{WP}.BK1 for Document 1 and WP{WP}.BK2 for Document 2, are automatically erased when you exit WordPerfect in a normal manner. In the event of a power failure, simply retrieve one of these files from the directory you specify with the Location of Files option (see "Location of Files" later in this appendix).

```
Setup: Backup

     Timed backup files are deleted when you exit WP normally.  If you
     have a power or machine failure, you will find the backup file in the
     backup directory indicated in Setup: Location of Auxiliary Files.

        Backup Directory

     1 - Timed Document Backup              No
           Minutes Between Backups          30


     Original backup will save the original document with a .BK! extension
     whenever you replace it during a Save or Exit.

     2 - Original Document Backup           No







Selection: 0
```

Figure A-2.   The Backup Options screen

You can also configure the program to automatically create, and retain, a backup copy of your work based on the last version prior to a save. This is called an "original backup." If you find that you've made unwanted changes in a document after you've saved it, you can go back to the previously saved copy. Unlike the timed backup file, the original backup file is not erased when you exit the program. Note that this option can take up a lot of room on your disk, because each document ends up being saved twice.

CURSOR SPEED

When you hold down a key, whether it is an arrow key or an actual letter or number, the computer automatically repeats that key. The speed at which it repeats is called the *cursor speed*. By default, the cursor is set to move at 30 characters per second. However, it can be adjusted to move faster or slower.

To set the speed, type **2** for "Cursor Speed" from the Setup menu. You can then enter a number corresponding to the desired speed. The "Normal" speed is about 10 characters per second, which is the computer's normal key repeat rate. If you are using WordPerfect Corporation's "Repeat Performance" (a utility that adjusts the cursor speed for any program), the setting should be left at "Normal". Note that some keyboards are not compatible with the option to speed up the cursor. If you have this problem, start WordPerfect with WP /NK to disable the Cursor Speed feature.

DISPLAY

To modify the attributes of your screen display, type **3** for "Display" from the Setup menu, and the Display menu will appear as shown in Figure A-3. Select one of the following options.

Automatically Format and Rewrite

When you enter text, WordPerfect automatically rewrites the screen so that text fits within the specified margins and tab settings. On some machines this process can cause a slight delay, especially when you're typing text into existing text formatted for multiple columns. That's why it's possible to turn off the Automatic Format feature.

To change this feature, type **1** for "Automatically Format and Rewrite," and then type **Y** or **N**.

Colors/Fonts/Attributes

Type **2** for "Colors/Fonts/Attributes" to change your options for colors and fonts. The choices that will be presented depend on the

---

```
Setup: Display

      1 - Automatically Format and Rewrite    Yes

      2 - Colors/Fonts/Attributes

      3 - Display Document Comments            Yes

      4 - Filename on the Status Line          Yes

      5 - Graphics Screen Type                 Hercules 720x348 mono

      6 - Hard Return Display Character

      7 - Menu Letter Display                  BOLD

      8 - Side-by-side Columns Display         Yes




Selection: 0
```

Figure A-3.   The Display menu

type of display card and monitor you have. If you have a text-only display, your options will be quite limited.

Display Document Comments

To change whether Document Comments are shown on the screen, type **3** for "Display Document Comments." Then type **Y** or **N** to indicate whether you want Document Comments to be displayed in double-lined boxes on the screen, or hidden. If you choose not to display Document Comments, you can still see where they are located in your document by using the Reveal Codes function.

Filename on the Status Line

The path name and file name of the current document are normally displayed in the lower left-hand corner of the screen. Some people may find this distracting, however, so this option allows you to suppress the display. To change whether or not the path name and file name are shown, type **4** for "Filename on the Status Line," then type **Y** or **N**.

Graphics Screen Type

WordPerfect will normally be able to determine automatically what type of display adapter you have; it will display its selection next to the Graphics Screen Type option. So it's unlikely that you'll have to set this yourself. However, there are some cases (such as when you have two monitors) when you need to change the default. To do so, type **5** for "Graphics Screen Type," and the Graphics Screen Type screen will appear, similar to the one shown in Figure A-4.

The list shown on this screen reflects all of the monitor types which WordPerfect comes prepared to support, in addition to those for which there are .WPD files in the WordPerfect directory. (You may need to copy the correct .WPD file from the Fonts/Graphics disk to select your monitor type.) When you've positioned the cursor bar on the name of your monitor type, type **1** (or simply press ENTER). The "Text (no graphics)" option will work with any type of monitor display, but graphics images will be displayed in rough form, and the Print View function will be more limited.

Hard Return Display Character

Hard Return codes ([HRt]'s) are not displayed on the normal Document Editing screen. To see them, you must normally use Reveal Codes. (Hard Returns are inserted whenever you press the ENTER key in the document, usually to end a short line or para-

---

```
Setup: Graphics Screen Type

   Text (no graphics)
×  Hercules 720x348 mono
   Hercules InColor 720x348 16 color
   IBM CGA 640x200 mono
   IBM EGA 640x350 mono
   IBM EGA 640x200 16 color
   IBM EGA 640x350 4 color
   IBM EGA 640x350 16 color
   IBM VGA 640x480 mono
   IBM VGA 640x480 16 color
   IBM VGA 320x200 256 color
   AT&T 6300 640x400 mono
   Compaq Prtble plasma 640x400 mono




1 Select: 1
```

Figure A-4.   The Graphics Screen Type screen

graph, or make a blank line.) However, you can use this option to display a visible character on the editing screen wherever a Hard Return is placed.

To change the displayed character, type **6** for "Hard Return Display Character." If you want to use a character from the keyboard, just type it and it will be displayed on the screen. You can also use the Compose option to insert a special character not normally available on the keyboard. To use Compose, press the <Compose> key (CTRL+2) and enter the appropriate two letters. Another option is to hold down the ALT key and type the ASCII code for the symbol you wish to use. A common setting is the paragraph mark, which can be created by holding down the ALT key, typing **2** and then typing **0** on the numeric keypad (ASCII code 20). To return to the default option (no character displayed), simply press SPACE BAR.

Menu Letter Display

All of WordPerfect's menu choices can be selected by typing single letters (called *mnemonics*), in addition to the numbers shown. Initially, WordPerfect displays these letters in boldface, but you can change that attribute. To do so, type **7** for "Menu Letter Display," and you'll see a partial Font menu appear. Use the Size or Appearance choices to change the attribute. The actual effect of the attribute you choose will be determined by the attribute selections you made with the Colors/Fonts/Attributes function.

Side-by-Side Columns
Display

Normally, WordPerfect displays newspaper-style and parallel text columns side-by-side on screen. However, because displaying columns in this way can sometimes slow you down when you're entering and editing text in the columns, WordPerfect has the option of disabling the side-by-side display.

To change this option, type **8** for "Side-by-Side Columns Display," then type **Y** or **N**. When you turn off the option, columns will appear to be on separate pages on the screen. However, the status indicators at the bottom of the screen will always reflect the correct column and page numbers. Regardless of whether or not columns are displayed side-by-side on the screen, they will always appear side-by-side on the printed page.

FAST SAVE (UNFORMATTED)

With the Fast Save option turned on, WordPerfect is much faster at saving documents. It attains this improved speed by foregoing the normal formatting process, which breaks the lines and pages of the document. One side effect of this is that you cannot print unformatted documents from disk. If you try, you'll see a message which tells you that the document was fast-saved. If you decide to leave the Fast Save option turned on, you can always manually format a document by pressing HOME, HOME, DOWN ARROW before saving. With Fast Save turned off (the default), documents are formatted before being saved.

To change this option, type **4** for "Fast Save," and then type **Y** or **N**.

INITIAL SETTINGS

You use the Initial Settings screen to set the default values for a number of WordPerfect's options. Most of the choices you make will remain in effect for all future editing sessions, with all documents you create and edit. Some of them can be changed for individual documents.

To modify your initial settings, type **5** for "Initial Settings," and you'll see the Initial Settings screen as shown in Figure A-5. The choices shown on this screen are described in the sections that follow.

Beep Options

This option allows you to specify whether WordPerfect will beep when an error occurs, hyphenation is requested, or a search fails. To change this option, type **1** for "Beep Options," and the Beep Options menu will appear. Type the appropriate number, and then type either **Y** or **N**.

Date Format

WordPerfect is able to enter the date and time anywhere in a document. You can control the format of the date via the Initial Settings menu or you can change it "on the fly," as needed. (When you change it with the <Date/Outline> key, the format you set remains in effect only for the remainder of the editing session.)

```
Setup: Initial Settings

      1 - Beep Options

      2 - Date Format              3 1, 4

      3 - Document Summary

      4 - Initial Codes

      5 - Repeat Value             8

      6 - Table of Authorities
```



```
Selection: 0
```

Figure A-5.   The Initial Settings screen

To change the format, type **2** for "Date Format." The chart on your screen shows the meaning of each character in the format, and examples are displayed at the bottom of the screen. The default format ("3 1, 4") is the typical format for dates at the beginning of a letter. The "3" is for the month, the "1" is for day of the month, the comma (,) inserts a comma after the date, and the "4" is for the year. Thus, the date for Christmas 1990 would be displayed as "December 25, 1990". You can mix any codes or words you wish. For example you could enter "It is 8:9 0 on 6, 3 1,4" to have WordPerfect display and print, "It is 5:30 PM on Tuesday, December 25, 1990." When you've typed the desired format, press ENTER.

Document Summary

WordPerfect's Document Summary function allows you to specify summary information about each document you create (see Chapter 6, "Office Features"). You can change the initial settings so that WordPerfect prompts you to create or modify the document summary whenever the document is saved. You can also tell the program what text to search for in order to determine the subject of each document. By default, WordPerfect searches for "RE:" to determine the subject. The text that it finds on the line containing this string is inserted automatically into option 2, "Subject/ Account" of the document's summary.

To change one of these options, type **3** for "Document Summary." You can then type **1** followed by either **Y** or **N** to change whether or not the Document Summary screen will appear automatically. You can also type **2**, and then type the text that the program should use to find the subject of a document. Press ENTER when you've finished typing the text.

Initial Codes

You can use the Initial Codes option to specify the initial codes for all new documents. When a document is first created (that is, when you begin typing on a blank screen), all of the Initial Codes specified with the Setup function are transferred into the document's Initial Codes (viewed and modified with the <Format> key). From that point forward, the document will always use its own Initial Codes and *will not be affected* by changes made to Initial Codes in Setup. This makes the document "portable," so that it can be retrieved by other copies of WordPerfect whose Initial Codes may be set differently.

To change the Initial Codes, type **4** for "Initial Codes," and you'll see a blank screen with the Reveal Codes function active. You can now perform many formatting commands, and the codes they generate will become the initial codes. When you're through, press the <Exit> key (F7).

Note that while you can insert many codes on this screen, there are some that are not allowed. For the most part, WordPerfect will not allow you to invoke functions which generate the prohibited codes. However, if you do insert one that is not allowed, it will be deleted automatically when you exit the Initial Codes screen. When you return to the screen, they will no longer appear.

Typical changes to the Initial Codes settings would include turning off justification, turning on page numbering, or setting the left and right margins. You cannot change the Base Font in the Initial Codes function with the Setup key. Instead, the Base Font for a new document is determined by the Initial Font for the currently selected printer. The Initial Font function on the <Format> key is used to specify the initial base font for a document after it has been created. See Chapter 11, "Using Printers," for a description of Base Fonts.

Repeat Value

While editing, you can indicate that you are going to repeat an operation by pressing ESC followed by a character or command. Repeat Value is the number of times a command or character is repeated. You can change the program's default setting in Initial Settings, or "on the fly" by typing a number after pressing ESC, and pressing ENTER.

To change the Repeat Value in Initial Settings, type 5, type a number from 1 to 9999, then press ENTER.

Table of Authorities

The format options available in the Table of Authorities can be modified within the Initial Settings function. These options affect the default values presented whenever you define a Table of Authorities in a document. To change them, type 6 for "Table of Authorities." See Chapter 5, "Document Accessories," for a description of the Table of Authorities function.

KEYBOARD LAYOUT

You can use the Keyboard Layout command to modify the actions performed by keys. You can use this command simply to move keys to different locations (for instance, moving the <Help> key to F1), or you can attach complex macros to keys. See Chapter 2, "Macros," for a description of the Keyboard Layout command.

LOCATION OF FILES

WordPerfect depends on different types of files to do its work. If you wish, each type of file can be placed in a separate directory on your hard disk. These include your backup files, hyphenation modules, the files that contain your keyboard macros, your main dictionary (or dictionaries), printer files, Style Library file, supplementary dictionary (or dictionaries), and thesaurus.

To specify the locations of these files, type 7 for "Location of Files." Next, type the number of the option for which you want to set a new location. Once you enter a number for the file type, enter the name of the directory. Be sure to include a backslash (\ ) before the directory name. If it is not on the default drive, add the drive designator (for instance, D:) before the backslash. When you are through, press ENTER, and WordPerfect will check the location you specified. If the location does not exist (for example, if you have not yet created the directory), you'll see an error message.

Unlike the other locations, the Style Library file is a complete *file name* (including path), not just a directory. You only need to specify a name at this prompt if you plan to use a Style Library file. See Chapter 7, "Styles," for a description of the use of this file.

UNITS OF MEASURE

You can change the units which WordPerfect uses for various measurements. You can specify the units for all measurement options, such as tabs, margins, line spacing, and so on. In addition, you can also specify a separate unit of measure for the status line display, which is shown at the bottom of the screen.

To change the units of measure, type 8 for "Units of Measure," and the Units of Measure screen will appear. Type 1 to change the units for measured options or 2 to change the units for the status line display. Then type the character that corresponds to the unit of measure you want to use.

You can always override the default units of measure when you enter a measurement for a format option. To do this, simply follow a number with one of the characters shown on this screen. However, WordPerfect will automatically translate all measurements in format options into the units you specified in Setup.

B

USING WORD SEARCH

The Word Search function on the List Files screen (see the "File Management" section of Chapter 1, "Basics Refresher") allows you to search through many files on disk to find ones which match certain criteria.

For example, you might want to search for documents which contain a specific word or phrase, such as a client's name. Or you may want to search for documents based on the information entered into the summary screen of each one, such as the name of the person who typed the document. You can also use Word Search to locate documents within a certain date range. If you wish, you can combine any of these search criteria.

PERFORMING THE WORD SEARCH

To use the Word Search function, begin on the List Files screen. Be sure that the list of files reflects the disk or directory in which you want to perform the search (use the Other Directory option, if necessary). If you wish to limit the search to specific files, mark the files by positioning the cursor bar on each one, and then typing an asterisk (*). (You can move to the next marked file by pressing TAB, and to the previous one by pressing SHIFT+TAB.)

Next, type **9** for "Word Search," and a menu will appear at the bottom of the screen. From this menu, you can choose to search for text only within the summaries of the documents, on the first page of all of the documents, or anywhere in the entire text of the documents. If you select choice 1, the search will locate text in any of the Document Summary items. If you select choice 2, it will look on the first page only (or within the first 4000 characters, if the first page is larger than that). If you select choice 3, it will look through the entire document. Naturally, choices 1 and 2 will locate text faster than choice 3, because a smaller quantity of text is searched.

Type one of the numbers to indicate the location to search, and you'll see a "Word pattern:" prompt. At the prompt, type the text you want to locate (see the next section), and press ENTER. Word-Perfect will search through the indicated files and then mark with an asterisk those files that match your request. You can then proceed to look at or retrieve any of them, or to perform any appropriate List Files function. If you perform another search, it will be limited to the currently marked files.

If you want to conduct a more detailed search, type **9** for "Word Search," and then **4** for "Conditions." A Word Search Conditions screen will appear, similar to the one shown in Figure B-1. On this screen, you can specify in even more detail which documents you want to locate. To specify the search conditions, type a number from 4 to 7.

To specify a date range, type **4** for "File Date," and press ENTER to move to the "From" option. Now type the earliest date that you want to locate (in the form MM/DD/YY), and press ENTER. Next, type the most recent date that you want to locate, and press ENTER. To search for all files *up to* a certain date, simply press ENTER at the "From:" prompt, and "(All)" will remain its selected option. To search for all files *since* a certain date, simply press ENTER at the "To:" prompt, and "(All)" will remain its selected option. To specify a month, omit the date (for example, 5//88 indicates May 1988). To specify a year, omit the month and date (for example, //89 indicates 1989).

```
Word Search

   1 - Perform Search on              All 38 File(s)

   2 - Undo Last Search

   3 - Reset Search Conditions

   4 - File Date                      No
       From (MM/DD/YY):               (All)
       To   (MM/DD/YY):               (All)

                  Word Pattern(s)

   5 - First Page
   6 - Entire Doc
   7 - Document Summary
       Creation Date (e.g. Nov)
       Descriptive Name
       Subject/Account
       Author
       Typist
       Comments

Selection: 1
```

Figure B-1.   The Word Search Conditions screen

To specify a word pattern, type a number from 5 to 7. The first line in choice 7 is for text that you want to locate anywhere in the document summaries (this is similar to choice 1 when you select "Word Search" from List Files). You can use the UP ARROW and DOWN ARROW keys to position the cursor on the different lines. Type the word pattern (see the next section), and press ENTER.

When you're ready to perform the word search, type **1**, and the search will begin. When the search is complete, the documents that matched the specified search criteria will be marked with an asterisk.

To perform a new search, type **9** for "Word Search," and then **4** for "Conditions." You can see that the number of marked files is indicated next to the first option. To return to the last set of marked files, type **2** for "Undo Last Search." (You can undo up to three levels of searches.) To reset all search conditions on the screen, type **3** for "Reset Search Conditions." Modify the conditions as desired, and then repeat the search by typing **1**.

WORD PATTERNS

You can type up to 39 characters for any word pattern. The program does not distinguish between uppercase and lowercase letters. In addition, the word pattern can contain special operators which affect how the text is evaluated.

To search for files that contain two or more specified words, separate them with a space or semicolon. Only files that contain all the words, not necessarily in succession or in the order you enter them, will be found. For example, if you type **drops murder weapon**, you are telling the Word Search function to locate all files that contain "drops" AND "murder" AND "weapon".

However, if you enclose the words in double quotes (for example, **"drops murder weapon"**), the Word Search function considers the words a *phrase* and will only find files that contain the words in succession, just as you've entered them.

Just as the space or semicolon is used as a logical AND operator, a comma is used as a logical OR operator. To find all files that contain either "drops" OR "murder" OR "weapon", you would type **drops,murder,weapon**.

You can also combine logical operators. For example, to find all files that contain either "drop" and "dead" or "take a hike", you would type **drop dead,"take a hike"**. When you combine operators, the word pattern is always evaluated from left to right.

You can also use wildcard characters in the word pattern, just as in DOS or in the Spell function. The ? character replaces any single character, and the * character replaces one or more characters. For example, typing **r?t** would find files that contain "rat", "rut", and "rot". Typing **gra*** would find files that contain "gracious", "graft", and "graphically".

You can create word patterns using any combination of double quotes, logical operators, and wildcard characters.

C

WORDPERFECT
CORPORATION
PROGRAMS

Besides WordPerfect, WordPerfect Corporation sells several other useful programs. These programs share a common user interface, which means that many of the keys that you use in WordPerfect are also used in these other programs. For example, all of them use the F7 key to exit the program, and the F3 key to summon help. A common user interface makes it easy for the user to move between programs.

The programs described in this appendix are PlanPerfect, DataPerfect, WordPerfect Library, and WordPerfect Office. Plan-Perfect is a powerful spreadsheet program with extensive calculation, graphing, and customization features. DataPerfect is an easy-to-use database program that allows multiple files to be linked in various ways. The programs in WordPerfect Library serve as utilities for the rest of the company's products, and WordPerfect Office is a modified version of Library for use in a network environment.

Other products from WordPerfect Corporation not described in this appendix are WordPerfect Executive, an integrated collection of programs popular with users of laptop computers; Personal

WordPerfect, a simpler and less expensive version of the full package; and Repeat Performance, a utility which increases the key repeat rate of the keyboard (a feature included in WordPerfect 5.0).

PLANPERFECT

PlanPerfect is a powerful and flexible spreadsheet program. Spreadsheet programs allow you to enter data in structured rows and columns, using formulas to perform calculations. PlanPerfect also allows you to transform a series of numbers into a variety of graphs and charts, such as a bar or pie chart, which you can then import into WordPerfect by using the Graphics Box feature (see Chapter 10, "Presentation Features"). Note that to incorporate a PlanPerfect graph into WordPerfect, you must have access to the META.SYS graphics driver file. This file is on PlanPerfect's Alternate Graphics Disk 1, which you can order from WordPerfect Corporation at no charge.

DATAPERFECT

DataPerfect, a powerful database program, allows you to store information divided into fields and records (much like a WordPerfect secondary merge file). You may, for example, want to use DataPerfect to store a mailing list.

In DataPerfect the user creates *panels*, which are used to enter and edit information. You can create several different panels and build links between them. You can, for instance, create one file for your clients and a separate linked file for invoices. Further, you can easily export your information from DataPerfect to WordPerfect's secondary merge file format, and use the data in a merge. You could, in this way, send a form letter to all of your clients.

The Notebook program, which is included with WordPerfect Library, is also used to maintain information such as mailing lists. However, Notebook is much more limited than DataPerfect in a number of ways. Notebook slows down dramatically when it has to handle large files containing more than 800 to 1000 records. Also, Notebook has fewer selection features, very limited sorting capability, and cannot link files together. It does, however, have the advantage of storing its files in the same format as the Word-Perfect Merge function, making exporting unnecessary.

WORDPERFECT LIBRARY

WordPerfect Library contains a collection of useful utilities that include

- Shell, a hard disk menu program that lets you keep many WordPerfect Corporation programs in memory at one time
- M-Edit, a macro editing program for macros that are created in WordPerfect, PlanPerfect, Shell, and other WordPerfect Corporation programs
- Notebook, a program that permits you to manipulate WordPerfect secondary merge files more easily
- File Manager, a utility similar to WordPerfect's List Files function
- Calendar, a useful calendar and appointment-scheduling program
- Calculator, a full-function financial, statistical, scientific, and programming calculator
- Beast, an addictive game

Three of these programs, Shell, M-Edit, and Notebook, are described in following sections.

Shell

Shell is a menu program for organizing the applications on a hard disk. It can also divide your RAM into sections so that more than one program can be loaded at a time. If you wish, you can leave WordPerfect Corporation programs resident in memory (as well as other programs with a "Drop-to-DOS" feature) while you execute other applications. You can then switch instantly between the loaded programs. You can load as many programs as will fit into available RAM.

Shell can take advantage of expanded memory boards that follow the LIM (Lotus-Intel-Microsoft) standard. These boards provide you with memory above the usual 640K limit. With expanded memory, you will be able to load even more WordPerfect Corporation programs into RAM at one time.

M-Edit

M-Edit allows you to edit macros created in any of WordPerfect Corporation's programs. The macro keystrokes are represented on screen by full-word descriptions of each key (as they are in WordPerfect's own internal macro editor).

M-Edit has numerous advantages over WordPerfect's internal editor. With M-Edit you can

- Edit and view two macros at the same time
- Copy and move a series of macro steps from one location to another within a macro, or between two different macros
- Undelete steps that you've accidentally deleted
- Edit macros longer than 5K in size (the limit of the internal editor)
- Print out the steps of a macro

The most convenient way to use M-Edit with other WordPerfect Corporation programs like WordPerfect is with Shell, which will enable you to quickly switch between editing a macro in M-Edit and trying it out in the application.

Notebook

Notebook allows you to manage WordPerfect secondary merge files easily (see the section "Secondary Merge Files" in Chapter 3, "Merge"). With Notebook, you can view records from your secondary merge file either in a row-and-column format (as you do in a spreadsheet program) or in a record layout, where you can view each record on a custom-designed screen (as you do in a database program).

A secondary merge file saved from Notebook can be used immediately by WordPerfect in a merge operation, without prior translation. Notebook inserts a header record containing special information, such as the record layout, field sizes, and field names. During the merge operation, this header record is ignored. A section in Chapter 12, "Integration with Other Products," describes this header record and how to work with it in WordPerfect.

WORDPERFECT OFFICE

WordPerfect Office is a version of WordPerfect Library, enhanced and modified for use in a network environment. In addition to all of the components of WordPerfect Library, WordPerfect Office includes the following programs:

- Mail, a program which permits you to send and receive messages and files on a network
- Scheduler, a program which allows you to manage event scheduling for a group of people, using the Calendar files and the Mail system
- Other network management utilities

If you use WordPerfect in a network environment, you can probably benefit from this integrated collection of programs.

D

WORDPERFECT
RESOURCES

You can use several phone numbers to contact WordPerfect Corporation. To receive technical support, you can call (800) 321-5906. Because toll-free lines can sometimes be busy and cannot be used outside of the U.S., the company also maintains a non-toll-free phone number, which is (801) 226-6800. Support is available from 7:00 a.m. to 6:00 p.m. Mountain Standard Time, Monday through Friday, and 8:00 a.m. to 12:00 p.m. on Saturday.

To get information about updates to WordPerfect, information about any current or future WordPerfect Corporation product, or for any other questions, call Information Services at (801) 225-5000. This office is open from 7:30 a.m. to 5:30 p.m. Mountain Standard Time, Monday through Friday.

The company's address is

WordPerfect Corporation
1555 North Technology Way
Orem, Utah 84057

Be sure to specify the department you wish to address, such as Technical Support.

THE WORDPERFECT
SUPPORT GROUP

The WordPerfect Support Group is an independent organization that provides support for WordPerfect Corporation products. With more than 18,000 members, it is the largest WordPerfect-oriented user group in the country. The group's newsletter, "The WordPerfectionist," contains tips, tricks, and articles that discuss various topics relating to the use of WordPerfect. You can contact the group by writing to

The WordPerfect Support Group
P.O. Box 1577
Baltimore, MD 21203

The WordPerfect Support Group also leads a WordPerfect-oriented forum on CompuServe, a nationwide on-line communication service. After you log onto CompuServe, you can access the forum by typing **GO WPSG**.

TRADEMARKS

1-2-3®	Lotus Development Corp.
Amiga®	Commodore Electronics Ltd.
Apple II®	Apple Computer, Inc.
Apple IIGS™	Apple Computer, Inc.
Atari® ST™	Atari Corp.
CompuServe®	CompuServe, Inc.
CP/M®	Digital Research, Inc.
dBASE II®	Ashton-Tate
dBASE III®	Ashton-Tate
DESQview™	Quarterdeck Office Systems
IBM®	International Business Machines Corp.
Lotus®	Lotus Development Corp.
Macintosh®	Apple Computer, Inc.
MailMerge®	MicroPro International Corp.
MS-DOS®	Microsoft Corp.
MultiMate®	MultiMate International Corp.
PostScript®	Adobe Systems, Inc.
ProKey™	RoseSoft, Inc.
SideKick®	Borland International, Inc.
SuperKey®	Borland International, Inc.
VAX™	Digital Equipment Corp.
VisiCalc®	VisiCorp
WordPerfect®	WordPerfect Corp.
WordStar®	MicroPro International Corp.

INDEX

The manuscript for this book was prepared and submitted to Osborne/McGraw-Hill in electronic form. The acquisitions editor for this project was Cindy Hudson, the technical reviewer was Kevin Shafer, and the project editor was Lindy Clinton.

Text design uses Century Expanded for text body and display.

Cover art by Bay Graphics Design Associates. Color separation by Colour Image. Cover supplier, Phoenix Color Corp. Screens produced with InSet, from InSet Systems, Inc. Book printed and bound by R.R. Donnelley & Sons Company, Crawfordsville, Indiana.

QUICK REFERENCE CARD

WordPerfect Key Names

Key Name		Key Name	
<→ Search >	F2	<Math/Columns>	ALT+F7
<← Search >	SHIFT+F2	<Merge Codes>	SHIFT+F9
<→ Indent >	F4	<Merge End-of-Field>	F9
<→ Indent ←>	SHIFT+F4	<Merge/Sort>	CTRL+F9
<Block>	ALT+F4	<Move>	CTRL+F4
<Bold>	F6	<Print>	SHIFT+F7
<Cancel/Undelete>	F1	<Replace>	ALT+F2
<Center>	SHIFT+F6	<Retrieve Text>	SHIFT+F10
<Date/Outline>	SHIFT+F5	<Reveal Codes>	ALT+F3
<Exit>	F7	<Save Text>	F10
<Flush Right>	ALT+F6	<Screen>	CTRL+F3
<Font>	CTRL+F8	<Setup>	SHIFT+F1
<Footnote>	CTRL+F7	<Shell>	CTRL+F1
<Format>	SHIFT+F8	<Spell>	CTRL+F2
<Graphics>	ALT+F9	<Style>	ALT+F8
<Help>	F3	<Switch>	SHIFT+F3
<List Files>	F5	<Tab Align>	CTRL+F6
<Macro Def>	CTRL+F10	<Text In/Out>	CTRL+F5
<Macro>	ALT+F10	<Thesaurus>	ALT+F1
<Mark Text>	ALT+F5	<Underline>	F8

Macro Commands

Command	Description
{;}comment~	Allows you to insert non-executing comments (comment is any amount of comment text).
{ASSIGN}variable~ value~	Assigns a value to a variable (variable is a single digit from 0 to 9, value is a text string without quotes, a number, or a formula).
{BELL}	Causes the computer to beep.
{BREAK}	Causes execution to continue after the next {END IF} command.
{CALL}label~	Executes macro section (identified by label) as a subroutine.
{CANCEL OFF}	Disables the <Cancel> key.
{CANCEL ON}	Enables the <Cancel> key.

© Osborne McGraw-Hill

Advanced WordPerfect

Macro Commands (continued)

{CASE}*val~cs1~lb1~...csN~lbN~*

Compares *val* with *cs1* through *csN* (values, in quotes if text). Macro section at location identified with *lb1* to *lbN* is executed if a match is found.

{CASE CALL}*val~cs1~lb1~...csN~lbN~*

Compares *val* with *cs1* through *csN* (values, in quotes if text). Macro section at location identified with *lb1* to *lbN* is executed as a subroutine if a match is found.

{CHAIN}*file~*

Causes macro *file* to be executed when the current macro is finished.

{CHAR}*variable~message*

Displays *message* as a prompt, waits for single character which is assigned to *variable* (single digit from 0 to 9).

{DISPLAY OFF}

Turns off display.

{DISPLAY ON}

Turns on display.

{ELSE}

Used with {IF} and {IF EXISTS}.

{END IF}

Used with {IF} and {IF EXISTS}.

{GO}*label~*

Causes execution to continue at macro location identified by *label*.

{IF}*value~*

Performs a conditional test. If *value* evaluates to a non-zero value, the following steps are executed. If zero, the steps following the next {ELSE} or {END IF} are executed.

{IF EXISTS}*var~*

Tests whether variable *var* has a value. If it does, the following steps are executed. If it does not, the steps following the next {ELSE} or {END IF} are executed.

{LABEL}*label~*

Identifies a macro location with the name *label*. Used by the {GO}, {CALL}, {CASE}, and {CASE CALL} commands.

{LOOK}*var~*

If a key has been typed during macro execution, it is assigned to variable *var* (single digit from 0 to 9).

{NEST}*file~*

Causes macro *file* to be executed as a subroutine. Execution continues after the {NEST} command when the macro is done.

{ON CANCEL} *action~*

Specifies an *action* to be performed when a Cancel condition occurs.

{ON ERROR} *action~*

Specifies an *action* to be performed when an Error condition occurs.

{ON NOT FOUND} *action~*

Specifies an *action* to be performed when a Not Found condition occurs.

{ORIGINAL KEY}

Executes the original definition of the last key pressed.

Macro Commands (continued)

{PAUSE}
Causes a macro to pause and wait for input from the user, ending with ENTER.

{PROMPT} message~
Displays message as a prompt on the screen.

{QUIT}
Causes execution of the macro to end.

{RESTART}
Causes macro to terminate when the current subroutine is finished.

{RETURN}
Causes execution to continue after the last executed {CALL} or {CASE CALL} command.

{RETURN CANCEL}
Causes execution to continue after the last executed {CALL} or {CASE CALL} command, and then indicates a Cancel condition.

{RETURN ERROR}
Causes execution to continue after the last executed {CALL} or {CASE CALL} command, and then indicates an Error condition.

{RETURN NOT FOUND}
Causes execution to continue after the last executed {CALL} or {CASE CALL} command, and then indicates a Not Found condition.

{SPEED}10ths~
Causes a macro to insert a delay of 100ths of a second between each subsequent keystroke in the macro.

{STATE}
Returns a number indicating the program's current state.

{STEP OFF}
Turns off single-step execution.

{STEP ON}
Turns on single-step execution, for debugging macros.

{TEXT}variable~ message~
Displays message as a prompt, waits for input from user ending with ENTER, and assigns the entered text to variable (single digit from 0 to 9).

{WAIT}10ths~
Causes macro to pause for 10ths of a second.

Values Returned by {STATE}

Value	Description
3	Active Document (1, 2, or 3)
4	Main editing screen is active (no menu or prompt is displayed)
8	Editing structure other than document itself is active (Footnote, Header, Footer, or Style Editing Screen, for example)
16	Macro definition is active (never set)
32	Macro execution is active (always set)
64	Merge is active
128	Block is active
256	Typeover is active
512	Reveal Codes is active
1024	A prompt with a Yes/No question is being displayed

Message String Control Characters

Character	Display	Action
		Cursor-positioning
^H	{HOME}	Positions cursor to upper-left corner of screen.
^J	{Enter}	Positions cursor to beginning of next line.
^K	{DEL TO EOL}	Clears from cursor position to end of current line.
^L	{DEL TO EOP}	Clears entire screen, positions cursor to upper-left corner of screen.
^M	{^M}	Positions cursor to beginning of current line.
^W	{UP}	Positions cursor up one line.
^Z	{DOWN}	Positions cursor down one line.
^X	{RIGHT}	Positions cursor right one character.
^Y	{LEFT}	Positions cursor left one character.

Message String Control Characters (continued)

Character	Display	Action
Cursor-positioning		
^P	{^P}	Positions cursor to specific column and row position on the screen. Followed by two characters or codes: one for column position, another for row position (relative to active window). Uses ASCII characters and codes to represent the positions.
Display Attributes		
^R	{^R}	Reverse video—on
^S	{^S}	Reverse video—off
^T	{^T}	Underline—on
^U	{^U}	Underline—off
^]	{^]}	Bold—on
^\	{^\}	Bold—off

Character	Display Attributes	Action
^V	{^V}	Turns on attribute specified for mneumonic menu letters in Setup. (Use ^Q to turn off.)
^N	{^N}	Turns on specific display attribute for text. Follow with one of the following: ^L—Bold ^N—Underline ^P—Blink ^Q—Reverse video.
^O	{^O}	Turns off specific display attribute for following text. Follow with one of the codes listed under ^N.
^Q	{^Q}	Turns off all active display attributes.

Merge Code Summary

Code	Action
^C	Request input from Console (keyboard).
^D	Insert Date.
^E	Mark the End of a record in a secondary file.
^Fn^	Merge Field n from the secondary file into the current primary file at the position of the code.

Merge Code Summary (continued)

^Gmacroname^G	Goto (start) a macro from within a merge. The macro will begin after the merge is completed.	
^N	Use the Next record in the secondary file.	
^Omessage^O	Output a message to the screen.	
^Pfilename^P	Change to a new Primary file.	
^Q	Quit the merge.	
^R	Mark the Return (end) of a field in a secondary file.	

^Sfilename^S	Change to a new Secondary file.
^T	Type (print) and delete the text merged to that point.
^U	Update (rewrite) the screen wherever it is encountered in the merge.
^V merge code^V	Inserts the merge code(s) into the merged document without executing them. These codes can then be used for a dual merge.

WordPerfect Startup Options

WP	No action
WP/B-*n*	Backup every *n* minutes
WP/D-*path*	Store temporary files in *path*
WP *filename*	Load *filename* after starting WP
WP/I	Install WP with current path for DOS 2.X
WP/M-*macroname*	Execute *macroname* after starting WP
WP/NC	Disable Cursor Speed function
WP/NE	Prevents WordPerfect from using Expanded Memory

WP/NF	Non-flash — used with some windowing programs
WP/NK	Disable enhanced keyboard calls
WP/R	Load 300K of WP into Expanded RAM
WP/SS-*r,c*	Set screen size to *r* rows and *c* columns
WP/X	Restore default settings for single session

All options can be combined.